Education of Exceptional Children

A basic text on the Rights of the Handicapped and the Gifted

Education of Exceptional Children

A basic text on the Rights of the Handicapped and the Gifted

PROF. K. C. PANDA

VIKAS® PUBLISHING HOUSE PVT LTD

VIKAS® PUBLISHING HOUSE PRIVATE LIMITED
E-28, Sector-8, Noida-201301 (UP), India
Phone: +91-120-4078900 • Fax: +91-120-4078999
VIKAS® Registered Office: A-27, 2nd Floor, Mohan Co-operative Industrial Estate, New Delhi-110044
E-mail: helpline@vikaspublishing.com • Website: www.vikaspublishing.com

SALES AND MARKETING OFFICES OF VIKAS® AND S CHAND AND COMPANY LIMITED

Chennai	:	Ph: 044-2363 2120, chennai@schandpublishing.com
Guwahati	:	Ph: 0361-2738 811, 2735 640, guwahati@schandpublishing.com
Hyderabad	:	Ph: 040-4018 6018, hyderabad@schandpublishing.com
Jalandhar	:	Ph: 0181-4645 630, jalandhar@schandpublishing.com
Kolkata	:	Ph: 033-2335 7458, 2335 3914, kolkata@schandpublishing.com
Lucknow	:	Ph: 0522-4003 633, lucknow@schandpublishing.com
Mumbai	:	Ph: 022-2500 0297, mumbai@schandpublishing.com
Patna	:	Ph: 0612-2260 011, patna@schandpublishing.com

Education of Exceptional Children
ISBN: 978-81259-0358-1

Product Code: V7EEC69TEDU10ENAA97O

First Published 1997
Reprinted several times between 1997 and 2020, 2022, 2023
Reprint 2025

PRINTED IN INDIA
By Vikas Publishing House Private Limited, Plot 20/4, Site-IV, Industrial Area Sahibabad, Ghaziabad-201010 and Published by Vikas Publishing House Private Limited, E-28, Sector-8, Noida-201301

Contents

Preface

This text is a response to the requests made by my students and colleagues who are working in the field of special education. It was they who motivated me through constant persuasion to undertake this venture. I first got interested in this field in 1968-70 while in the USA, doing my doctoral work with mental retardates at Indiana University, and teaching courses in special education at the Commonwealth University in Virginia. Upon returning to my country, I got involved in the planning of special education, curriculum development in special education, research and extension activities, and was associated with various departments of special education, National institutes. These included the Rehabilitation Council, the NCERT and selected NGOs in the field. I also guided several students for doctoral research in special education.

This book is intended for all those interested in special education, specially teacher trainees, at the Diploma, B.Ed., M.Ed. or Certificate level. It is the first comprehensive attempt in this field. I am indebted to my daughter Sabita, a Ph.D. in Pre-school education from the faculty of Home Science, who specialised in the education of exceptional children for her assistance in writing this book.

The text covers 15 chapters. Chapter high-lights, review questions and references are included with each chapter. Chapters I to III give an account of the foundations of special education, development of special education for exceptional pupils in our country, policies and programmes, critical issues and innovative steps. Chapters IV to XIII deal with all areas of exceptionality. Chapters XIV and XV cover teacher training and research areas in education of exceptional children. The major focus is on mainstreaming or integrating the milder categories of handicapped children in regular schools.

The content coverage covers the syllabi of all existing courses in the field. Hence, the text is expected to serve the needs of students, even research scholars, and teacher educators in special education. The text is an asset to those individuals and organisation who fight for establishing human rights and establishing a new order for the disabled.

Prof. K.C. Panda

Chapter 1

Conceptual Foundations of Education of Exceptional Children

This chapter deals with :

- The meaning of "Exceptional Children"
- The various terms used in the field of Special Education
- Meaning of Special Education
- Categories of Exceptional Children
- Children with Special Education needs
- Various Special Education Services
- Variations in the service delivery system such as portage, pre-school intervention
- Development of Special Education in the West
- Special Education in India

Exceptional Children Defined

Education of exceptional children is a challenging field. The term "Exceptional Children" refers to children whose needs are very different from those of the majority of children in society. These children deviate from average children to the extent they cannot receive classroom instruction in regular schools. This was the belief prevalent for several years.

Many children are hard of hearing but every such child is not exceptional unless the loss is such as to impair communication skills. Within a particular group of exceptional children, there are also variations. There are different degrees of hearing loss. Hence, it is appropriate to define exceptional children as those who differ from the average to such a degree in physical and psychological characteristics that the traditional school programme does not allow all round development and progress for them. They need special education or special ancillary services to grow according to their ability.

Special education refers to instruction that is specifically designed to meet the needs of exceptional children. It involves designing the physical environment in the classroom (e.g., use of ramps) teaching procedures, teaching content and equipment (hearing aids for the deaf) for a particular type of disability.

Several terms have been used to describe exceptionality: subnormal, handicapped, disabled, exceptional, special, impaired etc. These have added confusion to understanding and placing the children who are different from the average. As a result of widespread debate, discussions and research, the World Health Organisation has clearly distinguished the use of three terms: impairment, disability and handicap.

Impairment means, abnormalities of body structure and appearance and organ or system function resulting from any cause in principle. Impairment represents disturbances at the organ level (WHO, 1976).

Disability reflects the consequences of impairment in terms of functional performance and activity by the individual (WHO, 1976).

Handicap on the otherhand, refers to disadvantages experienced by the individual as a result of impairments and disabilities; handicaps thus reflect interaction with an adaptation to the individual's surroundings (WHO, 1976).

These terms are based on an organic model having functional inter-relationship.

Impairment → Disability → Handicap

The inter-relationship between the three can be explained by means of examples:

- A child born with a finger-nail missing has a malformation—a structural impairment—but this does not in any way interfere with the function of the hand and so there is no disability; the impairment is not particularly evident, and so disadvantage or handicap would be unlikely.
- A myope or a diabetic individual suffers a functional impairment but, because this can be corrected or abolished by aids, appliances, or drugs, he would not necessarily be disabled; however, the disadvantage is considerable, e.g., he may not be allowed to take part in group activities or may have to give himself regular injections.
- An individual with colour blindness has an impairment but it would be unlikely to lead to activity restriction; whether the impairment constitutes a handicap would depend on circumstances—if his occupations were agricultural he might well be unaware of his impairment, but he would be at a disadvantage if he aspired to drive a railway engine, because he would be prevented from following this occupation.

"Subnormality of intelligence is an impairment, but it may not lead to appreciable activity restriction; factors other than the impairment may determine the handicap because the disadvantage may be minimal if the individual lives in a remote rural community, whereas it could be severe if he lives in the midst of university graduates living in a large city, of whom more might be expected."

Hence, children are considered exceptional when they have some characteristics that deviate from the normal or average child. It is for this reason the term "Exceptional Children" is used more often. It is more inclusive in the sense that it consists of the handicapped in one extreme and of the gifted at the other. These children are classified into certain categories for the purpose of placement and educational care.

Types of Exceptional Children

The following categories of children represent the various types of exceptional children:

- The Educable Mentally Retarded
- The Trainable Mentally Retarded
- The Profound or Severely Mentally Retarded
- The Visually Handicapped
- The Hearing Handicapped
- The Emotionally Handicapped
- The Disabled Learner
- The Physically or Neurologically Handicapped
- The Speech and Language Handicapped
- The Slow Learner
- The Gifted
- The Multiple Handicapped
- The Socially Handicapped

The operational definitions of all these categories and a brief overview of their characteristics are given below in order to help the reader understand the text easily.

The Educable Mentally Retarded

The Educable Mentally Retarded (EMR) children have IQs between 60 to 85 (earlier 50-75) accompanied by impaired behaviour. These children can learn minimal academic skills by their late teens with special educational support. They are capable of social and vocational independence with proper education and training. Some of them need supervision and guidance. On an average 2.5 per cent children are within educable range. They come from low socio-economic backgrounds and are classified as non-pathological or cultural-familial. They are slightly below normal children in physical development. Their greatest difficulty is with learning of abstract concepts. They have a higher expectancy of failure than the intellectually normal. They need to make more effort, immediate and tangible reward and language training. Special teachers work hard to teach the EMR social-emotional adjustment, academic knowledge, physical and motor activities. These children are deficient in information processing habits and have low aspirations. Their rate of forgetting is rapid. But they do profit from training.

The Trainable Mentally Retarded

Trainable Mentally Retarded children have IQs between 40-60 approximately. By adulthood they have the intelligence of 4 to 8 year old. They can only learn selfcare socialisation and oral communication skills. They need personal attention and care throughout their lives. They can be partially self-supporting after training in sheltered workshops. They contribute 0.5 per cent of the retarded children population. They usually live with parents, relatives or are cared for by some social agencies. They display behaviour problems withdrawal, distractibility, and unusual emotional states. Special school setting sometimes is the answer to their training and care.

The Visually Handicapped

Visual handicap is defined in terms of visual acuity, field of vision, and visual efficiency. Visual ability is the ability of the eye to see distant objects clearly using Snellen chart. Individuals who see the letter capital 'E' from a 20 feet distance instead of 200 feet are legally blind. There are children who have low vision or residual vision. These children are sighted and their visual acuity does not exceed 20/70. These children have orientation and mobility problems. Low vision is defined in terms of clarity whereas partial sightedness is defined in terms of distance from the Snellen Chart. Education of these children is based on multi sensory approach, use of plus curriculum, use of Braille, etc.

The Emotionally Disturbed

An emotionally disturbed child is one whose reactions to life situations are unrewarding to himself and unacceptable to his peers and other members of society. They vary in degree. They show over a long period of time and to a marked degree certain characteristics which affect their academic performances. These are:

a. Inability to learn, that cannot be explained by intellectual, sensory or health factors.
b. Inability to build and maintain satisfactory interpersonal relationship with peers and teachers.
c. Inappropriate behaviour or feelings under normal circumstances.
d. General and pervasive mood of unhappiness or depression.
e. Tendency to develop fear associated with personal and school problems.

Educational programmes are planned quite cautiously to handle these children.

The Hearing Handicapped

Hearing handicap is defined in terms of degree of hearing loss. These are classified as mild (20-30 dB), marginal (30-40 dB), the moderate (40-50 dB), severe (60-75 dB), and profound 75 + dB. The deaf hardly profit from auditory training but the hard of hearings do. They have poor self concept, inferiority feeling, temper tantrums, submissiveness, lack of cognitive functioning and language reading difficulties. Interventions and psycho-educational programmes have proved helpful for them, including speech therapy.

The Learning Disabled

Learning disabled children exihibit disorder in one or more of the basic psychological processes involved in understanding and using the spoken or written languages. These disorders are manifested in listening, thinking, talking, reading, writing, spelling, arithmatic. They include conditions which are referred to as perceptual problems, brain injury, minimal brain dysfunction, dyslexia, developmental aphasia. They do not include learning problems which are primarily due to visual, hearing or motor handicaps, to mental retardation, emotional disturbance or to environmental disadvantage. These children are near or above average in intelligence, impulsive, distractible, poor in language organisation, and abstract ideas, hyperactive as well as hypo-active in different situations. They have severe reading problems. Emotionally unstable, these children are over dependent. They display deficiency in memory processes and thinking.

Physical, Neurological and Health Handicapped

A variety of interchangeable terms have been used to describe persons with physical handicaps e.g., physically handicapped, crippled, orthopaedically handicapped, multiple handicapped. But the legal definition for orthopaedically impaired is a severe orthopaedic impairment that adversely affects child's educational performance. The term includes clubfoot, poliomyelities, bone tuberculosis, cerebral palsy, amputations, fractures or burns that cause contractions.

Health handicap is manifested by severe communication and other developmental and educational problems, or having limited strength, vitality or alertness because of heart condition, tuberculosis, rheumatic fever, asthma, epilepsy, lemophillia, lead poisoning, leukemia or diabetes.

From an educational point of view, crippling and neurological handicaps would include all children with non-sensory physical handicaps whether or not they are accompanied by a neurological damage whether they result in chronic health condition or crippling. Muscle weakness, paralysis, non-coordination are grouped under neuro-muscular impairment. The difficulty usually occurs in nerves which innervate the muscles. This may result from infection or injury at any time during the individual's life. Poliomyelitis otherwise known as infantile paralysis comes under neurological impairment. Spina Bifida, Cerebral Palsy and Epilepsy are known neurological handicaps. They require special educational services and treatment. These chidlren show perceptual problems, inability for spatial orientation and judgement.

The Speech and Language Handicapped

Speech impairment is the most common disorder among exceptional children. Speech is defective when it deviates so far from the speech of other people that it calls attention to itself, interferes with communication, or causes the child to be maladjusted. Much can be done for these children by the regular classroom teacher and speech therapist. These children have articulation problems, stuttering, voice disorders, delayed speech and language problems. Language disorders are characterised by abnormal comprehension and/or production of symbols, grammatical structure and words. These are corrected by appropriate language training and intervention from early stages. Speech defects are corrected by speech therapy.

The Slow Learner

Slow learners are seen in the classroom. They are regarded in numerous ways. Slow learner refers to children and adolescents who learn or underachieve in one or more academic areas. Intellectually they are within 80 and 95 IQ points range i.e., on the borderline between average low average classification of intelligence. Slow learners are not special education students. They receive remedial education and for them the regular classroom curriculum and learning are applicable. There is no diagnostic or descriptive profile that characterises the slow learner. They are under achievers and they come from low socio-economic backgrounds. They have low self-concepts. They need educational attention but not special educational services.

The Gifted

Gifted are those children whose cognitive abilities place them in the upper three to five per cent of the population. The gifted children have an IQ of 130 and above. They have superior cognitive ability, creativity in thinking and production. They display superior ability in problem solving and possess high aspiration, high motivation, goal oriented behaviour, analytical ability, perseverance, action oriented, linguistic competence and physical abilties. They learn faster and remember for longer time than average or normal children. But for rare exceptions they are well adjusted in home and school. They can be future problem solvers, innovators, and evaluators of culture if adequate educational experiences are provided.

The Multiple Handicapped

The presence of more than one type of disability in an individual is referred to as multiple handicap. Most multiple handicapped children are characterised by mental retardation along with another physical disability. Emotional disturbance is also often associated with other disabilities i.e., cerebral palsy, epilepsy and mental retardation. Much thought is currently being given to the education of multiple handicapped children. The term does not include deaf-blind children.

Socially Disadvantaged

Social Disadvantaged Children refer to children who come from socio-economically backward sections of the community who cannot profit from school because of deprivation of one sort or another. They live in interior tribal and rural areas of the country where educational facilities are minimal. These children have been identified by various types of tests which are either in conflict with one another or are not comprehensive enough, (Panda, 1995). The disadvantaged children show progressive decline in intellectual functioning, cumulative academic deficits, and premature school termination and high dropout rates. Besides these, the behavioural characteristics include: distractibility, poor self-concept, low motivation, and impulsive behaviour.

Concept of Children with Special Needs

Can these children be called as "Children with Special Needs"? It is true that these children have special educational needs and the term special needs children is also used simultaneously for exceptional children. A brief discussion on this point is imperative.

The concept "children with special educational needs" is of British origin. Prior to 1944, provision of education was made on the basis of a specific handicap i.e., visual and hearing impairment, essentially through charitable initiatives. The emphasis was more on training than on education. Originally, provision for children with sensory and physical disabilities and mental handicaps were made, and subsequently extended to those with emotional and behavioural problems.

In the period following World War-II an increasing amount of research was directed at children with special education needs, particularly in the USA. It was recognised that this could not be achieved through the classification of children into handicap categories which had no direct educational implications. Parents became conscious and concerned that their children's educational needs should be met and in the period following the War many parents' organisations were started which then exerted pressure to improve educational provisions. This was the second cycle of development in special education.

Research on social deprivation indicated that children's educational progress did not reflect factors within the child but within the child's environment. This led to the Head Start programme in USA and "the educational priority area" programme in Britain. The third development was growing concern for the rights of the minorities. Equal educational opportunities were seen as essential to realising the rights through participation in the general system of education.

Integrated education was regarded as necessary to enable an individual to become an accepted member of society. These views led to a strong demand that those with special educational needs should be educated in ordinary schools. Integrated education in different forms was introduced, but in Britain it waited to be implemented till the 1988 Education Act was formulated about special education needs.

While use of the term "Special Education Need", or "children with special needs" sound very pleasant and affirmative, there are certain conceptual and practical problems while making a decision as to whether a child has certain special educational need (SEN). The conceptual issues are:

a. nature of special educational needs,
b. the rights of those with special educational needs and their parents,
c. the effectiveness of identifying, assessing, and meeting special educational needs.

The current definition of special educational needs is widely considered to constitute a major change from the previous framework based on educational handicap. The concept of SEN is more positive as it is concerned with everything about the child abilities—and disabilities—as well as resources and constraints in the environment which affect educational progress.

There are four arguments against the use of categories :

1. Children often suffer from more than one disability (multiple handicapped). This raises difficulties in placing them.
2. Categories promote the idea that all children in the same category have similar educational needs which is not true.
3. Categories as the basis for special provisions draw resources away from children not covered by the statutory categories e.g., special assistance for visually handicapped.
4. Categories have the effect of labelling children and schools adversely. This has a stigmatizing effect.

There are two reasons in favour of categorisation as well.

1. Categories help to focus attention on the needs of different groups of children with difficulties.
2. Categories offer a valuable means of safeguarding the rights of handicapped children to an education suited to individual needs.

But if one examines it critically the term SEN is also a category. In any case, separation of categories is an inherent part of the practical administrative arrangements for meeting special educational needs. Hence, the main change in using special educational needs is to loosen the connection between special education provision (SEP) and special school and units. What underlies the abandoning of categories in special needs education is the move to separating the delivery of special education provision from the location of delivery in special schools. The main issue currently is the nature of exceptional educational needs and the kinds and organisation of provision to meet these needs. Hence, the term exceptional children will be used throughout this book.

Special Education Services

How do we train these children? What kind of provision can be visualised? There are some accepted procedures and settings for treating children's problems. An examination of special education in the school system reveals an incremental continuum or ordered array of special education classes designed to serve the individual needs of children. Special educators agree that a range or continuum of placement alternatives must exist for exceptional children (Deno, 1973).

Four aspects are unique about special education: specialized educators, special curricular content, special instructional methods, and special instructional materials. Prior to the mainstreaming trend these four services were almost always provided to children within the context of special classes or schools. These classes and schools were categorized along a continuum reflecting their degree of separation from the mainstream. Resource rooms, self-contained classes, special day schools, and residential treatment centres reflect this continuum, with resource rooms being a relatively less restrictive environment than residential centres. The goal is to place a child in the least restrictive environment relative to the severity of his or her handicapped condition. Therefore, even with the current trend toward mainstream programmes, many exceptional children will receive some of their education in one or more of the special environments outside regular classes.

Residential Schools

The residential school has two purposes:

a. The residential schools are primarily meant to provide 24 hour comprehensive education and care.
b. In certain cases where the care and management of the severely disabled child poses problems, it is necessary to send disabled children to residential institutions. In this case, the aim is not education. It is just a residential facility for care. Education is an adjunct to the total programme.

The children of either category are permitted to have as much contact with parents as possible, either by home visits, parental visits or both. But the greatest disadvantage of residential institutions is that they deprive children to of a chance to mingle with normal children.

Home Bound or Hospitalised Instructions

The instruction is provided to children in Home/Hospitals in case they are under prolonged treatment for emotional problems, heart ailments, poliomyletes, chronic health problems. The special teacher goes to Home/Hospital to teach these children for a short period. It is psychologically and educationally useful.

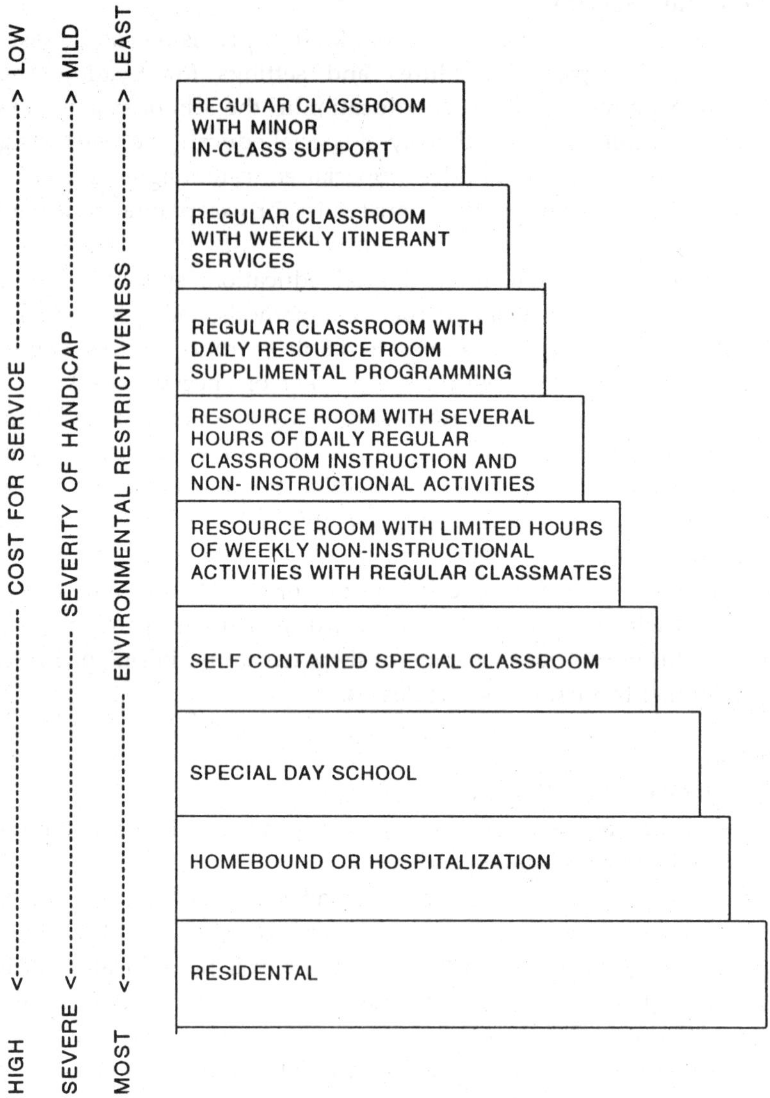

Figure 1: Continuum of Special Education Services

Special Day Schools

In many countries special day schools for various categories of handicapped children have been set up. These tend to be cheaper than special residential schools. In large cities, special day schools cater to the needs of one type of disability but in small cities they are meant for two disabilities. The defect in this system is that children are isolated from normal children.

Special Classes

Special class is a self-contained classroom in a regular school where a category of disabled children are admitted. There may be more than one special class depending on the number of children and the type of disability. This is specially meant for mentally retarded children. The children receive instruction in the special class and are separated from normal peers.

Resource Room

In this programme exceptional children, or children with special needs usually belonging to a single category, may be placed in a school for normal children. They participate in the regular classroom programme to the extent possible. For some time they go to a resource room where a specially qualified teacher instructs them in the use of special equipments and in overcoming special problems they may encounter in keeping up with academic or extra-curricular activities.

The resource room activities can be of three levels:

a. Resource room with limited hours of weekly non-instructional activities with regular classmates.
b. Resource room with several hours of daily regular classroom instruction and non-instructional activities.
c. Regular classroom with daily resource room supplementary programmes.

In this system which varies in degree of integration and use of resource room, the exceptional child is enrolled in the regular classroom. He receives much of his instruction there but he goes to the resource room to receive specialised instruction and use specialised equipments.

This plan is suitable for any type of child who can succeed in regular classes when provided with extra assistance. The resource room is well equipped with staff and equipment. The child becomes integrated with normal children academically and socially, in addition to his physical integration.

Regular classroom with weekly itinerant specialist

Under this system an exceptional child receives assistance from an itinerant teacher but is enrolled for all his classes under a regular teacher in the neighbourhood public school. In view of the fact that disabled children are often widely scattered it is not feasible to organise a resource teacher programme in every school. In such a situation it is advisable to have a travelling teacher assisting handicapped children in resource rooms in different schools. These schools should not be located at great distances from one another. It is quite similar to the resource room programme. Regular classroom teachers may also be trained to handle exceptional children in the regular class itself with more support from the special teachers.

The various types of special education services mentioned are representative ones. Three critical dimensions that define this continuum of special education services are: Environmental Restrictiveness, Severity of Handicap, and Cost of Service. Each dimension has been qualitatively anchored with reference to regular education classes. Thus, as placements get further away from the mainstream, they become increasingly more restrictive and costly, and are generally designed to handle more severe types of handicap. Ideally, placement decisions should be based on an analysis of an individual's needs and a system of methods for treating such needs.

Individualized educational programming calls for flexible use of settings and supporting staff. It seems logical that when support staff is skillful and motivated, the possibility of successfully educating a child in the mainstream is high. In a typical resource room arrangement, the exceptional child is enrolled in a regular program but is provided with additional educational and emotional support in one or may be two areas of weakness. The resource class would most likely be organized in a small group. In the self-contained special class arrangement, exceptional children are usually physically segregated from other groups of children and receive all academic instruction from special educators. But on a limited basis throughout the day they share in other activities such as sports and assemblies with non-handicapped peers.

Special day schools have been organised for different groups of exceptional children, especially the emotionally disturbed, physically handicapped, trainable mentally retarded, and multiple handicapped. Special schools are located some distance from the regular schools; this segregates children and staff, and limited interaction with non-handicapped peers takes place. Homebound or hospital services are provided primarily for children with serious health complications and/or multihandicapped preschoolers. Finally, there are residential schools or institutions for children with various severe handicapping conditions. Children live at the school and thus are able to receive intensive, daily educational, psychological, and medical services. Researchers have begun to investigate the effectiveness of services for exceptional children in the mainstream, and its variants.

Variants in the Service Delivery Systems

Portage

Portage training is used for children at risk, or for those having learning difficulties, developmental delays or mental retardation. It is a need based participatory family training in child care and development. It is home based. Yet it can be institution or centre based, non-formal, a cost effective pre-school early intervention programme for removing obvious learning difficulties or reducing delays in various areas of development such as cognition, motor, social, language etc. It involves parents, grandparents, siblings who act as the child's primary therapeutic teachers. The model is community based and it involves the utilisation of existing community resources.

Besides this, para professionals, professionals, non-professionals all cooperate and act as a team in this programme. It aims at motivating awakening and mobilising the community, parents, for changing the development of their children through service delivery. In the field of special needs children the programme has tremendous utility.

The Portage Model assumes that competencies are simply transmitted from professionals to parents, easily measurable and retained once learned. Children's development does not occur in a linear manner, but results from mutual transactions between children and their social and care giving environments.

Pre-School Intervention

Besides the educational services provided to the disabled children, attempts have been made to minimise disability by way of pre-school intervention. The portage project is one much innovation.

A comprehensive peripatetic teaching service has been conceived which would cater wherever possible, exclusively for children below school age with disabilities or significant difficulties.

These peripatetic teachers should

(i) assess children's educational needs on the basis of trained observation,

(ii) work with parents towards an educational programme for the child in the light of his assessed needs,

(iii) work directly with and teach children on a regular basis,

(iv) maintain contact with other professionals in the various services concerned with meeting the needs of young children with disabilities and their parents,

(v) encourage and participate in meetings of groups of parents of young children with special needs,

(vi) put parents in touch with toy libraries, local forms of pre-school provision—play groups, opportunity groups, day nurseries,, nursery schools, classes in ordinary or special schools and voluntary organisations.

Development of Special Education

The West

Education, Care, Training and Rehabilitation of exceptional children has a long past, but a short scientific history. An understanding of the origin and development of the special education movement would help to understand where we stand now in the field, particularly in India. Children with defects were not cared for in prehistoric societies. Defects like mental illness in the good old days were considered the result of some kind of sin. Children suffering from them were either killed or punished. The physicians and scholars in ancient Greek and Roman societies made some efforts to treat and preserve the lives of the handicapped and provided asylums for them. The Renaissance brought a small change in the earlier attitudes. This was the state of affairs until the late 18th and early 19th centuries.

The early history of special education started with the hearing handicapped as early as 1555 when the Spanish monk Pedro Ponce de Leon (1520-1584) taught a small number of deaf children to read, write and speak and learn academic subjects. Jnan Pablo Bonet in 1620 wrote the first book on the education of the deaf and developed a one handed manual alphabet that is being used even today. In England John Bulwer published another book on the education of the deaf in 1644, followed by the Deaf and Dumb Man's Tutor by George Dalgarno in 1680 which set out instructional methods.

The first school for the deaf in Great Britain was established in 1767 in Edinburgh by Thomas Braidwood. Braidwood's method combined oral and manual method teaching alphabets and signs.

At about same time Samuel Heinicke (1729-1784) developed the oral method emphasising lip reading and speaking skills in Germany at Leipzig in 1778 which was further developed by F.M. Hill (1805-1874).

In France, Michel del' Epee (1712-1789) who established the first school in Paris in 1755, and Ambroise Sicard (1742-1822) were developing sign language. The French system also emphasised training of the senses of sight and touch which became the forerunner to Montessorie's sensory training approach.

Education of deaf children in USA started with Gallandet (1787-1851) using the French method. Gallandet established the first school of the deaf in 1847 (which is today known as the American School for the deaf). The New York School for the deaf opened the next year. By 1863 there were 22 schools for the deaf in USA. The first oral school of the deaf in Massachussets was established in 1867. Day school classes for the deaf were started in 1869 at Berton. Adult education for the deaf began in New York City in 1874.

Subsequently Grahma Bell (1847-1922) worked tirelessly for the deaf. Helen Keller (1880-1957) who was deaf and blind herself from early childhood, was a living example of the effectiveness of special education in overcoming the disability. The development of services for the deaf were hindered because the conflict over oral and manual method of instruction, but these have been reconciled over the years. In 1880, an international congress of education of the deaf was held in Milan, Italy. It made two recommendations:

a. Oral method must be preferred to the manual method.
b. Oral method must be preferred to lip reading/sign language.

In Europe, oral method continued to prevail unchallenged during more than half the 20th century. After World War II the progress in electoacoustic technology gave new impetus to oralism. The increased belief that early education and intervention would allow most deaf children to attend ordinary schools for normal hearing or special units to these schools. The mainstreaming movement progressively gathered more and more strength in great Britain, then in the United States, and continental Europe.

Education of the blind began in France with Valentin Hany (1745-1822) a French philanthrophist who in 1784 founded the National Institution for the Blind in Paris. It is an integrated school and its success led to the establishment of seven schools in Europe during the next 15 years. The first school for the blind in Watertown, Massachussets was instituted in 1829 by Samuel Grindley Howe (1801-1876). This gave rise to residential schools for the partially sighted until the development of special classes in public schools in 1900 at Chicago. Special classes for the partially sighted was begun 13 years later in Boston. Hany developed embossed letters to be read with fingers and using this he printed the first book for the blind. Louise Braille (1809-1852) blind from childhood himself developed the system of Braille using raised dots to represent letters or alphabets, manually prepared for many years. The Braille typewriter was developed by Frank Hall (1843-1911), and a Braille printing system was standardised internationally in 1932.

Education of children with mental retardation began with the attempt by a French physician Dr. Itard (1775-1835) to educate an 11 year old boy who had been found living as a savage in the woods. This was documented in the book *"The Wild Boy of Aveyron"*. Edward Seguin (1812-1880) followed the technique in France and United States and Maria Montessorie (1870-1952) in Italy. Seguin published his book "Idiocy and its treatment by the Physiological method" in 1866. It contained ideas which are relevant even now—total education of the child, individualisation of instruction, beginning instruction at the child's current level of functioning, and rapport between teacher and pupil. These were included in the famous method of Montessories for the education of the handicapped and non-handicapped.

Decroly (1871-1932) in Belgium developed a curriculum for mentally retarded children early in the 20th century and established schools throughout Europe. Binet (1857-1911) made an immense contribution with the invention of intelligence testing.

In 1839 the first blind and mentally retarded (MR) child was enrolled in the Perkins Institute for the Blind in the USA. In 1848 the first residential school for the MR was opened in Massachusetts. By 1917 all states except four provided instructional care for the mentally retarded in the USA.

The first public school with special classes for children with mental retardation was formed in Germany in 1859 and thereafter in other European nations in the next decades. In the USA the first public school with special classes for the MR was opened in 1896 at Providence, Rhodes Island.

There were very few special treatments and provisions for the orthopaedically handicapped and the health impaired prior to the 20th century. In the USA the first special class was established in Chicago in 1899, for children with low vitality in 1908 at Providence, Rhodes Island, and a class for children with epilepsy in Baltimore, Maryland in 1909.

Esquirol (1772-1840) published the first description of childhood psychosis in 1838 in a volume on scientific treatment of mental illness. For the first time in 1871 the New Haven connecticut Public Schools provided a class for emotionally disturbed (ED) boys in New York City in 1874. These were first attempts made in USA. It was not until the 1930s that ED children were studied in a systematic way. The years since World War II have been characterised by the rapid development of services for handicapped children.

Special education services expanded rapidly after World War II both in numbers and types of children served. Legislative measures, parental involvement, early education or pre-school education for handicapped children all took off, including the education of those suffering from cerebral palsy, the learning disabled and the physically handicapped. By the 1970s facilities were available for all categories of the handicapped in the advanced countries of the world, and after 1981 in the developing nations.

Vocational Rehabilitation, occupational therapy, physical therapy were brought into the services for the handicapped. Expanded technology, use of computers, transportation devices, learning and visual aid technology, telecommunication systems, tele typewriters for the Deaf all came into use. Talking boons for the blind, which convert print into vibrating images that can be read with fingers were invented. The Kurzwell Reading Machine which converts print into spoken Engish, mobility aids etc. have further revolutionised the education of the disabled.

Besides, the 1970s have seen the emergence of mainstreaming and least restrictive environment as dominant concepts in special education. The special class has doubtful efficacy and that is why there is a shift from placement in residential schools and special day schools and increased enrollment in regular classes. Segregation is now discouraged unless the handicap is very, very severe.

Indian Scenario

School Education

The first attempts at educating handicapped children were made in the last two decades of the nineteenth century with the establishment of the first school for the hearing impaired in Bombay in 1885, followed by the first school for the visually impaired in Amritsar in 1887. Growth of schools for the handicapped in the sixty years until the advent of independence was extremely slow and sporadic. By 1947 India had just 32 schools for the blind. The number rose to 170 in 1980. Now there are 243 schools for the visually impaired in the country. Prior to independence there were only eight codes available in the country but Bharati Braille has replaced all other codes now. Thirteen Braille presses are available in the country.

The number of schools for the hearing impaired was only 35 in 1947 but had risen to 180 by 1980. The present figure of schools for the hearing impaired is about 478 as per the Rehabilitation Council of India (RCI) directory of which 97 are secondary schools. The largest number are in the state of Maharashtra (139 schools).

Schools for the mentally retarded were just three in 1947, but rose to 200 by 1980 and at present there are 600 schools for mentally retarded children. The first school for the cerebral palsied was started in 1973. There are 12 schools run for the cerebral palsied at present, but no facility is yet available for autistic children. As regards the orthopaedically handicapped most of them go to ordinary schools.

Teacher Training

Since 1981, systematic attempts have been made in the field of teacher training for handling special needs children. The leadership in this direction has been taken up by NCERT in designing courses of short term duration, mainly to implement the Integrated Education (IED) Scheme floated by the Govt. of India under centrally sponsored schemes (which has been now named as (PIED) project integrated education of the Disabled). NCERT has designed three level courses which are:

- Level I. One week training of all primary teachers in the project area,
- Level II. In-service training for six weeks for selected teachers,
- Level III. One year multi-category training of teachers since 1987 in its Regional Colleges of Education.

Besides, a six months training course has been given to key persons at the NCERT headquarters. Several courses have been designed by the Rehabilitation Council of India. Degree courses have been started in some universities leading to B.Ed. and M.Ed. in special education.

Rehabilitation

Vocational Rehabilitation Centres (VRC) have been established. National Institutes have started functioning. A three per cent job reservations for the handicapped has been brought in and special employment exchanges set up. National Awards, Tax concessions, self employment schemes, sheltered workshops are also available for the handicapped. District Rehabilitation Centres (DRC) have been set up.

Community Based Rehabilitations (CBR) are in operation, where it is the responsibility of the community to rehabilitate the disabled of all categories. Each level is eqipped with Trained Personnel. Regional Research Training Centres (RRTC) have been set up in the four regions of the country. A rehabilitation technology centre and the National Information Centre on Disabled and Rehabilitation (NICDR) have been set up at Delhi. The NGOs have done commendable work in the area of disability over the years.

Documentation

The National Information Centre on Disability and Rehabilitation (NICDR) undertakes collection, classification and storage of data on 12 different aspects of disability.

1. Concessions and facilities provided to the disabled by the central and state govt.
2. Organisations and institutions working for the disabled.
3. Professionals working for the disabled.
4. Statistics about beneficiaries of various rehabilitation schemes and programmes.
5. Demographic statistics about the disabled.
6. Aids and appliances available for the disabled.
7. Statistics about national awards and awardees.
8. Schemes of scholarships—beneficiaries.
9. Scheme of assistance for purchase/fitting of aids/appliances.
10. Scheme of organisations working for the disabled.
11. Employment statistics.
12. Research and Development Projects.

It is proposed to have Regional Centres of NICDR too.

Non-Government Organisations (NGOs) have contributed substantially to the care, training and rehabilitation of the disabled in India. There are 315 voluntary organisations working for the disabled in the country at present. Among them, prominent are the Mahavir Viklang Kendra, Jaipur, Nevedic Prosthetic Centre, Chandigarh, Thakur Hariprasad Institute of Mental Retardation, Hyderabad, Amar Jyoti School, New Delhi. Pandey and Advani (1995) have given an exhaustive list of the voluntary organisations in this sector.

An All India Federation of the Deaf has also come up.

The Rehabilitation Council of India is now regulating the training, recognition and derecognition of the special education centres, institutes.

Training programmes for physiotherapists, occupational therapists, prosthetic and orthotic professionals, speech therapists, audiologists, mobility instructors of the blind, vocational instructioners and counsellors, placement officers, clinical psychologists, rehabilitation workers and others are being held in various National Institutes and Universities as per the norms of the Rehabilitation Council of India.

The major changes as regards exceptional children have been: change from medical diagnosis to multi-professional assessment and treatment,; treatment to education, meeting categorical needs to individual needs and change from category specific curricula and methods to appropriate variations in curriculum for all. There is a growing recognition of special education needs, training of special needs teachers, reorganisation of remedial teaching services, development of much closer relationships between the staff and pupils with special needs.

Highlights of the Chapter

Children who differ from the average or normal in their physical sensory motor and psychological characteristics (intelligence memory, learning, thinking, personality etc.) are designated as exceptional children such as: mentally retarded, visually handicapped, hearing handicapped, physically handicapped, learning disabled, gifted etc. Some of them are called handicapped when they fall below the average in terms of competencies and a few other are called gifted when they deviate in higher direction particularly on intellectual competence.

Not all children are disabled or handicapped to the same degree. It depends upon the degree of impairments. Not all impairments lead to be disabled and/or handicapped. These exceptional children are at times grouped as children with special needs, but the term exceptional children is more comprehensive.

There are different categories of special educational services for education training and care of exceptional children: Residential School, Special Day School, Special Class, Itinerant Teacher, Resource Room Teaching, commonly known as Cascade System based on degree of their separation from the mainstream.

The recent trend however is deinstitutionalisation, mainstreaming and integration is of the exceptional children in the regular school system where least restrictive environment are provided for their growth and development.

Comprehensive care and educational readiness is planned involving community and parents under the portage system and pre-school intervention programmes. These attempts to educate, take care and rehabilitation of the handicapped have started since the early sixteenth and seventeenth centuries in the West and India towards the closure of the 19th century.

Rapid strides and challenging development in education of exceptional children particularly have taken place only after the mid twentieth century in the West and after and IYDP-1981 in India, both by the Governmental sector and voluntary organisations. NICDR established in Delhi augmented the expansion of the programme with full information support and the establishment of National Institutes in major areas of handicap: hearing, visual, mental, orthopaedic, and the Rehabilitation Council of India, under the Ministry of Welfare have brought man power development programmes into the wheel.

Review Questions

1. Explain the concept of exceptional children. Mention the types of children who come under this category.
2. Differentiate between Impairment, Disability and Handicap. Are these terms interrelated?
3. Explain the conceptual and practical issues in the use of terminology "children with special needs".
4. What kind of special educational services can be provided to the exceptional children?
5. Outline the origin and development of special education in the west.
6. Briefly outline development of special education in India.
7. State and explain some variants of special education services.
8. Write short notes on:

   Educable Mentally Retarded
   Trainable Mentally Retarded
   Emotionally Disturbed
   Slow Learning Children
   Disadvantaged Children
   Gifted
   Hearing Handicapped
   Visually Handicapped
   Orthopaedically Handicapped
   Learning Disabled
   Speech and Language Handicapped
   Special School
   Portage System
   Resource Room
   Special Class
   Itinerant Teacher

References

Deno, E., (1973), *Instructional alternatives for exceptional children,* Reston, VA, CEF.

Pandey, R.S. and Advani, L., (1995), *Perspectives in Disability and Rehabilitation,* New Delhi: Vikas Publishing House.

Warnock, M., (1978), *Special Education Needs, Department of Education and Science,* the Warnock Report, London.

WHO, (1976), *International Classification of Procedures in Medicine,* Geneva, Vol. 1 and 2.

Chapter 2

Issues and Innovations in Education of Exceptional Children

This chapter deals with various issues and measures relating to the education of exceptional children. The focus is on issues such as:

- The concept of labelling a child and referring him/her for placement.
- Assessment in Special Education.
- The effects of special class placement of exceptional children.
- Deinstitutionalisation.
- Mainstreaming and/or Integration of exceptional children in regular schools.

Issues relating to integration and innovation are also covered such as:

- Small group instruction.
- Mastery learning strategy.
- Resource room instruction.
- The role of the resource teacher.
- The role of the regular teacher.
- Peer tutoring.
- Programmed Instruction.

Micro Computer in Education.
Ecology and Special Education.
Physical Education in Special Education.

Labelling

"Labelling refers to the act of assigning a child or a condition to a general category or to a particular position in the classification system"—(Hobbs, 1975). By implication it is generally negative. A label indicates that a stigma is present, particularly with mild handicapping classifications e.g., mental retardation, specific learning disabilities, emotional disturbance. In day to day life we often use labels for various purposes. Labels exert direct influence on our behaviour towards persons, objects, situations and issues. In the case of the handicapped the theory of deviance explains the attributions we make.

Referrals precede a child being labeled as disabled in one way or the other. It is initiated when significant learning or behavioural problems in the classroom are noticed. Although anyone can refer a child for special education, it is usually the regular teacher or parent who exercises this responsibility. A regular classroom teacher can use observation, criterion-referenced assessment, curriculum-based assessment for referral purposes. A teacher can observe systematically and collect baseline data, and develop the Criterion Referenced Test (CRT) to know how well or poorly a child is doing compared to others. Recently, the Concept-Based Assessment (CBA) has received considerable attention. This is an assessment procedure in terms of the expected curricular outcome of the school. The teacher simply monitors the progress with respect to school's curriculum.

After referral, the children are labelled on the basis of their eligibility and educational needs. Labels are used to provide some degree of communication among professionals. There are both positive and negative sides to labelling. Hobbs (1975) stated that labels led to improved legislation, imrpoved communication, and the development of advocacy agencies. On the negative side, there are possibilities of stigmatisation, peer rejection, and wrong labelling of minority group children on the basis of inappropriate tests. The labelling process is not that easy as there are overlapping characteristics i.e., Mild mental retardation and learning disabilities. Hence, to provide a specific educational programme based on a label alone is obviously and inappropriate step.

Most severely handicapped students are identified prior to school age by parents and physicians. The majority of mildly handicapped students are usually identified by administration of educational and psychological tests. The physical or sensory disabilities are identified by non-educational procedures. Psychological and educational tests are non-referenced tests. These are relevant to most exceptional stuents. Labels are given according to test scores obtained by the child.

Some of the commonly used tests of intelligence and achievement used in assessing children for labelling purposes are:

1. Wechsler Intelligence Scale for Children—Revised.
2. Kaufman Assessment Battery for Chidlren (sequential and simultaneous processing).
3. Wide Range Achievement Test—(Revised).
4. Peabody Individual Achievement Test—Revised.
5. AAMD Adaptive Behaviour Scale.

Following placement, the education of exceptional students is largely placed in the hands of the special education teacher. Of course, the regular teacher too takes responsibility, as well as the school counsellor, specialists and therapists wherever available. However, once a student has been deemed eligible to receive special education it is essential to develop an Individual Education Program

(IEP). After the labelling and placement in a special setting, the question is asked how much of its is justifiable? Are there efficacy studies to substantiate this? Is the assessment correct?

Assessment in Special Education

Assessing children for identifying handicaps is a necessary step for placement. These are done in various ways. As a matter of fact, assessment in the field of special education has been more controversial than any other area of special education. For effective placement of a child in special education institution and for mainstreaming, two issues are of special concern: (i) assessment principles, and (ii) assessment procedures. Test measures or scores are not the sine qua non of assessment—as assessment here means much more than simply a calculated figure. It requires proper screening for identification of all possible plus and minus points to prescribe guidelines for immediate and intermediate interventions and for the child's future placement in continuum of special education delivery processes.

An attempt has been made in this chapter to present an analysis of the salient features of psycho-educational assessment used for various categories of the handicapped and make the readers, practioners and professionals aware of the shortcomings.

Traditionally assessment and intervention were regarded as independent processes but in Special Education both are integrated and dynamic. Assessment forms an integral part of the process of intervention. Assessment data should dictate intervention and the nature of pupil on the other hand would specify the assessment procedures. The form of psychological assessment now most prevalent in education fails utterly to do this.

The Deviations are:

1. Use of the test for purposes other than those for which they were designed e.g., use of intelligence tests for remedial and compensatory intervention whereas its function is for classification and placement. Intelligence score does not tell the teacher how best to teach. It simply shows the extent to which an individual child differs from others who took the test.
2. Use of technically inadequate tests in decision making, and lack of concern for the type of culture to which the child is exposed as well as using inadequately constructed norms as reference points. Diagnostic Personnel should not routinely administer in such tests to children, nor use normative scores, and interpret and make important decisions. Careful consideration of the target group is necessary with reference to its cultural background. Measurement instruments must have empirical evidence for their validity and reliability for use in such groups.

3. Use of Deficit Score to identify handicapped children is very much in vogue in case of learning disabled children. Discrepancy between capabilities (IQ test) and achievement levels are often used to identify the disabled learners. In fact, measurement errors accumulate when difference scores are used to identify children. One needs to carefully use the different scores.
4. Bias in assessment has been a subject of regular debate. Tests used should not only be non-discriminatory but decision makers should not be biased while making decisions basing their judgement on race, sex, SES, physical characteristics, parental power etc. Labelling has a tremendous effect on teacher's expectation and assessment of cognitive competence and achievement.
5. Assessment of abilities versus skills is another issue. It is better to use skill development models than the ability training model for design of instruction of the disabled. These are related to:
   a. To what extent does ability deficit account for achievement of academic skills?
   b. Does change in ability scores improve achievement skills?
   c. Should we design intervention on the basis of norm reference tests?
   d. Is intervention necessary when efficacy of intervention is marginal?
6. Competence of persons who assess the child varies very widely in our country. There is virtually no certification for test users in India.
7. Should we avoid assessment of disabled children? Certainly such a step is not desirable but a test administrator should know the kind of data to be collected; the kind of behaviour to be sampled; adequacy of tests to measure such traits; relevance of tests; and test administration and scoring procedures.
8. Certain ethical issues also deserve attention. These include:
   — No placement or denial of placement should occur without a full and individual evaluation of each child's special educational needs.
   — Evaluation must be in the primary language of the child.
   — All evaluation devices must be professionally and properly validated for the specific purpose for which the school proposes to use them.
   — Tests should be administered by trained personnel.
   — Assessment should contain more than an IQ test.
   — No one test can be used for placement.
   — Adaptive behaviour, physical condition, and cultural background are to be ascertained.
   — Re-evaluation should be a necessary condition of psycho-educational assessment and diagnosis because "when a programme talks about labeling someone as a particular type and such label could remain with him for the remainder of his life, the margin of error must be almost nil".

9. Cost effectiveness and feasibility in terms of time and objective of assessment need attention. For screening purposes one can use the Group Administered Norm referenced test; or the Multiple Skill Test (Iowa Test of Basic Skills); Cognitive Abilities Test; California Achievement Test; Stanford Achievement Test; Peabody Picture Vocabulary Test.
10. For placement purposes, for example, use of the Norm referenced criteria is appropriate enough using the Wepman Auditory Discrimination Test; Illinois Test of Psycholinguistic Abilities; Development Test of Visual Motor Integration; Development Test of Visual Percepton; Bender Gestalt Test; American Association of Mental Deficiency; Adaptive Behaviour Scale; Edward's Personal Preference Schedule; California Personality Inventory, Thematic Appreception Test; or the Rorschack Ink Blot Test.

Efficacy Studies of Special Class Placement

Special education services were designed to help handicapped children. But much can be said about the effectiveness of special education. It is effective, and it is not effective. There are several reasons for the equivocal nature of this generalisation. One important reason is the vaguely defined parameter of the group "the mildly handicapped": mildly retarded, learning disabled, emotionally disturbed etc. These mask treatment effectiveness, and do not provide an accurate picture of intervention efficacy in general.

Secondly, the Illinois Test of Psycholinguistic Abilities (ITPA) has served as the clinical test in various intervention programmes. The belief is that language training provides better scope for helping special children. This is not so. Efficacy studies on the basis of language intervention are divided. Meta analysis of the findings revealed that ITPA total score and subtest scores based on psycholinguistic training are quite effective and encouraging. For a basic area like language, the average elementary pupils gains about one standard deviation over the school year and exceeds about 84 per cent of the pupil's score made on the language achievement measure at the beginning of school year (Hamill and Larsen, 1978). Perceptual motor training has essentially no effect on achievement and cognitive outcomes and only a modest effect on the areas of which training is directed i.e., perceptual motor ability.

Visual or auditory training failed to produce any significant difference, in achievement on reading skill. But when a child's preferred mode of learning matched with the teaching method, modest improvement for auditory mode, visual mode or kinaesthetic mode of teaching were observed. But special class placement was most disadvantageous for handicapped children whose primary problem was lowered IQ levels. (EMR—.14, slow learner (76-90 IQ)—.34). The emotional and behaviour disordered pupils in a special class were better off than those in a regular class.

One significant factor which appears to lower the efficacy of special class placement is the lowered expectancy. It diverts instructional efforts away from academic pursuits towards a maintenance function. On the other hand, teacher's expectation are not dampened for learning disabled, behaviour and emotionally disturbed children of normal intelligence. This gives a direct focus to a system focusing on individual learning needs and abilities, in order to design the most effective programme of academic improvement necessary to overcome academic deficits. Hence, special education must seek out not new technology, but a frame of reference emphasising the potential for growth in all its clientele. Such a position must be "special" in special education to operate more effectively. It must come out of labelling effects.

It has been observed that a special education intervention that works in one place may or may not work in another. The variability inherent in special education practices is compounded by the fact that it is essentially indeterminate. Special education interventions may or may not produce benefits but the final outcome is largely unpredictable. Hence, special education does not require prescriptive pronouncement (Dunn, 1968).

Therefore, during the present decade great stress has been given to mainstreaming, normalisation, and integration of special needs children under the rubric of least restrictive environment. This trend is in sharp contrast to that of the past years prior to 1980. Concern is being expressed in implementing programmes that truly enhance the academic and social skills. The concept of handicap has undergone a change, the responsibilities of the special educator and regular education have also received recognition. Special education services in the form of integrated education are a response to this need.

Research attempting to observe developmental change sin self-concept and peer acceptance before and after labeling has resulted in mixed results. Labeling either improves or has no significant effect on self-concept and pper acceptance. It is true that there is a strong case against use of labels, but some kind of generic classification and categorisation system is necessary for placement and for organising programmes for the handicapped. Negative connotations cannot be totally avoided but they can be reduced to a minimum if they are directly related to the special educational programme.

Deinstitutionalisation

Several concepts are used in this field to connote mainstreaming or integration such as deinstitutionalisation, normalisation, least restrictive environment (LRE). They are interrelated to the extent that a discussion of one is difficult without reference to the others. "Deinstitutionalisation" means that removing retarded persons from institutions and placing them in other environments. "Mainstreaming" means educating retarded persons as much as possible in classes with non-retarded persons. "Integration" basically means mainstreaming. "Normalisation" means that the individual's total environment should be as close as possible to that of non-handicapped person's environment. Segregation is only desirable when the nature of the handicap is such that education in regular classes with the use of supplementary aids and services cannot be achieved satisfactorily.

Deinstitutionalisation is a trend which grew in reaction to institutionalisation. In institutions, disabled children were considered physically or mentally ill and received treatment but no care and education. Around 1800 such institutions sprouted and as they grew in size they became less cost effective and housed people without much of treatment either. The trend continued. In the 1950s and 1960s a number of social movements took place to help the retarded e.g. President Kennedy's approach to mental illness which led to the establishment of community centres which provided impatient and outpatient care, treatment, consultation and education.

Deinstitutionalisation includes three processes (1) reversing institutionalisation by finding alternative placement, (2) returning to the community all residents who have developed the skills necessary for successful transition, (3) establishing residential environments that protect rights and lead to a rapid transition to the community. At the initial phase there also negative reports on deinstitutionalisation; (a) placement in nursing homes where the quality of care is less than at institutions, (b) primarily medication was the treatment, (c) readmissions to institutions since community facilities are not available, (d) poor medical diagnosis, (e) regression in adaptive behaviour, and (f) incompetent staff to look after the inmates.

Mainstreaming

Over the years, things have improved, diagnosis has become multi-disciplinary, education has become the emphasis, trained professionals are available. Hence, the need for integration and mainstreaming is more felt. Mainstreaming is an approach that emphasizes integration and as such it is the antithesis of the earlier institutionalisation movement which emphasized segregation. But not until the 1970s was it thought fit to integrate retarded children, even though it was known earlier that special classes were not superior to regular classes, and that placement in special classes stigmatised those children. Hence, efforts are directed toward a less restricted educational environment.

The Council for Exceptional Children (CEC) has specified the essentials of mainstreaming the mildly disabled.

1. Providing the most appropriate education for each child in the least restrictive environment (LRE).
2. Concentrating on specific educational needs than on labelling.

3. Developing means by which regular classroom personnel can serve students with adjustment problems.
4. Writing the skills of regular and special educators to best serve the students.

Has mainstreaming a sound footing in research in special education? As early as 1968, Lloyd Dunn, the doyen of the special education movement, wrote a paper based on a decade of research called 'Special Education for the Mildly Retarded, Is much of it Justifiable'? His arguments were quite understandable that in terms of cost, energy training of specialists and resource allocation, special schools and special classes for the mildly retarded did not yield substantial results in the area of academic achievement although improvements did occur in the areas of personal-social adjustment. Attempts were made to make the efficacy studies more objective but the findings virtually remained the same. Rather, placement of a mildly disabled child in a regular class contributed to a slightly better educational performance with the assistance of resource teachers, aids, and care. The differences appeared to be bridged due to pre-school intervention, built-in programmes of language, physical-motor coordination exercises, and manipulating personal social interaction among the peers in the classroom. Hence, in the late 1970's the cry was not for special education of the midly disabled but integration and mainstreaming.

Mainstreaming is a relatively recent development in special education. In fact, the origin of the term 'mainstreaming' is not known. During the mid-twentieth century, several factors came together to precipitate change in the direction of mainstreaming. The research literature that relates most specifically to the mainstreaming movement deals with the mentally retarded.

"*Mainstreaming* is the education of mildly handicapped children in the regular classroom. It is a concept that is compatible with the *least restrictive environment* .... All the handicapped can be educated with their normal peers whenever possible. It is based on the philosophy of equal educational opportunity that is implemented through individual planning to promote appropriate learning, achievement and social normalisation". (Stephens, Blackhurt, and Magliocia, 1983, p. 3).

Mainstreaming does not mean placement of all exceptional students in regular classes. The key to mainstreaming is the placement of the mildly retarded in the regular classroom environment that best fits their needs. It can even be a regular classroom for the part of the day. Sometimes, it may not include a regular classroom but a special class in the regular setting, and extracurricular activities determined by consideration of how best we may promote learning, achievement, and social normalisation.

Mainstreaming is a particular orientation towards supplying special education to the majority of the mildly retarded in particular and the handicapped in general. Environmental stimulation has significant positive effects on the development of retarded children. This was observed in the 1940s and gave a hard blow to the concepts of institutionalisation and segregation prevalent then. It opposed the idea that retardation was permanent and irreversible. Although the Skeels and Dye (1939) study was a landmark, the subsequent studies furthered the research into environmental factors which serve to diminish retardation. Multisensory approaches reduced learning disability. VAKT Multisensory approach (Visual-Auditory-Kinaesthetic-Tactual) approach became widespread.

While sociometirc studies admittedly showed low acceptance, by non-handicapped peers of handicapped children in mainstream classes they also showed that in special classes there is lower academic achievement and few social models from whom the handicapped could learn interpersonal skills. Efficacy studies have shown better academic achievement of regular class special children than those in special classes as highlighted by Dunn, 1968. Dunn's article was frequently cited as *the* consciousness—raising article that began the mainstreaming movement in earnest. It virtually led to an unwarranted assumption that all mildly handicapped children should be placed in the mainstream.

Mainstreaming, is no longer a fad or slogan. It has outgrown that stage. Mainstreaming is a workable process. It needs a comprehensive support system for its success in the school. Are the schools ready for it? What is meant by readiness? It means an individualised education programme, the least restricted environment and parental effort, particularly in the context of a developing country. Further the concept of integration and mainstreaming aim at bridging the differences between milder conditions of disability and the normal peers by providing access to equal educational opportunity under the least restrictive environment. The delivery models of such integration include placement of a mildly disabled child in a regular class with resource teachers for all purposes of acquisition of academic and social skills, an itinerant special teacher plan for a cluster of schools; partial integration where the disabled child lives in a residential setting but attends most of his classes in the regular class of a day school; on special classes with the children however, taking part in cocurricular and other activities of the school.

The objectives are bridge up the initial entry differences in—

a. academic achievement,
b. social skills, and
c. economic sufficiency through development of vocational skills within the limits of the special children's educability.

The aim is never to replace special education classes or schools which could meet the demands of the severely disabled/retarded. In a word, the objective of integration and mainstreaming is normalisation under the least restrictive environment (LRE).

Mainstreaming had its roots in the civil rights movements of the 1950s and 1960s which recognised segregation as illegal. Although the terms mainstreaming and LRE share historical antecedents they are not equivalent. LRE mandates that, to the maximum extent appropriate, handicapped children should be educated with non-handicapped children. In cases of severe handicap, the educational agency may remove a student to a special institution. Resource room or itinerant instruction, in which a visiting teacher takes special classes, is to be provided as a supplementary service to instruction in the regular classroom. Thus, if school personnel or others involved in evaluating and developing individualised educational programmes (IEPs) for students can justify a more restrictive placement than a regular classroom, that placement is acceptable with parental consent.

Mainstreaming has often been interpreted to mean that handicapped students must be instructed is regular classroom settings. According to the US Department of Education (1984) 68% of handicapped students receive most of their education in regular classes in the US, while an additional 25% are enrolled in special classes located in the same buildings as regular education classrooms. Placement in regular classrooms or in school buildings within thse classrooms is presumed to give handicapped students more opportunities to be in contact with non-handicapped peers. Such exposure is thought to present behaviour patterns for handicapped students to emulate.

Placing handicapped students in the same clasroom as non-handicapped students seems to result is desegregation. These students may occupy the same space but they may not be engaged in activities with one another. However, placement in regular classroom per se does not result in improved achievement or social status.

Handicapped students' social status has been improved when programmes were planned to help integrate them into the regular class setting. Kaufman, Gottlieb, Agard, and Kukic (1975) and Wang (1981) emphasized this as follows:

1. "Mainstreaming refers to the temporal, instructional and social integration of eligible exceptional children with normal peers. It is based on an ongoing individually determined educational needs assessment, requiring classification of responsibility for coordinated planning and programming by regular and special education administrative, instructional, and support personnel (Kauffman et. al., 1975; pp. 40-41)."
2. "The term mainstreaming is used to mean an integration of regular and exceptional children in a school setting where all children share the same resources and opportunities for learning on a full-time basis", (Wang, 1981, p. 196).

Several excellent works have discussed the historical and philosphical underpinnings of mainstreaming and LRE, and have analysed research studies conducted on the mainstreaming of handicapped students in regular classroom settings.

Integration

Integration is another expression used to mean mainstreaming. Integration cannot be reduced simply to an educational issue, or an employment issue. Its achievement will require the successful coordination of a whole series of transitions for the handicapped, ranging from early identification, to early intervention, to school programmes, to community, jobs and finally to community living.

An approach to integration that takes the individual needs of the special child into full consideration may result in one or more of following:

Physical integration—Planning for the location of special programmes in school buildings with regular education programmes.

Social integration—Planning for regular personal interactions between students who have handicaps and those who do not.

Academic integration—Planning to ensure students with an without handicaps simultaneously use school resources.

Societal integration—Planning designed to enable students with moderate and severe handicaps to work, live, and spend leisure time with their fellow non-handicapped citizens.

What does integration really mean ?

Integration means:

- Providing special services within the regular schools.
- Supporting regular teachers and administrators.
- Having students with disabilities follow the same schedule as non-disabled students.
- Involving disabled students in as many academic classes and extra curricular activities as possible including music, art, field trips, assemblies and exercises.
- Arranging for disabled students to use library, playground, and other facilities at the same time as non-disabled students.
- Encouraging helper and buddy relationships between disabled and non-disabled students.
- Arranging for disabled students to receive their education in regular community environments when appropriate.
- Teaching all children to understand and accept human diferences.
- Enrolling disabled children in the same schools they would attend if they did not have disabilities.
- Taking parents' concerns seriously.
- Providing an appropriate individualised programme.

Integration does not Mean:

- Dumping students with disabilities into regular programmes without preparation or support.

- Locating special education classes in a separate wing at a regular school.
- Grouping children with a wide range of disabilities and needs in the same programme.
- Exposing children to unnecessary hazards and risks.
- Ignoring children's individual needs.
- Placing too much demands on teachers and administrators.
- Ignoring parent's concerns.
- Isolating children with disabilities in regular schools.
- Putting older students with disabilities in classes for younger children i.e., age appropriate placement.
- Maintaining separate schedules for students in special education and regular education.

How to achieve mainstreaming and/or integration ?

Reynolds (1980) has suggested a set of specific targets in 10 different areas for effective mainstreaming and/or integration.

1. *Curriculum*—The preparation of all teachers should include the study of, and first hand experience with curricular principles, guides, and structures from pre-school through secondary school levels. The means and procedures by which curriculum is developed, adopted, and changed should be understood and there should be practice in designing and modifying curriculum and materials, especially to suit the individual needs of students.
2. *Teaching Basic Skills*—The preparation of all teachers should include necessary elements to assure competency in teaching the basic skills (defined to include literacy, life-maintenance, and personal-development skills).
3. *Class Management*—All teachers should be proficient in class management procedures, including a variety of ecological interventions, group techniques, crisis interventions, etc.
4. *Professional Consultation and Communication*—It is essential now that all teachers have opportunities to master the knowledge and practices involved in effective consultation and other forms of professional communication. All teachers should be skilled at group problem-solving.
5. *Teacher-Parent-Student Relationship*—All teachers should have skills and sensitivity for dealing with parents and siblings of handicapped students.
6. *Student/Student Relationships*—All teachers should be able to convey to students the positive attitudes necessary for productive interactions with normal peers.

7. *Exceptional Conditions*—All prospective teachers should have full knowledge about exceptional children, about school procedures for accommodating children's special needs, and in the functions of specialists who serve exceptional children. Moreoever, opportunities for direct experience with the children and with specialists should be provided.
8. *Referral*—Teachers need to learn the procedures for referrals, the responsibilities involved, and the ways to capitalize on referral resources to obtain better education for individual pupils.
9. *Individualised Teaching*—All teachers should be competent in the assessment of the individual student's educational needs and in adapting instruction to the individual. Teachers should have working knowledge of the IEP development process.
10. *Professional Values*—Professional educators' values ought to reflect a primary emphasis on the needs and rights of individual students.

The following issues emerge from the above for the purpose of implementing the integrated/mainstreamed education scheme.

1. Degree of segregation in the educational setting has to be spelled out for the mildly disabled. What type of integration would best fulfil the objectives needs to be decided.
2. Supportive systems and services for psychological, recreational, and vocational skill development have to be visualised and introduced.
3. Instructional procedures have been stereotyped due to the lack of exposure of existing teachers to special teaching techniques. There is need for inservice as well as preservice teacher training.
4. Existing negative attitudes of teachers and normal peers towards mildly disabled children's capacities need to be changed.
5. Parental involvement and community participation in the total scheme of integrated education is important. The parents constitute a vital factor in the child's care and acceptance at home.
6. Integrated schools should use sensory stimulation and life skill training.
7. Routine placement of a mildly disabled child in regular school without due process of identification and diagnosis, and prescriptive teaching, is meaningless.
8. Normal and mildly disabled teacher-pupil ratio, in classes needs major attention.
9. Preparation for early intervention programmes, quality of intervention, and management must be made.
10. Behaviour management resource specialists should be used and resource rooms installed.
11. Professional intolerance and alienation among specialists of different disciplines should be minimised.

12. Delineation of activities by different service delivery systems in the total scheme of integrated education is required.
13. Development of infrastructure and instructional materials in regional and state languages for the resource room is needed.

Innovations in Special Education

Innovative steps have been visualised and are in operation in recent years to make mainstreaming and/or integration effective. Teachers who know how to individualise instruction will have little difficulty integrating disabled pupils in the classroom. Individualised instruction in a classroom does not mean 30 students doing 30 different things at the same time. It means that after a general discussion, the class can be divided into three to five small groups for part of their instruction. It is in the small groups that the most pressing needs of the children can be met.

Teachers should be managers of learning, facilitaters of the learning experience rather than disbursers of information. All teachers need time to work with individual pupils or groups of pupils. Experienced teachers keep catch up time in the few minutes before recess, during lunch, or after school to help those pupils who need extra instruction. During this time they also help children to begin homework.

Small group instruction

Using small group instruction is another way to make mainstreaming more effective. Before using this technique the teachers should have sufficiently developed their classroom grouping skills to enable small pupil groups to function smoothly. They should be taught how to work in groups. The following instructions could be a starting point:

- Choose your two most trustworthy pupils.
- Assign them each a specific task to be completed outside class, such as preparing for a science demonstration.
- Excuse the pupils from regular class work. Make the assignment a choice one.
- Have the pupils put on their demonstration.
- Compliment pupils for a job well done.
- Get ready for complaints from others for such choice assignments. Now the stage is set.
- Select a reliable pupil and one of the less reliable ones.
- Gradually extend this procedure over five or six weeks to more and more small groups.
- Make sure that having a group assignment remain a privilege; this will encourage good behaviour.

Mastery Learning Strategy

Mastery learning techniques offer a systematic way to give pupils longer periods of time to master skills and concepts without penalty. In the long run mastery learning can save time by reducing the time for revision. Bloom (1964) has found that mastery learning hinges on pupil perserverance and aptitude, and on the clarity of the teacher's instructions. Pupil's perseverance tends to increase as pupils realise that they are learning.

In order to use mastery learning the following steps may be used. Use Mastery Learning by—

- Restricting mastery learning to the basic curriculum.
- Beginning with the most essential basic skills.
- Providing pupils with a short list of skills to learn.
- Having each pupil study, practice, self-test, recycle, and retest, with final checking (testing) by the teacher until mastery is achieved.
- Initially, allowing about 10 to 15 per cent more time for handicapped children.
- Drawing on assistance of tutors from other grades or the same grade, teacher aides, parent volunteers, programmed instructional units, micro-computer drills.

Mastery learning is an optimistic theory about teaching and learning that any teacher can virtually get all students to learn excellently, swiftly and self-confidently. Both exceptional and non-exceptional children can benefit from the system of instruction if it is systematic, if the tasks are broken into small steps, if goals are clearly stated, if sufficient time is given to the learners and there is some criteria of what constitutes mastery.

Bloom asserts that native intelligence matters in learning. But when instruction is matched to learner's present level of functioning, all students can learn fast. Mastery learning programmes are used successfully in special education programmes under IEP. Some of the materials used in special education classes are based on mastery learning principles. In order to make it more effective a resource room with a resource teacher are required.

Resource Room

The concept of resource room gained popularity following the declaration that the tracking system was illegal. ("Tracking" system is one by which children, based on IQ test achievements, are placed in different classes, according to their ability. This was judged to violate the law on education of the disabled). This was the forerunner to mainstreaming and LRE. The resource room concept is a promising alternative to placement in self-contained classes or regular classes without support services. Usually students attending resource rooms are mildly handicapped and gifted exceptional children.

A resource room is a class which special needs students attend for less than 50% of their school hours. The resource room is staffed by a resource room teacher. Attendance in the resource room is determined by a multi-disciplinary staff according to the student's individual needs. Students attend in specific time slots when they receive remedial instruction from a trained specialist in their deficit areas. A resource room should be well equipped with a wide variety of instructional material. Individualised instruction may include perceptual training, language development, motor training, social and emotional development, and academic skills development. Resource room class size should be small. A recommended size per teacher would be no more than 20 students at any one time. Class sessions are either individual or in small groups of up to five students per session. The sessions continue for a minimum of 20 minutes and a maximum of 45 minutes in length. The resource room should have the same comfortable characteristics of a regular classroom—should be at least 150 square feet size with adequate lighting, and ventilation. The resource room should be easily accessible to techers and students and possess adequate storage space for folders and materials. In general, the resource room should provide a positive learning environment.

Placement in the resource room is intended to be of short duration. As students progress toward specified goals they are returned to full-time placement in the regular classroom. Return to the regular classroom should progress through a gradual phasing out of support services. The resource room is to be considered as one type of service delivery within the continuum of services available.

Resource Teacher

'A resource teacher's role is open ended and limited only by time, talent and acceptance of the teacher by the school administration and staff. The resource teacher is a trained specialist who works with, and acts as a consultant to other teachers, providing materials and methods to those who are having difficulties within the regular classroom. Usually the resource teacher works with the mildly handicapped population in a centralised resource room.

The role of Resource Teacher has been identified as follows:

a. He should conduct and participate in the screening of children with learning disabilities, determine their learning abilities and prepare final report for referral.
b. He should provide instruction in small groups and individually.
c. He should prepare lessons for a child who cannot function in a regular classroom.
d. He should provide resource room help till the child is fully integrated in the regular class.
e. He should provide consultation to the regular classroom teacher and parents.

Requirements of Equipment for Resource Room Disability-Wise Inventory of Equipment and Material

Disability	*Aids and Equipments Individuals*	*Materials Shared within a School*	*Materials Shared amongst schools*	*Instruct-Material*
Orthopaedic	Adjustable furniture, special writing material, thick pen.	Adjustable furniture provision for development of improvised prosthetics.		
Visual Impaired Blind.	Braille slate and stylus Abacus, Taylor frame, Mobility canes.	Brailler, Abacus, Taylor frame, Cassettee and Talking books, Maps, Recreational material, Embossed recreational materials.	Braille sheets, Thermoform machine, Indu Brailon Maintenance services for Brailler, Embossed recreational materials.	Braille Material on cassette and talking books.
Partially sighted and low vision children.	Special adaptive equipment like hand magnifiers to be used with spectacles, reading lamps.	Specially designed desks with adjustable magnifiers, white boards in	Special arrangements for producing large print materials,	Large print materials.
Hearing Impaired.	Individual hearing aids.	Voice trainer, Mirror 3′ × 6′ size for speech therapy, big mirrors 10′ × 6′ in each classroom, Group hearing aids, cell hearing aids.	Audiometer Voice trainer Maintenance facilities for hearing aids.	Special learning materials like flash charts, educational games, handouts of classroom activities.
Mentally Retarded		Sensory apparatus and kits prepared on the lines of Maria Montessori Kits or produced by NCERT for early Childhood Education Programme.		Material written on a lower reading level than average.

The resource teacher may be categorical, non-categorical, itinerant, teacher consultant to regular class teachers, parents and other personnel connected with the education of the child.

A resource teacher is a highly trained professional who is capable of diagnosing the child, planning and implementing the teaching programme, assisting the classroom teachers, providing continuous evaluation of the child and conducting in service sessions with other educators, and the community. The role of the resource teacher includes direct service to individuals and small groups of children, consultant services to classroom teachers, and assessment and delivery of individualised programmes.

The special education/Resource-room Teacher should :

- find out if the student has the skills to function in the classroom,
- identify the physical or academic adaptations needed for the student to function in the regular class,
- identify the student's strengths and weaknesses;
- provide the handicapped student an opportunity to visit the regular education class and meet the teacher before he is enrolled there,
- determine the adapted equipment or the special services needed by students to function in the regular class,
- participate in planning for mainstreaming activities,
- participate in parent and community orientation programmes on mainstreaming,
- seek out consultative relationships with specialists on the school staff,
- develop programmes to prepare special students for entry into regular classes,
- prepare members of regular classes for the entry of special students into the class,
- gather information to determine the educational needs of each students,
- evaluate each student's present level of functioning,
- determine goals for each student that are appropriate, realistic and measurable,
- determine group goals for the class as a whole and for subsets within the class,
- involve parents in setting goals for their children,
- design teaching procedures that provide for individual differences among students,
- prepare a variety of activities that will involve the entire class in grouping patterns that are varied and flexible,
- design a variety of alternative teaching strategies,
- develop plans for using human and material resources,
- develop a flexible time schedule that provides for learning, as well as the physical and social needs of each student.

Regular Class Teacher

The regular class teacher where a child with special needs has been admitted should:

- learn about the student's handicapping condition,
- its common characteristics,
- the child's expected performance,
- common difficulties the disabled child will experience,
- learn about the appliances and special materials the child uses, e.g., pushing a wheel chair up or down stairs, storing wheel chairs, etc.,
- determine if any special methods, techniques, or adaptations are needed for the disabled child to function more independently and successfully,
- meet the special education teacher to determine specific strengths, weakness and needs of the handicapped student,
- prepare the classroom, remove obstacles, make necessary adaptations to furniture, rearrange furniture to help the special needs student, and so on,
- use various techniques to manage individual and group behaviour:
    (i) Reward self-directed behaviour;
    (ii) Teach how to respond to disruptive behaviour;
    (iii) Use peer role models to advance goals;
    (iv) Teach students to relieve aggression in acceptable ways.
- acknowledge appropriate behaviour in order to stimulate continuous effort;
- conduct class activities in ways to encourage student interaction;
- provide instruction in the development of coping strategies;
- plan with the students for systematic appraisal and improvement of the psychological climate of the class;
- collect and record data to evaluate student progress;
- develop a feedback system that will furnish continuous data to students, teachers, and parents;
- use evaluation data to assess the attainment of goals and to set new goals.

Stating it more realistically the regular as well as the special and resource room teachers for teaching exceptional children must be cognizant of their Rights, Roles, and Responsibilities. Mainstreaming therefore is the "End of the Quiet Revolution". The Rights of the exceptional learners are to be safeguarded while mainstreaming them in terms of their right to

Public education,
Individual education programme (IEP),
Non-discriminatory evaluation,
Due process of law,
Least restrictive environment.

The IEP is the management tool that specifies the child's educational needs, annual goals for the child, the service provided and effectiveness of the programme. The IEP holds that individual educational needs of the child should be determined rather than the needs of categories of children.

Teaching exceptional children in the regular classroom does not mean watering down or slowing down the rate of curricula presented to the student. The disabled learner has problems with language facility, learning styles, motivation, consistent work and therefore the teacher has new roles to play. He does not simply slow down the speed.

The teacher must be careful and give specific directions to the student, many times if necessary. These should be presented both visually and verbally. The task must be presented at the students response level. The need of frequent praising and reserving criticism is important in motivating students who keep failing in school related tasks.

New learning tasks must be analysed by the teacher and broken into small sequential steps. Different sensory modalities may be used in combination. Repetition of difficult materials, review of earlier materials, use of several response modes ie.g., tape recorded response, models, and drawing, for knowing comprehension may be used.

The teacher must evaluate the student's performance fairly. The teacher has to create a climate of acceptance for the learning disabled students without which they will feel rejected and isolated in the regular classroom.

Teamwork with other professionals gets importance in mainstreaming, particularly the principal, special-education teacher and school psychologists. Teachers dealing with exceptional pupils must be adequately trained through in service programmes. They should be acquainted with referral processes.

In a regular school the critical person is the special teacher or resource room teacher. A resource room setting involves movement of students through the resource room from the regular class on regular basis. Constant liason between the regular and resource teacher is required to help the exceptional child. There are other specialists who can assist the regular teacher i.e., speech therapists, language teachers, parents etc.

But the greatest obstacle to mainstreaming should be first removed i.e., negative attitudes towards the handicapped. Many students who are mainstreamed are identified prior to the time that they enter school, although the majority of them are identified by classroom teachers and are referred thereafter for assessment and placement.

Just as the resource room/special teacher, the regular teacher and other staff members have specific roles to play for successful mainstreaming, the special and regular students are no less important.

The Regular Education Students should :

- listen to a special education teacher when he speaks to the class about the physically handicapped program;

- use a set of crutches or a wheel chair, to have experience of how it feels to be in a wheel chair or on crutches;
- spend a day in the special education class, simulating the handicap for the entire day, and then report the experience to the regular education class;
- read materials about handicaps.

The Special Education Studend should :

- engage in normal activities in the regular classroom, such as copying from the board, completing assignments with little assistance;
- invite one or more pupils from the regular class to become acquainted with students before mainstreaming. This is best accomplished through cooperative involvement in a task. The students will have buddies in the regular classroom; and
- get an opportunity to meet the regular classroom teacher before placement.

Peer Tutoring

Training pupils to teach one another, one to one or in small groups provides an extensive opportunity for individualised instruction. Peer tutoring is defined here as two, three, and sometimes four, or five pupils working together on the same task. Typically one pupil is being taught by another. Peer tutoring is mutual and interactive. In order to ensure it, the classroom teacher has to work out how to start, monitor, evaluate and terminate. Peer tutoring has salutory effects.

Organisation of a Resource Unit

A resource unit for various subject areas from which a teacher can make a selection for a target group of impaired children in mainstreamed classroom can be developed by following certain guidelines and activities.

These are:

- Decide the subject area for the resource unit.
- Prepare the curriculum by writing behavioural objectives for possible knowledge, skills, and concepts, for each unit.
- List related study skills that might be developed while completing the unit e.g., letter writing, public speaking, library use.
- Describe ways to initiate the unity to create pupil interest e.g., Bulletin boards, dramatizations, reading a poem or story etc.
- Prepare an extensive list of activities for the unit.
- Prepare list of available publications for pupils.
- Prepare a list of resources to include sites for a study trips, records, filmstrips, tapes, songs and dances, charts, maps, and so on.
- Describe a variety of ways to evaluate the unit.

Programmed Instructions

Programmed instruction is well suited for individualised instruction and for mastery learning. Programmed instruction can be effective in meeting the needs of several types of exceptional pupils:

- Because the material content has been thoroughly task-analyzed, slow learning pupils experience success.
- Visually impaired pupils can benefit from those programmed materials that have verbal responses using auditory presentation.
- Hearing impaired pupils can benefit from visual responses formats.
- Pupils with superior abilities can often experience an enriched curriculum by using programmed material.
- Programmed materials also help pupils who have health problems to catch up on content when they have been absent for a period of time.
- Physically handicapped pupils whose upper extremities are affected can benefit from programmed materials that do not require written responses, especially if the machine is easily advanced to the next frame.

Programmed materials can provide regular classroom teachers with another method of meeting the individual needs of a variety of pupils. The up to date mode for presenting programmed instruction is the microcomputer.

Use of Microcomputer

Microcomputers in the classroom are another very powerful tool for the mainstreaming teacher. The computer is probably the most powerful tool ever developed for helping pupils of widely varying needs, achievement levels, learning problems, or interests. The computer promises to bring teachers extra pairs of quality hands. It is highly motivating to most pupils.

For Pupils

The computer,

- Writes extremely large words on a screen particularly for the partially visually impaired pupil.
- Provides auditory accompaniment to visual symbols on the screen. What is typed on the computer is read back immediately by the micro computer.
- Allows 30 pupils to work at 30 different skill levels in spelling, arithmetic, or other subject areas.
- Provides practice in typing.
- Provides eye-motor coordination skill drills.
- Increases reading speed and comprehension.
- Provides opportunities for creative thinking.
- Presents visual simulations of difficult concepts in animated form, slow or fast, repeatedly.

- Furnishes endless drill and practice on virtually any skill or concept to be mastered.
- Provides practice in problem solving.

For Teachers, the Computer

- Facilitates data-based management such as storage and retrieval of individual and class pupil records with the data analysed, summarized, and in consumable form for easy interpretation.
- Provides information retrieval such as finding specific references to go with special pupil needs.
- Develops daily pupil schedules.
- Observes demonstration teaching. There is a large screen which magnities everything on the microcomputer so the entire class can see what is happening. Using this, teachers can show and explain very abstract ideas, repeating them as often as necessary.

Why does the Microcomputer Work ?

The major reason why microcomputers really work as educational tools are stated below:

1. The machine is interactive; it is not passive like television.
2. The machine can be infinitely patient, unlike a human being.
3. The pupil tends to become more relaxed, less tense and uptight than the presence of a human being.
4. The drill and practice programmes are similar to programmed instructional materials and work for the same reasons of immediate feedback, reinforcement, and pacing.
5. Many of the learning activities resemble actual games; there is a fascination about these games which we have yet to define precisely.
6. Micros are different in kind, not just in degree, from any learning system.
7. Sound programmes have been field-tested, revised and revised until they do work, until pupils do learn.
8. Microcomputers are incredibly fast and accurate.
9. Microcomputers enable both competency-based mastery learning of skills and open-ended, divergent-type thinking.

Technology for the Disabled

During the last 15 years things have changed greatly. Silicon chips and micro processors have changed society. Technology is gradually changing the life of disabled. The Computer has two characteristics that have significance and meaning for the disabled (a) decrease in size of hardware (b) increasing sophistication, while makes it easier to use. Micro computers can be attached to wheel chairs to improve mobility. They are more accessible for use by handicaps because mere key strokes are needed to perform computer functions.

The micro processor facilitates communication (a) as a compensatory device for sensory disabilities (b) as an assistive device for individuals whose physical impairments make communication difficult. Talking computer terminals can translate text into speech, special adaptive devices for micro computers that can provide visual displays of auditory information by translating sound into text. For motoric disabilities communication aids have developed that allow them to operate computers with single switch input devices. Key board enhancers and emulators help individuals with restricted movement by reducing the number of actuations necessary for communication, e.g., minispeak system adaptive communication devices can be linked to micro computers that can help the disabled to control his living environment in some ways: answering telephone calls, etc.

Telecommunication system helps the disabled to gather information and disseminate information. These should not be confined to schools alone. Computer networking also enables people to use information from far off remote places. Electronic Bulleting Boards and electronic mails, use of word processors and telecommunication software are beneficial to the disabled in sending and receiving information from large information libraries using telecommunication hook ups.

Often telecommunication is tele text, a one way transmission to television viewers. Current tele text applications include: news headlines, weather forecasts, school holidays. Closed captioning in a tele text is useful to hearing impaired individuals.

A video disk is a table top device that is interfaced with a monitor to play video programmes stored on 12 inch disks. When interfaced with a micro computer it becomes a powerful tool for instructional use. It can allow students to move ahead or go back according to learner's needs. Information can also be shown in slow motion. California school for the deaf has developed a system to use the video disk to teach language development and reading. With this system, students use light pens to write their responses on the screen. It is available on low cost at present.

Artificial intelligence refers to the use of computer to solve the same types of problems and to make the same kinds of decisions faced by humans. This has potential benefits to disabled individuals. Robots is a device that can be programmed to move in specified direction and to manipulate objects. To some extent, robots are being used in classrooms to teach computer logic. Robots are able to acquire information, understand it, and plan and implement appropriate actions.

Ecology and Special Education

Ecology means study of relationship between an organism and the environment. Its applications to special education is relatively new although it originated from Strauss, Lehtinen, and Cruickshank with brain injured children in 1940s.

Hobbs (1966) started the first Re-Ed project with emotionally disturbed children and recognised socialisation problems did not occur within child; it existed rather in the environment and its interactions with the labeled child. It is an environmental misfit. Therefore, the child has to be removed from the environment for helping him to be temporarily away from it, and then change the environment to suit him. Segregation was to be as brief as possible; normalisation was always the goal. Normalisation was possible for ED children through ecological intervention.

Broadly, the approach emphasized that disturbance or defect is not intrinsic perse, but the description of the interaction of a particular child with a particular environment. The search is for the mismatch in the eco-system. "The study of the child occurs not in the sterility of the psychological laboratory, but in the naturalistic real world, holistic settings in which the problems occur. This is not to deny that emotional disturbance, mental retardation, learning disability are not real. The ecological focus in special education tries to show that looking only at internal factors cannot give the whole picture and that treatment approaches based on simplified, historical, etiological views can limit the success that parents and professional might face with disabled children.

Special education ecologist looks at both how child acts on the environment and how the environment acts on the child. They look for establishing an equilibrium by using appropriate coping skills, which may be taught to the child and engineered in the environment.

The ecological special educator studies the cultural relativity of the child's behaviour and tries to promote cultural conformity and adaptation between the child and the environment. It is not limited to emotionally disturbed only but to all areas of disability. School related factors produced disability, learning and behaviour. Infact, we place regular and special education students for about 1100 hours per year in school without changing the school environment or designing the school environment. Partial attempts have been made for the physically handicapped children. Special educators must move away from the child focus approach to more of a pedagogy in which they test, observe and teach in the real world settings where skills must altimately be generalised and demonstrated successfully.

Physical Education for the Disabled

The aim of physical education for the handicapped is to aid in achieving physical, social, and emotional growth commensurate with their potential. Accordingly handicapped students are required to take a Battery of motor, physical fitness, and perceptual motor tests for the making of the Yearly IEP.

Physical education programme has 3 basic functions: (i) input functions (ii) abilities (iii) motor skill. Basic input functions include equilibrium reflexes, vestibular system, vision, audition, tactile and kinaesthetic success. Perceptual motor abilities include: balance, laterality, directionality, body image, spatial awareness, cross-lateral integration. Physical fitness parameters consist of strength, muscle and cardiovascular endurance, and flexibility. Motor abilities include: speed, power, agility and motor coordination. It both there are intact, then skill acquisition occurs through movement and sports exercises. Hence, physical education instruction is a must for the disabled. The regular sports activities should be suitably modified to suit to the capabilities of the disabled. Play and sports for the disabled should be more organised and structured than those of the normal child.

Understanding special education processes are significant in planning the programmes for the handicapped. Infact, identification, referrals, placement, management in a particular service system is of crucial importance. More important at the moment is application of technology, computer, mastery learning techniques, programmed texts and several other innovations to the advantage of special needs children and their education. It is necessary, that practioners, teachers resource team should have a thorough understanding of the various aspects of disability and processes. The chapter highlights the need for mainstreaming the mildly handicapped.

Highlights of the Chapter

Several issues are at the crossroads in the development of education of exceptional children. Use of labels such as Mentally Retarded, Physically Handicapped etc. put children at a disadvantage for no fault of theirs. Labeling has a negative/stigmatising effect which further accentuates the shortcoming of the handicapped children.

Labels are used sometimes by way of discrimination, and have racial, ethnic, social class or personal basis and are the result of inadequate assessment procedures. The prevailing referral system based on use of psychometric assessment suffers from poor use and selection of tests, improper test, administrative bias in testing, etc., leading to wrongful placement of the handicapped child in a special school or special class. Assessment should be culture representative and comprehensive.

Studies on the efficacy of the special class have often led to improvement in sociometirc relationships whereas arguments favouring better achievement of the handicapped in the regular setting are becoming common and sensible for the mildly handicapped children.

Advocacy programmes for mainstreaming the handicapped have gained momentum in theory and practice, although in most cases, integration has remained by and large at the physical level. This is but a transitional phenomenon. Mainstreaming provides most appropriate education for each under LRE; fulfils specific educational needs; helps in adjustment problems; develops skills in the handicapped. Effective mainstreaming and/or integration would further involve: curricular changes, class management, teaching of basic skills, teacher-parent-student relationships, appropriate referral services, individualised teaching and assistance in resource rooms.

In order to further speed up the process of normalisation, various innovative procedures are under way in the field which include: teaching handicapped children in small groups, using peers as tutors, adapting mastery learning and task analysis techniques, utilising resource rooms, resource teacher competencies, programmed materials, micro computers, and revitalising the regular classroom teacher in terms of new experimential inputs for handling the handicapped children in the regular classroom. Ecological understanding with a view to providing wholesome conducive educational environment and design of suitable physical activities for the handicapped have been a few major breakthroughs in special education.

Review Questions

1. Explain the concept of labelling. What is the effect of labelling?
2. Is the special education system justified for handicapped children?
3. What is mainstreaming or integrated education? How can it be effective?
4. How can a resource room plan contribute to effective mainstreaming?
5. What are the uses of micro-computers in special education?
6. What kind of technology can be used for the education of the disabled?
7. Explain ecology and special education from the point of view of integrating the disabled into the community.
8. What is the role of physical education for the disabled?
9. What is the role of a regular teacher in a mainstreamed class for the disabled?
10. What is the role of a resource teacher in a mainstreamed class for the disabled?
11. What is the role of the peer group on disabled pers in a mainstreamed classroom? What is the role of normal peers in this setting?
12. Write notes on:

Least restrictive environment	Normalisation
Small group instruction	Peer tutoring
Mastery learning	Deinstitutionalisation
Resource teacher	Resource unit
Resource room	Programmed instruction

References

Bloom, B.S., (1964), *Stability and Change in Human Characteristics*, NY, Wiley.

Dunn, L., (1968), "Special education for the mildly retarded. Is much of its justifiable?" *Exceptional Children*, 35, 5-22.

Hamill, D.O. and Larsen, S.C. (1978), "The effectiveness of Psycholinguistic Training. A reaffirmation of position". *Exceptional Children*, 44, 402-414.

Hobbs, N.L., (1966), "Helping disturbed children, Psychological and ecological strategies." *American Psychologist*, 21, 1105-1115.

Hobbs, N.L., (1975), *The future of children*, San Francissco: Jossey Bass.

Kauffman, M.J., Gottlieb, J., Agard, J.A., and Kukic, M., (1975), "Mainstreaming: Toward an explication of the construct". In E.L. Meyen, G.A. Vergason, and R.J. Whelan (Eds.), *Alternatives of teaching exceptional children*, (pp. 34-54). Denver: Love.

Reynolds, N., (1980), *A Common Body of Practice for Teachers, The challenge of public law—94-142* to teacher education Minneapolis, National Support System.

Skeels, H. and Dye, H. (1939), "A study of the effects differential stimulation on mentally retarded children," Proceedings of the American Association of Mental Deficiency, 44, 136-144.

Stephens, T.M., Blackhurt, A.E. and Magliocia, L.A., (1983), *Teaching Mainstreamed Students*, New York: John Wiley & Sons.

U.S. Department of Education, (1984), Sixth annual report to Congress ont he implementation of Public Law 94-142. The Education for All Handicapped Chidlren Act, Washington, DC: Author.

Wang, M.C., (1981), "Mainstreaming exceptional children: some instructional design and implementation considerations", *Elementary School Journal*, 81, 195-221.

Chapter 3

Policies and Programmes in the Education of Exceptional Children

Education and Training are the corner stones in the development of the potentialities of children, more so of children with special needs, or those categoriesed as exceptionals. Several policies and programmes have been undertaken in this field in our country. This chapter briefly describes these programmes.

- Recommendations of the Education Commission on the Handicapped.
- The National Policy for Children
- Objectives of education for handicapped children in the International Year of Disabled Persons, 1981 with specific reference to India.
- Recommendations of the Working Group on Education of the Handicapped, 1981.
- Report of the Advisory Committee, 1981 on the Handicapped.
- National Policy on Education, 1986 on the Handicapped.
- Report of the Ramamurty Committee, 1991.
- The Jannardan Reddy Committee Report 1992.
- Programme of Action, 1992.
- The Integrated Education Scheme 1992 for the Mildly Handicapped.
- Human Rights as per the United Nations' Standard Rules, 1994.

The Indian Education Commission (1964-66)

The Education Commission was the first to suggest that the education of handicapped children has to be organised not merely on humanitarian grounds, but also on grounds of utility. Proper education would enable handicapped children to overcome their disability, and make them useful citizens. It has to be remembered that the Constitutional directive on compulsory education includes handicapped children as well. Very little has been done in this field so far; and on account of several difficulties, any great improvement in the situation does not seem to be likely in the near future. All the same, it is important that a serious beginning is made. There is much in the field that can be learned from the educationally advanced countries which in recent years have developed new methods and techniques, based on advances in science and medicine.

It was further emphasized by the commission that, the primary task of education for a handicapped child is to prepare him for adjustment to a socio-cultural environment designed to meet the needs of the normal. It is essential, therefore, that the education of handicapped children should be an inseparable part of the general educational system. The differences lie in the methods employed to teach the child and the means the child uses to acquire information. These differences in methodology do not influence the content or the goals of education. This form of education is, therefore, conveniently referred to as "Special Education". The Commission suggested educational facilities to be extended to four groups: the Blind, the Deaf, the Orthopaedically Handicapped, and the Mentally Retarded.

At the time, Education Commission (1964-66) made its recommendation, there were 115 schools for the Blind, 70 schools for the Deaf, 25 schools for the Orthopaedically Handicapped and 27 for the Mentally Retarded int he whole country. The Education Commission felt that the existing facilities were extremely inadequate. A carefully thought out plan for the development of educational services for the handicapped was therefore needed.

The Education Commission further felt that the progress in providing educational facilities to handicapped children will be limited by two main considerations: lack of *teachers* and of *financial resources*. A reasonable target will, therefore, be to provide by 1986, education for about 15 per cent of the blind, deaf and orthopaedically handicapped children and to about 5 per cent of the mentally retarded ones. This would mean the provision of educational facilities for about 10 per cent of the total number of handicapped children. As a part of the programme, it should be possible to have at least one good institution for the education of handicapped children in each district.

This goal was expected to be reached through the adoption of two programmes, *the special* and *the integrated*. In the special programme, the handicapped children are isolated from the normal ones and one placed in special institutions. In the other, handicapped children can be enrolled in regular school programmes. The second has everal advantages of which two are important: reduction of costs, and promotion of mutual understanding between the handicapped and the non-handicapped children. There have also been disadvantages: for instance, many handicapped children find it psychologically disturbing to be placed in an ordinary school. An overall view of the problem show that experimentation with the integrated programmes is required and every attempt should be made to bring in as many children into integrated programmes as possible. With these salient suggestions the Commission left then implementation to planners of the country.

National Policy for Children

India is one of the few countries in the world with a comprehensive policy for children. The National Policy adopted in August 1974 is designed to provide guidelines to the Ministries of the Central Government, State Government and other agencies for an integrated approach to child development. The Ministry of Social Welfare coordinates action for the speedy implementation of measures contemplated in the National Policy for children. The measures are intended to cover all children belonging to the weaker sections of society and those who are handicapped. Then came the seminal International Year for Disabled Persons IYDP) in 1981.

IYDP—National Draft Plan for Education of Handicapped

The General Assembly of the United Nations proclaimed 1981 as International Year for Disabled Persons in their Resolution No. 31/123 dated 16 December 1976. The United Nations General Assembly set forth the following objectives:

- — Helping disabled persons in their physical and psychological adjustments to society.
- — Promoting all national and international efforts to provide disabled persons with proper assistance, training, care and guidance, to make available opportunities for suitable work and to ensure their full integration in society.
- — Encouraging study and research projects designed to facilitate the practical participation of disabled persons in daily life, e.g. by improving their access to public buildings and transportation systems.
- — Educating and informing the public about the rights of disabled persons to participate in and contribute to various aspects of economic, social and political life.
- — Promoting effective measures for the prevention of disability and for the rehabilitation of disabled persons.

The theme of the year was "full participation with equality". In other words:

- integration should replace the present trends towards segregations;
- enrollment of handicapped children in ordinary schools should replace special residential schools;
- the development of sheltered workshops would remain a desirable programme;
- greater efforts would be made towards securing open employment for the handicapped.

India was one of the signatories to the resolution proclaiming IYDP, 1981. The Government of India endorsed the objectives set forth in the resolution of the General Assembly. Within the framework of the general objectives declared by the United Nations, the specific objectives to be achieved by India in the light of its present resources were the following:

- To evolve a National Policy on the handicapped, to include education, training, employment, measures to achieve full social integration, and protection and guarantees under the law.
- On the basis of this, to lay the foundation of a network of services for the handicapped that reaches the grassroot level, so that a comprehensive rehabilitation service is eventually provided by preparing a prospective development plan for rehabilitation.
- To initiate in this chain a few practical programmes that would carry immediate and significant benefit to handicapped people themselves.
- To initiate concrete programmes aimed at bringing about the integration of of handicapped people into the community and then utilisation in every way possible. Currently, there is a strong tendency to institutionalise handicapped people. This tends to inculcate among the handicapped a sense of dependence which prevents them from fully participating in community life even after they leave the protective walls of institutions. It also leads to maladjustment at work and in other social settings.
- To give a positive rural bias to services for the handicapped, since in India a great majority of handicapped persons live in rural communities. At present, practically all institutional programmes are located in urban areas. Most handicapped people from rural areas have to migrate to cities.
- To develop a strong national disability prevention programme. Currently, only a National Programme for the prevention of Blindness is in operation. What is important is to develop and put into operation a comprehensive and pragmatic programme for the prevention of disabilities, where necessary, through legislative sanction so that wherever needed, social reforms could be brought to eliminate physical and mental disabilities.
- To prepare a base for research and development through the National Institutes, Institutes of Technology and other bodies so that in the years to come programmes for the rehabilitation of the handicapped should be responsive to change in the social or economic climate and to developments of techniques and technologies in various disciplines bearing on this field.
- To develop and initiate a planned network of information and publicity services for dissemination of information on new techniques, equipment programmes for the handicapped and for employers, teachers and social workers. The service should not only disseminate information but should also stimulate a greater awareness among opinion groups of the employment potential of the handicapped. Campaigns to eradicate social prejudice should form an integral part of the plan.

— To collect, with as wide a base as possible, all relevant data on the handicapped in the country.

In conformity with the National Plan of Action, State Governments have developed their own plan of action keeping in view the concepts and the priority areas as indicated in the plan of action. Special Education Cells have been set up in the states.

Working Group on the Education of the Disabled Child, 1981

Following the IYDP a working group was set up by the Govt. of India:

1. To suggest steps for
   — the adoption of proper legislative measures for the education and training of disabled,
   — publicity, and
   — action research.
2. To formulate the detailed action plan on "Education for the Disabled Child", including the Development of Skills in the context of observing 1981 as the International Year of the Disabled Persons, particularly with a view to enriching the existing services for the disabled; and
3. To give an idea of the financial requirements for implementing the various items of the Action Plan, keeping in view the feasibility of starting the programmes in IYDP, 1981.

The foremost task that emerged relates to the collection of reliable data on the basis of sample surveys in all the existing diversities of the country, according to social, economic, cultural and geographical factors.

The committee recommended that the following categories of handicapped children should be sovered:

1. The blind or the visually handicapped.
2. The deaf or the hearing handicapped.
3. The orthopaedically handicapped.
4. Educable and trainable mentally retarded children.
5. The cerebral Palsied.
6. The neurologically handicapped, including the epileptic.
7. Children with speech and language disorders.
8. Children with speech and language disorders.
9. Children with minimal brain dysfunction including learning disabilities.

Expereince indicated that quite a large number of multiple handicapped children need special services. Their problems are more complex.

What is of greatest importance is that a flexible and child-centred approach should be adopted. A child with a disability poses many complex intra-family, physical, social, economic and educational problems. To come to terms with such a staggering variety of problems no single approach is adequate. It is recommended, therefore, that for the pre-school handicapped children the following types of services may be organised:

1. Wide dissemination of information about the management and stimulation of various types of handicapped children at home may be undertaken through adequate literature in all Indian languages and publicity through all media of mass communication. In fact training of parents in the management and stimulation of disabled children may be a part of the functional literacy programmes being undertaken as part of various projects.
2. The publicity programme should be supported, by the worker at the district, block or village level, whose task should be to watch out for tell-tale signs of disability in children and to advise parents on the possibility of their children being at risk. This worker should undertake inter-personal discussion with an counselling of parents and other relatives or siblings.
3. Short courses for the training of parents, workshops and conferences for parents, and other forms of interaction between the parents and the professionals should be systematically organised with a view to enhancing the capability of parents to manage and enrich the pre-school education of disabled children at home.
4. Wherever possible, disabled children between three and six years of age may be integrated into ordinary nurseries or pre-schools. To the extent possible, they should also be integrated into balwadis and other pre-school centres in rural areas.
5. Special pre-schools and balwadis may be set up for more severely handicapped children. These should be operated as day schools and maximum interaction between the disabled and normal children should be promoted.
6. For a small percentage of disabled children whose parents are totally unable to care for them, residential nursery schools should be set up, preferably one in each block, on to begin with, one in each district. Disabled children should be sent to residential nursery schools only as a last resort when they cannot benefit from other programmes.

For school age children the traditional approach has been to place handicapped children in special schools and especially in special residential schools. This has tended to isolate the disabled child. This trend is probably one of the most important factors contributing to the prevailing prejudice against disabled people. Moreover, our resources are limited and the cost of keeping disabled children in special residential schools is considerably greater than that in integrated settings and day schools. It is imperative, therefore, that a wide range of programmes should be taken up to suit the differing requirements of children with varying disabilities as well as in different social, cultural and economic circumstances.

The following types of programmes were recommended.

Integrated Programmes

a. Resource Teacher Programme
b. Itinerant Teacher Programme
c. The Special Class
d. Partial Integration

Special Schools

a. Day School
b. Special Residential Schools

While the placement of disabled children in integrated settings is expected to promote their social and psychological acceptance, it is often stressed that education of severely handicapped children needs certain supportive services like those of social workers, psychologists, physiotherapists, occupational therapists, speech therapists, and the like. It becomes the special responsibility of special schools, both day and residential to offer these supportive services in order to make the education of disabled children beneficial.

Further, special schools have often served as laboratories. They evolve special techniques which can later be applied even in integrated settings. Unfortunately, on account of the pressure of work in ordinary schools, it is by no means easy even for special teachers in integrated settings to devote time and energy to the development of new techniques and technologies.

The role of an innovative teacher in the education of disabled children can hardly be overemphasised. A great deal of research is needed to arrive at the most effective techniques of imparting general education as well as vocational and professional skills to children with diverse disabilities. Some areas of specific research are listed below:

1. The chain of interpersonal interactions set off by the advent and management of a disabled child in the family.
2. Comparative study of academic and affective development of disabled children in various programmes.

The programme was proposed for a 20-year span.

Advisory Committee on Blind, Deaf, Orthopaedically Handicapped, and Mentally Retarded

The Ministry of Social Welfare and the Ministry of Education and Culture had appointed advisory committees to go into the details of the problems in these areas. These committees have met and discussed the following aspects in June and July, 1981.

a. Early detection, prevention, medical and physical rehabilitation.
b. Education and training of handicapped children and adults, including teacher training.
c. Employment.
d. General matters: role of voluntary organisations, creation of public awareness.

The salient recommendations with respect to training of teachers on education of the handicapped were:

a. Except for the severely orthopaedically handicapped and multiple handicapped children, no special education component is necessary. They should be integrated into regular schools. But for successful integration, teachers of regular schools should receive proper orientation. It was suggested that short term in-service teacher training programmes be conducted to meet this need.
b. In the area of education of the Blind, Deaf and Mentally Retarded, the prevailing conditions in rural areas were such that special schools were not available for hearing impaired children. Therefore, these children had to attend regular schools and teachers must be acquainted with the special needs and problems of these categories of handicapped.
c. The need for teacher training was highlighted by the inadequacies existing in the system. The dearth of teacher educators was stressed. The need for excellent models of teacher education and the need to strengthen the existing teacher training programmes were also recommended.
d. Appropriate curricula should be developed for use in special schools special classes and remedial classes in rural and urban areas, by an agency such as NCERT and Regional College of Education.
e. There should be cooperation and coordination between all teacher training programmes in the country. It was suggested that the Ministry of Social Welfare and NCERT could undertake this.

National Policy on Education, 1986, 1992 (R)

The objective should be to integrate the physically and mentally handicapped with the general community as equal partners, to prepare them for normal growth and to enable them to face life with courage and confidence. The following measures were to be taken in this regard:

(i) Wherever it was feasible, the education of children with motor handicaps and other mild handicaps would be common with that of others.
(ii) Special schools with hostels would be provided, as far as possible at district headquarters, for the severely handicapped children.
(iii) Adequate arrangements would be made to give vocational training to the disabled.
(iv) Teacher's training programmes would be reoriented, in particular for teachers of primary classes, to deal with the special difficulties of handicapped children; and
(v) Voluntary effort for the education of the disabled would be encouraged in every possible manner.

Recommendations of Ramamurthy Committee, 1991

The Govt. of India set up the Ramamurty Committee to comment upon NPE/POA stipulations. Some of the specific observations made on the handicapped as stated in the NPE 1986 were as follows.

NPE advocated the policy of integrating the physically and mentally handicapped with the general community as equal partners.

The POA mentioned the detailed measures to be taken, important amongst them being massive in-service training for teachers, orientation programmes for the administrators, development of supervisory expertise in the resource institutions like the SCERT and DIET, etc. It also called for provision of incentives like supply of aids, appliances, text books and free uniforms.

The reasons for the low coverage of handicapped children in education are the following:

— Education of the handicapped is viewed as a social welfare activity.

— Child to child help leading to sensitization of the future generation, child to parent help for community sensitation and special and general pedagogy reinforcement were missed.

— Most of the special centres for the handicapped are located in metropolitan cities and urban centres. The non-government organisations barring a few exceptions have not significantly begun to operate at district or sub-district levels. Reportedly, 215 districts in the country do not have special schools for any disability though there are over 1000 documented special schools.

— The scheme of Integrated Education for Disabled children which was conceptualised by the Department of Social Welfare in 1974 was implemented for several years in terms of running 'Mini Special Schools' within general schools. The reason was that there was no provision for sensitisation and involvement of all the teachers.

The NPE, so far as it relates to education of the handicapped, is inadequate in the following respects:

- It has not stressed the mobilisation of the total general education system for the education of the handicapped.
- Special schools have been treated in isolation from other educational institutions from the point of view of providing the educational supervisory infrastructure, leaving it to the Ministries of Welfare and HRD to co-operatively develop the same.

The merit of the POA is in its call for establishment of special schools at district and sub-district levels: curriculum development apart from provision of infrastructural facilities; and specific target setting for universal primary education of the handicapped. While special schools for the education of those with severe handicaps are rightly emphasised by the POA, they have not laid emphasis on multiple delivery of services in special schools. While single disability mode is required for research, development and rehabilitation work, for delivery of educational services, multi-service mode in special schools should be given importance. This is particularly so because doctors, dispensaries, public health centres and development functionaries are multi-purpose in nature. The POA has not called for redefinition of the role of special schools.

The Department of Education has been implementing a scheme for the integrated education of the disabled under which 100% assistance is given to the States. The scheme is at present being implemented in nineteen States and Union Territories. The annual provision under the scheme is of the order of Rs. 2 crores and as of now 20,000 children are being covered. Assistance provided to the states under the scheme is expected to be utilised to provide for salaries and incentives for teachers, setting up of resource rooms, carrying out assessment of handicapped children, training of teachers, provision of instructional material, etc.

Having comprehensively taken into account the problems faced in providing education to the handicapped with reference to their special and diversified needs, and having studied the history of implementation of the educational programmes for the handicapped, the Committee gave the following recommendations:

(i) People should be made aware of the problems of the handicapped. The media should be effectively used for this purpose.

(ii) Every family with a handicapped child should be provided support through incentives, dialogue and periodic training and evaluation. Parents' groups and community education groups should be formed.

(iii) The educational system of the handicapped should be flexible. It should offer a range of education provisions—special schools for those who cannot be educated in general schools, special classes in general schools and integrated education for the disabled, vocational centres, etc.

(iv) Educational packages should be offered for hearing impaired children in a differentiated way—
Purely oral oriented programmes for profoundly deaf children.
Combined oral-manual programmes for profoundly deaf children for the education of whom pure oral programmes will not be adequate.
Segregated programmes for those children form whom such programmes are essential.
Integrated programmes for those whom this modality promises better emotive, cognitive, social and linguistic development.

(v) For making boys and girls of impaired hearing economically independent, vocational training has to be specially organised. Vocational training which is job-oriented and matched to the abilities and aptitudes of the hearing impaired, should be organised in a significantly diversified way.

(vi) Bharati Braille has been developed, at the National Institute for the Visually Handicapped (NIVH), Dehradun. This should be utilised maximally.

(vii) While work has been initiated for the development of Braille notations for mathematics and science, not much progress has been made.

(viii) For the moderately mentally retarded, special curricula should be developed and standardised—not merely for the purpose of basic education in the three R's but also for training in self-care skills like motor integration, perceptual and motor skills, language, communication and conceptual skills.

(ix) Vocational schools for mentally retarded adults are not many. For their benefit jobs in sheltered workshops, farms and industries should be provided.

(x) In the pre-service teacher training programme, education of the handicapped, should be made part of the pedagogy and methodology.

(xi) A programme of sensitisation should be implemented for in-service teachers as well. This should include various components, namely, Non-formal Education, Vocationalisation of Education and Distance Education.

(xii) Teachers' training colleges should have special courses for teaching handicapped children; a special component on the education of the handicapped should be included in the B.Ed. courses as well.

(xiii) At least one resource faculty should be provided in each DIET to provide teacher training inputs in the context of education for the handicapped.

(xiv) The role of the special schools should be clearly redefined as spelt out below:

  (i) Early identification of chidlren with handicaps and formulation of stimulation programmes for them.

  (ii) Education of the handicapped children who cannot be educated in general schools up to the point when they can be integrated—thus breaking the insulation between the general and special schools.

  (iii) Providing service as resource agencies for implementing the integrated education programmes in general schools.

  (iv) Bringing about mutual reinforcement of the pedagogies of special and general education.

(xv) A lot of development is taking place in the application of technology for the benefit of the handicapped. Several technological aids are already available, e.g., Brailleix produced in Germany which facilitates recording of whole encyclopaedia on cassettes, pritning conversion devices like 'tactacon' which facilitates presentation of printed matrial in vibro-tactile form so as to enable blind persons to read, devices facilitating mobility of blind persons, etc. The technologies and techno-aids available for meeting the special needs of handicapped children should be reviewed, and measures for dissemination of information should be formulated.

(xiv) Sustained researches should be undertaken to determine the needs of the physically handicapped and produce technological aids capable of helping in overcoming handicaps.

These recommendations were very comprehensive to shape the programme planning effectively. Subsequently another Committee was set up by the government the Janardan Reddy Committee, which submitted its report in 1992.

The NPERC, 1992 felt that the NPE was inadequate in the following respects:

- NPE had not stressed the mobilisation of the total general education system for the education of the handicapped.
- Special schools had been treated in isolation from other educational institutions from the point of view of providing the educational supervisory infrastructure, leaving it to the Ministries of Welfare and HRD to co-operatively develop the same.

The NPERC made very useful recommendations relating to the modalities of implementing programmes for the education of the handicapped. *Inter alia,* it had advocated the use of media in creating awareness about the problems of the handicapped, providing suport to every family with a handicapped child through incentives, dialogue and training and adopting a flexible approach to the education of the physically handicapped the NPERC examined at length the needs of different categories of the disabled such as the deaf, the blind and the mentally retarded, and made specific recommendations. The NPERC had also made important recommendations on the role of training, and of technological development in the education of the physicall handicapped.

The Programme of Action which was formulated in 1992 by MHRD, Government of India took all these historical antecedents into account and focussed on an operational framework for implementing the plan of education of handicapped.

Programme of Action—1992 Salient Features

The POA made a state of the art analysis of the situation. At the end of 1991-92 about 30,000 children with disability were availing special benefits under the scheme of Integrated Education for Disabled Children (IEDC). In addition, about 60,000 children with mild disabilities received resource support without special benefits. A large number of children with disability were also receiving education in special schools which numbered about 1035. The Project Integrated

Education for Disabled (PIED) is being implemented, as a field demonstration, in one block each in ten States and Union Territories. In these blocks about 90 per cent of children with disability are receiving education in general schools. The cost per pupil in these blocks is now around Rs. 2000 but is likely to come down as the number of beneficiaries increases. General teachers feel confident and motivated as their status in the community has improved due to the services they provide. The innovative multi-category training of resource teachers has been found to be effective and has been institutionalised in the Regional Colleges and the training programmes organised by Non-governmental Organisations. Each DIET has been provided a resource centre for orienting elementary teachers and establishing field demonstrations in lab areas. Faculty from 102 DIETs have so far received induction training at the NCERT.

The Ministry of Welfare had taken steps to ensure supply of trained manpower to special schools and improve standards in these schools through the National Institute for the Handicapped and increased support to NGOs.

The Ministry of Labour manages 17 Vocational Rehabilitation Centres (VRCs) for the handicapped and helps in their placement. About 66,000 persons with disabilities had been rehabilitated under this scheme by September, 1991. Three per cent of seats for admission to ITIs and under the Apprenticeship Training Scheme are available for Handicapped persons. These seats are being fully utilised.

The evaluation of special schools and the scheme of IEDC has revealed some grey areas. The general education system has not yet been mobilised, to a noticeable extent, for education of the handicapped either at the Central or State Level. Inputs from different schemes like CBR, DRC, ECCE, non-formal education, adult education, vocational and technical education, etc. are not being brought together for the education of the physically handicapped. Some states are still reluctant to implement the Integrated Education for Disabled Children (IEDC) System, while some are implementing it rather indifferently. Few NGOs are active in rural areas. The standard of education in special schools needs improvement. Facilities for the education of children with multiple handicaps are yet to be developed. The early detection and intervention programmes so essential for education of these children have yet to be started. The goal of universalisation of elementary education for this disadvantaged group remains an unachievable dream unless concerted and urgent measures are taken.

For achieving equalisation of educational opportunities, children with disability should have access to quality education comparable to other children. However, considering the financial resources likely to be available the targets for education of disabled children should be as follows:

(i) Children who can be educated in general primary schools:

(a) Universal enrolment by the end of ninth Five Year Plan.

(b) Ensuring achievement of minimum level of learning through adjustment and adaptation of curriculum and teaching to special needs.

(ii) Children who requite to be educated in special schools or special classes in general schools:

(a) Universal enrolment by the end of the ninth Five Year Plan.

(b) Ensuring achievement of level of learning commensurate with their potential.

(iii) Reduction of drop out rates to a level on par with other children:

(iv) Providing disabled children access to secondary and senior secondary schools with resource support and making special provision for vocational training of these children, particularly those with intellectual disabilities.

(v) Reorienting pre-service and in-service teacher education programmes including pre-school teachers training programmes to meet special needs.

(vi) Reorienting adult and non-formal education programmes to meet educational and vocational training needs of persons with disability.

The strategy of area-specific and population specific micro-planning for UEE is equally relevant for this disadvantaged group. Planning for UEE and adult literacy at all levels—centre, state, district, block and project—should provide for the educational needs of this category of children.

Education of children with disability will be a component in the training of educational planners and administrators as well as preservice and inservice teachers. District Institutes of Education and Training (DIETs), Colleges of Teacher Education (CTEs) and the Institute of Advanced STudy in Education (IASE) which have been provided with facilities for this component will have to pay particular attention to this aspect of teacher training. While drawing up schemes for strengthening SCERTs, cells for education of the handicapped may be considered as envisaged in IEDC.

The material supplied under Operation Blackboard will have to take into consideration special needs of these children. School buildings will have to take note of architectural adjustments needed to ensure access to children with disabilities, at the construction stage itself so as to avoid expenditure on modifications later on. Special schools need to be opened in the districts which have no special school facilities. The education of the handicapped should form an essential component in all externally assisted basic education projects being implemented or proposed to be implemented.

The following actions are needed for achieving the targets laid down:

(i) Adequate allocation or resources.

(ii) Provision for education of persons with disability should be made an integral component in externally assisted basic education projects.

(iii) Provision for education of the disabled should be made in the Centrally Sponsored Schemes of Operation Blackboard, Vocationalisation of Education and Non-formal Education.

(iv) There should be coordinated implementation of schemes like Community Based Rehabilitation, ECCE, VRCs and IEDC, so as to reduce cost and achieve higher coverage. This would require coordination among the Ministries/Departments of Health, Welfare, Education, Women and Child Development and Labour.

(v) The NGOs have to be encouraged to implement IEDC, particularly in rural areas. The NGOs involved in other educational activities should be encouraged to work in this area also and should be assisted in developing their expertise.

The Ministry of Labour is providing vocational training for the handicapped through the Craftsman Training Scheme (CTS), the Apprenticeship Training Scheme and separate Vocational Rehabilitation Centres (VRCs). Three per cent of the seats for admission to ITIs under the Craftsman Training Scheme and Apprenticeship Training Scheme are reserved for candidates who are handicapped but have the aptitude and are otherwise fit to undergo the required training. The States/UTs have been advised from time to time to implement this reservation for the handicapped which will be continued during the eight plan also. Seventeen VRCs will continue to provide training to a larger number of handicapped persons during the eight plan. The instructors in ITIs will receive orientation to meet special needs of handicapped persons. This components will be added in ITI instructor's training programme. Adjustment and adaptation of equipment to provide full access to disabled persons will be ensured.

Training of Teachers

All the DIETs to be established by the end of the eighth Plan will have a resource room and trained faculty to teach the essential components of education of children with disability. They will also run orientation programmes for teachers, at least from lab areas and practising schools, to establish field demonstration of the IEDC programme. The SCERTs will support field demonstrations under the scheme of IEDC. Similar actions is suggested for the 250 CTEs and 50 IASEs. The budget provision is available in the scheme itself. The pre-service training curriculum will induct essential components in these areas, wherever it has not been done so far.

All in-service teachers should receive awareness inputs on the education of children with disability in orientation programmes. In each area/institution where IEDC is implemented all teachers should receive orientation as envisaged in the scheme of IEDC. The Heads of Institutions and educational administrators should also receive training.

Special Teachers

The NIHs and regional training centres have built up the capacity to train single disability special teachers for special schools. Besides meeting demands of the new special schools, the existing untrained teachers will be trained and backlog cleared by the end of the eighth Plan. Inservice training of special teachers will be planned in a way that each teacher receives a three-week course every four years.

Content and Process

Curriculum flexibility is of special significance for these children. Special needs of these children will be met, if child centred education is practised. The curriculum adjustment and adaptation of teaching methods and material will be worked out, field tried and provided to the users. The following actions will be taken:

(i) Guidelines for child centred education, including special needs in the classroom are being developed at the NCERT.

(ii) Guidelines for adjustment of curriculum and instructional material and methods for the visually and hearing handicapped at the primary level have been developed. These are avaialble for use by teachers in IED/Special Schools.

(iii) The achievement of minimum levels of learning by children with mild disabilities should be ensured through resource support and alternative learning materials, wherever needed.

(iv) The Boards of Examination should make adjustments and adaptations in examinations for the handicapped children.

(v) Study of more than one language should not be compulsory for deaf children.

(vi) Teaching of Science and Mathematics is either not available to handicapped children or they opt for an easier substitute. Special efforts should be made by the NIHs and the NCERT to develop an action programme to improve access of disabled children to these important areas.

(vii) Child-to-child held in education of children with disabilities is an effective resource in view of large classes and multigrade teaching. NCERT should develop a package and make it available to teachers by end of 1993.

(viii) The special learning aids and equipment like braille books, braille kit, audio visual material will be developed and made available to schools by NIHs and NCERT.

Use of Mass Media

Radio and television are being used in a limited way both for advocacy as well as educational purposes. The CIETs, SIETs, NIHs and other organisations will develop a variety of programmes so that they can be regularly telecast/ broadcast. The MHRD will approach the Ministry of Information and Broadcasting for providing adequate time for this purpose.

Field publicity units should be utilised by states for advocacy programmes. Newspapers and magazines have started popular advocacy and educational writing in this area. The NCERT and the NIHs will develop packages and hand them over to journalists.

Monitoring and Evaluation

The availability of a reliable data base is essential for proper monitoring and evaluation of educational programmes for persons with disabilities. Towards this end the District Education Office, must with the help of other agencies, collect data about the number of disabled persons in the districts—disability wise, sex wise and age group wise, beneficiaries under IEDC, special schools, ITIs, VRCs, etc., number of special and resource teachers, their qualifications and pay scale, and budget utilisation. Similar information should also be included in the statistics collected by MHRD as also the Educational Surveys conducted by NCERT.

The MHRD and the Ministry of Welfare should make grants under IEDC and special schools contingent on the latter regularly giving the information. An inter-departmental Committee should be set up at the State and Central levels for monitoring. In addition, regular visits by the officers of the MHRD, NCERT, Regional Colleges of Education and field offices, should lead to status reports.

Evaluation studies by external agencies, universities conducting courses on education, and rehabilitation of persons in specific geographical areas will be commissioned by MHRD and the Ministry of Welfare.

Integrated Education for the Disabled Children (IEDC) 1992

The Government of India has given the education of diabled children special attention to achieve the goal of education for all. The objective is to integrate the handicapped with the general community at all levels as equal partners, to prepare them for normal growth and to enable them to face life with courage and confidence. This is operating through the centrally sponsored IEDC scheme. In addition, the disabled children who are placed in special schools should also be integrated in common schools once they acquire required communication and daily living skills. The Central Government assists the States/Union Territories in their implementation as per conditions laid down in the scheme. The scheme is implemented through the State Government/s UT Administrations/ Autonomous Organisations of stature having experience in the field of education and/or rehabilitation of the disabled. Because this scheme has to be implemented in schools, the Education Department is the implementing agency. The state

Governments may take the assistance of voluntary organisations also for this purpose.

The Scheme provides, educational facilities for children with disabilities who can be integrated in general schools. While rehabilitation assistance will be made available to all children with disabilities, student benefits will be extended on the recommendation by the Assessment Team. The scope of the scheme includes pre-school training for the disabled children and counselling for the parents. It would include, among other things, special training for hearing handicapped children, mobility and orientation training for the visually handicapped, daily living and communication skills training required by chidlren with other disabilities, parental counselling and training in home management of these children. The education of the disabled children under this scheme will continue tup to the senior secondary school level and include vocational courses equivalent to the senor secondary stage. A disabled child in receipt of any scholarship/assistance under some other scheme relating to disability from the State/Central Government will not be eligible for any of the benefits under this scheme unless he/she is willing to forego the other sources of assistance.

Implementing the Scheme

The implementing agency has set up an administrative cell under an officer not below the rank of Deputy Director to implement, monitor and evaluate the programme. These officials are chosen for their special qualifications in this field, or if they are not so qualified, will be trained in a course conducted by the National Council of Educational Research and Training (NCERT). This cell will identify the areas and institutions for implementing the scheme.

It is preferable that in order to properly plan and supervise the implementation of the scheme a number of developmental blocks should be selected for its operation, rather than scattering the schools under this scheme all over the State. Within the area of the selected block all the desired inputs should be provided to the schools covered.

To identify disabled chidlren in the blocks/districts where the scheme is yet to be implemented, the first task should be to provide suitable orientation to all school teachers in the area for conducting a survey to identify disabled children in general schools. Teachers may be provided a small honorarium for conducting the survey. The IEDC cell should provide printed survey forms for identification of these children. Assistance up to Rs. 10,000 may be provided to the IEDC cell for this purpose. These efforts should be supplemented by publicity through the mass media.

The State-level cell will make arrangements for equipment, learning materials, staff, etc. in order to provide education to disabled children. The cell will also set up the machinery for assessment of a disabled children. Wherever a survey has been conducted by any other agency it should be utilised and augmented with the survey of disabilities not covered by the earlier survey. Monitoring and evaluation of the scheme at the State level will be carried out by the cell. The cell will ensure that the information regarding the scheme is widely known.

The Administrative Cell to be set up by the State Education Department will have a Deputy Director, a Coordinator (who will be a psychologist) a Special Educator, a Stenographer and a Lower Division Clerk.

Assessment of the Disabled Children

The Coordinator of the programme will be responsible for arranging for the assessment of the children and monitoring their progress. A three-member assessment team, comprising a doctor, a psychologist and a special educator will be formed. The State/UT assessment team will function under the Administrative Cell. Specialists will be drawn upon in consultation with the State Health Department. Wherever district rehabilitation centres have been established, its resources for assessment may be used. The non-government organisations (NGOs) with infrastructural facilities may also be used for assessment purposes.

The average cost of an assessment should not exceed Rs. 150 per disabled child. It will be necessary to examine a large number of children to select those considered suitable for placement in an integrated programme.

The assessment report should be comprehensive enough for educational programming; a profile of what a particular child can or cannot do during testing situations should be adequately reported. The report should specifically indicate whether the child can be put directly into school or should receive preparation in special school/special preparatory class in the Early Childhood Education Centre specially equippped for this purpose. Functional assessment can be carried out by the teacher if formal assessment is to take a long time so that the educational programme can be started for these children.

Facilities for Disabled Children

1. A disabled child may be given the following kinds of facilities. The facilities should, as far as possible, be given in kind. In case similar incentives are not being offered by the State Government/UT Administration under any other scheme, the following rates could be adopted.
   a. Actual expenses on books and stationery up to Rs. 400 per annum.
   b. Actual expenses on uniform up to Rs. 200 per annum.
   c. Transport allowance up to Rs. 50 per month (if a disabled child admitted under the scheme resides in the school hostel within the school premises, no transportation charges would be admissible).

d. Reader allowance of Rs. 50 per month in case of blind children after class V.
e. Escort allowance for severaly handicapped children with lower extremely disabilities at the rate of Rs. 75 per month.
f. Actual cost of equipment, subject to a maximum of Rs. 2000 per student for a period of five years.

2. In the case of severely orthopaedically handicapped children, it may be necessary to allow one attendant for 10 children in a school.
3. Disabled children residing in school hostels within the same institution where they are studying may also be paid boarding and lodging charges. Where there is no state, scheme of scholarships to hostel dwellers, the disabled children whose parental income does not exceed Rs. 5,000 per month may be paid actual boarding and lodging charges subject to a maximum of Rs. 200 per month. However disabled children should generally not be placed in hostels unless the required educational facilities are not available in nearby schools.
4. Severely orthopaedically handicapped children residing in school hostels may need the assistance of a helper or an ayah. A special pay of Rs. 50 per month is admissible to any employee of the hostel willing to extend such help to children in addition to his/her duties.

Special Teacher

Except for children with locomotor disabilities, special education teachers may be appointed in schools where the scheme is in operation to provide specific attention to the disabled children.

The teacher-pupil ratio for special education teachers envisaged under this scheme is 1:8. This ratio will be the same for normal classes as well as for preparatory pre-school classes. The same teacher will provide counselling to the parents. In accordance with this ratio the requisite number of special teachrs may be appointed in schools (or for a cluster of schools) for children requiring special teacher support as per qualifications specified in the scheme.

The same scales of pay as available to the teachers of the corresponding category in that State/UT will be given to special teachers. Considering the special type of duties, these teachers will be given a special pay of Rs. 150 per month in urban areas and Rs. 200 per month in rural areas. The State Education Department may recruit such teachers for this purpose following the normal recruitment procedures.

Educational Measures

A resource room having all the essential equipment, learning aids and materials may be provided for a cluster of schools implementing the scheme of integrated education. The NCERT has prepared a handbook which also indicates the type of facilities which may be provided in the resource room. A list of equipments required for various disabilities is already described in chapter 1. The average cost of such equipment is estimated at Rs. 30,000. The need for equipment would depend upon the disability types of the students enrolled in the associated schools. The resource room may be set up preferably in an existing room in the school. A new room may be built only where no accommodation is available to the satisfaction of the State Government. Grant shall be available for construction of a resource room in a school in such circumstances subject to a maximum of Rs. 50,000. NGOs/special schools wherever available should be used as resource centres for the IED programme in general schools.

Visually and hearing impaired children should be allowed to take only one language as already recommended. Provision for alternative modes of examination for blind and other children with physical disabilities coming in the way of writing should be considered and provided by the Boards of Examination.

Preparation of disabled children for education being essential, preference should be given to the blocks where the schemes of Integrated Child Development (ICD) and Early Childhood Centres of Education (ECCE) exist while selecting blocks for implementation of the scheme. Support for services for disabled children will be available for instructional materials and training of teachers. Procedures of grant are governed as per scheme IEDC, 1992.

United Nations Standard rules, November, 1994

The Rights of Disabled children have been greatly recognised and the UNO has stimulated several conditions on the Nation and State to plan for it. The following are the United Nations Standard Rules on the Euqalisation of Opportunities for persons with disabilities duly adopted by the XI World Congress on Mental Retardation.

Equal Participation

1. States should take action to raise awareness in society about persons with disabilities; their rights, their needs their potential and their contribution.
2. States should ensure the provision of effective medical care to persons with disabilities.
3. States should ensure the provision of rehabilitation services to persons with disabilities in order for them to reach and substain their optimum level of independence and functioning.
4. Stats should ensure the development and supply of support services, including assistive devices for persons with disabilities, to assist them to increase their level of independence in their daily living and to exercise their rights.

Target Areas

5. States should recognize the overall importance of accessibility in the process of the equalization of opportunities in all spheres of society. For persons with disabilities of any kind states should (a) introduce programmes of action to make the physical environment accessible; and (b) undertake measures to provide access to information and communication.
6. States should recognize the principle of equal primary, secondary and tertiary educational opportunities for children, youth and adults with disabilities, in integrated settings. They should ensure that the education of persons with disabilities is an integral part of the educational system.
7. States should recognize the principle that persons with disabilities must be empowered to exercise their human rights, particularly in the field of employment, in both rural and urban areas they must have equal opportunities for productive and gainful employment in the labour market.
8. States are responsible for the provision of social security and income maintenance for persons with disabilities.
9. States should promote the full participation of persons with disabilities in family life. They should promote their right to personal integrity and ensure that laws do not discriminate against persons with disabilities with respect to sexual relationships, marriage and parenthood.
10. States will ensure that persons with disabilities are integrated into and can participate in cultural activities on an equal basis.
11. States will take measures to ensure that persons with disabilities have equal opportunities for recreation and sports.
12. States will take measures for equal participation by persons with disabilities in the religious life of their communities.

Implementation Measures

13. States assume the ultimate responsibility for the collection and dissemination of information on the living conditions of persons with disabilities and promote comprehensive research on all aspects, including obstacles that affect the lives of persons with disabilities.
14. States will ensure that disability aspects are include in all relevant policy making and national planning.
15. States have a responsibility to create the legal bases for measures to achieve the objectives of full participation and equality for persons with disabilities.
16. States have the financial responsibility for national programmes and measures to create equal opportunities for persons with disabilities.

17. States are responsible for the establishment and strengthening of national coordinating committees, or similar bodies, to serve as a national focal point on disability matters.
18. States should recognize the right of the organizations of persons with disabilities to represent persons with disabilities at national, regional and local levels. States should also recognize the advisory role of organizations of person with disabilities in decision-making on disablity matters.
19. States are responsible for ensuring the adequate training of personnel, at all levels, involved in the planning and provision of programmes and services concerning persons with disabilities.
20. States are responsible for the continuous monitoring and evaluation of the implementation of national programmes and services concerning the equalization of opportunities for persons with disabilities.
21. States, both industrialized and developing, have the responsibility to cooperate in an take measures for the improvement of the living conditions of persons with disabilities in developing countries.
22. States will participate actively in international cooperation concerning policies for the equalization of opportunities for perons with disabilities.

Development of special education perspectives have been well explained and described through the commissions, committees, programmes, policies of Government since Education Commission made is recommendation. The adoption of Integrated Education Schemes, and detailed programme of action have added seriousness of purpose to the education of disabled. Add to this is the role of United Nation's emphasis and declaration for the State to take up the responsibilities. The future only will show the progress.

Highlights of the Chapter

Interest in the education of the handicapped had a programatic development in our country. In 1964-66 the Education Commission made an analysis of the state of art in special education in the areas of Blind, Deaf, Mentally Retarded and Orthopaedically Handicapped and observed inadequacy in the quantity and quality of institutions compared to magnitude of the problem. It was quite emphatic of the expansion of the movement which became consistent with National Policy on Children, 1974.

The IYDP, 1981 recommended education of the disabled, prevention, rehabilitation, and full participation with equality. India was one of the signatories which made series of attempts to evolve a National Policy on the Handicapped and a strong national disability prevention programme. Currently, prevention programme on Blindness is on its march. Specific planned network was established to provide education, legal protection, and employment.

The working groups, and various sub-committees set up by the Ministry of Welfare priortised the categories of disability to be taken care of. Initially, the Deaf, the Blind, the Orthopaedics and the Mentally Retarded were enrolled in different special schools. Long-term and Short-term teacher training courses were also conceptualised alongwith emphasis on awareness, generation and dissemination of information. Voluntary organisations also grew up in pace.

The National Policy on Education, 1986; 1992 (R) made recommendations on-education of mild disabled children in regular schools, special residential schools in District HQs, vocational training, teacher training and initiating voluntary effort which were corroborated further by Ramamurty and Janardan Reddy Committee Reports leading to a Programme of Action (POA) 1992. The POA made plans for implementation in the areas of: Integrated Education of the Disabled, support to families of disabled, development of educational packages, development of Braille, vocational schools, preservice teacher training programmes, inservice programme, early identification, use of technology in education of the handicapped, setting up VRCs, reorientation of the general education to take care of disability, Field Publicity Programmes, Convergence of ECCE, ICDS with PIED programmes etc. The PIED Scheme is a Centrally Sponsored Scheme.

The United Nations Standard Rules, 1994 operationalised and made mandatory recommendations to various States and Nations for protecting Rights of the Disabled in terms of equal participation in life, provision of equal educational opportunities for the disabled and responsibility of the State for complete care of diabled children and population. The National Disability Bill, 1996, in India is a step in this direction in our country.

Review Questions

1. What has been the recommendations of various committees and commissions on the education of handicapped since the Education Commission upto the IYDP, 1981?
2. What are the policy guidelines on the education of handicapped on the education of handicapped as per 1986 (1992-R) NPE and its revision?
3. Briefly state the integrated education scheme, 1992 on the education of the mildly handicapped.
4. State the Rights of Disabled as per United Nations Standard Rules, 1994.
5. Briefly state the evolution of Special Education for exceptional children (Handicapped) since the Education Commission to present times in India.

References

Education and National Development, Report of the Education Commission (1964-66), Ministry of Education and Culture, Government of India.

Janardan Reddy Committee Report, 1992, Ministry of Human Resource Development, Government of India, New Delhi.

National Policy on Education (1986, 1992), Ministry of Human Resource Development, Government of India, New Delhi.

Programme of Action (1992), Ministry of Human Resource Development, Government of India, New Delhi.

Ramamurty Committee Report, 1992, Ministry of Human Resource Development, Government of India, New Delhi.

Report of the Advisory Committee on Blind, Deaf, Orthopaedically Handicapped and Mentally Retarded (1981), Ministry of Social Welfare, Government of India, New Delhi.

Scheme of Integrated Education for the Disabled (1992), Ministry of Human Resource Development, Government of India, New Delhi.

United Nations Standard Rules on the equalisation of opportunities for persons with disabilities, XI World Congress on Mental Retardation, Nov., 1994.

Working Group on the Education of Disabled Child (1981), Ministry of Social Welfare and Ministry of Education and Culture, Government of India, New Delhi.

Chapter 4

Mentally Retarded Children

There are children who cannot mentally function as well as most children we find in society. These children are subnormal in intelligence and behaviour. This retardation is pervasive and is een in all societies and cultures in varying proportions. Students will get a comprehensive and clear idea about mentally retarded children after reading the text presented here. The present chapter deals with:

- the meaning of mental retardation, along with its variations,
- the six hour retarded child,
- the prevalence and causes of mental retardation,
- the measures used to prevent it,
- the psycho-educational characteristics i.e., how mentally retardates learn, remember, perceive and think,
- the kind of educational provisions needed for them, including mainstreaming,
- the roles of regular and resource room teachers,
- education of the severely retarded.

Who is a Mentally Retarded Child?

Mental retardation has been known for centuries and different terms have been used to explain it. Early in the twentieth century, the terms moron, imbecile, and idiot explained the three levels of retardation. During the 1940s the term feeble-minded was used. In recent years terms like 'mental subnormality' and 'developmental disability' are being used.

Until the twentieth century, retardation was defined in terms of an individual's inability to meet the minimal demands of society. In 1905, Alfred Binet developed a method of identifying students who could be expected to fail in the regular school curriculum and who therefore required a special instructional programme, which was translated and used in the USA by Henry Herbert Goddard. Terman's 1916 edition of the Standord Binet Intelligence Scale was quickly adopted as a standardized, objective, norm-referenced way of identifying retarded children. IQ became a standard for classification of mental retardation. However, David Wechsler, who devised a series of intelligence tests, warned against the rigid use of intelligence test scores as the sole criterion for diagnosing retardation.

The Mental Deficiency Act of 1921 in England considered "Mental defectiveness as a condition of arrested or incomplete development of mind existing before the age of eighteen years, whether arising from inherrent causes or induced by disease or injury."

One of the earliest definitions was given by Doll (1941). According to him mentally retarded children show different characteristics. These are:

1. Social incompetency
2. Mental subnormality
3. The deficiency is developmentally linked
4. The retardation finally comes on maturity
5. Retardation is constitutional in origin
6. It is essentially incurable

Encyclopedia Britanica defines mental deficiency as "A state of subnormal evaluation of the human organism in consequence of which the individual affected is incapable of assuming the responsibilities expected of a socially adequate person, such as self-direction, self-support and social participation." Sarason and Dorris (1969) defined, "Mental retardation refers to individuals who for temporary or long standing reasons function intellectually below the average of their peer groups, but social adequacy is not in question or if it is in question, there is little likelihood that the individual can learn to function independently and adequately in the community."

All these definitions were prevalent at different times and in different countries. But none of them could adequately explain mental retardation. The characteristics pointed out by different authors are also unrelated to one another. Therefore, the American Association of Mental Deficiency (AAMD) set up a committee under the Chairmanship of Rick Heber to develop a comprehensive definition of mental retardation. Heber defined mental retardation as "significantly sub-average general functioning existing concurrently with deficits in adaptive behaviour and manifested during the developmental period" (Heber, 1959).

This definition was subsequently restated as: "Mental retardation refers to significantly sub-average general intellectual functioning, resulting in or associated with, concurrent impairments in adaptive behaviour and manifested during the developmental period." This definition has three aspects:

a. Sub-average intellectual functioning,
b. Developmental in origin,
c. Impairment in adaptive behaviour.

A standard intelligence test is applied to assess the IQ of children. If the IQ falls below two or more standard deviations from the normal then the child has subaverage intelligence. In Stanford-Binet and Wechsler tests the IQ points are respectively 68 and 70. The low intelligence manifests during the first 18 years of life, and the child in order to be categoriesed as mentally retarded must also show impariment in adaptive behaviour. Adaptive behaviour is defined as "the effectiveness of degree with which an individual meets the standards of personal independence and social responsibility expected for an age and cultural group" (Grossman, 1977). Adaptive behaviour means social adjustment which varies from simple self-help skills to that of personal social adjustment in adulthood. These are determined on the basis of scores on an adaptive behaviour scale developed by the AAMD Vineland Social Maturity Scale, or Adaptive behaviour inventory of children.

Adaptive behaviour refers to the effectiveness of the individual or the degree to which a person meets the standards of personal independence and social responsibility expected for his age and cultural group. Expectations differ for different ages. Deficits are reflected during infancy and preschool years in the areas of sensorimotor skills, communication skills, self-help skills, and early socialisation skills. During early school and adolescent years, adaptive behaviour deficits are reflected in academic skills, activities of daily living, the use of appropriate reasoning and judgement in mastery of the environment, and the use of social skills. During late adolescence and adulthood, adaptive behaviour deficits may be reflected in any of the skills cited for younger persons or social responsibilities and performance, or vocational activities.

Retarded children who function at different levels of retardation require different educational programmes, curricula, methods, and materials. In recent years, differences observed among them have led to the use of four levels: mild, modertate, severe, and profound retardation. The mild group, which makes up approximately 75 to 85% of the total retardation population, is called educable mentally retarded (EMR) in school settings. These children are in the IQ range of about 55 to 80. IQ students in the EMR range are capable of learning basic academic skills of reading, writing and arithmatic. Most children can learn vocational skills.

These children may enter school at the usual age, but formal reading and writing instruction may be delayed until about age eight or nine. During school years, they may be given instruction in simple arithmatical concepts, understanding of the home and community, and development of good work habits. Curricula are designed to provide basic skills for coping with the environment. Educable children usually develop language skills.

The moderate level of retardation (IQ range about 35 to 60) includes essentially the same group as those called trainable mentally retarded (TMR) in schools. Until the 1950s, this group was usually not admitted to public schools.

Gradually separate classes were started for them under the public school system. The curricula for TMR students differ from that of EMR curricula. TMR students are unlikely to develop independence as adults. They are unlikely to learn to handle finances beyond simple purchases and usually need some supervisory help. The academic skills taught include learning to recognise signs and common symbols, learning to recognize and use coins, and telling time to the half or quarter-hour. In addition to development of skills of self-care and simple occupational skills, it is especially important for the curriculum to include leisure skills. TMR students eventually develop language skill,s but articulation problems are more common than that in the EMR children. Teachers use experience as well as reinforcement techniques to teach the TMR.

Severely retarded (IQ range about 20 to 35) and profoundly retarded (IQ below 20) children are not considered for school placement. Educators usually referred to all retarded children below the TMR level as custodial. It was assumed that all such children would be in residential institutions. Although today about 80% of individuals who are in residential facilities are severely or profoundly retarded, many others have remained at home. With the deinstitutionalization movement, many children in western countries are provided education through public schools.

The Six Hour Retarded Child

A good description of mental retardation is given in the "The Six Hour Retarded Child" where the students who perform poorly in school may function adequately at home, and within the community. If they are able to meet family and social needs in every area except in school, they are not considered as retarded.

The term "6-hour retarded" first appeared in the report of the conference on "Problem of Education of Children in the Inner City", President's Committee on Mental Retardation, 1969. The conference recommended:

1. provide early childhood stimulation education as part of the public education programme;
2. conduct a study of the histories of successful inner-city families who have learned to cope effectively;
3. restructure education of teachers, administrators, and counsellors;
4. re-examine present systems of intelligence testing and classification;
5. commit substantial additional funding for research and developmental in educational improvement for the disadvantaged;
6. delineate what constitutes accountability and hold the school accountable for providing quality education for all children; and
7. involve parents, citizens, citizen groups, students, and general and special educators in a total educational effort.

The concept of the 6-hour retarded child has survived into the late 1980s. Today many psychologists and educators have accepted that children identified as mildly retarded during the school-age years manifest retarded functioning only in the school setting and that outside of school, during childhood and in their work as adults, function successfully. Often their retardation is invisible to their employers, families, neighbours, and friends.

Some of the recent studies such as the work by Edgerton (1984) suggests that regular and special education programmes should prepare children with limited potential for the roles they will play as adults. In fact, no one concerned about the future of the mildly retarded pupil can be content in the belief that their problems exist only in school, and that outside of this setting they function as capably as their age mates. How then do we go about helping the retarded to learn the necessary competence to live successfully within the limits of their abilities?

Interest in the study of mental retardation came from the pioner work of Itard, the French Physician in his study on the care of The Wild Boy of Aveyron. Seguin subsequently focussed on appropriate educational placement and provisions for the low intelligent group of children. Recent years have seen much more progress in this field: legal, organisational and educational, because of interest groups and National Associations in the U.S. and U.K. In our country special education and rehabilitation programme for the handicapped have already been introduced through the integrated educational programme and special schools.

Prevalence

On the average 2.5% of all children are mild and moderately retarded and 0.5% are severely retarded. There has been no systematic National Survey conducted to determine the prevalence of mental retardation in India. It has been estimated however that there are about 20 million persons who are mildly retarded and about four million persons who are moderately and severely retarded. The figures of prevalence of mental retardation in India vary from 0.22 to 32.8 per thousand population. Family density and retardation had high association. Those born to mothers below 19 years of age had more chances of being retarded. In rural areas incidence of retardation is more. Within 0-14 age group the NSSO 1991 states that in rural areas the incidence of MR is 3.1% and in urban it is 0.9%. The NIMH mentions 2% of general population as MR, three quarters of them, Mildly so, and one fourth severe. There are over 600 schools for the mentally retarded, unevenly distributed among the States.

Causes of Mental Retardation

Mental Retardation occurs due to genetic and environmental factors which come into play at pre-natal, perinatal and postnatal stages of development.

Genetic

One of the most visible conditions associated with mental retardation is Down's Syndrome. Down, in 1865, was the first to use the term mongolian idiocy to name a particular form of mental retardation, now referred to as mongolism or Down's Syndrome. Down's Syndrome contains the non-sex determining chromosome. Chromosomal anomaly explains many forms of mental disorders. In non-dysjunction Down's Syndrome one pair of genes fails to separate at conception, resulting in an extra or 47th chromosome after forty-six known as Tirsomy-21. The face of the child has palpebral fissures that are oblique and narrow laterally, speckled iris, flatness of the nose bridge, enlarged tongue, small ears, and short and broad neck. Other common anomalies are flattening of the occiput, broad hands with the little finger curved, short broad feet with a wide space between the first and second toes, pelvic anomalies, and congenital heart anomalies in almost 25% of patients. Intellectual development is impaired (IQ 25-69).

There is a clear cut association between Mental Age and Trisomy-21.

Down's Syndrome incidence per 1000	*Below 20*	*20-24*	*25-29*	*30-34*	*35-39*	*40+*
	0.46	0.65	0.88	1.26	3.92	17.60

Whatever the IQ value, it seems safe to say that Trisomy-21 children will not be able to enjoy an independent life, even if some of them reach borderline intelligence. Mongolism or Down's Syndrome is due to the presence of three types of chromosomal anomalies. Three main cytogenetic forms are known: with 47 chromosomes and a standard trisomy-21 (95% of all cases); with normal mosaics, with 46 chromosomes/trisomy-21 (two three per cent), and with translocations (two to three per cent). Although it is not known that the causes are, a close association between maternal age and trisomy 21 has been repeatedly demonstrated.

These children need extra care. Parental support is a vital need to ensure that infant stimulation programmes emphasizing self-help skills, language acquisition, feeding, toilet training, and positive socialization, are provided. Down's syndrome individuals are educable and should have exposure to their non-handicapped peers from their early years. In the past, professionals advised parents to place their Down's syndrome child in 24-hour institutional care based on the false assumption that the Down's syndrome individual would be severely or profoundly retarded. Custodial care is seldom warranted unless severe medical, psychological or social problems occur.

The greatest general development is found in Down's Syndrome individuals who are reared at home and well stimulated. Optimum progress occurs when facilities are positive and training begins early and is comprehensive.

Translocation is common. It occurs because of faulty cell division in which one chromosome is attached to another. In Mosaicism, the cell receives an extra twenty first chromosomes, but there are fewr abnormalities in this form of Down's Syndrome.

Turner's Syndrome

Turner's Syndrome results from the absence of an X-chromosome in the female (XO). Learning problems are usually seen, including impaired hearing. Treatment includes use of female hormones to develop female sex characteristics. Klinefelter's Syndrome is seen in males due to the presence of an additional X-chromosome (XXY) and a chromosome count of 47. The male usually develops female characteristics. Mental retardation due to this factor remains within the moderate range.

Congenital Defects

Microcephaly and Hydrocephaly are two types of disorders which involve cranial and congenital defects. These are of unknown origin and they exist before birth. Primary microcephaly is inherited whereas secondary microcephaly is acquired. In the case of primary microcephaly the brain tissue is under-developed in relation to size of the cranium. Retardation ranges from mild to severe. Overproduction or under absorption of cerebrospinal fluid is termed as hydrocephaly. The head is globe shaped, the bridge of the nose is flat and the eyes are pushed downward, and become more widely spated. It is not hereditary. Surgery is applied to prevent further disorders. Hydrocephaly if not conrolled will lead to profound retardation and death.

Microcephaly is one cranial aberration which can have both genetic and environmental causes. In such cases mental retardation ranges from moderate to severe. It might be due prenatal radiation also.

Metabolic and Nutritional Disorders

Galactosemia is a carbohydrate disorder which is transmitted genetically. In such cases, the infants fail to metabolise the galactose in milk. Unless the child is placed on a low lactose diet, mental retardation sets in. Similarly when the body fails to change phenylalaline into tyrosine, it leads to phenylketonuria (PKU). PKU which can be detected easily by urine culture or blood analysis.

Phenylketonuria (PKU)

Phenylketonuria (PKU) is one of the biochemical irregularities associated with mental retardation. It was first noted in 1934 that a few institutionalised retardates passed urine with a peculiar "mousy" odor. This was found to arise from the excretion of phenylacetic acid. PKU results from the absence of the enzyme phenylanine bydroxylase, which normally converts phenylalnine, an essential amino acid common to most proteins and many other foods, into tyrosine and its constituent components. High levels of phenylalanine damage developing brain tissue. Since brain damage is irreversible, permanent and severe mental retardation is a predictable outcome.

It is an autosomal recessive inborn error. If the disorder is undiagnosed and untreated, progressive brain damage begins. Until the 1950s, prognosis was poor; most affected individuals had IQs of about 30 and were institutionalised.

Neonatal screening using urine test is now universal. Guthrie test is now used, which reveals excess phenylalanine through a blood test 24 to 48 hours after birth. If PKU is diagnosed, the infant is placed on a low phenylalanine diet. Dietary treatment must begin within a few days of birth for maximal effectiveness. Adult IQ of early treated PKU individuals is about 90; IQ becomes lower with delay of treatment so that by about three years of age, maximal damage has occurred.

The problems may become more serious when PKU is not treated. Pregnant women transmit unmetabolized phenylalanine to their embryos and fetuses at the critical pre-natal period causing adverse influences on brain development. A common recommendation now is for PKU women to keep a low caloric diet throughout their child bearing period. The safest recommendation is for PKU women not to have children. Low protein diet acts as a prevention of such disorders. Hypothyroidism or Cretinism is a common disorder leading to low IQ. Use of Thyroxin can lessen Cretinism.

Gestational Factors

Gestational disorders like premature birth also cause mental retardation. Even post mature births are harmful in the sense that survery is used for birth and because of extra growth, there is prolonged labour and consequent adverse effects on the brain of the newborn. Severe environmental deprivation, special sensory handicaps (deafness and blindness) contribute to retarded development. Multiple handicaps such as epilepsy, and cerebral palsy also account for some degree of retardation. After birth the child can cntract diseases such as menigitis and encephalities which can also result in retardation.

Lead Poisoning

Lead is found in the soil, water and atmosphere. It occurs more frequently in the natural environment than other heavy metals. Lead is one of the few metals that seems to have toxic effects. It can enter the body through one's diet, eating of lead-based paint, and exposure to an environment containing a high lead content. Foundries, brass works, battery factories, printing operations, and other plants have been shown to increase the amount of lead in the surrounding environment. Today most victims of lead poisoning are infants and toddlers who are likely to take edible objects into their mouths. Common sources of lead poisoning are lead paints in the wall, furniture, crib rails, toys, battery cases, which the infant licks up, or chewing of lead pencils etc. The symptoms of lead poisoning are treated by using medicines and by maintaining a healthy diet. Lead free environment is to be ensured. Prevention is most important since it leads to permanent damage of the brain. Drug abuse, lead poisoning, and mercury poisoning all lead to brain damage.

Rubella

Rubella (German measles) is a viral infection. The postnatal rubella virus is transmitted through contact with blood, body waste excretions, nasopharyngeal secretions of infected persons, and their clothing. Human beings are the only known hosts for the rubella virus. Nearly 20 to 30% chance of damage to the foetus occurs when a mother contracts the infection during the first trimester of pregnancy. These were first reported by Sir Norman Gregg, an Australian ophthalmologist, 1941. The congenital rubella syndrome as described by Gregg consists of foetal anomalies, ocular defects, and hearing impairment. Mental retardation is a common result of early damage to the foetus. The virus is transferred from the mother's bloodstream to the placenta and then enters to the foetal bloodstream. It is apparent that the earlier in the pregnancy the mother contracts the viral infection, the more pervasive the damage to the foetus.

Prevention seems to be the key to reducing the impact of congenital rubella, as there is little hope of reversing the effects. Of course, corrective surgery can be performed in cases where the foetus suffers cardiac damage or has cataracts, and hearing aids can be given to the hearing-impaired child, but damage is not reversible.

Immunization procedures such as large doses of gamma globulin have been shown to be ineffective in preventing damage to the foetus once the mother has contracted the virus. Chemotherapeutic procedures also have proven inadequate as protection against the devasting effects of congenital rubella.

Infection and Intoxication

During the prenatal period the foetus is succeptible to damage from maternal infection and intoxication. Within the first three months of pregnancy, the mother's infection of rubella can lead to serious complications, such as: mental retardation, heart disorders, seizures etc. About 85 per cent of rubella babies suffer from these types of ailments. Continuous moderate intake of alcohol can also produce these deficiencies. Mental retardation occurs due to congenital syphilis, although syphilis can be controlled. Postnatal infections caused by viruses, bacteria, parasites and fungi may also lead to mental retardation. Toxic agents cause damage to the foetus.

Mother-foetal blood group incompatibility

Mother-foetal blood group incompatibility can lead to death and spontaneous abortion of the foetus. This is inherited. These are of two types.

ABO incompatibility

A.B.O. incompatibility concerns the blood of the mother and foetus blood types. If the mother's and foetus's blood types (A, B, AB, O) are different, various problems can ensue. A.B.O. incompatibility occurs with second and later pregnancies. However, if the mother has O-type blood and fetus has A-type blood, incompatibility can even occur even during first pregnancy. Once again bilirubin is produced which can cause brain damage unless detected and controlled. In case of high bilirubin, the child can be placed under direct sunlight that will break down the excess bilrubin in the blood.

RH-incompatibility

Typically if the mother carries Rh-negative blood she is administered RhoGam within 72 hours after birth of a Rh positive child. More recent practice indicates that RhoGam can be administered periodically during pregnancy.

X-ray, Birth Injuries and Trauma

Exposure to X-ray in the early months of pregnancy, using harmful drugs, especially those used in treatments of cancer, antiepileptic drugs and hormones can damage the growing foetus. Untreated fits of the mother, and accidents from falls resulting in injury to the abdomen can damage the growing foetus and lead to mental retardation.

Pre-natal, perinatal, and postnatal injury can cause trauma. Mechanical injury or birth injuries can cause brain damage. Anoxia i.e., lack of oxygen, is also responsible for mental retardation. Postnatal anoxia is caused by shock and respiratory difficulties. The extent of brain injury during birth will determine the degree of retardation.

Brain Disease

Neurofibromatosis and Tuberous sclerosis are two examples of gross brain disease. Neurofibromatosis is hereditary and is characterised by brownish spots on the skin, and tumours in the brain and nervous system. Tuberous scelorsis is characterised by reddish-orange modules in a butterfly pattern on the face and cheeks.This is hereditary. Its treatment consists of removal of tumours wherever possible and use of anticonvulsants in case of seizures.

Deprivation

Low Socio Economic Status (SES) through poor language environment, large number of children in the family, emotional suffering of mother during pregnancy, and nutritional deficiencies of the mother during pregnancy, cause impairment in intellectual functioning. Environmental influences explain by far the greatest number of cases for which no etiological classification is given.* Prevention focuses upon the enrichment of the impoverished environment and the provision of high quality educational and social services.

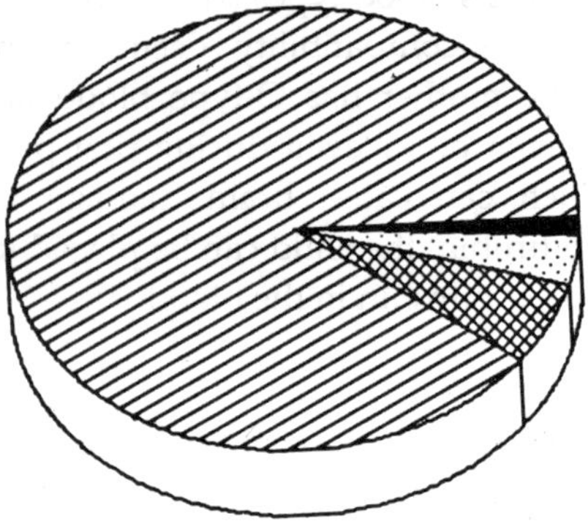

Figure 2: Percentage of Mental Retardation

Preventive Measures

It follows from the causes that certain preventive measures can be taken. These are:

1. Early screening and detection.
2. Vaccination against rubella.
3. Surgical procedure to correct hydrocephaly.
4. Amniocentosis to detect chromosomal aberrations in the foetus i.e., blood examination.
5. Use of drugs to control the effect of childhood illness. Urine test for metabolic disorders: PKU, Galactosemia.
6. Blood transfusion of Rh-factor babies and vaccination of Rh-sensitised mothers.
7. Laws that prohibit the use of lead based paint on baby toys and furniture.
8. Dietary treatment of PKU and galactosemia.
9. Improved maternal nutrition and parental health care.
10. Genetic counselling for persons who are carriers of potential genetic defects.
11. Enrichment of impoverished environments.
12. Dermatoglyphics.
13. Serological and Viral tests for intra uterine infection.
14. X-ray of the skull and EEG.
15. Examination of the cerebrospinal fluid.
16. Chromosomal studies for detecting anomalies.

Identification

How to know who is really mentally retarded? Despite the controversy over the concept of IQ, IQ continues to be a criterion for identification of retardation and its classification. The concept of adaptive behaviour is also used in classification and identification. It refers to the effectiveness with which an individual copes with the natural and social demands of his environment. There are also certain tell-tale signs observable in these children.

Behavioural Signs

Certain behavioural signs give an indication of the presence of mental retardation among children. These can be observed by teachers and parents.

1. General academic retardation characterised by slow rate of learning, poor problem solving skills, slow reaction to environmental demands.
2. Poor memory. Inability to retain things mentally for long periods.
3. Difficulty in developing concepts, especially abstract concepts. Absence of clarity.
4. Inability to arrive at generalisations and see common elements among different objects or events.
5. Slow language development-usually the language is limited in terms of vocabulary and variety.
6. Below average in imagination and creaive thinking.
7. Inability to delay gratification and satisfaction by immediate reward.
8. Short attention span and intolerance of frustration.
9. Limited play and social interests.
10. Lack of concentration, heightened distractibility and incapacity for comprehension.
11. Lack of coordination in self-help skills (sucking, chewing, eating, use of hands, legs, fingers, etc.).
12. Some have physical features like a small or large head, smal eyes, straight hair, fissured tongue, low set ears, and short stature, physical deformities and paralysis of one or more limbs.
13. In case of school going children there are repeated failures and inability to cope with the lessons.

Testing

For the mentally retarded, assessment includes basically intelligence and adaptive behaviour along with developmental material supplied by parents, teachers, social workers and professionals. The two most widely used intelligence tests are: the Stanford Binet, and the Weschler Intelligence Scale for Children. These individual tests along with functional assessment tests developed by the National Institute for Mentally Handicapped can be used.

Adaptive behaviour is assessed using adaptive behaviour scales. In these scales, assessment is made on the basis of maturational and developmental skills in the areas of communication, motor ability and self-help in early childhood. In later periods, learning and social skills receive greater emphasis. During adolescence, social and vocational adjustments are emphasised. AAMD adaptive behaviour scale and the Vineland Social Maturity Scale are quite well known tests of measuring adaptive behaviour. The adaptive behaviour dimensions, according to AAMD behaviour scale, are related to the following dimensions.

Components of the A.A.M.D. Adaptive Behaviour Scale

Part 'A'	*Part 'B'*
Independent functioning—Eating, Toilet use, Cleanliness, Appearance and Care of clothing, Dressing and Undressing, Travel, General independent functionining;	Violent and Destructive behaviour;
Physical development—Sensory Motor;	Antisocial behaviour;
Economic activity—Money handling and Budgeting shopping skills;	Rebellious behaviour;
Language development—Expression, Comprehension, Social language development;	Untrustworthy behaviour;
Number and Time;	Withdrawal;
Domestic activity—Cleaning, Kitchen duties, other domestic activities;	Sterotyped behaviour and odd mannerisms;
Vocational activities;	Inapproperiate interpersonal manners;
Self-direction—Initiative, perseverance, Leisure time;	Unacceptable vocal habits;
Responsibility;	Unacceptable or eccentric habits;
Socialisation.	Self-abusive behaviour;
	Hyper-activity tendencies;
	Sexually aberrant behaviour;
	Psychological disturbances;
	Use of Medication.

Levels of Adaptive Behaviour from Birth to Adulthood

Description Terminology.	*Preschool Age (0-5) Maturation and Development.*	*School Age (5-21) Training and Education.*	*Adult (21 and over) Adequacy.*
Mildy retarded	Can develop social and communication skills, minimal retardation in sensori-motor areas; rarely distinguished from normal until later.	Can learn minimal academic skills by late teens; needs special education, particularly at secondary age school age school age levels.	Capable of social and vocational independence with proper education and training; some need supervision and guidance.
Moderately retarded	Can talk or learn to communicate; poor social awareness; may learn to walk and feed self. Toilet training is minimal.	Can learn academic skills by late teens if given special education, although still functionally illiterate.	Capable of self maintenance in unskilled occupations, but needs supervision and guidance.
Severely retarded	Poor motor development speech is minimal; generally unable to profit from training in self-help; little or no communication skills; may learn to walk.	Can talk or learn to communicate; can be trained in elemental health habits; cannot learn functionally academic skills; profits from systematic habit training.	Can contribute partially to self support under complete supervision as by developing skills to a minimal useful level in sheltered workship, needs permanent care.
Profoundly retarded	Gross retardation: rarely develops feeding, speaking, toilet, or other self-help skills, often bed bound.	Some slow motor development; remains bed bound; cannot profit from training in social help, needs total care.	Little motor or speech development, totally incapable of self maintenance, needs permanent care.

In this direction the National Institute for Mentally Handicapped (NIMH) at Secunderabad has done commendable work in developing behavioural assessment scales for Indian Children with Mental Retardation, Functional assessment tools, Assessment of the Mentally Retarded Individuals for grouping and teaching; Problem Behaviour Checklist; Maladaptive Behaviour Checklist; Behaviour disorder checklist; Adaptive Behaviour Scale (Indian Revision); etc. The skill development tests for Gross and Fine motor skills, Meal time skills, Toilet Training, Tooth Brushing, Bathing, Grooming and Social skills, activities developed in a series of bookets by Thakur Hariprasad Institute for the Welfare of Mentally Handicapped would also go a long way in bridging the gap between testing and training for the development of skills.

Educational assessment of the mentally retarded needs to be more functional than verbal. School readiness measures developed by Muralidharan, the Harison reading readiness profile, and Durrell analysis of reading difficulty can be given to M.R. children as high as up to the sixth grade. The Illinois test of Psycholinguistic abilities form of adaption available in our country can be used for diagnosis and related language processes. There are tests which can be profitably used: The Peabody Picture Vocabulory Test (PPVT), Auditory discrimination test, verbal language developmental scale.The crux of the issue lies in developing systematic testing methods, devising certain norms, modifying them in terms of progress achieved, adapting them to the regional languages and variations.

The approach so far has been the use of psychometric tests even though adaptive behaviour assessment has formed a basic component in testing for screening, placing and making any intervention. Although AAMD Adaptive Behaviour Scale, Vineland Social Maturity Scale and a few others have been adapted in our country, there have been wide shortcomings in their use. There are culturally atypical children, hyperactive children to whom such tests can be administered with lots of difficulties. Their motivation and attitude are different. The apprehension of parents about testing because of bias or apprehension of stigma, use of tests for identification by Psuedo professinals, Para-professinals as a measure of social welfare activiites attached to such identification have further posed problems.

Classification of Mental Retardation

There are different methods of classification of mental retardation. The medical classification is based on the cause, the psychological classification on the level of intelligence, and the educational classification on the current level of functioning of the mentally retarded person/child. The proportion of children who fall under the various categories of mental retardation are depicted below.

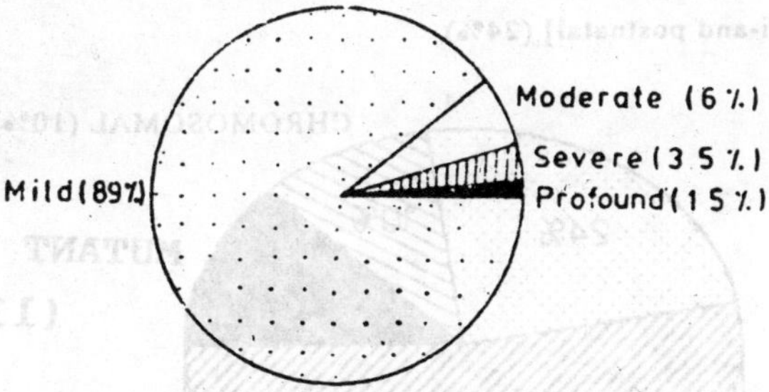

Figure 3: Clinical Classification of Mental Retardation (per cent)

Medical	*Educational*	*Psychological*	
		Wechsler	*Standord Binet*
1. Infections and Intoxications	1. Educable-IQ 60-85	1. Mild IQ 55-69	IQ-52-67
2. Trauma or physical agent	2. Trainable-IQ 30-59	2. Moderate IQ 40-54	IQ-36-51
3. Metabolism or Nutrition	3. Custodial-IQ Below 30	3. Severe IQ 25-39	IQ-20-35
4. Grossbrain disease (Post natal)		4. Profound IQ Below 25	IQ-20-35
5. Unknown prenatal influence			
6. Chromosomal anomaly			
7. Gestational disorder			
8. Environmental influence			

The various classifications provide an understanding of the level at which the mentally retarded person functions with respect to his education, appropriate behaviour and the degree of his independence. The characteristics of mentally retarded persons vary depending upon the level of retardation, country, age, culture etc. The terms currently used to described the various degrees of mental retardation are mild, moderate, severe and profound.

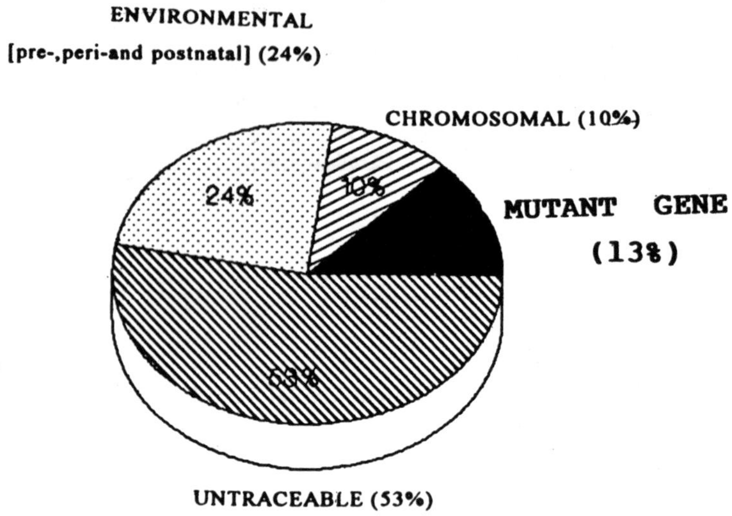

Figure 4: Etiological Factors of Mental Retardation in India

Psychoeducational Characteristics

Learning and Memory

Mildly retarded children have poor learning ability and they forget things quickly. They have a slow rate of responding. Hence, learning difficulty in the mildly retarded can be partly overcome by slowing down the rate of presentation. Pictorial presentation of materials has facilitatory effect on recall. Sen and Sen (1969a) displayed pictures on two occasions with a gap of one month. Recall improved when larger numbers of pictures were displayed. Sen and Sen (1969b) in an experimental study tried to determine the effect of prior learning on subsequent learning in MR. The results showed that a higher degree of prior learning, led to a positive transfer in learning of the second list. Repeated learning improves memory in the mentally retarded. They are deficient in short term memory. Mentally retarded children have rehearsal deficit. If they are taught rehearsal strategies, they improve in memory. Presentation of materials using concrete objects improve both learning and memory followed by pictorial and symbolic material presentations.

Das (1965) found that the retarded had longer reaction time. The retardates were found to be more sensitive than normal children to evaluative verbal stimuli like "good" and "bad". Retardates could name colours faster than they could read words, and showed relatively less interference than normals in naming the colours of words. Intelligence level among the retarded was related to the ability to acquire and distinguish verbal conditioned responses. The mildly retarded children suffered from lack of sustained and analytic attention. In the words of Zeaman and House (1963) they have attention deficit. Failure to attend to details is responsible for poor learning. Further these children have low threshold for failure and they attribute their failure to external sources.

They learn better under conditions of tangible and immediate reward. And they do not have the ability to delay gratification. Non contingent approval and attention also improves their learning. They have poor concentration and short attention spans.

If these are the characteristics they display, then what is to be done to help them? Because of their slow rate of learning, mentally retarded children need more extended periods of activities for academic preparation. There is a need to develop their reasoning ability. Primary school teachers need to emphasize manipulation of concrete objects. Varied experiences should be provided to enhance their imaginative powers. The motto for them should be "learning by doing". The goals of learning should be adjusted to a basic level because of the slow rate of learning, the need for more repetition, and the mastery of less material.

A few concrete example of visual discrimination training would be:

a. Matching pictures, patterns on the floor,
b. Circling all 'a's or 'b's in a printed page,
c. Having pupils match lower and upper case letters,
d. Having pupils find hidden objcts in pictures,
e. Having pupils reproduce block designs/pictures.

Auditory discrimination training would consist of:

a. Identifying the voices of classmates,
b. Making pupils differentiate sounds after listening to rhymes.

Learning and Memory Training would involve:

a. Asking children to write words on small strips of paper; then cutting the words into syllables, mixing up the pieces and asking them to reconstruct the words.
b. Distributing some cards with arithmetical problems and some with answers randomly among pupils in the class, then asking children to move from their seats to another place in the room and read the problems on their cards. Then the children with the correct answers should carry their cards to the child with the problem.

c. Making children choose the correct letters the teacher names from a scrambled group of letters.
d. Demonstrating the concept of cooperation by conducting a three-legged race.
e. Making pupils form two lines of unequal length to illustrate the concepts of longer and shorter.
f. Developing comprehension of sequence: giving several pupils sentence strips, each containing a historical fact or an event in a story. The pupils must then physically arrange themselves in the order in which the events occurred.

Mentally retarded children have difficulty with memory. In order to translate short term storage to long term storage the teacher has to: (1) Involve the child in doing certain activities, (2) Asking him to move, and verbalize a number line instead of merely verbalizing, (3) Asking him to set a goal before engaging in a task, (4) Giving a reward contingent upon successful completion of a task, (5) Presenting material in varying tones instead of using a monotonous pattern of presentation.

Materials learned can be made more meaningful by giving examples. Material becomes more relevant when it is related to past knowledge and experience. For example,

— Have pupils close their eyes and form a mental image or picture of the attributes of a word, or form a mental picture associating a word with experience.
— Use verbalization to relate facts. Columbus sailed in the blue ocean in 1492.
— Describe an event in the pupils' own words instead of restating the event exactly as presented in the book or in your own words.
— Use drill and overlearning for most school learning. Practice should be spaced over a period of time, with more frequent repetition in the initial stages. Practice should continue until pupils can retrieve the information with ease.

Recognize a pattern. See the similarity in the names Ram and Sham. Notice that all building numbers on one side of the street or odd. Enhance mental imagery. Use color, size, and shape in visual presentations. Use variation in auditory presentations. Use Chunking (repetition of units or syllables). Use Rehearsal. Have pupils vocalize or repeat the information to themselves during practice. Ask pupils to write, copy or trace the material to be learned.

Instructional techniques can be used by the teacher during teaching-learning process in case of mildly mentally retarded children.

1. Use material that matches the developmental level of the pupil.
2. Limit the length of the learning task to an extent commensurate with the pupil's attention span.

3. Present the task in small, sequential steps.
4. Introduce a few elements of a concept in any one period.
5. Early learning should bring success experience.
6. Present concepts using concrete materials.
7. Provide distributed practice.
8. Provide for transfer of learning by presenting the same concept in a variety of settings.
9. Present learning tasks that are useful in real life situations.

Effective instructional techniques in arithmetic should utilize the following principles. They should be structured, developmental and sequential, concrete, in short segments with limited changes between steps, repetitive and practical. The major difficulties encountered in teaching arithmetic to mildly retarded pupils are their low levels of abstraction and their level of reading.

Other practices that will facilitate the learning of arithmetic by mildly retarded pupils are using consistent language, routine formats, and color coding. Consistent language prevents confusion. For example, "times", "multiply", and "find the product" are some of terms one might use to explain a multiplication problem. It is best to use the same term until pupils have a thorough understanding of the process. Different language can then be paired with what was previously used, for example, 12 times 11 can be restated as 11 multiplied by 12.

Personality and Motivation

Certain basic differences are observed in the Mildly retarded and the normals. The retarded scored higher on extraversion and lower on neuroticism scales. In other words retardates are more extraverted than normals. They are more persistent. The retarded are very rigid both physiologically and in their personality make up. They are more hostile than normals to diagnostic tests. They need help in resolving their conflicts. They are more afraid of failure, anxious and withdrawn. Panda and Lynch (1972, 1974) found that retardates had greater faith in luck and expect failure much more than success.

Retarded children have a poor self concept and are very impulsive. They show a global style of looking at things. They do have an external locus of control (Panda, 1971a, b).

A positive learning environment that provides successful experience is helpful. Much of this low esteem might be prevented if instruction could be modified for pupils who learn more slowly and need more repetition and concrete experience than average pupils. They must learn to deal with failure and criticism and accept it.

Physical Fitness

Normal boys are significantly superior to retarded boys in such physical tests as gripping strength, vertical jump, and ankle flexion. What is the relationship between motor skills and intelligence? How do retardates compare in motor skills with normal children of similar chronological age? And does motor skill proficiency relate to peer acceptance?

Educable mentally retarded children as a group are inferior to children of normal intelligence and similar chronological age in physical fitness and motor skill proficiency. Also, the relationship between intelligence and motor proficiency of retarded children is somewhat higher than it is in normal children.

Research has indicated that retardates seem to be less proficient in fine motor activities than they are in gross motor activities. Educable mentally retarded children, as a group seem to be one to two years behind their normal counterparts in physical development. The physical development pattern for retarded children is similr to that of normal children, but at a lower level.

The question is whether or not motor skills proficiency of educable mentally retarded children can be improved.

Lillie (1966) administered 65 diagnostically based motor development lessons to a group of 16 preschool culturally deprived children. The lessons were evaluated in terms of a gross motor score and a fine motor score on the Lincoln Oseretsky Motor Development Scale. The contrast groups were a kindergarten control group and a home control group.

The results of this study indicated that all groups made significant gains in gross motor proficiency, but no difference existed among the groups in fine motor proficiency as a result of training. However, the fine motor proficiency of the experimental group was significantly superior to the home control group.

Mentally retarded children do make significantly greater gains on several gross motor tests including all six balance tests on the Lincoln Oseretsky as a result of training.

Based on the intervention research the following conclusions may be drawn:

1. Specially planned and implemented motor development programmes are beneficial in improving the gross and fine motor skill proficiency of educable mentally retarded children.
2. Specially planned programmes of physical education and physical training are beneficial in improving the physical fitness of educable mentally retarded children. In some cases, such improvement compares favourably with the performance of normal children of similar chronological age.
3. No cause and effect relationship has been demonstrated between physical education programmes and improved intellectual functioning.

Creative Thinking

Early writers in this field have used such terms as imagination and creativity to explain the phenomenon we now term productive thinking.

Creative thinking has four major components: Flexibility, Originality, Elaboration, and Fluency. Flexibility is a measure of the ability to change from one form of thinking to another. Originality indicates the uniqueness of a response. The response may be of high, medium or low quality. Elaboration is a measure of the number of ideas used to build the basic response. Fluency is the number of relevant responses given within a specified time.

The great majority of the studies done in this field have been on intellectually gifted children. It seems that most investigators have not considered the possibility that children of below average intellectual functioning may exhibit some degree of productive thinking ability.

How do retarded children compare with normal children in productive thinking abilities? And can the productive thinking abilities of educable mentally retarded children be improved?

A comparison of the productive thinking abilities of retarded and normal children was attempted by Crawley (1966). One verbal and two non-verbal measures of productive thinking were administered to a group of 26 special class retardates, a group of 26 regular class retardates, and a group of 26 children of normal intelligence. The three groups were of the some mental age. Crawley found that no significant difference existed among the groups on the measures used. He also found no significant correlation between mental age, IQ, and the productive thinking modes utilised.

Tisdall (1962) was one of the first to investigate the effect of schooling on the productive thinking abilities of retarded children. He administered Torrance tests to a group of retarded children in regular classes, a group of retarded children in special classes, and a group of normal children. He found no significant difference among the groups in non-verbal measures. However, the average performances for the normal and special class groups were significantly better than the average of the regular class retarded groups on measures of verbal productive thinking.

A more direct attempt to influence the productive thinking abilities of retarded children was attempted by Rouse (1965). The experimental classes were exposed to a six week programme of productive thinking activities devised by the investigator. The regular classroom teachers were trained to administer the programme. The results indicated that the experimental group performed significantly better than the control group.

The following conclusions seem appropriate:

a. There seems to be a weak relationship between productive thinking, and IQ and academic achievement.
b. Educable mentally retarded children demonstrated a lower level of verbal productive thinking than normal children, but seemed to be equal to normal children on measures of non-verbal productive thinking.

c. Conflicting evidence exists with regard to whether or not productive thinking abilities of retarded children can be improved.

Social and Emotional Characteristics

Retarded children appear to be especially vulnerable to emotional problems because of their intellectual handiaps. Their deficiencies in judgement, in understanding of their environment, and in anticipation of the results of their behaviour constantly lead them into situations in which they experience failure and punishment.

Most of the research that has been done on social and emotional adjustment of EMR children can be categorised as studies to determine one of the following: (a) the adjustment of EMR children in regular classes, (b) the adjustment of EMR children in special classes, or (c) the adjustment of EMR children in partially integrated arrangements.

The findings of the studies dealing with administrative arrangements can be summarised as follows:

1. The mentally retarded child in the regular classroom is not accepted as readily as his more capable peers.
2. Placing a child in a special class does not necessarily mean that his acceptance or self concept will improve.
3. The special class, seems to promote better "sociometric" adjustment of a retarded child; that is, the retarded child will be more accepted and less rejected in a special class than in a regular class, partly because of the decrease in number and a different reference group.
4. The self concept of the retarded child is better if he is left in a regular class only if interventions are introduced.
5. The special class retarded child probably interacts less with his neighbourhood peers than he would if he were in a regular class.
6. Partially integrated arrangements do not give a retarded child sociometric equality with the normal child, but they do improve the retarded child's self concept.
7. Achievement motivation is poorer for EMR's placed in special classes.
8. Parents of EMR's are satisfied with their child's progress and placement in some special classes.

Many of the recent studies reported in the literature on social and emotional adjustment of the retarded, deal with ways of improving the adjustment of EMR children. This is an encouraging sign. Too often the reaction of educationally oriented professionals, among others, to poorly adjusted EMR's has been really negative. Many seemed to feel that if they ignored the problem it would go away. The problem usually "went away" in the form of a drop-out following, or probably because of, the lack of an intervention programme on the part of the school. The studies presented in this section generally will not be presented in detail; most of them are not controversial, but what is of interest usually is whether or not something was found 'that worked', and to which group the results may be generalised.

The retarded child lacks social skills in comparison with normals. This can be inferred from his poor scores on sociometric devices. That the mentally retarded are rejected because of their antisocial behaviour is another indication of their lack of adequate social skills. Aprasia (ability to perceive persons as separate entities but not in meaningful or significant interaction in group activity) may contribute to social skill deficits. There is a greater incidence and degree of aprasia among retardates than among normals of the same chronologial age. Another factor which contributes to poor social skills is poor logical thinking, which is probably correlated with aprasia. Social skills can be taught to EMR children. Mentally retarded children would benefit from the inclusion in the curriculum of a formal training programme designed to improve knowledge of appropriate social behaviour. It seems reasonable that as a result of this training programme the prevalence of aprasia among EMRs would also decrease.

Certain instructional methods help improve social skills in the retarded. Group counselling, grouping the retarded with popular children, vocational counselling, etc., are appropriate for upper trainable and educable groups. The social reinforcement techniques can be used for all levels of retardation and in all environments: home, school, or institution. The various techniques probably produce different levels of change, and bring about these changes with varying amounts of time and/or effort invested. Once behaviour modification techniques are learned, they can be applied relatively easily to bring about rather immediate changes in sociometric standings.

Certain opportunities can be created to develop more appropriate social skills in the retarded. These are:

Exchanging proper greetings
Engaging in play activities
Seeking alternative strategies to fifhting
Developing a sense of whom to trust
Participating in small group work
Engaging in social interaction.

Many mentally retarded pupils will be unaware of the nuances of emotional reactions of other individuals. To facilitate recognition, understanding, and proper response of emotional reactions, use pictures or role playing of situations explaining happiness, sadness, anger, fear and disgust.

Language Characteristics

Children with MR in the absence of demonstrable biological pathology, but having a parent or sibling who is retarded, are labelled the culturally familial type. Their behaviour is due to uncertain or presumed psychological causes. The educable mentally retarded are of this kind. These children have experiences in common and the two appear to be interrelated. If we can determine what the linguistic deficits are and what the deficits in experiences are, then we ought to be able to determine how to eradicate linguistic deficits by providing the necessary experiences among the retardates and deprived.

By far the most influential and pervasive theory of the linguistic deficits of the deprived is that of Bernstein. He hypothesised the existence of a "public" language which is different in a number of specifiable ways from the more "formal" language of the middle class. The language of the deprived and retarded consist of short, gramatically simple, often unfinished sentences, a poor syntactical construction with a form stressing the active, rigid and limited use of adjectives and adverbs, low order of generality of symbolism, and a low level of conceptualisation.

One of the earliest intervention studies was done by Smith (1962). This was an attempt to study the effects of a group language programme on the language abilities of a group of deprived children. Specifically, Smith hypothesised that a language development programme would enhance total language age scores as measured by the ITPA, that IQ would be unrelated to language age score gains, and that initial language age scores would be unrelated to total language age score gains.

Sixteen matched pairs were used. All were students in special classes, between the ages of 7 and 10 and had received Binet scores between 50 to 80. Over a three month period the children were taken from their special classes into groups of eight each three times a week for 45 minutes. They were exposed to a language programme which was designed to be stimulating and enriching. Each child was urged to be an active participant in the programme. The lessons were planned to include a wide range of activities with visual and auditory stimuli and were aimed at decoding, association and encoding of linguistic symbols.

Decoding activities were such things as answering oral questions, carrying out instructions, and recognising objects or naming. Association activities included such tasks as relating objects to their spoken names, naming pictorial stimuli, and listening to stories and answering questions. Encoding activities included naming and describing pictured objects, rhythmic activities and finger play.

Results at the end of the three month period showed that the experimental group gained 6.75 months on the total language age score as measured by the ITPA; the control group lost four months. This is a significant differene. The mean language age gain of the experimental group was thus more than seven months over the gain of the matched control group. The experimental group showed gain for all nine subtest scores, with the greatest gains on the vocal encoding subtest (number of concepts enumerated to an object) and the visual motor association subtest (choosing a picture which has a conceptual communality to a first picture). For the control group, performance on five of the nine subtests remained the same or decreased, with minimal gains shown on the other four subtests. It was found that neither IQ or initial language age (LA) was related to the LA gain.

It is important to note that the experimental group received another differential type of treatment besides the language lessons which might account for results. They were removed from their special classes for these lessons whereas the control group subjects were not. It must also be noted, however, that the greatest gains seemed to be made by the experimental group on subtests which were similar in task orientation as the lessons. For example, one might expect a child who had received more experience in describing pictured objects to do better at a task which required him to enumerate a large number of concepts in response to an object. It therefore appears that the types of gains made are related to the emphasis of the lessons that the children have been exposed to.

Mueller and Smith (1964) attempted to measure whether the gains made in the Smith study were stable over time. Thirteen matched pairs from the original Smith subjects were used, and they were administered the ITPA 13 to 14 months after the original testing. The same examiner administered the test as in the first study.

Differences between the total LA scores of the Smith pretest, the Smith post-test and the Mueller and Smith Follow-up scores were compared: as we have noted the differences between the Smith pre and post test LA scores were significant, but this difference did not show up on the follow-up test, although the experimental group still tended to score above the controls. Mueller and Smith did an analysis of the individual improvement scores and found that eight children showed no improvement while eight improved from 6 to 16 months. Further, an analysis of IQ and class placement showed no differences between these two groups, and this is taken as evidence that the children were stimulated differentially by the programme. What this result implies is that language stimulation programmes of preschool are to be continued in regular classrooms if gains are to be maintained.

One study which uses an at home control (HC) group and also a kindergarten control (KC) is one by Stearns (1966). He described a diagnostically based series of language lessons. The lessons concentrated in teaching visual and tactical discrimination, labels for objects in terms of shape, size, colour, and increasing ranges of adjectives and adverbs and prepositions used by the children. The lessons also attempted to increased sentence length and build correct grammatical order and syntax. Lessons were based upon the capabilities and weaknesses of the children's performance: teachers used corrective feedback techniques and reinforced social contact; children were asked to discriminate among familiar objects and were trained to describe features of objects.

Children were chosen on the basis of a psychosocial deprivation criteria. All had IQs of 50-85, with a mean CA of 64 months. The ITPA was administered pre-mid-term and post term and in a follow up. Pre to mid term and mid-term to post gains were not significant, but gains over the entire year were sigificant; the experimental group gained 19 months in total LA while the KC group gained 13 and the at home control gained 12 months. During the four months in whch the lessons were given (mid-term to post), children made the greatest gains on subtests measuring meaningful levels of organisation, and this appears to indicate that the greatest gains are made ont hose subtests which require the child to perform tasks similar to those stressed in his lessons.

In a follow-up study done one year after the post test results, gain for this period were found to be significantly smaller than the gains made over the period of the year before. Thus again the gains were not maintained, and this appears to indicate that a continuous programme of language stimulation is necessary to maintain gain over time.

The last intervention study (Dunn and Mueller, 1966) concerns itself with the examination of the ability of a specific type of reading instruction to enhance reading ability and the use of the Peabody Language Development Kit (PLDK) in increasing oral language development and raising IQs. Three experimental groups received the Initial Teaching Alphabet (ITA) in isolation, the PLDK in isolation, and the two together. Group four was a control group.

The ITA concentrates on teaching the individual sound symbols before he is taught to put them together in words and sentences. The reading programme is continued in a normal way, although the teachers stress sounds in isolation and combination. The PLDK is designed to stimulate oral language, and attempts to train the psycholinguistic processes of convergent, divergent and associative thinking, and vocal and motor expression through auditory, visual and motor channels. The system consists of daily lessons containing such activities as brainstorming, classification, critical thinking, listening, describing, conversing and memory work.

Evaluation data was gathered at pre, post and one year periods on achievement measures (Metropolitan Achievement Test), language measures (ITPA and PPVT), and on intelligence measures (Binet). Findings indicated that on achievement measures, the ITA groups were clearly superior to those groups which did not receive it, and further analysis indicated that this is because of differential performance on the MAT with the ITA groups performing significantly better on word discrimination tasks. On language age measures, specifically the ITPA, the PLDK groups were found to perform significantly better than the non-PLDK group but not on the PPVT.

The experiments noted that the ITA is therefore effective in stimulating reading ability apparently because it helps develop word skills, and that the use of the PLDK stimulates most aspects of language skills. These findings appear to indicate that these measures are effective in combination and that sound discrimination will indeed pull up scores on achievement and IQ. It indicates what educators have long suspected that there is an intimate relation between language and learning to read, and that learning to read should be enhanced by language stimulation. For teaching reading and language, functional approach is quite useful. Language exeprience stories provide an excellent format.

Attention and Perception

Mild mentally retarded children have low attention span. They display a global perceptual style and fail to develop simultaneous processing habits. They are mostly impulsive while perceiving objects and act as levellers. Attention span can be enhanced by using certain specific training procedures. These children profit when tasks are short. The complexity and length of the task is slowly increased. They are trained to listen, watch, reflect, look at different aspects of the object. This can be done by using a timer 'start-stop'. Gradually time given to complete a task can be reduced. Teach them at concrete level rather than at an abstract level.

In order to improve their discrimination skills one can use repetition and matching techniques using different objects. Use of letter discrimination, form discrimination, identification of letters, patterns, finding out hidden figures, reproducing blocks or designs, copying figures, locating names from a telephone directory, attending to relevant cues, and concentrating on objects, discriminating sounds and symbols, have proved quite useful for improving perceptual processes. Mild and Moderate MRs show attention deficit to relevant dimension in discrimination learning. They also show poor self questioning skills.

Poor information processing is seen among the manifestations of mental retardation. Multisensory teaching techniques have often been recommended to improve information processing habits. For example, use of the language master, motion pictures, filmstrips, talking calculators, using role play and dramatisations, tracing letters and pronouncing them are some of the techniques which are being used independently and together in dealing with mentally retarded children. Piagetian tasks are also used to enhance information processing ability.

Educational Provisions

General educational goals are applicable for the educational programmes of the mildly retarded. The academic levels of the mildly retarded in special classes were not as high as those of their counterparts in regular classes. The objectives of education for these children are self-realisation, human relationships, economic efficiency, and civic responsibility.

The following guidelines are suggested:

Level of Education	—	System and area of concentration preschool centres, Anganwadis, ICDS centres.
Preschool (Age 3 to 6)	—	Communication skills, self-help, and socialisation skills, perceptual exeriences.
Primary (Age 6 to 9)	—	Integrated school system, special development of basic skills, resource room teaching.
(Age 9 to 12)	—	Formal academic training in reading; written and oral communication; arithmatic; motor and perceptual development. Children should be placed in regular classes.
Secondary (Age 13+)	—	Pre-vocational training skills, formal learning. Sheltered workshop situation is also recommended.

Interventions

One of the major trends in the education of mentally retarded children has been the addition of educational services for the EMR. The impetus for this began in the summer of 1965 when the Head Start programme was introduced by the office of Economic Opportunity in the USA. The Head start programme was originally meant to benefit the economically deprived children but it did profit a larger number of EMR as well.

The role o the intervention programme in bringing cognitive, affective and psychomotor changes will be dealt here under four main sub-heads:

a. Preschool intervention
b. School intervention: special class/special school
c. Post school adjustment
d. Mainstreaming/integration in Regular School.

Preschool

Blatt and Garfunkel (1967) studied the effect of non-automated responsive environment on the intellectual and social competence of EMR children. In addition they also planned to see if preschool intervention would reduce the occurrence of intellectual and academic deficits. 59 preschool children having Mean IQ 77 were assigned to two year preschool intervention programmes i.e. E_1 preschool intervention in cognitive and affective processes; E_2 preschool intervention with responsive environment, and C. at home control. The experimental groups gained 7 IQ points over the ones at home, but the gains did not continue after the programme was discontinued.

Weikart (1967) reported the results of longitudinal study on the efficacy of the preschool programe designed to compensate for the cultural deprivation.

Increase in IQ was not stable over a period of time even though IQ gains were noticed for the experimental group. Similar was the case of language ability. But in arithmatic, reading, and language skills, and personal-social adjustment significant gains were noticed.

Hodges, McCandles and Spicker (1966) assessed the effectiveness of a diagnostic curriculum to remedy cognitive, affective and motoric deficits among culturally deprived children having low IQ and attempted to improve the progressive deficits. 142 psychosocially deprived children, with IQs between 50-58 were selected for the study over a three year period initially. The three groups of children were divided into Experimental, Kindergarden and Contrast at home control (AHC), with Mean IQs of 73.57, 75.27 and 74.18 respectively. The experimental group received a structured curriculum designed to remedy the specific deficits of individual children in areas of language and motor development, concept formation, and socialisation. The Kindergarten groups received the traditional school curriculum and the at home control group did not get any training. The EXPL group had significantly higher IQ that the KG and AHC group, and the KG group was higher in IQ than the AHC group but after two years of school entrance the differences were washed out. Language ability scores had similar fate. Achievement in the first grade had been different significantly in case of EXPL group. Personal social adjustment scores continued to be better for the EXPL children.

The experimental group demonstrated higher fine motor proficiency than the KG and AHC group. However, in a nutshell it can be stated that, significant IQ gains can be made with intellectually subnormal children and the gains can be continued if the programe is long term. Adjustment and achievement gains are worth noticing in the intervention programme. Hence, whether preschool programmes are necessary or not has to be carefully examined before the expensive programmes are introduced on a massive scale.

School Interventions: Special Education

The typical solution to the problems of retarded children in the public schools has been the creation of special classes in which the special needs of these children are satisfied by specially trained teachers. Retarded chidlen placed in the regular classes or integrated classrooms perform better standardised achievement tests. Special class children received higher ranks in personal socioal adjustment compared to their peers in the regular classroom. This may arise out of placement differences i.e., good retarded children placed in regular classes and the dull among them sent to special classes.

In Illinois, Goldstein, Moss and Jordan (1965) carefully designed an experiment to avoid the pitfalls of previous studies. Children with an IQ of 85 were tested for four years in their respective classes on IQ, achievement, social knowledge, parental perception, relationship with neighbourhood peers, response to success and failure experiences and productive thinking. The findings showed that both special class and regular class children gained in IQ to the same extent. There was no significant difference in achievement, but special class children showed less interest in interacting with their neighbourhood peers, than those in special classes. Hence, special classes do not seem to be justified in terms of cost, training of teachers, equipment, etc.

Studies reported by Jordan (1960) and Johnson (1961) on sociometric index of retarded children showed that lower IQ children feel more rejected and are lower in social status than their brighter peers in the special class—the same pattern that exists in the regular class. The majority of studies show:

a. There is a positive relationship between intelligence and peer acceptance.
b. Retarded children in special classes are more often favourably chosen by their peers than retarded children in the regular grades when sociometric measures are employed.
c. Retarded children who are segregated from their brighter peers have a significantly poorer self concept.

Teaching reading and arithmetic to EMR children has also been investigated but no general approach has been recommended. For example, if a child is aurally inclined he profits from the phonic approach. If he is visually inclined he may profit from a visual approach i.e., programmed materials. In so far as arithmetic achievement is concerned it is suggested that arithmetical understanding is to be developed than mere arithmetical manipulation of symbols. Training in language ability has already been discussed in this chapter. It can be said that group language development programmes used systematically do produce significant language gains.

Retarded children represent a group that is heterogenous with respect to specific abilities, motivational patterns, learning styles and strategies and social histories. Hence, any serious attempt to elicit maximum achievement from a given child while deriving benefit from what is known about retarded children generally, will have to strengthen such application with a knowledge of the specific child's response patterns and performance level.

Further, the teachers ought not to have negative expectancy as result of the label 'Mentally Retarded'. They should motivate these children with reward, affection, attention, approval and acceptance. These children suffer from a cloak of incompetence—highlighted in Edgerton's "The Cloak of Incompetence: Stigma in the life of the retarded", 1967. All the children studied in this book, had a sad tale to tell. In planning for the education and training of mentally retardates due consideration has to be given to their motivational and need patterns and programmes must be engineered in the appropriate directions.

In addition to these, proper motivation may also be provided for achieving success in school. This can be done by accepting the children, by rewarding them when they succeed, and by giving them social responsibility and leadership roles. The classroom of the mildly retarded children should also be larger than the normal classroom. It should contain high-interest, low vocabulary reading material along with games of therapeutic value. Arts and crafts can be used for self expression. Home and family life education may also be included in the curriculum. Parents and teachers need to use social reinforcements with these children.

Their language is so poorly developed that enriched language lessons are recommended. These children may be encouraged to speak during field trips, dinner time, and to describe what they do at different times.

Post School Adjustment

Post school follow-up studies with EMR children have been conducted primarily to demonstrate that such individuals lose their identity as retardates, becoming economically self sufficient and socially adequate members of society once they become adults. A few of these studies were conducted to demonstrate that special education services were instrumental in helping the EMR attain successful adult adjustments in unskilled and semiskilled occupations. However, these successful adjustments seem to occur regardless of whether the individual had received his education in special or regular classes. The major variable identified to date, which seems to affect post school adjustment, is the length of stay in school with those dropping out early (AT CA 15 or 16) less able to make a successful adult adjustment. However, according to the long term follow-up study of Baller, Charles, and Miller (1966), even these individuals eventually become successful members of society when compared with comparable socio-economic class intellectually normal adults.

Post school studies with TMR adults have generally found that approximately two-thirds of these individuals have remained in the community, and that the other one-third had either died or been placed in a residential institution. Of those remaining at home, approximately 30% worked or had worked for pay, and approximately 75% had learned adequate self care skills and had developed sufficient social skills to get along unsupervised in their immediate neighbourhood. Again, these attainments seemed unrelated to whether they received or did not receive special educational services.

The Moderately Retarded

These children possess IQ of 40 to 54 (Wechsler) or 36 to 51 (Binet). They are deficient in adapting behaviour, physical, motor, and language development, learning and occupational expectations, social and personality adjustments.

Children who are moderately retarded have hearing and vision impairment. Such children get tired easily and have health and respiratory infections. Language development is delayed both speech and understanding. Their expected level of achievement is about 1/3rd of the normal. Usually they continue upto fourth grade and do not have independent vocational pursuits.

Moderately retarded children are more dependent upon others and they do not acquire personal social skills. They do not foresee consequences and make social adjustments.

The educational provisions for these children are primarily meant for making them vocationally productive by placing them in sheltered workshops. The following programme may be followed.

Levels of Children		*Areas of Concentration*
Preschool (Age 3 to 5)	—	Half day classes. Development of self-help skills. Speech and language development. Motor and socialisation skills.
Primary (Age 6 to 9)	—	Fie hours of schooling a day. Training in preschool-level skills. Development of visual and auditory skills.
(Age 9 to 12)	—	Full day classes. Functional academic training. Reading, writing and arithmetic. Physical education and skill development.
Secondary (Age 13+)	—	Training in prevocational and vocational skills in sheltered workshops. Development of community relationships.

The following guidelines should be considered by the teacher:

1. Examine the needs of the child.
2. Set realistic goals.
3. Understand the child's behaviour in relation to development.
4. Provide support during learning experience.
5. Allow adequate time for the child to complete the task.
6. Select proper stimuli to elicit response.
7. Provide consistency in discipline and supportive roles.

The Profound and Severely Retarded

This category of children reveal substantial deficiencies in the areas of physical development, communication, self care and intellectual functioning. They remain mostly in institutions under constant care. The severely retarded group includes children between IQ range 20 to 40.

Integration in these cases means either establishing special classrooms within the regular school which will help them to experience a normalised environment and the accompanying stimuli which may help them to develop appropriate behaviours. There is the possibility to interact with peers with no handicaps and it may improve attitude of children without handicap towards children with severe retardation. Small group instruction has also been found to be effective with sense MRs. Community based environment training is also another dimension that has been tried out. Two teaching procedures have been found effective with sense profound retardates (a) Task analysis and (b) Prompt analysis. In task analysis, target behaviours are borken down into bits and sequences. In prompt analysis, promptings are given to help initiate a response. For the severe and profound, retardates, it includes physically helping the child to perform the behaviour, modelling (demonstrating in their presence what to do) and verbal or gestural directions (telling them what you want them to do). Prompts are useful.

The educational provisions for profoundly retarded children are meant for the development of self-help skills or communication skills. Sensory training technique is used for these children. For the trainable, training in gross motor activities, self-help and social skills, communication skills are given depending upon the developmental level. Behaviour modification techniques and reinforcement techniques are applied for development of behaviour, and teaching toilet skills. For teaching skills to these children task analysis and programming are necessary. They are further trained in sheltered workshops.

In recent years, there has been emphasis on the education and care of the educable mentally retardates in India. Attempts are being made to open special schools for these children and train teachers to handle them. However, the sole objective is mainstreaming the retardates into normal schools. In severe cases where mainstreaming seems extremely difficult, special schools have been recommended.

Mainstreaming and Integrating Mildly Mentally Retarded in Regular Schools

Remarkable progress has been achieved in our understanding of early education for handicapped children since the classic pioneering works of Kirk, Skeels and Dye, supported by investigators from numerous fields by placing significant changes through early intervention. Extensive reviews of these programmes have revealed a general gain followed by a general decline overtime when programmes were discontinued. Early intense and prolonged programmes produce modest but stable favourable gains. An important implication of the transactional or otherwise interactive models is that a radical alteration of the educational environment of handicapped child may create a new interaction pattern that could significantly determine the course of development. One such change is mainstreaming or integration.

What evidence is available? The following paragraphs will briefly but pointedly cite assumptions and evidence based on empirical studies.

The setting of the regular classroom is less isolating for the handicapped children

In general, studies do indicate that social acceptance increases, modestly when the handicapped join a mainstreamed class. The degree of acceptance depends upon the degree of impairment. When the handicap is mild and not physically obvious, acceptance increases. The problem of social is alienation or isolation as longitudinal studies show is life long and inescapable for the moderately, severely handicapped.

Academically and socially the handicapped child will benefit more from integration with regular students

Exposure to normal children who serve as behavioural models, should help mildly handicapped students improve academic and social achievement. There is evidence that mildly handicapped children to as well in regular classroom as in a special class ... it must be gauged solely in relation to individual capacities.

A greater degree of acceptance of the handicapped by normal children is relfected in some findings but these are few, and deal almost exclusively with the mildly handicapped while overt name calling and labelling may increase basic negative attitudes towards the handicapped.

Regular teachers in general oppose integrations. Even after a course in special education, negative attitudes persist. But those who volunteer to teach such children often maintain a positive motivation. There has been a shift in the philosophy of special education for EMR children away from the selfcontained special class and toward integrating EMR students' into regular classes for as much of the day as possible.

Several generalisations and facts are cited for and against special classes and mainstreaming. These are:

1. In a regular classroom retarded children will fall continually behind their age mates and in the higher grades much of what goes on in a regular classroom will be incomprehensible to them because of their limited basic skills.
2. In a self-contained special class, EMR children not only get more special attention because there are usually fewer students but they can be exposed to methods and materials specifically designed for slower-learning students.
3. The quality of education in the regular classroom can be improved if the slower students who often demand a disproportionate amount of the teacher's time can be removed.
4. Since retarded children tend to be socially isolated anyway there is little social damage done by removing them from a regular classroom and they will not have to suffer the constant humiliations associated with being slower than the other students.

However, there are some equally compelling arguments against the self-contained special class and in favour of mainstreaming. These are:

a. Education is far more likely tobe individualized and will take account of differences between students today than was done in the past and as a result the regular classroom is better able to cope with the slower student.

b. There has been a realization that all retarded children do not learn in the same way, and thus it makes little educational sense to place them all in the same classroom.
c. It is usually necessary to label children mentally retarded before they can be placed in a special class, and this label is stigmatizing and humiliating.
d. Once children are placed in a special class, less will be expected of them, and they are less likely to be challenged.
e. Special classes represent a form of segregation in some communities because a grossly disproportionate percentage of special class students are from particular groups.
f. If handicapped children are placed in regular classes, the other children will acquire a better understanding of the nature of their various disabilities, and thus, they will be more tolerant of handicapped people.
g. Research in which the educational performance of retarded children in special classes was compared to retarded children in regular classes has failed to demonstrate that retarded children benefit academically from special class placement.

Because of these empirical evidences there is gradually a change in thinking it is now felt that unless it is a case of multiple handicap, the mild mentally retarded can be educated in the regular class.

There is a growing emphasis on the similarities between the mentally retarded and non-retarded rather than on their differences; a recognition that retarded people can improve their level of functioning; a questioning on the concept of M.R. based on IQ; a de-emphasis on labelling and tolerance for deviation; increased individualisation; the recognition that some MR live successfully in society; an emphasis on prevention and care, planning and coordination of services.

What has been done then in order to fulfil the objectives? Realising the massive nature and extent of the problem as well, the government of India has introduced and spread integrated education for major categories of disability e.g., visually impaired, hearing impaired, orthopaedically and neuro-muscularly impaired, children with multiple handicaps, and the mildly mentally retarded who have a rightful place in the regular class has been ignored. The plan is to equip regular schools on a selected basis with resource teachers and equipments, books and assessment facilities and not to deny opportunity on the basis of stigma or ignorance.

It is the responsibility of the States and central agencies to implement the scheme. In order to bridge the differences successfully, preschool training and parental counselling are to be introduced as preparatory activities.

The scheme further visualised establishment of a cell in the Directorate of Education with one assessment team under its control. State government officials who remain in charge of the programme should undergo training along with teachers of the integrated schools. Priority being given to rural sectors, the scheme at the initial stage emphasizes disabled children remaining at home and attending regular classes. There is no restriction on a school in respect of disabled children belonging to different categories depending upon the existing physical and technical facilities. Number of disabled children who can be admitted to a regular clăss has not been specified although the commonsense understanding is that they should be no more than 8 to 10. Incentives for resource and special teachers, qualifications, scholarships for identified disability groups have been laid down in details. Teacher training programme is necessary to solve the immediate problem of shortage of teachers.

Dunn's article is frequently cited as the consciousness raising article that began the mainstreaming movement in earnest.

This led to a broader array of special services to support the exceptional child; non-discriminatory testing; antilabelling movement; and participatory decision making in placement on the part of parents.

The most important research of the last two decades that has productively expedited mainstreaming has been in two areas: differentiated programming, and functional non-categorial approaches to educating the exceptional student.

Effective mainstreaming requires an enabling philosophy, a continuum of special education services, participatory leadership and adequate communication mechanisms.

- — Basic academic skills should therefore include as a pre requisite behaviours concepts, langauge, and arithmetic content. Assssment should include observation, assessment of products, student records.
- — Assessment information is to be used by teachers for planning individual education programmes. Teaching system must include task analysis, and shaping procedures.
- — The physical environment in classrooms should be arranged to facilitate instructional objectives and increase learning opportunities.
- — Parents have to participate in the IEP development for their retarded children.

Classroom Organisation for Mainstreaming

In order to make the mainstreaming programme effective for the mildly mentally retarded, certain organisational activities are necessary. These would include: scheduling time (catch up time in the few minutes before closure of the school each day, using paraprofessionals, hiring an itinerant teacher) to meet individual needs; providing for mastery learning (combining mastery of basics, most essentially skills, giving extra time, ensuring assistance, study, practice, self test-recycle and retest); using small group instrution (proceeding slowly, asigning clear, discrete short term tasks, extending the group work from two or three pupils to more in a group); peer tutoring; developing resource units; organising learning activities (mathematics, reading, science etc.) for active participation; using programmed instruction; using micro computers (wherever feasible). Teachers have to ensure and understand that individualised instruction does not mean teaching each pupil individually. Organisational arrangements for individualising instruction can provide multimedia materials for pupils who learn best by seeing, doing, listening and talking. Adaptive aids can be integrated for exceptional pupils into classroom instruction.

Besides, a classroom for mainstreaming the mild mentally retarded would necessitate use of special teaching methods: use of developmentally appropriate examples and materials, ensuring success, limiting learning test to attention span, presentation of learning tasks in small, sequential steps, use of concrete concepts and modes, repetition, showing parallels with daily life and providing readiness for learning: reasoning, environmental experience, language, attention, visual discrimination, auditory discrimination. Each of these readiness can be developed in the mildly mentally retarded through systematic activities. Research evidences substantiate these basics.

Teaching for information processing is also achieved by using multisensory teaching techniques. Social skills and mental health and adjustments have been developed in these children with the limits of their educability. Cognitive learning is also achieved among EMR children though successful manipulation of informational and affective reinforcement techniques (Panda, 1971a, b). Manpulation of achievement responsibility to the advantage of their achievement has been a positive strength for mildly retarded (Panda and Lynch, 1972; 1973; 1974). Further, a clear model has been suggested to understand the dynamics of mildly retarded by looking into their family (Panda, 1974).

The Role of the Resource Teacher

A large number of different approaches to teaching mildly retarded children in the resource room and integrated class setting have been proposed by various experts. Among them the significant ones are which the resource room ought to adopt in addition to all other techniques mentioned at different places in this chapter.

1. The physiological method of Seguin—an educational program stressing the training of the senses and motor training.
2. Montessorie's auto-educational system—a teaching method based onthe assumption that education should be enjoyable and that children should choose for themselves those activities that are best for them.
3. Piaget's approach which stresses that children learn by doing rather than by being taught to and that children must discover logical relationships for themselves.

4. The unit method of Ingram—a teaching method emphasizing practical knowledge and the application of academic subjects to real life.
5. Perceptual motor training—an educational system emphasizing special perceptual and motor exercises to fill in gaps in normal development.

The Role of the Regular Classroom Teacher

Mild Mental Retardation

1. Shaping and allowing appropriate interaction experiences among students with and without handicap.
2. Developing planned instructions.
3. Assessing change of attitudes among peer groups and developing appropriate attitudes among non-retarded children.
4. Accepting instructional responsibility for mainstreamed pupils. It is challenge but one must know how to meet the challenge.
5. The teacher must use the developmental skill training approach in sequencing skill training, attention training, attention training, rehearsal training, learning to learn, and instrumental enrichment. He must try to back to basics and teach social adaptation skills.
6. He must use cognitive strategy approach. Self instruction, problem solving, are some of the relevant techniques.

Mental retardation is the most prevalent form of disability in the population. This varies from educable range through trainable to custodial group. The genesis of mental retardation is genetic in severe cases and sociocultural in mild cases. These children until recently were institutionalised and educated either in special school or special classes. It is only after 1980's mainstreaming the midly retarded has been increasing in developed and developing countries of the world. Various intervention strategies have been introduced in different areas of abilities. Resource room and regular classroom teacher roles have been specified and are of great importance in the education of mild mentally retarded. The education and care of the severely retarded has also been stated.

Highlights of the Chapter

Mentally retarded children differ from normals in intelligence and adaptive behaviour which are observed during 18 years of their lives: (educable IQ 60-85, trainable IQ 30-59, custodial IQ below 30). The description fits well to the "Six hour Retarded Child" who functions below the normal in school. Nearly 2.5 per cent children are mild and moderately retarded and .5 per cent are severely retarded.

Mental retardation occurs due to chromosomal anomalies: e.g., Trisomy-21, translocation, mosicism, turner's syndrome, congenital defects: Microcephaly and Hydrocephaly, metabolic disorders; galactosemia. Biochemical irregularities:

PKU, galactosemia, and certain infections: lead poisoning, Rubella, intoxication, blood group incompatibility: ABO and Rh; X-ray, Birth injuries and trauma, Brain disease, malnutrition and deprivation. There are also unknown factors.

Preventive measures include—vaccination against Rubella, aminocentosis, Blood transfusion, Dietary treatment of PKU and galactosemia, improved maternal nutrition, early screening and detection and several others.

Assessment is done using standardised IQ tests, adaptive behaviour tests and functional assessment kits.

Mildly mentally retarded and/or EMRs have deficits in learning and memory, attention, deficit, inability to delay gratification, distractibility, poor self concept, impulsivity and external fate control, poor five muscular coordination, low creative and physical ability restricted language code etc.

These deficits are not organic or fixed. Improvements have taken place through repetition, overlearning, discrimination training, motivational measures using social reinforcement, peer modeling perceptual training, motor coordination training, language enrichment and personality building programmes besides early school intervention, presentations of learning materials using concrete, pictorial and symbolic sequences and planned interventions in all areas of behaviour.

For mild retarded and/or EMR group, integrated education partial integration i.e., combination of special and regular classes have been emphasized whereas for TMR special school or residential setting is more realistic measure. Mainstreaming has been the focus for mild mentally retarded chidlren than self-contained special classes.

To make mainstreaming/integration successful for EMR proper assessment, placement, parent involvement, resource room instruction, individualised education programme are a must. The regular classroom teachers and the resource room teachers are to be tuned to the needs of the EMR children.

Review Questions

1. Define mental retardation and illustrate the various categories.
2. How would you identify a mentally retarded child? Explain the procedures.
3. Describe learning and memory characteristics of EMR children? How would you reduce their deficiencies?
4. State the social and emotional characteristics of EMR children. What measures would you take to reduce the deficiency?
5. What is the nature of creative thinking in Mentally Retarded childen?
6. What are the motivational characteristics of EMR children?
7. What are the various instructional techniques used for helping the retarded child?
8. What are the various educational measures used for mentally retarded children?
9. State the etiology and prevention of Mental Retardation.
10. Explain the concept of mainstreaming for MR.
11. Describe the role of the regular teacher in teaching EMR in a mainstreamed class.

12. Write notes on:
    a. Physical characteristics of MR.
    b. Trainable MR.
    c. The six hour retarded child.
13. State the educational provision for severely retarded children.
14. What kind of classroom organisation is required for mainstreaming EMR?
15. Write notes on:

Down's Syndrome	Galactosemia
Turner's Syndrome	Microcephaly
Trisomy-21	Hydrocephaly
PKU	Rubella
Intoxication	Lead poisoning

References

Ballar, W.R., Charles, D.C. and Miller, E.L. (1987), *Midlife attainment of the mentally retarded: A longitudinal study,* Genetic Psychology Mongoraphs, 75, 235-329.

Blatt, B. and Garfunkel, F. (1967), "Educational Intelligence: Determinants of school behaviour of disadvantaged children". Exceptional Children, 33, 601-08.

Crawley, J.F., (1966), *Productive thinking in Retarded and Non-retarded children,* University of Connectieut.

Das, J.P., (1965), "Discrimination learning in retardates and normal with the use of evaluative verbal cues", *Journal of Mental Deficiency Research,* 91, 31-38.

Doll, E.A., (1941), "The essentials of an inclusive concepts of Mental Deficiency", *American Journal of Mental Deficiency,* 45, 214-219.

Dunn, L. and Mueller, M., (1966), *The efficacy of the ITA and Peabody language development, Kit with Good and Disadvantaged Children after one year,* IMRID Science Monograph, 2.

Edgerton, R.B., (ed.), 1981, *Lives in Process: Mildly retarded adults in a large city,* Washington, DC, American Association on Mental Deficiency.

Goldstein, H., Moss, J.W. and Jordan, L.J., (1965), *The efficiency of special class training on the development of mentally retarded children,* Washington, U.S. Office of Education.

Grossman, J. (ed.), (1977), *Manual of terminology and classification in mental retardation,* Washington DC, the American Association on Mentally Deficiency.

Heber, R., (1959), *A manual on Terminology and Classification in Mental Retardation,* American Journal of Mental Deficiency, 64, 55-64.

Hodges, W., McCa ndles, B. and Spicker, H. (1966), *The development and evaluation of a diagnostically based curriculum for preschool psychologically deprived children,* Final Report, USOE.

Johnson, G.O., (1961), *A comparative study of the personal and social adjustment of mentally handicapped children placed in special classes with mentally handicapped children who remain in regular classes,* Syracuse: Syracuse University, Research Institute.

Jordan, J.B., (1960), *Intelligence as a Factor in Social Position—a Sociometric study in Special Classes for the Mentally Handicapped,* Ph.D. Thesis, University of Illinois.

Lillie, D.L., (1966), *The Effects of Motor Development Lessons on the Motor Proficiency of Preschool Culturally Deprived children,* Unpubished doctoral dissertation, Indiana University.

Mueller, M. and Smith, J., (1964), *The stability of language age modification over time,* American Journal of Mental Deficiency, 68, 537-539.

Narayanan, H.S., (1981), "A study of the prevalence of mental retardation in Southern India", *International Journal of Mental Health,* 10, 28-36.

Panda, K.C., (1971), *Effects of social reinforcement, Locus of control and congnitive style on concept learning among educable mentally retarded children,* EPS series No. 12, American Psychological Association.

Panda, K.C., (1971), "Social reinforcement: Theoretical issues and research implications", *Psychological Studies,* 15, 55-67.

Panda, K.C., (1974), "A process model approach for research in retardates, parental family. Theoretical and methodological consideration", *Indian Journal of Mental Retardation,* 71, 14-24.

Panda, K.C. and Lynch, W.W., (1973), "Relationship among scores on intellectual achievement responsibility and cognitive style measures in educable mentally retarded children", *Indian Journal of Mental Retardation,* 6, 55-66.

Panda, K.C. and Lynch, W.W., (1972), "Effects of social reinforcement on the performance of mentally retarded children, a review of research with implications for classroom practice", *American Journal of Education and Training of the Mentally Retarded*, 7, 115-123.

Panda, K.C. and Lynch, W.W., (1974), "Effects of the race and sex on attribution of intellectual achievement responsibility for success and failure situations among educable mentally retarded children", *Indian Journal of Mental Retardation*, 7, 72-80.

Rouse, S.T., (1965), "Effects of training programme on the production thinking of EMRS", *American Journal of Mental Deficiency*, 69, 66-73.

Sarason, S.B., and Dorris, J., (1969), *Psychological problems of mental deficiency*, New York: Harper and Row.

Sen, A.K., and Sen, A., (1969a), "Associative transfer as a function of prior learning in paired associate task among mental defectives", *Psychological Studies*, 3, 16-19(b).

Sen, A.K., and Sen, A, (1969b), "The relationship between memory and intelligence among mental retardates", *Indian Journal of Mental Retardation*, 2, 1-5(c).

Smith, J.O., (1962), "Group language development for educable mentally retardates", *Exceptional Children*, 29, 95-101.

Stearns, K.E., (1966), *Experimental Group Language Development of Psychosocially Deprived Preschool Children*, Ph.D. Dissertation, Indian University.

Tisdall, W.J., (1962), "Productive Thinking in Retarded Children", *Exceptional Children*, 29, 36-41.

Weikart, D.P., (1967), *Preliminary results from a longitudinal study of disadvantaged preschool children*, Paper read at Council of Exceptional Children, St. Louis, Missouri.

Zeaman, D., and House, B., (1963), "The role of attention in retardate discrimiantion, learning", in N.R. Ellis (ed.), *Handbook on Mental Deficiency*, New York: McGraw Hill.

Chapter 5

Visually Handicapped Children

Some children are compeltely blind. They cannot see anything. Some can see only the difference between light and dark or day and night and cannot see the shape of things. Many others have some problems in seeing things clearly. This chapter will enable the students to know precisely what blindness is, including different degrees of visual impairment. Specifically it deals with:

- **Meaning of visual handicap, its identification and classification.**
- **Causes or etiology of visual handicap.**
- **Characteristics of visually handicapped children**
- **Educational Provisions and mainstreaming issues for visually handicapped children.**
- The role of Resource/Special and Regular classroom teachers.

Who is a visually handicapped child?

Visual handicap is defined in terms of visual acuity, field of vision, and visual efficiency. 'Visual ability' of the eye to see distant objects clearly is assessed using the Snellen chart, developed by Herbart Snellen, a Dutch doctor. The chart starts with a big 'E' which a normal eye can see at a distance of 200 ft. When vision of a person is so impaired that to see the 'E' clearly he has to come within 20 ft. of it or nearer, he is then considered legally blind. His vision is assessed as 20/200 in the better eye. It simply means a legally blind person sees something at 20 ft. distance which can be seen by a normal eye at 200 ft. easily. Visual impairment is a condition in which a student's vision is deficient to such a degree that it significantly affects his school functioning. The handicap is reflected in the child's accuracy at school work. Another descriptor may also be used to classify an individual as blind. If the visual field (amount of side to side space that can be seen at one time) is severely limited, that person may be considered blind even if visual acuity is better than 20/200. This visual field limitation is often called tunnel vision. If the visual field is no greater than 20 degrees in width, the individual can still be classified as being blind even though visual acuity is not within typical range of blindness. 'Visually efficacy' means how well one can use one's vision. This means how the visual information is processed, analysed and interpreted in the brain.

Functionally, visual handicap presents a different problem. There are children who have low vision or residual vision. These children can read large prints, and sometimes are not benefitted by visual aids in reading and writing. These children are partially sighted and their visual acuity does not exceed 20/70.

As opposed to touch reading they use pring. Low vision and partial sightedness are not synonymous. Low vision is defined in terms of clarity reduction whereas partial sightedness is defined in terms of distance from the Snellen Chart.

Educationally speaking, blind children are those visually handicapped children who use Braille, and partially seeing are those who use print. That is why a partially sighted child is known as print handicapped.

Classification

Visually handicapped children can be classified according to following categories as per Government of India circular.

Visual Impairment Categories
All with Corrections

	Better Eye	*Worse Eye*	*Percentage Impairment*
Category D	6/9-6/18	6.24 to 6/36	20%
Category I	6/18-6/36	6/60 to Nil	40%
Category II	6/60-4/60 or Field of vision 110-20	3/60 to Nil	75%
Category III	3/60 to 1/60 or Field of vision 100	F.C. at 1 ft. to Nil	100%
Category IV	F.C. at 1 ft. to Nil or Field of vision 100	Field of vision 100	
One eyed person	6/6	F.C. at 1 ft. to Nil	30%

The method of evaluation shall be the same as recommended in handbook of medical examination.

Impairment of 20%—40% or less only may be entitled to aids and appliances.

Prevalence

Visual handicap is cosnidered a low prevalence handicapping condition existing in approximately one in every 1000 school children population. But as per the National Sample Survey, (1991) the visual handicap in India is 4.005 million in CA 0-14 which constitutes 3 per cent of school children.

Causes of Impairment

Causes of visual handiap can be both genetic and environmental. Visual impairment may be due to accommodation or convergence problems. The major accommodation problems are myopia, hyperopia, and astigmatism. In myopia, or nearsightedness, the individual can see visual stimuli at close range but has trouble in seeing things at a distance. Among partially sighted children myopia is common. Hyperopia is just the opposite of myopia. In astigmatism, the individual faces focusing rpobelms. Hence, there is blurred or distroted vision. Accommodation problems have a genetic basis. Usually these are corrected by the use of eye glases, contact lenses, or surgery. There are of course some infections (diabates, syphilis) which cause accommodation problems which are usually difficult to be treated.

Convergence refers to the movement of eye balls to achieve binocular vision and depth perception. If convergence problems are not corrected, serious problems can result including blindness in the affected eye. Various conditions describe convergence problems. In nystagmus, the eyes tend to moe abruptly in continual jerky motions, with the ovement being involuntary. In heterphoris, one eye tends to deviate in direction from the other when the individual focuses on some visual stimulus. There are different types of other ailments such as esophonia, an inward drift of one eye, exphoria or outward drift. In hyperphonia one eye tends to drift up, whereas with hyphoria one eye tends to drift downward. With strabismus both eyes tend to converge either inward or outward. There are both genetic and environmental causes (accidents or injuries causing muscle paralysis) for these. If not corrected loss of binocular vision may result. There are also physiological problems: contract, glaucoma, etc. having both genetic and environmental causation.

The causes of visual impairment can also be classified as Ocular, General and Injuries.

Ocular

Congenital and developmental disorders have been stated to be one of the major causes of visual impairment in children. These are:

Anaphathalmia — In which the eyes do not develop at all.

Microphathalmia — In which the eye ball is abnormally small.

Oxycephaly — An nomaly of the skull bones resulting in optic atrophy.

Antridia — In which the iris fails to develop and visual acuity becomes poor and there is rapid involuntary movement of the eye ball.

There are various others eye disorders: Byphathalmia, Albinism Retinblastoma (malignant tumour), Congenital Cataract—(due to Rubella infection).

These are certain congenital and developmental anomalies. But there are other eye disease which impair visual acuity. Conjuctivitis of the new born which is now prevented just after birth by droping a one per cent silver Nitrate Solution to the baby's eyes. Sometimes there is a fibrous mesh behind the lens called Retrolental Fibroplastic.

It is caused due to excessive use of Oxygen on premature babies while in incubators. "Trachoma" results out of crowded home conditions and as a reslt of chronic contagious diseases of the conjunctiva and cornea. It is a common cause of blindness and is preventable. It is spread by flies or touch. Eyes should be kept clean. "Glaucoma" is a potent factor of blindness in middle age. In early stages, it can be cured. "Cataract" is a disease of old age, yet it can occur at any time due to a rupture of the lens.

General Diseases

Syphillis and Gonorrhoea are considered common causes of blindness in India. Both are passed on by parents and become manifest during the fifth and 15th year of life. Atrophy of the optic nerve is associated with neurotyphillis. Chronic diarrhea is a cause of blindness in rural India. Substistence on barley water alone results in loss of vitamin-A which softens the cornea. Hypertension, diabetes and kidney diseases cause visual impairment.

Malnutrition is the cause in most cases not only of visual impairment but also of several sensory and cognitive dysfunctions. In a country like ours malnutrition and ignorance about eye care cause blindness. Deficiency in vitamin-A, vitamin-B, B_2, C, and D are also associated with impaired visual functioning.

Injuries and accidents especially which create trauma and chemical disturbances or burns, tobacco, methyl alcohol, dyes, National Sample Survey 1991 found cataract, old age, and injuries as major causes of visual impairment.

What can be done to prevent and/or cure Visual Impairment?

Blindness is preventable if care is taken in time. The care must be both medical and educational. In our country, poverty, malnutrition and ignorance are the main causes of visual impairment. Health of the mother during pregnancy is also of primary importance. Distribution of vitamin-A to children is the most suitable preventive measure. Fat in the child's food along with leafy vegetables prevents blindness in children. Care should be taken to educate the community on the basic hygiene of vision. Of course too much of vitamin-A can poison the child.

Eyes should be washed with cold water every day as many times as possible. They should not rubbed excessively. Don't apply anything to the eyes without doctor's advise. Errors of refraction or balance should be corrected early. Illumintion of the classroom should be free from glare and flicker. Prints for reading should be spaced for avoiding eye strain.

Vaccinate children against all infectious diseases and protect the eyes of the new born with tetracycline eye ointment or one per cent silver nitrate drops at birth.

Identiiication

Besides, clinical assessment, how can a teacher undertake functional assessment? There are certain tips for teachers. There are certain tell-tale signs which parents, teachers can observe. In such cases,

- the child rubs the eyes excessively,
- has watery eyes,
- reddened eyelids,
- covers one eye and tilts the head forward,
- holds objects and books close to his eyes,
- asks other children for help while taking notes from the blackboards,
- blinks more frequently,
- squints,
- complains about headache following classroom eye work,
- bumps into objects or people,
- moves head forward and backward while looking at distant objects,
- frowns or looses his place while reading or writing,
- has poor eye-hand coordination,
- places head close to reading material.

Snellen Chart

Clinical assessment is done by using the Snellen Chart. The Snellen Chart is a measuring device used to determine an individual's central distance visual acuity. The chart contains eight rows of letters of the alphabet in graduated sizes. There is one version for young children and for people who cannot read. That replaces the alphabet with the letter E in different orientations and sizes. The letter sizes on the chart correspond to the estimate of the ability of a typical person to read the materials. The chart is constructed so that at a distance of 20 feet a person reading the figures on the chart corresponding to what a normal eye sees at 20 ft. is said to have 20'/2-' vision. A person with 20'/20' vision and both eyes working in a coordinated fashion is considered to be normaly sighted. When a person sees at 20 ft. what a normal person sees at 70 ft. or 200 fit. that person has 20'/70' or 20'/200' vision. Individuals who have low vision or who are visually limited may be legally blind (visual acuity of 20'/200' or less), or partially sighted (visual acuity between 20'/70' and 20'/200').

The Snellen chart is widely used as a screening device for detecting eye problems because of the ease and speed with which it can be administered, its low cost, and its wide range of applicability. The Snellen chart gives no indication of near-point or peripheral vision, convergence ability, fusion ability or muscular imbalance.

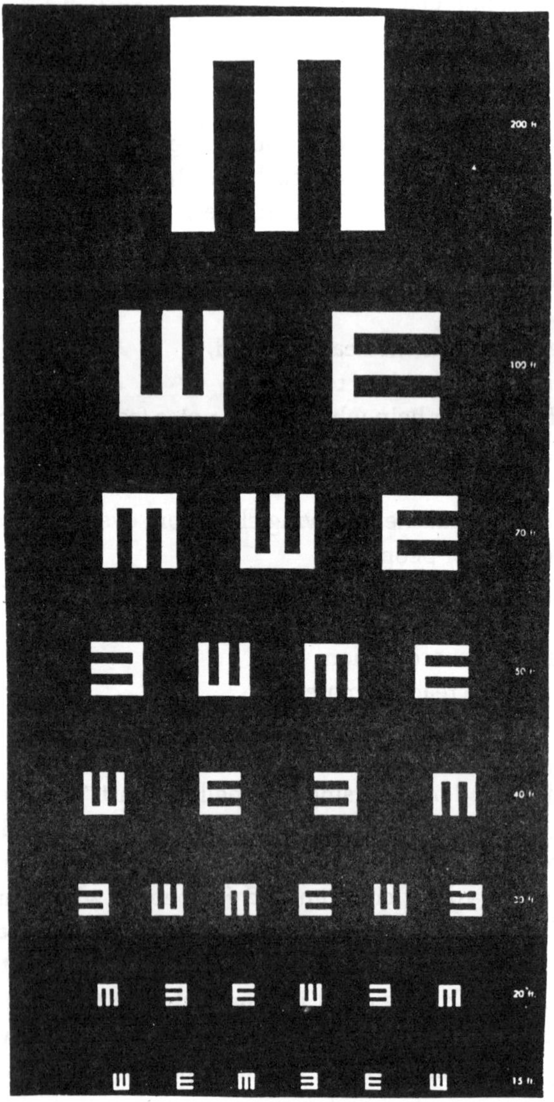

Figure 5: Snellen Chart

Bryan and Bryan (1979) list three shortcomings of the Snellen chart:

1. It is not a good predictor of competence in visual processng of objects and tasks.
2. It does not tell how a child uses vision in terms of discriminating light or darkness, estimating size, or determining spatial location.
3. The results are not translatable into educational programmes. Children with the same visual acuity may respond differently to school tasks, and therefore, require different programming.

Getman (1985) argued that visual acuity is not the only criteria for measuring acquisition of basic visual skills. He estimated that 80% of the assignments in contemporary classrooms are visually centered and that every child should have the opportunity to improve all of the visual skills on which success will depend. However, the most important initial screening device for detecting eye problems is one that measures central visual acuity.

The following tests are used for intellectual abilities:

1. Interim Hayes-Binet for IQ Age 6+.
2. Perkins-Binet-Carl Davis-revision.
3. WISC.
4. Vithoba Pannikar Performance Test of intelligence for the Blind.
5. The Blind Learning Aptitute Test (BLAT) (CA 6-20).
6. The Haptic Intelligence Scale for the Adult Blind.
7. Koh's Block Design Test.
8. The Slossan Intelligence Test.
9. PPVT (Partially sighted).
10. Illinois Test of Psycholinguistic Abilities.
11. Bohem's Test Basic Concept.
12. C.M. Bhatia-Performance Tests of Intelligence, 1955.
13. Kamat's measuring intelligence among Indian children.

Behaviour and Social Development Characteristics are assessed by using the following tests:

1. Bayley Scales of Infant Development.
2. Denver Development Screening Test.
3. Maxfield-Buch Holz social maturity scale for blind pre-school children.
4. Wide Range Achievement Test.

Vision characteristics are considered on the basis of:

1. Visual Efficiency Scale.
2. Evaluating Functional Vision.

Assessment is one of the major challenges facing those who work with visually impaired children today. Assessment for what? Much of the developmental assessment uses chronological age as the basis of comparison. For comparison this is all right but there is a wide degree of variability around the age norm. The observed deficiencies are obviously the natural consequence of visual impairment and its attendant circumstances. It is impossible to evaluate visually impaired and sighted children on a set of common measures, even if they are suitably adopted. Further, ability measured may serve an entirely different ecological function for visually impaired children than it does for sighted children.

In other words (1) we should reject the sighted comparison in the assessment of visually impaired children; (2) group norm based approach is not necessarily the best approach for visually impaired children since visually impaired children are heterogeneous e.g., residual vision, visual history, pre and post birth blindness, visual, cognitive, emotional impairment, parents' reaction to impairment, etiological differences even under one homogeneous CA. There is need for individual assessment of all these abilities.

Characteristics

Vision is the most actively used sense by man. Cognition depends upon his visual experiences. Impairment imposes three basic limitations on the individual. Visually impaired children are experientially deprived in terms of range and variety of experience. Their ability to get along is also limited because of restricted mobility. They are unable to control their own environment and themselves in relation to it. These are significant deficits. Community attitudes and reactions depend upon tradition, culture and belief. Gradually with advancement and progress in welfare activities attitudes are changing towards the blind. Still there are certain sterotypes which reflect in terms of attitudes and responses. People still believe that a blind person is nothing, can do nothing and can be nothing. Visually impaired children thus have a low self-concept, poor personality make up, low need for achievement (low n-ach) than normal peers.

Sometimes, parents feel that a blind child is born due to some sin committed. Therefore he is ignored and not taken care of. Neglect causes certain personality problems. The child has to develop certain personal self help skills. Over-protection is also dangerous. It denies the child all kinds of natural demands. The blind child suffers from behavioural deficiency because of extreme neglect or over-protection.

A significant deficit appears to be in understanding abstract concepts. There is no difference between the language abilities of visually impaired children and normal children including communication skills, although certain physical or gestural features may not appear in communiction. They do have howeer have difficulty in generating word meanings. Partially sighted and blind children are normally one year behind in mathematics and two years behind in reading than their normal peers, (Daugherty and Moran, 1982).

Educational Provisions

The educational facilities existing is the country consist of special schools for the visually handicapped. By and large these schools are residential in character. Specially trained teachers using Braille teach at these schools the same curriculum meant for the normal school. Children are given all assistance and support for academics, mobility training and orientation, music, social activities and so on.

The other alternative has been the integrated schooling for visually handicapped and the partially sighted with resource room facilities.

Integrated Education for the Visually Handicapped (Mainstreaming)

Visually handicapped children can be educated in the regular class. The curriculum should be the same. But the visually impaired child receives the information predominantly from touch and hearing. Hence, there is no need of a special curriculum but approach to teaching should be multi-sensory and he should be exposed to a plus curriculum.

Plus curriculum is used to help the visually impaired and is not extra but compensatory. This skill development always facilitates better learning. Areas of plus curriculum include:

a. Braille
b. Use of equipments
c. Orientation and mobility
d. Social skills
e. Daily living skill
f. Sensory training.

Co-curricular activities should include intellectual activities (Music, debate, writing etc.). Combined physical and intellectual activities like exercises, dancing, can be developed in blind children. Slow pace should be the criteria for teaching the blind children in an integrated setting.

Use of equipments

Technology has come up in a big way to help the blind and partially sighted students. Raised numeral watches, calculators, that aurally announce data entries and results of computation, low vision aids magnifiers, electronic magnifiers which run on the printed page and the image is enlarged and projected on to a monitor in the small video camera, portable telescope.

Laser Cane

This long cane sends out three light beams that warn of the objects straight ahead, objects at head level, and changes in walking elevations. When the beam's path is broken by an object, sounds are emitted and the individual avoids obstacles.

Sonic Glasses

Worn like typical eye glasses these glasses send out ultrasonic sound waves that cannot be heard by anyone. Once these sound waves hit objects, however, they are changed into sounds that can be heard by the blind individual as echoes. The individual is trained to hear echoes to determine how far or near the objct is, its relative direction and some of its characteristics. Sonic guide is similar in principle as sonic glasses but is worn like a hat over the head.

Kurzweil Reading Machine

It translates printed text material into aural English. It is able to deliver the speech messages at the normal human speech rate.

Optacon

This is a small machine held in the hand which translates letter by letter images from the scanner into tactile stimuli. The major advantage is any type of printed matter can be read by the visually impaired student without having to be first translated into Braille (Barraga, 1983).

Micro Computer and computer Braille translator can be used to a great advantage by the visually impaired students.

Orientation and Mobility

The visually impaired have to develop orientation and mobility skills. This should be based on sense of hearing, touch, smell, taste, kinaesthesis, to be developed by using different techniques such as:

Guide dogs: sighted guide techniques; long cane techniques; safety techniques; electronic aids for mobility, laser cane, yields beam of light, infra red light to detect objects and a pair of glasses known as Sonic guide, which is mounted on ultrasonic sensors. Safety, security and gracefulness are the three main outcomes of mobility training.

A teacher with keen observational skills may notice the discrepancy in a pupil's ability to perform distance vision tasks such as copying from the chalkboard and near point vision tasks such as reading.

The visually handicapped children may not experience the same degree of independence in moving about as pupils with normal sight. Orientation difficulties can impose one of the greatest limitations to mobility. Such difficulties in spatial activities suggest a vision problem.

Some of the specific procedures which are to be used to help the visually handicapped child to master the school environment are:

1. Guide the pupil in walking around the classroom until he is comfortable doing it.
2. Have the pupil walk around the classroom by himself until he is comfortable doing it.

3. Repeat the same procedure of guiding the pupil while explaining the lay out for other areas of the school.
4. Concentrate on movement in one area at a time.
5. Be sure to rehearse.
6. Give specific verbal descriptions.
7. Use the pupil's name when speaking to him as he may not know that you are looking at him.
8. Use a 'buddy' as a guide when the child goes out.
9. Familiarise the pupil with any changes that are made in the school.

Daily Living Skills

These skills include eating, tailoring, dressing, body hygiene-cleanliness, taking baths, washing clothese, handling money, shopping, using electrical appliances, using telephones, shaving, food preparation, clearing a place, and using medicines.

A daily living skill training programme can take into account the following considerations:

— Give an idea of the daily living skills to the visually impaired.
— Diagnose his difficulties in mastering them.
— Provide pre-requisites in terms of training.
— Grade the skills.
— Use aids in teaching skills.
— See that the gain is sustained.

Social Skills

Occasionally visually handicapped children display deficiency in social skills. This is due to lack of experience and over protection. They should be rewarded verbally for any positive social gesture. Seer acceptance should be encouraged. Verbal cues can be provided to partially sighted or low vision children. Allow them to speak to the class. They have to develop self confidence.

Sensory Training

Use of multisensory materials have added advantage for the visually handicapped pupils. Commercial kits and language masters are also available. Television also provides a source of multi-sensotry learning. Computers has also come to the service of the disabled. In teaching visually handicapped children one must remember that each child is unique. Each has strenghts and weaknesses. His handicap should therefore, not interfere with teaching him to grow up.

A teacher should practice the following to develop visual efficiency of low and partially sighted children:

1. Expose the children to various lighting conditions; encourage children to see, discuss what they see, increase vocabulary.
2. Give them enough time to observe, provide coloured lights, and present attractive toys for identification.
3. Draw pictures/figures and ask the child to trace them.
4. Discriminate three dimensional objects, teach gradation in size, teacher names of colours and intensity concepts.
5. Use flash cards, increase memory, complexity, and decrease duration, and specify order.
6. Draw form in dotted lines, draw forms free hand, teach them to throw and catch ball, and reinforce vocabulary.
7. Find omission of parts and present objects in ascending, descending order.
8. Teach form constancy.
9. Teach figure and ground discrimination.
10. Teach visual motor coordination—paper shapes, clay modeling, folding paper, bead-stringing, tracing, wiring ropes.

These measures help the partially sighted children develop competence and they gain much from schooling.

Least Restrictive Environment

Visually handicapped children may need assistance in mastering the school environment. The following activities are helpful: Magnifying glass and/or spherical lense can be provided for students with low vision aids to answer and correct their own scripts. Several factors should be considered for providing appropirate environment to the visually handicapped children varying in degree of handicap.

— Illumination should be bright, diffused and free from glare and shadows.
— Figure and ground contrast is a must especially for partially sighted pupils.
— Up to a point the larger the print, the better it is for pupils to see. If it is very large pupils can not see it at all.
— Pupils with partial visual impairment should be asked to sit close to the black-board.
— Blue and white stencils, multi-coloured chalks, and grey pencils are difficult to see.

A normal classmate can-work as a 'buddy' for a visually impaired child and assist him in drills, taking notes, tutoring him, creating awareness of what is happening. For developing concepts in visually handicapped children one should use concrete experience. Visually handicapped children should be helpful to associate words with tactile experience. Structured activities where pupils can learn by doing and experience, and teaching them by units are helpful.

Resource Room

A resource room forms a part of the integrated education programme when there are sufficient number of visually impaired children. It is necessary for

a. Preparation of material,
b. Teaching plus curriculum,
c. Locating the braille materials, and
d. Remedical teaching.

Equipments necessary in the Resource Room in order to assist the resource teacher in teaching the visually impaired children are the following aids and appliances.

1. Braille writer for teacher.
2. Braille slates and stylus for pupils.
3. Abacus for teaching maths.
4. Braille sheets of paper.
5. Classroom furniture.
6. Low vision aids.
7. Large print books.
8. Bulletin boards (Braille).
9. Braille Books.
10. Hammer, saw, pliers etc. for teaching industrial art.
11. Tape-recorders and cassettes.
12. Duplicating machines (Braille type).
13. Teaching aids.

General Teaching Procedures

The roles of special teacher, the regular teacher and resource teacher are difficult to spell out in a tight schedule but there are certain general teaching factors all should remember. Regardless of the degree of visual impairment one teaching procedure that has been recommended for both partially sighted and blind students is increased time allotment for task completion.

For the partial sighted the actual size of the printed word or image has to be increased whereas for the severely impaired, braille has to be used. More recently Severs (1987) described the use of computer technology in the form of a braille translator printer.

There may not be any difference in the level of content but tactile input and concrete examples are necessary. For partially sighted students listening skills can be developed in isolation from and in conjunction with presentation of visual stimuli. During reading exercises emphasis can be placed on both reading and listening skills as the teacher orally reads along with the student. For blind students listening skill becomes paramount. They might use talking books or tapes.

Compressed speech presentations have been used to speed up listening skills. Orientation and mobility training through Hoover Cane and Guidedog are also essential. Laser cane is a latest arrival which enables the blind to avoid obstacles.

Regular classroom teachers do not have to learn Braille. They have to make certain arrangements in the classroom. For example, use of magnifiers, keeping background noise minimum, furniture adjusted to provide maximum visual efficiency. Visually impaired children rely on sound to a great extent. Hence, teacher has to use distinct sounds while reading instructions. Children must learn to focus attention on all letters of a word. Use of large print materials also aid learning for the partially sighted. Talking books, cassette players, audio tapes, strips are available. Compressed speech recorders are also available.

Different instructions are necessary for teaching different curriculum areas.

For mathematics teaching, the Resource Teacher as well as the regular teacher should—

1. Use clips, spools, magnetic boards.
2. Provide a desk copy of whatever you write on the board.
3. Teach mental arithmetic.
4. Use an adapted abacus.
5. When you teach through pictures, linees, use dark chalk or pencils and preferably use two or three dimensional models.
6. Embossed graph paper slide rules are available. Raised clock and talking calculators are available.

Teaching of mathematics is different and difficult. In special school certain topics are omitted for the visually impaired child but in integrated setting this is not done. Teaching of mathematics to normal children is mostly done through blackboard supplemented by oral instructions. Normal children learn quickly by organising and sequencing. Visually impaired children have difficulty in these. Hence, the teachers should omit certain lessons and teach only such exercises where the child can succeed. The second caution that a teacher ought to take is that presentation of mathematics for learning must be at a slow rate. Sufficient drill and formative evaluation is needed.

The resource teacher is not a mathematics teacher. He is in fact a consultant to the regular class teacher in mathematics. Normally children with visual impairment should not be admitted after standard six. They should be taught by the Abacus method. Resource teacher should know before hand what is to be taught in the regular class. He should study the content and prepare reading materials. He should use model illustrations. The child should not be sent to regular class without proper reading and writing materials. Extra drill may be conducted and the child must be asked to explain the procedure. Mathematics learning then will be easier for the visually impaired children.

Teaching language to the visually impaired involves for the visually handicapped two skills: receptive process i.e., braille reading and expressive process which is Braille writing and spelling. The visually impaired should be familiarised with books, the braille mechanism, concepts of positions, contexts, comparative terms e.g., big, tall, short, thin etc. and adequate listening skills. Listening skill improves his vocabulary. He should be trained in listening to sounds, in discriminating between sounds, locating the direction from which the sound is coming, sound tracking, and associating sounds with objects, sequencing sounds and reconstructing life situations through auditory clues. These enable the visually impaired child to acquire language comeptence and comprehension.

For writing, tactile materials are to be used. Hence, pupils use a stylus to write letters. Kinaesthetic feedback is desirable. Papers with raised lines help writing skills to develop.

For spelling skills—Articulate the words clearly. Point out the visual aspects of the words. Give oral spelling tests, practice spelling lists on a type writer. Repetition improves spelling and typing skills. Make the blind listen to audio tapes.

Teaching of Science is both a product and a process. The child has to imbibe information and he has to develop scientific reasoning. He can learn by first hand experience, undertaking field trips, explaining everything that come across. He can be taught through grouping with sighted peers. It is difficult for the visually impaired to conduct science experiments but it is not impossible. Notations are given in Braille and they do follow the procedures. Embossed diagrams, three dimensional models are used. Appropriate reading and discussion can compensate for the deficits imposed by lack of sight.

Because of experimental deprivation, verbalism of sosical science concepts are difficult for the visually impaired children. Printed materials are used in this case for which Brailled copies are not available nor talking books. Hence, readers and sighted classmates can be used for helping them.

As far as possible Braille materials are to be made available. Field trips are to be organised. Tactile geographical maps would be of great help to the visually impaired. Special maps designed and developed for the purpose of teaching the visually impaired may be obtained and the child can explore the map by himself. Inspite of the specialised training blind children find map reading difficult.

Creativity is manifested in thinking abilities like fluency, flexibility, orginality, elaboration. The blind are quite good at music and rhythm. Indigenous musical instruments can be used. Creative expression and production are very helpful for expression of feelings of the visually impaired.

The low vision students can paint, make sculptures, thread patterns. It requires cooperation of teachers and sighted peers.

Teaching aids are vital to enhance the learning of basic concepts. Teaching aids make teaching and learning quite effective. Mann (1987) has described kits for form discrimination, recognition, size and weight discrimination, seriation, mathematical concepts such as place values, finger-dexterity co-ordination, reading groups and maps by using fibre based boards, rubber bands, embossed map, magnetic maps, etc.

In the integrated education setting we have no right to change the curriculum but what one can do is to take the experiences of blind child very nearer to that of the normal child through modified experience, resource room teaching, remedial instruction, and multisensory approach. There should be a thorough understanding between the regular and resource room teacher.

The Resource Teacher at the Primary Level

Certain precautions as well as positive steps are required to be followed:

1. Teaching tactile discrimination—expose, the child to various 'touch' objects and experiences. Make him interact with sighted children.
2. Spend more time in the resource room, and promote individual instruction i.e., one to one correspondence.
3. Encourage note taking habits—Teacher should insist on them taking notes.
4. Presentation of material through various sense modalities.
5. Evaluation—The child should be evaluated on his own, not in comparison to sighted peers.
6. Supportive services—Effective involvement and cooperation among parents, resource room teacher, and regular teacher.

The resource room teacher ought to teach in addition to the above:

1. Introductory braille
2. Braille writing
3. Touch sensation
4. Listening skills
5. Daily living skills
6. Pre-cane mobility skills
7. Mathematical concepts and abacus
8. Mobility skills using long cane
9. Remedial teaching for slow learning visually impaired children.

A resource teacher is not specialist in any curricular subject, but in teaching skills and integrated education peculiar to blindness. He should have, however, a minimum knowledge of the subject matter. He may discuss the matter with regular teachers and act accordingly. Regular teachers can also engage these children in remedial instruction. There is no hard and fast rule regarding the nature of instruction in the resource room.

The Regular Classroom Teacher

Besides the roles already specified and dicussed under teaching principles, teacher behaviour, technological advances will accomplish very little unless certain changes in attitudes occur. The teacher should have a positive attitude that visually handicapped children will learn well as others. Verbalisation and conceptualisation difficulties are the most frequently faced problems with visually handicapped children. Some of the general principles the regular teacher should use are as follows:

1. Use concrete experience. Pupils can touch and manipulate with guided language, a meaningful whole.
2. Help pupils learn by doing. Actually experiencing a situation helps pupils put together bits of information and improves conceptualization.
3. Teach by study units. The unit method organizes learning activities into a meaningful whole. Study units need systematic structure.
4. Integrate study units. Integrating reading, writing, number work, the arts, and physical activities offers an excellent opportunity to fulfil experience.

If the partially sighted are to learn to read print material, several environmental factors need attention.

1. Be sure that proper aids i.e., magnifiers have been selected and that pupils know how to use them.
2. Be sure to keep background noise to a minimum, particulars for phonic events.
3. Fatigue may result from an awkward position that the pupil may assume to improve the visual field. In most cases, special adjustable desk tops can be used to achieve good posture and maximum visual efficiency.

Determine the developmental level of reading readiness for each pupil. Pupils with visual handicap have slightly more speech defects than the average pupil, particularly articulation problems. This probably results from inability to clearly observe facial expressions and speech articulations. Visually handicapped children must develop listening skills, focussing attention, and require a little more time for reading than the normal peers. The regular classroom teacher should be aware of these limitations.

Highlights of the Chapter

Children whose vision is so impaired that they can only see objects at a distance of 20 ft. which a normal eye can see at 200 ft. are legally blind. If the visual field is severely limited, that person can be called legally blind even if visual acuity is better than 20/200. There are children have low vision or residual vision. The visual acuity does not exceed 20/70 in the case of partially sighted children. As opposed to touch reading they use print. Low vision and partial sightedness are not the same. The totally blind children read Braille.

Three per cent of children have visual handicaps. Causes of visual handicap can be ocular or general or due to injuries. There are also physiological problems: cataract, glaucoma. General causes include—Syphillis, Gonorrhea, Chronic Diarrohoea, Hypertension, diabates, Kidney malfunctions, malnutrition, ignorance about eye care, injuries and accidents, chemical disturbances or burns. Methyl alcohol, paints, carbon monoxide, lead cause eye problems.

Visual handicap can be prevented by the use of Vitamin-A, guarding the health of the mother during pregnancy, providing fats and leafy vegetables in the diet, community education, eye care, vaccination against infectious diseases.

There are behavioural signs of visual handicap but the clinical assessment using the Snellen Chart has been most efficacious, although there are points of differences about its utility. Psychological Tests have been used to assess the characteristics of visually handicapped children.

Visually handicapped children are experientially deprived, have low self-concept, low n-ach, poor personality make up. They are one year behind normal children in mathematics and two years behind in reading.

Special education facilities include: Special schools for the blind, residential as well as day schools, and integrated education with the same curriculum. The visually handicapped children are given orientation and mobility training, Braille, use of aids and equipments, plus curriculum training in social and cultural activities, sensory training. The visually handicapped and partially sighted who are enrolled in integrated settings use resource room facilities, low vision aids. Specific training is given to train visually handicapped children master school environment, including daily living skills. Least restrictive environment is provided by using bright illumination, figure and ground contrast, larger prints, buddy, structured activities etc.

General teaching methods, computer technology, compressed speech presentations are adjusted to suit to the needs of visually handicapped children. Specific outlines are provided in the text for teaching mathematics, language, writing, spelling, science.

Precautionary measures such as teaching tactile discrimination, spending more time in the resource room, note taking habits, multisensory model presentation, supportive services are to be taken by the resource teacher in addition to the ascribed role. The regular classroom teacher should use concrete experience help pupil to learn by doing, use unit teaching, teaching aids for the partially sighted and develop learning skills of visually handicapped children.

Questions

1. Define visual handicap. How would you identify a visual handicapped child?
2. What testing techniques are used for assessing visual handicapped children?
3. What are the characteristics of visual handicapped children.
4. What are the educational provisions for helping visually handicapped children?
5. How would you develop visual efficiency in the partial sighted?
6. What equipments are necessary for the resource room for visually handicapped children?
7. How would you teach mobility and daily living skills to visually handicapped children?
8. What are the types of visual handicap? What are the causes? How would you prevent them?
9. What is type of regular teacher is reqired in an integrated class for teaching the visually handicapped?
10. What is the role of a resource teacher in teaching visually handicapped in a mainstreamed class?
11. Write notes on:
    a. Snellen Chart
    b. Orientation and Mobility
    c. Least restrictive environment
    d. Plus curriculum
    e. Aids and equipments
    f. Resource room

References

Barrage, N., (1983), *Visual handicaps and learning,* Austin, Texas: Exceptional Resources.

Bryan, J.H. and Bryan, L.H., (1979), *Exceptional Children,* Sherman Oaks, CA: Alfred.

Daugherty, and Moran, M., (1982), "Neuropsychological Learning and Developmental Characteristics of the Low Vision Child", *Journal of Visual Impairment and Blindness,* 76, 398-406.

Getman, G.N., (1985), "A Commentary on Vision-Training", *Journal of Learning Disabilities,* 18(9), 505-512.

Mann, R., (1987), "Teaching Technology Education to Visually Impaired Students", *Technology Teacher,* 47, 7-10.

Panda, S. and Panda, K.C., (1995), *Development of Education of Blind in India,* (In Press).

Pannikar, K.K., (1978), *Vithoba Pannikar Scale of Performance, Test for the Blind,* NAB, Bombay.

Report of the National Sample Survey Organisation, No. 393, of July Dec., 1991 on Disabled Persons.

Severs, M., (1987), "Computer Technology and Academic Skill Training for improving Disaled Students' Academic Performance, Applications and Limitations", Paper presented in 38th Conference on College Composition and Communiction, Atlanta.

Chapter 6

Hearing Handicapped Children

A few children are completely deaf. They do not hear at all. Neither do they turn their heads nor respond even to loud sounds. A few others are partly deaf. He/she may hear loud noises or voices but not soft or whispering tones. Children with hearing loss create a big problem for communication. In this chapter students will learn precisely:

- Meaning of hearing handicap.
- Prevalence of hearing handicap in the population and its forms.
- The causes of hearing handicap.
- The identification procedures—audiometer.
- Characteristics of hearing handicapped children.
- Educational measures and instructional techniques.
- Integration and mainstreaming of the hearing handicapped.
- Aids and appliances.
- The role of a resource/special teacher.
- The role of regualr classroom teacher.

Who is a hearing handicapped child?

Earlier it was believed that those who are deaf from birth also have an intellectual defect. Hence, the term deaf-mute carried the notion of a double infirmity. This belief continued until it was realized that the absence of speech in the born deaf, was not related to a deficiency of the vocal organs and was only the consequences of the lack of hearing.

Deafness or impairment in hearing capacity is defined in terms of degree of hearing loss. Total inability to hear is deafness but those whose sense of hearing is defective but who manage with or without hearing aids are called hard of hearing. Deafness might occur before the child acquires language or afterwards due to certain environmental problems. The hard of hearing are those in whom the sense of hearing although defective is functional with or without a hearing aid. Deaf individuals have hearing problems that are so severe that speech cannot be understood when it is transmitted through the ear, but hard of hearing individuals can still use the auditory channel as their major avenue for speech and language development.

According to the conference of Executives of American Schools for the Deaf, a deaf person is one whose hearing is disabled to an extent (usually 70 dB) that precludes the understanding of speech through the ear alone, with or without the use of a hearing aid; a hard-of-hearing person is one whose hearing is disabled to an extent (35 to 69 dB) that makes difficult, but does not preclude the understanding of speech through the ear alone, with or without a hearing aid.

Quigley and Kretschmer (1982) stated that for educational purposes, " a-deaf child or adult is one who sustained a profound (91 dB or greater) primarily sensorineural hearing impairment prelingually". This trend is probably related to development of early intervention programme and improvements of hearing aids resulting in earlier and better spoken language acquisition for an increasing number of the less profoundly hearing impaired.

The definition that was adopted by a UNESCO experts committee (1985) introduces the notion of relativity of deafness to prevalent socio-economic conditions.

"To be considered as deaf are those children whose spontaneous speech and language development have been very much retarded or is completely absent, due to their severe hearing impairment or hearing impairment combined with a lack of training and/or technical amplification. In countries with adequate resources for diagnosis, training, and provision of hearing aids, some children with hearing impairment would not be included in the above-mentioned group, whereas they would be regarded as functionally deaf in countries lacking these resources" (P. 5).

The WHO recommended that a distinction be made in all physical or mental defects, between impairment, disability and handicap. Deaf children and adults are impaired in having a pathological auditory system. They are consequently disabled by the difficulty of perceiving speech and environemntal sounds. This disability can make them more or less severely handicapped by limiting their overall personal and social functions. The disability can, however, be reduced by appropriate hearing aid fitting, training, and in the case of children education.

Hearing impairment may be from birth (congenital hearing impaired) or may be acquired at any age in life (adventitious hearing impaired). There is a difference in speech and communication between the two groups and they need entirely different instructional techniques. In integrated education programme children with smaller degree of hearing loss are benefitted. Children with severe handicap in hearing show poor progress in coping with regular school studies.

It is important to distinguish between those who were affected from birth or shortly thereafter, before they learnt language, and those who became hearing impaired later on. These are commonly called prelingually and postingually deaf, respectively. The prelingually deaf child cannot acquire language by the same natural process as the normal hearing. Lack of adequate stimulation during the early period of life results in great difficulties in the acquisition of spoken language skills. It also produces permanent structural changes in the central nervous system. These changes diminish the capacity of the brain to efficiently process speech-linked information later on, even if normal hearing could be restored, or artificial hearing produced (Perier et. al., 1984).

The postlingually deaf children have sensory impairment that interferes with their ability to perceive speech and other sounds, but they have a normal language function. The quality of their speech may become distorted, but they usually remain intelligible. They are good in reading and writing. The prelingually deaf children have difficulties in acquiring spoken language. Most of them, when they leave school as adolescents or young adults, have language deficiency, in addition to their sensory impairment. They are deficient in oral language skills, reading and writing capacities. This linguistic deficiency constitutes serious handicap for their integration with hearing individuals. It can be attentuated and largely prevented by early and adequate education. The sign language, may be used to develop the normal linguistic function which will allow full participation in the socio-cultural life of the deaf community.

Classification of Hearing Impairment

The medical legal definition of hearing impairment has been in terms of degree of hearing loss and ear problems. These are classified as Mild 20-30 dB; marginal 30-40 dB; severe 60-75 dB; and 75 and above dB, profound category. The deaf seldom or never profit from auditory training.

The following is an extract from the Ministry of Welfare Notification No. 4-2/83-HW. III date 6.8.86 regarding classification of hearing loss.

Pure tone average of hearing in 500, 1000 and 2000 Hz by air conduction should be taken as basis for consideration as per test recommendations.

Further, it should be noted that:

a. When there is only an island of hearing present in one or two frequencies in the better ear, it should be considered as total loss of hearing.
b. When there is no response (NR at any of the 3 frequencies (500, 1000, 2000 Hz), it should be considered as equivalent to 130 dB loss for the purpose of classification of disability and in arriving at the average. This is based on the fact that maximum intensity limits in most of the Audiometers is 110 dB's and some audiometers have additional facilities of +20 dB for testing.

Hearing Impaired Categories

Sl. No.	*Category*	*Type of impairment*	*dB level and/or*	*Speech discrimi-nation*	*Percentage of impair-ment*
1.	I	Mild Hearing Impairment	dB 26 to 40 dB in better ear	30 to 100% in better ear	Less than 40%
2.	II	Moderate Hearing Impairment	41 to 55 dB in better ear	50 to 80% better ear	40%-50%
3.	III	Severe Hearing Impairment	56 to 70 dB Hearing Impairment in better ear	40 to 50%	50 to 75%
4.	IV	(a) Total deafness	No hearing	No discrimi-nation	100%
		(b) Near total deafness better ear	91 dB and above in	No discrimi-nation	100%
		(c) Profound Hearing Impairment	71 to 90 dB	Less than 40% better ear	75%-100%

Prevalence

Several measures have been undertaken to assess incidence or prevalence of deafness. One of the estimates available indicates that five per cent of school children have different degrees of hearing loss or they suffer from some form of hearing problem. With regard to our country, the National Sample Survey (1981) reported 3.02 million hearing impaired children, except for the 0-4 age group. Its occurrence is more in rural areas than in urban areas. There is a need therefore not only for early identification but of prevention and are and finally education and training. The National Sample Survey 1991 estimated hearing impaired to be 3.242 million in India in the age group 0-14, and hearing and speech impaired 4.482 in CA 15-59.

It has also been found that the speech of prelingual hearing impaired is slow and of high pitch, with prolonged vowels, rythmic abonormality and defective articulation. The incidence of hearing impairment is more in males than in females.

Causes of Hearing Loss

Hearing loss may not necessarily be due to organic factors but to psychological and psychiatric reasons. There has been differential focus. The otologist looks for medical and surgical intervention, an audiologist suggests amplification and therapeutic management but for an educator or resource teacher emphasis on language development is crucial remedial step.

Neurological

Besides organic causes which are responsible for hearing loss, the sensorineural hearing loss is associated with actual neurological transmission of sound. Such hearing loss results from damage to the sensory walls within cochlea or to the auditory nerve both because of genetic and/or environmental factors.

There are certain causes which occur before birth.

Hereditary

11 to 60 per cent of sensory neural hearing impairments have a genetic cause (dominant gene—Alpert's syndrome) and recessive gene transmission—(Usher's syndrome) to the tune of 40% of deafness cases.

Rubella

Maternal rubella, a German measles virus that has its most devastating effect on an unborn child during first three months of pregnancy is most important cause. It accounts for 27% of all the known causes of hearing loss. If the mother has contracted genital herpes the child can have hearing loss.

Infectious Disease

Early infectious diseases like mumps, influenza of the mother affects the infant's hearing. Certain other diseases of the mother e.g., diabetes, kidney disease, liver diseases affect the baby's hearing capacity.

Drugs

Some research has shown that overdose of strong drugs like streptomycin, quinine, thalichloride and L.S.D. are associated with hearing impairment and therefore expectant mothers should remain away from these.

Malnutrition

Malnutrition is another such cause. In addition Rh-incompatibility, emotional trauma, brain fever, brain tumor and certain neurological factors do their part in affecting hearing capacity of the infant adversely.

During Birth

During birth there are certain factors which affect hearing loss. Lack of oxygen, use of forceps in delivery, instrumental delivery, premature delivery followed immediately by jaundice, use of anaesthetic agents in delivery do cause hearing problems.

After Birth

The cause which affect hearing loss after birth in children are measles, mumps, whooping cough, menigitis, typhoid fever, encephalitis, infections in nasal cavities, eustachian tube, middle ear infection, ear discharge etc. All these lead to hearing loss. Ear discharge is more prominent among the causes (NSSO, 1991).

Adequate awareness on the part of parents can prevent the hearing handicap. Early follow-up services for checkig expectant mother's health and health of the new born can prevent hearing impairment and associated problems.

Identification

How would one identify the hearing impaired children? Obviously there are some behavioural indicators and some measurements tools including audiometer. But before the child is referred to an audiometric clinic, certain signs are visible. These are called behavioural clues. The child displays one or more of the following.

1. Frequent ear aches.
2. Fluid discharge from ear.
3. Cold and soar throats occuring frequently.
4. Lack of equilibrium.
5. Inconsistency in following directions.
6. Always asking "what" — "what".
7. Observing the lip movement.
8. Speech defects.
9. Limited vocabulary.
10. Has trouble in paying attention.
11. Restless and lazy.
12. Over acting or withdrawal behaviour.
13. Use of earphones.
14. Undeveloped or underdeveloped language.
15. Does not respond when called.

Testing Techniques

Early diagnosis, intervention with proper identification is essential to help the hearing impaired is done at different levels. One has to look at the:

a. *High risk register*

This records the history of childhood hearing impairment: infection from Rubella, defect of ear, nose, throat, cleft lip or palate, less than 1500 grms. of births weight. In addition to neurologic, there is also neontal menigits. After this identification, they are tested by audiological tests. No such high risk survey programme has so far been undertaken in India.

b. *Screening Procedures*

Sounds are produced at various frequencies when the child is asleep and the capacity of the child is observed with regard to responding to the sound. It is not an independent measure but is a supplementary technique.

c. *Cribiogram Technique*

In this techniques sound boxes are kept in the crib and a recording device is attached to the bed on which the baby sleeps. When sound at 92 dB is produced at certain intervals the reaction of the baby is recorded automatically. There are no Indian studies on the cribiogram.

d. *EEG*

EEG is used to screen the child for auditory response. Audiometric tests and observations of infants behavioural response to various sounds during first six months, followed by audiometric tests are being used in our country.

After an early identification, early interaction and preparation using hearing aids, early stimulation, development of sensory motor skills, auditory training to monitor speech, play and constructive activities to develop concepts and abstraction are undertaken. The hearing aid should be very carefully selected to suit to the child's needs. Basic activities are also required to be started for the development of auditory verbal communication. More important is that the child with hearing loss needs to be accepted, in the family first and parents are to be trained in the use of hearing aid and early stimulation techniques.

Audiometer

Human ear is senesitive to respond to a wide range of frequencies which range from 20 to 2000 Hz. It is not equally sensitive to all frequencies nor all speech sounds be perceived at the same level of intensity. The human ear is sensitive to intensities from 0 db 130 db SPL. Various tests have been devised and used to find out solutions to identify the degree of loss in low middle and high frequenceis.

The most common tests are: tuning fork tests of Rinne in Germany: Lateralisation tests by Weber, the Bing test for different conductive and sensory-neural loss, Schwabach tests of sensory neural loss. All these techniques are developed in Germany and are used to identify type of hearing loss not the degree of hearing loss.

Audiometer which was developed in 1920 is an electronic device producing pure tones. It measures the Hearing Threshold Level (HTL), Hearing Level (HL) and Sound Pressure Level (SPL). An audiogram is prepared by testing the child which indicates the degree of hearing loss. Generally normal hearing sensitivity lies within the range of 10 dB to +20 dB at all frequencies when hearing sensitivity or capacity falls beyond 20 dB at two or more frequencies the person is said to have hearing loss. This may vary from time to time, ear to ear and frequency to frequency.

On the basis of all these i.e., degree of affection, site of lession, on-set and duration of loss, hearing impairment is classified as mild, moderate, severe and profound. It can also be categoriesed as conductive loss, mixed loss, sensory-neural loss and non-organic loss, cogenital loss (at the time birth), prelingual loss.

Speech audiometry gives us:

a. Speech Reception Threshold (SRT)
b. Speech Discriminatory Threshold (PB Max %)

Psychological Testing

The use of testing for the hearing handicapped poses a special challenge to the psychologist since these children have communication difficulties. The following tests are used to assess competence of the hearing impaired child.

1. Seguin Form Board—Age 5 to 15 years.
2. WISC-R—Age 6 to 16 years.
3. Vineland Social Maturity Scale (VSMS)—Birth to 30 years.
4. Bayley Scale of Infant Development upto 30 months.
5. Bender Visual Motor Gestalt—Age 4+.
6. Differential Aptitude Test.
7. Chatterjee's non Language Preference Record.
8. Personality—Projective Tests—Rorschack Ink Blot Test.
9. Behaviour checklist.
10. Revised Conner's Parents and Teacher Questionnaire—Age 6 to 12 years.

Certain non testing techniques are also used. Interview, case history, observation of day to day behaviours contribute to total assessment.

Language assessment is necessary in young children who show signs of delayed speech which could be due to hereditary and environmental factors. It is done to establish language problems relating to phonology, grammar, semantics. The teacher may observe these by oral testing, asking the child to name pictures, objects in the classroom and around him, response to a particular interaction, telling a story to the child and asking him to narrate it. He may use dictation as a method of testing, listening comprehension, receptive expression, tests of pronounciation, articulation, vocabulary tests, matching of items, testing grammatical structure, transformation of one pattern to another, complete the sentense by rearrangement of words. By using all these techniques the teacher can prepare a profile of language ability which eventually helps to plan for language intervention.

For measuring language ability of Hearing Impaired Children Edinburgh Articulation Test (CA 3-6); Auditory Comprehension of Language Test (A 3-7); Test for Reception of Grammar (TROG) CA-13; Linguistic Awareness in Reading Readiness Test (A 3-6). Auditory Discrimination Test (3-6), Hoston Test for Language Deveopment (upto 6 years); Comprehension Test of Basic Skills;

Readiness Test (K-1.3a); Word Recognition Test; Picture Aided Reading Test for the deaf (CA 11 years); Weale Analysis of Reading Ability (CA 5 and above); Standard Reading Test (CA upto 14 years); Illinois Test of Psycholinguistic Ability (ITPA) (CA 2-10); Full Range Picture Vocabulary Test; Reynell Developmental Language Scale-Revised, (CA 1-7); British Picture Vocabulary Scale (Ca 2.5-18); Aston Index (Ca 5-14) and Nebraska Test of Learning Aptitude for both hearing and HIC are used. But adaptations and new development of such tests are yet to emerge in our country. For measuring intelligence, PPVT-Revised (CA 2 1/2-40); Slosson Intelligence Test (1 to adult); Stanford-Binet Intelligence Scale-(CA 2-12); Wechsler Intelligence Scale for Children-Revised (CA 6-16.11) are available.

In India, one finds Auditory Discrimination Test used for the both dyslexic and normal readers for the auditory discrimination purpose. Word Analysis Test in Kannada and word synthesis test are used for the dyslexic children but greater sophistications and applications are in need.

Psycho-educational assessment with hearing impaired children should have two objectives. Is there a deaf personality? What are the effects of hearing impairments on cognitive and social development? There is nothing called deaf personality. They do reveal certain characteristics. They have similar problems like visual impaired children in terms of social and personal adjustment.

The intellectual function of deaf person has been evaluated by two streams of psychological activity (a) development of intelligence test to measure complex problem solving ability (b) development of cognitive functioning in the area of measures, perception, learning.

The favourite tests in intelligence are: WISC (performance scale), RPM, PPVT. The tests conditions are usually not possible to be met by deaf children. Indian norms are not available. Standardised administration cannot also be followed language translation is required. The examinees also cannot communicate much clearly. Hence, IQ only provides a crude estimate of intellectual ability. The low score has therefore to be interpreted with caution. Again a crude information is not also worthless if it is used in conjunction with a broad spectrum of adaptive behaviour that are indicative of intellectual functioning. Such areas include: social competence, self competence, physical competence, receptive communicative competence, expressive communicatively competence, adjustment competence, tests are to be developed to measure all these. The other source of information about deaf child's competence comes from experimental studies based essentially on the defect hypothesis than different hypothesis.

Other than test development, the following points are to be kept in mind:

a. Communicative efficiency of the tests.
b. Establishing rapport.
c. Motivating hearing impaired child to do well in tests.

d. Ensuring comparable task demands inspite of language differences.
e. Interpretation to data relative to some norm.

Characteristics of Hearing Impaired Children

There are certain behavioural problems which are associated with hearing impairment. They feel invariably inferior and helpless in adapting to circumstances that require verbal communication. They have a poor self-concept which damages the developm nt of personality (Loeb and Saregiani, 1986). They develop temper tantrums and are mostly submissive. A fair number of hearing impaired children have additional perceptual motor deficits due to brain damage or cerebral dynfunction. Delay in achieving motor milestones, poor gross motor coordination, delayed hand preference, hyperactivity, perseveration, short attention span, impressiveness, emotional lability are some of the other characteristics.

Their intelligence ranges from retarded to normal with specific learning disabilities on concept formation. Infact, it would be better to state that deaf children are as intelligent as hearing children, but there are a few who are low in intelligence. But if this is detected early they can be helped to certain extent to improve through special educational facilities.

Language development of the deaf child differs markedly from that of the normal. In fact, the normal child learns the language. The deaf child is taught language. They process language and linguistic utterancs visually. Whether the child is prelingually deaf or postlingual deaf they behave like deaf children in communication skills. But those who loose their hearing after experiencing speech can be trained a little easily. With training insecured and use of aids the deaf child acquired workable language and speech. The profound'y deaf must receive sound training and prosthetic aids as close to the age of two.

The deaf child as well as hard of hearing experience a lag in vocabulary skills compared to non-hearing impaired students. The deaf having a much greater lag. The vocabulary development gets worse as the hearing impaired child grows older. This eventually affects syntax, morphology development.

They have limited vocabulary and inability to comprehend meaning, concepts, abstract feelings, complex structure of language. In written language one often finds problems associated with sentence construction, knowledge, gender, tense, appropriate use of verbs, adjectives, nouns, idioms etc. All these affect the academic growth of hearing impaired children. Both reading and arithmatic performances are deficient in hearing impaired children.

As regards cognitive functioning, the hearing impaired children face deficits in understanding abstract concepts. Because of limited vocabulary they possess poor comprehension ability. They do not have any difficulty in adjusting to social situations. On all the aspects of development i.e., mental, intellectual, personality and educational achievement the hearing impaired children are inferior and are at a lower level. In vocational adjustment they face more difficulties.

They have high pitched voice with slow and laboured speech. The vowels used by them are either prolonged or distorted. They display abnormal rhythm in speech. There are nasal sounds, mispronuciations and montonous voice.

Pitch refers to variation in production or phonation of voice. Voice disorder could arise out of faulty habits, abuse of the voice, delayed speech, organic anomalies. Fluency disorders could be stuttering e.g., prolongation of sounds, compulsive repetition of syllables, difficulty in initiating utterances. Clutering e.g., excessive speed in speaking, disorganised sentence structure, slurred or ommitted sylables and sounds. These are due to faulty learning or organic conditions.

For the hearing impaired children with Arithmatic and Reading problems a programme of Distinct Instructional System to Arithmatic and Reading (DISTAR) is also available. Teaching is designed for small groups to HIC for daily 30 minutes sessions. The lessons are presented in a rigid and repetitive way. There are 160 lessons starting with objective identification. For hearing impaired children of learning difficulties and delayed language skill.

Some of the difficulties, the deaf child experiences, in learning to read may be explained by the greater problem he has in ordering terms through the process of 'visual scanning for the hearing child, this ordering and visual scanning itself are forced by the explicit motor speech pattern. There is no such motor pattern in the deaf to force an order of scanning, unless one is provided by an arbitrary process such as finger movement.

More specifically the hearing impaired children have certain specific characteristics with regard to language. He has problems of verbalising abstract concepts e.g., happiness, sorrow, mercy. He often makes mistaks in writing or speaking a simple sentence. The speech of a hearing impaired child is generally unintelligible to a new listener because of tone, pronunciation, use of prolonged vowels e.g., Wa-te-rz. The speech may be nasal. The consonants are not properly articulated e.g., 'and' for 'hand', 'arm' for 'harm' etc.

The deaf child has pronunciation problems. These may be substitution, ommission, addition, distortion. Substitution refers pronunciation "wabbit" for "rabbit", "deze" for "doze". In case of addition, 'ischool' for 'school'. Unintelligibel speech—'foah' in place of 'far'. Deaf children display more errors which relate to ommissions of consonant sounds. They also experience difficulty in perceiving speech sounds.

Educational Provisions

Hearing impairments can be viewed not only from an educational perspective but also from the larger perspective of their effects on the child's overall adjustment.

The speech and hearing behaviour of Deaf children needing special care varies according to category of hearing impairments. This is an extract from the book published by NCERT, on hearing impaired children.

Group		*Speech and Haring Behaviour*	*Special Needs*
I.	Hearing thresholds with in 25 dB with normal Hearing.	Speech is normal. Follows normal pattern of development with good auditory perceptive skills.	Needs no special attention.
II.	Hearing threshold 26 to 40 dB, Mild Hearing loss.	Exhibits difficulty in hearing faint speech, speech at a distance of speech with background noise. Speech and language developments are within normal limits. May exhibit occasional auditory perception problems some educational retardation likely.	Will benefit from special seating in the class. Hearing aid is beneficial. Parents and teachers should be educated on the Child's problems in understanding due to hearing loss.
III.	41 to 55 dB moderate hearing-loss.	Language development and speech are mildly affected. Difficulty with rarely used words, minor differences in meaning of words and idioms, defective articulation but still intelligible speech. Voice quality and inflection almost normal. Reading and writing are delayed. Vocabulary training, reading and writing to be specially attended to in addition to schooling.	They should well to hearing aids & amplification, early speech and language training and parent counselling indicated speech and language development to be monitored. Special seating, supportive teaching will help to integrate the child in a normal school.
IV.	56 to 70 dB. Moderately severe Hearing-loss.	Grammar, Vocabulary, articulation and voice are affected. Can understand loud speech. Early speech is unintelligible. Even with hearing aids, show difficulty in understanding. Reading and writing needs special assistance. Requires individual attention.	Only a few in regular school with special assistance will benefit. Requires preschool, speech and language training and special classes in early years in academic subjects.
V.	71 to 90 dB. Severe Hearing-loss.	Speech and language do not develop spontaneously. Are aware of sounds produced very loudly at a distance of	Initially educationally deaf, early training on hearing aid suditory

Group	*Speech and Haring Behaviour*	*Special Needs*
	1 ft. or near the ear. The voice will be high-pitched and articulation distorted.	training, language, development speech. Reading and special schooling for hearing-impaired are indicated. Preschool training and normal schooling may not be beneficial.
VI. 91 dB and above. Profound Hearing-loss.	They do not rely on hearing for their communication. Occassionally may hear thunder or explosion. Generally produced sounds are not recognised. Are educationally deaf. Language and speech develop only by training. Special schooling is required. Communicate mostly through gestures, voice, inflection, articulation greatly affected. Require consisten (regular) speech and language training and special coaching in subjects.	Special schooling and vocational guidance needed. Cannot function in a regular school. Hearing aid may prove to be beneficial only when fitted early and with proper training.

Home Based Programmes

Home based programmes are introduced at very early stages for the young infants depending on the degree of hearing impairment, developmental status of his intellectual level, degree of parental involvement. In this, some corrective exercises and stimulating environments are created. The infant is given auditory and speech training. Then after formal assessment is over, they are placed in schools depending upon the category of impairment.

Special Schools

Children who have severe disability in hearing are placed in special schools for the deaf. Usually, there is no other alternative. These children follow an entirely different curriculum and they can not keep pace with the normal school curriculum because of their language handicap.

Special Classes and Regular Class Combination

There are mildly hearing impaired children who can profit from regular class room teaching. They are given adequate preparations in some school subjects, personal-special skill development, communication skills. These children spend half a day in regular class and the remaining half in a special class with a special teacher and/or a resource teacher to prepare to cope with the regular class works.

Integrated Class Rooms

Children with minimal hearing loss are placed in the integrated classrooms alongwith the regular students. With minimum classroom arrangements, instruction, use of hearing aids these children are able to cope with the normal students in the regular classroom. Special assistance is given to such pupils.

Vocational Placement

For hearing impaired adolescents vocational placement is decided after assessing his intelligence level, range of interest, aptitude, social maturity and adaptability and communication skills. The vocational counsellor will assist him for appropriate placement. Ordinarily they can adjust to routine works in a sheltered workshop.

Least Restrictive Environment Setting

The least restrictive setting for hard of hearing students consists of:

a. A hard of hearing child has to be seated as close as to the teacher.
b. No undue attention is to be paid to him.
c. They learn by hearing and observing others.
d. Make only sensory structural changes within the classroom which can absorb sounds.
e. For these students the presentation of actual school material should follow three phases.
    i. The lesson by the teacher i.e., vocabulary and providing advance organisers.
    ii. Presentation of materials which have been previewed.
    iii. Material continuously.

The hard of hearing child may participate in a team response approach in a small group.

Sign Language

For the deaf child teaching of sign language is important. Language signs (using the hands, fingers, and the arms to form whole words or phrases) and finger spelling (using hands and fingers to form representations of individual letters). The American sign language system (ASL) is commonly used in these cases. The sign language system is given below.

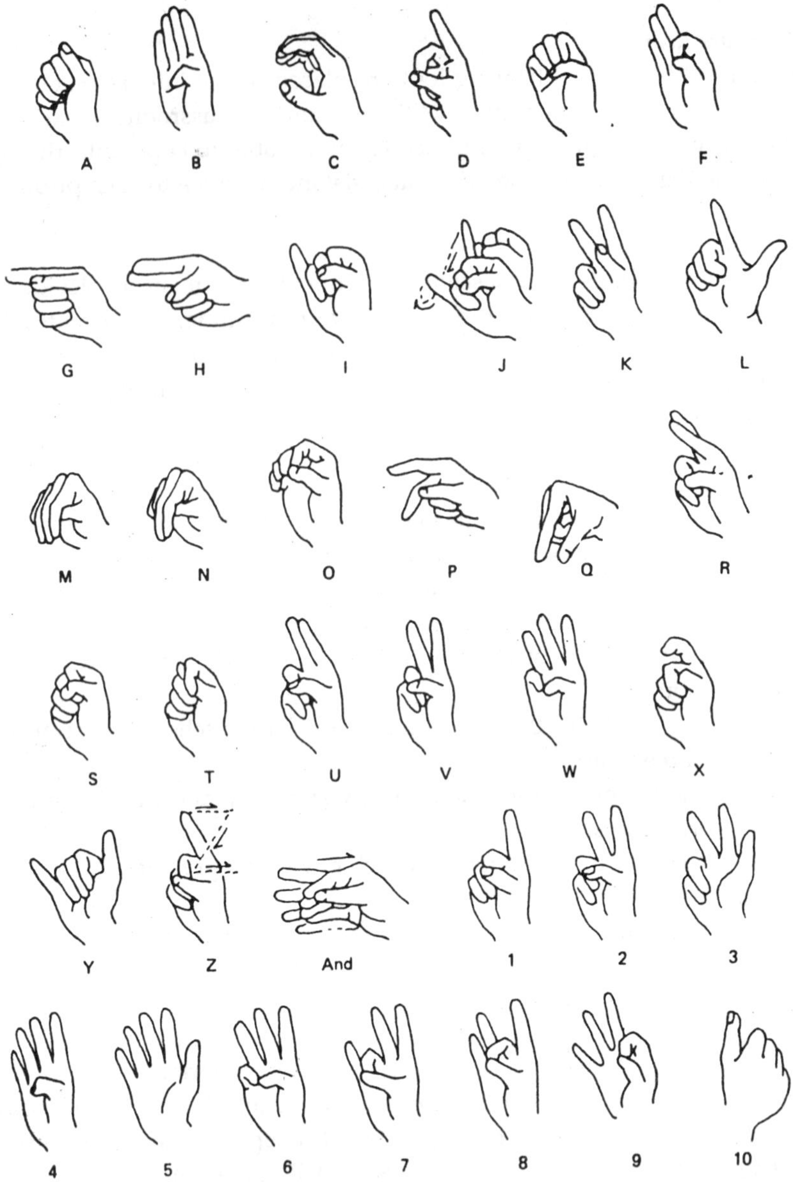

Figure 6: Sign Learning

Speech Reading (Lip Reading)

It is another technique within to normal communication. Teaching using this method is named as oral-aural method. The deaf child has to use some type of auditory aid so that he can listen to the speech stimulus. The child is trained in this auditory process. These two approaches have led to creation of various combinations and adaptations.

Hearing impaired children differ from one another in many ways in degree and type of hearing loss intelligence and home environment. These differences have influence on their acquisition of communicative ability and further course of education. In order to meet the needs of different hearing impaired children according to their acquisition potential, different methods of teaching are used for them.

There are five combination of methods which are used now in the education of deaf.

Auditory Unisensory or Acoupedic Methods

This relies on auditory training to develop spoken language. Speech reading is either not encouraged or suppressed during training periods. In the verbo-tonal method, perception of acoustic features through the tactile sense is used. The auditory global approach stands at the margin between the acoupedic and the oral-aural, since "the primary, although not always the exclusive, channel for speech development is auditory".

Oral-Aural Method

Auditory perception and speech reading are used but signs are excluded. Use of multisensory approach and active oral-aural dialogues are used. In cued speech and related systems, the oral-aural approach is combined with a system of hand shapes executed near the mouth synchronously with speech. The hadn brings only that part of the information that is not supplied by lip reading. The combination of this information allows the deaf child to clearly identify by sight the speech sounds and syllables that the hearing children identify through the ear. Finger spelling is executed by the teacher simultaneously with speech. The child then is asked to accompany his or her own speech by finger spelling. Since the latter is written language, reading and writing are strongly emphasized.

Unilingual Bimodal Communication

One language, that of the hearing society and of most deaf children's parents is simultaneously expressed in speech and signs. There are varieties of signed representations of spoken language. Some are close to the regional sign language of the deaf differing mostly in word order; others use additional signs to convey syntactical and morphological information. Still others are wholly contrived.

Bilingual Bimodal Communication

Spoken language in a an oral-aural approach is used by hearing persons. Sign language is used in other situations by deaf and hearing persons. In early education, parents use those signs they have learned in combination with their spoken language.

Visual Unisensory Communication by Sign Language Alone

While no educator advocates that deaf children should not learn the major language, a few favour the exclusive use of sign language for early education. Only after sign language is firmly established as a first language, the majority's language is taught as a second language. In some programs, teaching is first done in the written form and spoken language.

General Teaching Processes

Hearing impaired children utilise lip-readings or speech reading with clues to facilitate communication. Their speech reading will improve if we can look into and adapt certain precautionary measures while teaching speech reading.

Teachers of hearing impaired children should avoid keeping mustaches, hair styles, ornaments, beards to facilitate the child to look for cues of communication. They should not cover the face with book while reading a passage to prevent eye contact which aids oral communication. The teacher must face the child while teaching reading and do not make movements unless it is absolutely required. These measures aid in helping the hearing impaired for speech reading. Hearing impaired children get more tired easily. Hence, have short activities, combine visual illustrations with oral activities work sheets, individual game, physical activities, and relaxation exercises.

A hearing friend often called 'buddy' helps the hearing impaired child by taking notes for him, pointing out who speaks and what is being spoken. They help them to come back to the correct place in the lesson when it is being taught as they sit near them. Social interaction is also improved by rotating the buddy system in the classroom. If a teacher speaks slowly, the hearing impaired child gains a lot.

Certain general teaching techniques are to be practised by the teachers of hearng impaired children (Gearheart, 1980).

1. Combined visual presentation with oral materials
2. Use handouts for these children
3. Use multisensory approach when necessary
4. Focus on pupil's attention
5. Teach the major portion of the lesson
6. Make summary presentation
7. Use transition sentences
8. Use short and clear verbalisation
9. Ask questions to check comprehension
10. Explain things and repeat.

For accelerating language and oral communication skills among hearing impaired children language experience training should be incorporated as a regular feature in the school emphasing all the aspects of language competence, comprehension and skills of communication role playing, action, illustration cards, pictures, drills, picture-worn dictionaries, practice sheets, phonics, structural analysis are to be used. Several language training kits are available and can be profitable used.

Written comprehensions and expression can be enhanced by writing simple sentences on a topic and presenting them in a scrambled order and asking the hearing impaired child to rearrange the cards using semantic organisation. They can be given matching exercise order in of excercises, questions regarding what, when, where and how. Hanging of charts in the room also speed up the language acquisition.

For mathematical ability, training use of abacuses, plastic chip, coins and other small objects, value boxes, number lines, playing card, semiabstract materials facilitate learning. Hearing deficient chidlren are not poor in abstract and conceptual ability but because of language deficit their overall performance is retarded.

Speech therapy has been recommended for reinforcing speed and sound patterns. Close communication with speech therapist will result in consistent and concentrated programmes. Use of hearing aids individually and group hearing aids in the class room facilitate instruction and learning.

Integration/Mainstreaming of the Hearing Impaired

The integration of the hearing impaired children into ordinary classes was a major development in the education of the deaf in the 1960's. For implementing mainstreaming appointment of a specialist teacher of the deaf, a screening programme in cooperation with health authorities, guidance and counselling of parents of pre-school aged children from the age first diagnosis, a resource room, aids and equipments for facilitating hearing are some of the essential requirements.

Many hearing-impaired children, with early education, proper hearing aid fitting, and continued support, can successfully be educated with the normally hearing loss is an important factor but is by no means decisive in itself for mainstreaming. Some profoundly deaf children can succeed in ordinary schools, while others with more residual hearing may not be able to do so. It varies from country to country. West Germany maintains separate special school systems for the profoundly deaf and the hard of hearing. Italy allows officially all hearing impaired children to be mainstreamed. Development countries where special education has yet to be organized view mainstreaming as a tempting alternative to special schools.

Sign language interpretation services for the deaf have been developed primarily in the United States to assist the deaf in all circumstances in which they may benefit from them. In addition to sign language interpretation, other forms of interpretation are beginning to be developed in some countries: oral interpretation and oral interpretation with cued speech.

The trend toward mainstreaming has increased over the years. Further, early speech and hearing training have proved effective for reducing the language and education difficulties of most hearing impaired children. Conrad (1979), demonstrated that whatever method was used, whether oral or manual, the majority of deaf school graduates reached a mean reading age equivalent only to that of 9 to 10 year old hearing children. Quigley and Kretschmer (1982) showed that deaf children of deaf parents who had signs as their first language were not disadvantaged in the overall language evaluation when compared with deaf children of hearing parents.

The results, together with sign language, were instrumental in the brith and development of the total communication (TC) philosophy. It is the right of a deaf child to learn to use all forms of communication to develop language competence. This includes: child-devised gestures, speech, formal sign language, finger spelling, speech reading, reading, writing, as well as any other methods that may be developed in the future. Every deaf child should also be provided with the opportunity to learn to use any remnant of residual hearing he or she may have by employing the best possible electronic equipment for amplifying sound. Many schools in the United States, and a growing number throughout the world, have adhered to the principle of TC. Many are urging parents to learn to communicate with their children through signs in addition to speech. Such combination of signs and speech has been termed bimodal communication.

The academic content for hard of hearing students within mainstreamed settings should be similar to that of their non-handicapped peers although this does not display average performance in academic areas. The contents of deaf students are however not same as that of regular student.

There is a need for giving both hard of hearing children and deaf children speech and language development training: Speech perception and production, vocabulary development, syntax development, language usuage. The degree to which all these will be emphasized will depend upon the degree of the hearing loss.

The hard of hearing child should be given speech perception training. He has to listen sound, discriminate sounds and produce speech. Lip reading as a form of speech perception should not be used. It can at best become an adjunctive skills.

As regards vocabulary development, new vocabulary should be constantly presented. Printed or written presentation should follow aural presentation. Vocabulary should be presented in different contexts, e.g., 'cool' has different meanings in different context.

The hearing impaired children should be given training in syntax and morphology i.e., word forms and word orders and how they affect meaning of a statement.

The child has to be involved in the language interaction. He should participate than only receive language. This can be done by turn-taking, changing topic, entering and existing from concersation.

Aids and Appliances

Hearing aids are used by the hearing impaired children individually and in groups. They are classified into different types based on:

a. Place of wearing,
b. Portability,
c. Number of persons using.

According to place of wearing some aids are available:

(i) Body level (pocket) hearing aids,
(ii) Ear level hearing aids (spectacle type, behind the ear type, inside the ear aid. There are all individual portable aids.

The auditory trainer or speech trainer uses a table model individual aid, whereas group hearing aids are table models for group hearing group activities with large number of children.

The ear moulds also vary which is fitted with hearing aids. There are standard mould, shell type mould, Skeleton mould, canal lock mould, canal mould, vented mould, open ear mould. Moulds are selected on the basis of acoustical properties, conspicuoussess, and tight fitting on the ear. Many people want to hide it.

Hearing aids for children should be selected very carefully. The audiologist selects a limited number of hearing aids to be tried on each child to select an appropriate aid. It is based on:

a. type of hearing aid,
b. frequency response,
c. arrangement of wearable amplification, and
d. maximum power output.

Resource Teacher

For successful mainstreaming besides the above particularly for any disability, good will of parents of other children, the goodwill of teachers, the goodwill of the school as a system, and the goodwill of the local education authority are essential. These are closely linked. Teachers of mainstream schools are inadequately prepared and naive about the needs of hearing impaired children and exhibit behaviours which are not always appropriate. The role of the teacher in mainstreamed class is very challenging.

Parents and teachers are trained to observe and look for responses with different aids. It is a continuous process by well trained personnel. Rechecking is done at intervals but it will take some more time before our society provides such benefits and services to the hearing impaired child.

The resource teacher in school can take care to correct their speech to make it intelligible. He can make group practice for common pronunciation and individual practice for developing spoken skills. Resource teaching helps the hearing impaired children to overcome their lack by learning the oral and manual skills of language. The sensitisation of their residual hearing and visual channels also help them to participate suitably in IED settings.

The resource teacher is the key person in the integrated system for teaching the hearing impaired. In this situation the resource teacher should be a specialist on hearing impaired children. He should have the following competencies (P. 26).

1. Knowledge of different types and degree of hearing impairments,
2. Methods and instruments used in measuring hearing loss,
3. Speech development in normal children,
4. Problem of speech development in hearing impaired chidlren,
5. Process of communication and the tools used in it,
6. Developing language in hearing impaired children,
7. Different psycological tests used to assess language, intelligence and adjustment of hearing impaired children,
8. Articulatory phonetics used to correct the speech of the hearing impaired,
9. Different supportive services, and
10. Resource room and facilities.

He/she can handle maximum 8 to 10 hearing impaired children and keep a record of entry behaviour, functional hearing potentiality, level of language acquistion, level of intelligence, and psychological problems of the child. He is infact, a remedial teacher of the hearing impaired. He looks after all the curriculum and social development of the hearing impaired child.

The Regular Teacher

The role of regular teacher is more important in the mainstreamed class of hearing impaired children. Besides seing that amplification device works, he should face the child during classroom presentation. They have to question frequently the understanding of the concepts presented. They have to provide many more written exercises to make sure that the material is understood. He should not lower the expectation which can adversely affect the academic and social growth especially language skill.

The teacher should avoid calling attention to children with speech problems in the classroom. The teacher can use PPVT which improves expressive and receptive language.

The teachers have to modify some of their habitual modes of teaching—such as, talking to the class when facing the clalk board, asking the student to sit in front of the classroom, the good ear must be facing or near the teacher. The children should be trained in lipreading and picking up nonverbal cues. Do not exaggerate the pronunciation of your words, speak naturally. Exaggerated gestures are to be reduced to a minimum.

The regular teacher should tell other students to adjust with the hearing impaired child and explain to them the implications of hearing loss. So that they should adjust to the hearing impaired child well. He should ensure that the hearing impaired child understands his directions. He should instill self confidence in them. He should refer the child to the resource teacher and explain his deficiencies. He should kep a close rapport with the resource teacher. Classroom conditions should be conductive to his speech reading and hearing.

Providing education and training to the hearing impaired pupils a challenge not only to the regular classroom teacher but to special teachers as well. A consistent attempt, monitoring and feedback on the performance of hearing impaired children is needed. The parents and community have also great role to play in accepting such children. IED and the resource room teacher plan are positive steps in bringing hearing impaired to the mainstream.

Highlights of the Chapter

Deafness is defined in terms of degree of hearing loss. Total inability to hear is deafness (70/75 dB) but those whose sense of hearing is defective but can manage without hearing aids are called hard of hearing (35 to 69 dB). Hearing handicap makes it difficult to understand language. Hearing handicap may arise at birth or may be acquired at any age in life, but the problems of both are different.

Nearly five per cent of school going children have different degrees of hearing loss. There are 3.242 million hearing impaired children in the CA range of 0-14. Hearing and speech handicap combined the figure is 4.482 million in CA range 15-59.

Besides organic causes, damage to the sensory walls within the Cochlea, auditory nerve, dominant gene transmission (Alphert's Syndrome)—recessive genes (Usher's Syndrome), Rubella, infectious diseases, drugs, malnutrition, lack of oxygen during birth, use of forceps during delivery, prematurity, encephalities, mumps, meningitis, typhoid, measles can lead to hearing loss.

Audiometer is used to assess hearing loss besides the tell-tale signs which are used primarily for referral. The various testing techniques include: high risk register, screening, cribiogram, EEG, Audiometer. Certain Psychological tests and non-testing techniques are used to assess behavioural charactersitics of the hearing handicapped.

Hearing handicapped children feel inferior, helpless, have poor self-concept, temper tantrums, are submissive, have poor gross motor coordination, delayed hand preference, hyperactivity, short attention span, emotional inability, slightly low IQ, than normal children, poor language and communication skills. They experience difficulty in understanding abstract concepts, and have difficulties in vocational adjustments. The most significant defects appear in pronunciation.

Both special school and integrated education are recommended for the hearing handicapped including a combination of the special class and regular class provisions. The whole purpose is to provide LRE by allowing HH child to sit close to the teacher, help them to hear and observe signs, lip movement. Several aural-oral techniques are applied to teach HH language and communication.

General teaching methods include visual presentation with oral instruction, use of handouts, multisensory approaches, summary presentations, short and clear verbalisation etc. For mathematics, use of abacuses, plastic chips, number lines, playing cards, and for language disability speech therapists are used.

The HH can be well integrated into the regular school. Early speech and hearing have proved effective for helping HH to learn. There is no difference in their curriculum compared to normal children but special care has to be taken for vocabulary development and semantics. They should be trained as to how to make use of hearing aids and other appliances.

The resource teacher in an integrated setting has several important roles—understanding of aids, speech development techniques, techniques to improve language, phonetics etc. The regular teacher might as well concentrate upon teaching of curricular subjects, adaptive behaviour and skills.

Review Questions

1. Who is a hearing handicapped child? How would you identify a hearing handicapped child?
2. What are testing and assessment procedures for the hearing handicapped children?
3. State the causes of hearing handicap.
4. State some of the behavioural signs of the hearing handicapped children.
5. What are some of the educational provisions for the hearing handicapped children?
6. What are the characteristics of hearing handicapped children?
7. What is the role of the resource teacher in teaching hearing handicapped children in a mainstreamed class?
8. What is the role of regular teacher in teaching the hearing handicapped children in a mainstreamed class?
9. Write notes on:
   a. Audiometer
   b. Speech reading
   c. Accoupedic methods
   d. Lip reading
   e. Finger spelling
   f. Unilingual bimodal communication
   g. Bilingual bimodal communication
   g. Aids and appliances

References

Conard, R., (1979), *The deaf school child*, London: Harper and Row.

Gearherart, R.B., (1980), *Special education for the eighties*, C.V. Musby, London.

Loeb, R., and Sarigiani, P., (1986), "The impact of hearing impairment on self perception of children", *Volta Review*, 88, 89-91.

Perier, O., Algeria, J., Buyse, M.D., Alimonte, G., Gilson, D., and Serniclaes, W., (1984), Consequences of auditory deprivation in animals and humans, Acta Oto-laryngological, (No. 411), 60-70.

Quigley, S.P., and Kretschmer, R.F., (1982), *The education of deaf children: Issues, theory and practice*, London: Arnoid.

UNESCO, (1985), *Consultation on alternative approaches for the education of the deaf*, Paris: UNESCO.

Chapter 7

Emotionally Disturbed Children

Some children in the classroom are mischievious. They are hyperactive or hypoactive. They have temper tantrums and display unruly behaviour and self injurious behaviours quite often. These children pose problems for the classroom teacher. In this chapter attempt has been made to bring to the knowledge of students the salient features regarding:

- the meaning of emotional disturbance,
- the cause of emotional disturbance,
- the identification procedure,
- the types of emotional disturbance,
- the characteristics of emotionally disturbed children
- the educational provisions in regular school or self-contained classroom,
- the role of the resource/special teacher, and
- the role of the regular classroom teacher.

Who is an Emotionally Disturbed Child?

Emotional disturbance can be viewed from a variety of perspectives. In the past emotionally disturbed children were viewed as autistic. They were confined to institutional programmes and were under residential care. Very few of them received schooling, if at all. After 1975 when the Handicapped Children's Act was passed in USA there developed a new interest in the education of the emotionally disturbed in a separate school. The other view which is prevalent is mainstreaming or integrating the emotionally disturbed into a normal environment. In many cases there is no such clearcut decision regarding the care, treatment, education and rehabilitation of emotionally disturbed.

The term "Emotional Disturbance" has different meanings. For teachers, an emotionally disturbed child is one who is shy, withdrawn, or who is too aggressive. Emotionally distrubed behaviour was considered synonymous with misbehaviour or deviancy. By deviancy it is meant that "a student takes actions which are prohibited by the teacher". In this definition the locus of the problem was on the norms of the school. A different kind of definition was also given in terms of the ecology of the child. According to this, emotional disturbance is viewed in terms of environmental variables which create maladaptive emotional reactions. For example, the frustrating environment in the school or such other unfavourable circumstances lead to emotional disturbance. From the view point of the peer group certain behaviours are problem behaviour. According to this, a child who cannot make interpersonal adjustment with his age mates is considered as a emotionally disturbed child. When the child's sociometric relationship declines, he becomes emotionally disturbed.

Parents and others have their own conception of emotionally disturbed children. For parents, the child sometimes becomes a scapegoat and the problem is created because of marital conflicts and incongruent needs of the parents. Emotionally disturbed parents produce emotionally disturbed children.

Under this framework who should be considered as emotionally disturbed? The term refers to a condition exhibiting one or more of the following characteristics over a long period of time and to a marked degree that adversely affects educational performance.

a. an inability to learn that cannot be explained by intellectual, sensory or health factors,
b. an inability to build and maintain satisfactory interpersonal relationships with peers and teachers,
c. inappropriate behaviour of feelings under normal circumstances,
d. a general and pervasive mood of unhappiness or depression,
e. a tendency to develop physical symptoms of fear associated with personal or school problems.

This particular term emotional disturbance with all the emotional and behavioural characteristics does include Schizophrenic and autistic characteristics. It does not include the socially maladjusted unless serious emotional disturbance is accompanied with social maladjustment.

Further, a child is emotionally disturbed when his reactions to life situations are unrewarding to himself and unacceptable to his peers and other members of the society. These children lack flexibility to modify their behaviour. They are too excitable or too withdrawn, too brave or too fearful. For teachers, a child is emotionally disturbed when he would be disrupting the whole class, would place undue pressure on the teacher and disturb the general school atmosphere. The American Psychiatric Association defined emotional disturbance as follows: "It is a type of Psychiatric disturbances without clearly defined physical cause or without structural damage to the brain". In general, emotional disorder or disturbance in children can be defined in terms of certain observable characteristics such as: "hyperactivity, withdrawn behaviour, failure to achieve at a level reasonably commensurate with ability, tendency towards fighting and other aggressive behaviour, resentment and antagonism towards authority and rules and regulations, and general problems in learning and concentrating, not associated with known organic or sensory defects" (Phillips, 1967). Hence, an emotionally disturbed child is one who shows to an extreme degree, one or more of the characteristics listed above.

Emotional disturbance is not distributed evenly in all age groups, sex and social class groups. The behaviour problems are maximum during early puberty and these are found earlier among girls than among boys.

Parents having services and semiskilled occupations have more emotionally disturbed children compared to parents who hold professional and skilled occupations.

Types of Emotional Disturbances

Emotional disturbance cannot be classified on a continuum as MR, Hearing handicapped, or visual handicapped. It varies according to clinical symptoms which are grouped to define a type of emotional disturbances such as Autism, Psychosis, Childhood Schizophrenia etc.

Autism

Autism in children is one of the most severe forms of emotional disturbance. This is also otherwise known as childhood schizophrenia. This condition is presented with and is followed by delay in speech development, non-communicative use of speech, and withdrawal tendencies. Such children do not use language to convey meanings.

Kanner (1943) descrbed that an autistic child has:

— severe withdrawal of contact from other people
— an intense need to preserve sameness
— an inability to deal with people
— apparently good intellectual potential
— severe disturbance of language functioning.

In his book Kauffman (1977) states "attempts to pinpoint the origin of behaviour disorders in family relationships have met with little success. Family relationships are best viewed to as contributing to behavioural development. From another point of view autism in children may result purely out of language impairment and language training. It has been possible to reduce the occurrence of autism in children clinically. Many of the psychiatrists also treat autistic children and have made them quite acceptable.

Rutter (1978) emphasized delayed and deviant language, repetitive speech, stereotypic behaviour (body movements while speaking), echolaliac speech, resistance to change, delusions, hallucinations, loosening of associations and incoherence.

Psychosis

This is the most severe and debilitating of the emotional disturbances. Psychotic children have no contact with reality. Childhood schizophrenia is quite commonly seen. In early infantile autistic children, we find extreme withdrawal, peculiar communication, and improper use of language. They only react to their own private imaginary scheme of life.

Childhood Schizophrenia (Psychosis)

Unlike autism this disorder has its onset after 30 months of age and before 12 years. The child must exhibit at least three of the following sudden anxiety, inappropriate affect, resistance to change, oddities of motor movement, abnomalities of speech, hyper or hyposensitivity to sensory stimuli, self mutilation, impairment in social relations, absense of illusions, delusions, hallucinations and incoherence.

Psychophysiological Disturbance

These disorders result in physical malfunctioning but without any anxiety. These children have severe eczema, asthma without emotional overlay. They also exhibit anorexia nervoa, persistent loss of appetite, and are underweight. They have painful migraine. They mostly need medical treatment.

Psychoneuroses

In this type of disorder certain functions are distorted but the child is not isolated from reality. It is said that the psychoneurotic child builds castles in the air and the psychotic child lives in them. Many children are cautious, frightened and show uncontrollable crying etc. They have phobias, manias, panic syndrome, and conversion.

Personality Disorders

These children cannot adjust to society. They are extremely shy. They have delusions of persecutions and are rigid. They lack the resilience to develp better ways of meeting emotional problems or alternatively sometimes they appear as too outgoing. The second type feel no tension or anxiety.

Transient Situational Personality Disroder

These are acute reactions to catastrophnic or unpleasant incidents such as: death of a friend, rleative, accidents etc. These are situational and are responsible for chronic and acute personality disturbance.

Prevalence

In a survey conducted by the National Institute of Mental Health it has been observed that nearly 1.5% of population in the age group of 0-21 suffers from emotional disturbance.

Causes

Psychoanalytic

There are a variety of causes for emotional disturbance. Most of them are psychoanalytic and a few of them are explained by learning. The psychoanalytic causes include: anxiety as a source of emotional disturbance, distrust of adults because of traumatic experiences, frustration of libidinal desires, parental rejection, punishment, ridicule, and insecurity deprived from lack of affection or social prestige. Emotional disorders are explained by learning psychologists using conditioning. The same disorders are also reduced by counter conditioning or reconditioning.

Environmental

There is some evidence of mental illness occuring in particular families and behaviour characteristics of twins. Schizophrenia is one such example. On the other hand, modelling explains behaviour problems. The situation is more confusing than clear. Maternal malnutrition, anoxia, head injury as well as educational school related factors explain emotional disorders.

Among the family factors, Cullinan, Epstein, and Lloyd (1983) include (a) child's early separation from his parents due to desertion, death etc. (b) parent's conflict, divorce (c) parent hostility, abuse or neglect (d) parents who themselves may be incompetent or have behaviour problems.

Kauffman (1985) indicated six school related factors:

a. insensitivity by the school to the individual,
b. inappropriately high or low expectation for the student,
c. inconsistent behaviour management procedures,
d. meaningless or uninteresting materials and assignments,
e. reinforcement of inappropriate behaviour caused by teacher attention,
f. students modeling inappropriate behaviour.

Identification

How do we identify emotionally disturbed child? Generally the Illinois test of psycho-linguistic ability, measures of auditory closer, right left descrimination, eye hand coordination etc. tests are given. Much of the pathology of the emotionally disturbed child is due to the fact that these children cannot delay gratification and have poor pulse control and a disturbed time sense. They further manifest learning deficits on manageable behaviour, feeling of failure, diminished self-esteem and lack of communication with adults arising out of school failrue. These behaviour are manifested in the child's day to day environment. It is more important to know the way through which the emotionally disturbed children learn than what they learn. It has been found out that the emotionally disturbed children learn using an impulsive strategy or what other boys known as a rapid tempo with uncritical response. They are quite hyperactive and they have attention and motivational deficits rather than cognitive deficits.

The following behavioural characteristics are very effective in screening emotionally disturbed children.

- Needs an unusual amount of providing to get work completed.
- Is inattentive, indifferent, or apparently lasy.
- Exhibits nervous reactions such as nailbiting, sucking thumb or fingers, stuttering, extreme restlessness, muscle twitching, hair twisting, picking and scratching, deep and frequent sighing.
- Is actively excluded by most of the children wherever they get a chance.
- Failure in school for no apparent reason.
- Is absent from school frequently or dislikes scool intensity.
- Seems to be more unhappy than most of the children
- Achieves much less in school than his ability indicates he should.
- Jealous or over competitive.

Screening procedures can be moe intricate and perhaps more accurate by addition of teacher rating, peer rating, self-rating, using standardised personality tests and inventories. Three most widely used tests are: California Psychological Inventory. Very few tests are available for use at elementary level or when chidlren are quite young. However, children's Appreciation Test, Thematic Appreciation Test, WISC and Bender Gestalt Tests can be used quite effecively for identifying emotionally disturbed children.

Besides these, a few other tests are also in use of identification.

1. Revised Behaviour Problem Checklist from kindergarten age to grade VI with 89 items.
2. Burk's Behaviour Rating Scales with 110 items used from grade I to VIII.
3. Child Behaviour Checklist used from 4 years to 16 years.
4. Walker Problem Behaviour Identification Checklist 50 item and from preschool to grade six.
5. Personality inventory for children from 3 to 16 year olds 600 items broken down to 30 scales.
6. Rorschack Ink Blot Test.
7. Sentence Completion Test.

Behaviour assessment of children has been primarily based upon adult's judgement of children's behaviour not children's opinion of themselves or each other (peer rating). Adequate behavioural assessment of children must involve appraisal of the child's behaviour in more than one setting and requires evaluation or more than the social and emotional domains. Particularly for young children perceptual motor and language performance are more required to account for any behavioural deficit than intelligence. Hence,

1. Assessment of child's behaviour must be multifaceted and must be done in its own socio-interpersonal context.
2. It must have a social learning perspective i.e., how does the child function as a person rather than uncontrolled bits of information about a child's functioning.

There are norm referenced scale for assessing adequqncy of children's performance in some areas of functioning i.e., intelligence, language, perceptual-motor but in behavioural assessment norm referenced tests are not readily available and assessment is a matter of subjective clinical appraisal. Similarly reciprocal influence of environment, behaviour and the person variables is a matter of clinical judgement. However, some progress has been achieved in assessment of cognitive influences on behaviour. Neuro-psychological and neuro-physiological assessments are time consuming and usually do not reveal more information than standard psychological and behavioural assessment. Behaviour rating scales, checklists and interviews with parents and children are more meaningful accompanied by direct observation of behaviour.

After identifying the characteristics which would categoriese the child ED or not one must also examine a few questions. There are 14 different ways of classifying problem behaviours. These will enable us to know the ED children and use the data for referral. These are as follows:

	Criteria	*Normal*	*Problem*	*Referrable*
A.	*Intensity:*	Non-Disruptive:	Disruptive:	Extremely Disruptive:
	How disruptive of the child's other activities is the problem behaviour?	Behaviour does not intefere with the child's other activities.	Behaviour interfers with the child's other activities.	Behaviour completely disrupts child's other activities.
B.	*Appropriateness:* Is the behaviour a reasonable response to the situation?	Reasonable: Response is acceptable or expected for the situation.	Inappropriate: Response is undesirable for the situation.	Excessive: Response is out of proprotion to the situation.
C.	*Duration:*	Short-Lived:	Moderately Long:	Long-Lasting:
	How long does the behaviour episode last?	Episode lasts only a short time (short time within a class period).	Episode extends over a longer period (some carry over from one class to the next).	Episodes are long lasting (greater part of a day).

Criteria	*Normal*	*Problem*	*Referrable*
D. *Frequency:*	Inrequent:	Frequent:	Habitual:
How often does the behaviour occur?	Behaviour usually is not repeated (rarely repeated in a day: rarely repeated on other days).	Behaviour is repeated (may be repeated several times a day: may be repeated on several days).	Behaviour happens all the time (repeated on many days).
E. *Specifically/ Generally:*	*Occurs in Specific situation:*	*Occurs in Several situations:*	*Occurs in many situations:*
In how many types of situations does the behaviour occur?	Behaviour occurs in specific type of situation.	Behaviour occurs in more than one type of situation.	Behaviour occurs in many types of situation.
F. *Manageability:*	Easily Managed:	Difficult to manage:	Cannot be managea:
Howe easily does the behaviour respond to management effort.	Responds readily to management efforts.	Inconsistent or slow response to management efforts.	Does not respond to management efforts.
G. *Assessibility of Characteristics:*	Easily Assessed:	Difficulty to Assess:	Cannot to Assessed:
How easily can the circumstances that produced the behaviour be identified?	Easy to identify situation or condition producting behaviour.	Situation or condition producing behaviour difficult identify.	Cannot identify situation or condition producing behaviour.
H. *Comparision with Maturity Level of Class:*	No Deivation from Level of Class:	Below Level of Class:	Considerably below level of class:
How close to the norm of the class is the problem behaviour?	Behaviour is par for the group.	Behaviour is below the group level.	Behaviour is considerably below the group.
I. *Number of Problem behaviour exhibited.*	Rarely more than one.	Usually more than one.	Usually many and varied.
J. *Acceptance by Peers:*	Accepted:	Had Difficulty Gettng Along:	Not Accepted:
Does the child have difficulty being accepted by peers?	Is accepted by peers?	May have difficulty with particualr individuals.	Unaccepted by group.

	Criteria	*Normal*	*Problem*	*Referrable*
K.	*Recovery Time:*	Rapid:	Slow:	Delayed:
	How quick is the situation leading to the episode forgotten?	Gets over episode quickly.	Gets over episode more slowly.	Does not get over episode.
L.	*Contagion:*			
	Does the behaviur disrupt the activities of others?	Little or no effect on others:	Considerable effect on others:	Excessive Effect on others:
	Do others copy the problem behaviour?	Behaviour does not disturb or does not serve as a model for others.	Behaviour disturbs immediate neighbours or neighbours copy behaviour.	Behaviour disturbs whole class or whole class copies behaviour.
M.	*Degree of contact with reality:*	No foncusion between Real/Unreal:	Some confusion between real/unreal:	Confuses real/unreal:
	Does the behaviour represent a loss of contact with reality?			
N.	*Response to Learning Opportunities:* How readily does the child respond when learning opportunities are provided?	Responds positively to Enrichment/Remedial work.	Responds slowly or weakly to Enrichment/Remedial work.	Does not Respond to Enrichment/Remedial work.

Characteristics

Emotionally disturbed children are often seen as unpredictable that present serious problems. Emotionally disturbed children in contrast to the normal group have no close emotional proximity with their parents.

Failure in school is often thought to be a symptom of neurotic behaviour. Further, the self of the disturbed child is invariably negative. When self-evaluation questionnaires are given to emotionally disturbed children, they saw themselves as less likeable, and less able to arouse affection in others. They are either psychotic or emotionally indifferent. For this reason, quite a few programmes have been designed on classroom organisational pattern so that these children can function to their maximum but the research evidence on the learning characteristics of the emotionally disturbed children show lack of interest in academic matter and school performance, lower I.Q. and achievement.

Their reading and mathematics achievement are significantly below the average. The majority of the studies demonstrate however, that emotionally disturbed children as a group have little less than average intelligence. But primarily their personality and behavioural traits contribute maximum to discrepant achievement in reading and arithmatic achievement.

The emotionally disturbed children lack most of these attributes, such as:

- Ability to handle anxiety,
- Feeling of self work,
- Conformity to demands,
- Peer acceptance,
- Less conflict over independence,
- Engagement in activity of academic nature,
- Setting of realistic goal.

In fact, we sometimes overlook the emotional disturbance of gifted children or very bright children whereas we become we become more concerned about the learning disabled child who has emotional problems.

Studies on the learning of emotionally disturbed children further show that these children are resistant to remedial effect because of the extreme defensive nature. One of the consistent findings that has come up both from descriptive and survey studies is the progressive decline in reading and arithmatic achievement as children identified as emotionally disturbed progress through the grades. This also contributes to diminished feelings of self-regards as children progressed in school. In one of the studies at the university of California, Bower and his associates showed that the difference between emotionally disturbed and normal children is more between grade IV and VI. In another study by Feldhusen and associates (1967) it was found that the emotionally disturbed child is aggressive, destructive and also far behind in reading and arithmatic achievement specially before grade III. This is why attempts are made to group emotionally disturbed children into different categories such as schizoid, character disorder, borderline and psychosomatic complaints. Similarly these children have reading skill deficiency, deficiency in word recognition, perceptual deficiency, visual deficiency memory and hyperactivity. All these characteristics are responsible for problem behaviour.

In the area of academics, most students with emotional or behavioural problems have considerable difficulty. Kauffmann, Cullinan and Epstein (1987) found that academic deficits specifically reading were related to the students aggression, defiance, and violation of the social rules.

The authors also identified several characteristics that are seen in behaviour disordered students.

- Disrupts other children
- Is compulsive
- Does not compete the required task

- Is destructive to own and other's belongings
- Does not follow commands
- Is undependable
- Exhibits inappropriate behaviour
- Is unhappy or depressed
- Exhibits poor interpersonal relationships.

Mattison, Humphrey, Kales, and Wallace (1985) also noted the characteristics of behaviour disorders which are conduct disorders than anxiety, or withdrawal. However, anxiety disorder, avoidance behaviour, separation anxiety, overanxiety, withdrawal, depression are typical behaviour emotional problems.

They have slightly leas than average intelligence. Kauffman (1985) and Kauffman, Cullinan and Epstein (1987) found intelligence of emotionally disturbed children to be less than average or low average i.e., around 90 IQ, varying from 60 to 130 IQ.

Educational Provisions and Treatment

There are various methods of treating emotionally disturbed children. Emotional catharsis is a psychotherapeutic technique which is used quite often. In this technique the causes are known, these are released through expression and acceptance and the symptoms are extinguished. The other technique is interference through counter-conditioning, deconditioning, decensitization, etc. The latter method emphasises positive growth and relearning rather than the more extinction of pathological behaviour. The Rogerian method of non-directive counselling is very fruitful in such problem situations.

The educational programmes should be planned quite cautiously for these children. It may be of three different types:

a. Day schools which are exclusive for these children.
b. Special class in regular school for emotional disturbed.
c. Integrated setting or school for emotionally disturbed.

A few ideas are of great use in making educational provisions for the emotionally disturbed children.

1. Structuring limits in the classroom receives first priority. The classroom atmosphere should be more than negative restrictions. The classroom atmosphere must give support and direction to activities. Out of emotional chaos order will emerge among these children.
2. There is no value in concluding that emotionally disturbed children are educationally retarded. Subject matter itself should convey appropriate information for social and academic learning. These children should be given selected readings on social learning.
3. Group dynamic principles may be used for disturbed children e.g., seating arrangements, position of teachers, and pupils can be designed to encourage desired interactions between teachers and pupils, and among pupils.

4. Directed group activity can be used. This will break inhibitions. Role playing is also another technique for release of emotional problems.
5. Involve the child in work as soon as he reaches the school or when he is at home in any work. This way he will not get time for 'horse play' or day dreaming.
6. Offer support and reward when tey do good work; never attack the child as a person; focus correction on actual task and keep relationship task centred.
7. As the child increases in responsibility and self direction, plan for more long range activities but with manageable steps.

Emotional disturbances are just like any other problem. These are not unsurmountable. Parents and teachers can help the child reach firm strong, and self directing decisions. These decisions are merely a few suggestions.

Integration or Mainstreaming the Emotionally Disturbed Children

The council for exceptional children in U.S.A. has recently published in a statement, highlighting the major intentions of mainstreaming/integration.

1. Providing the most appropriate education for each child in the least restrictive setting.
2. Looking at the educational needs of children instead of clinical or diagnostic levels.
3. Looking for an creating alternatives that will help general educators serve children with learning or adjustment problems with regualr setting.
4. Utilising the skills of general and special education so that all children may have equal educational opportunity.

However, the recent researches show quite disappointing consequences although the normal children in the classroom do respond quite favourably to the emotionally disturbed children. But the success of the programme depends more on facilitating different types of children. There are various interventions which aim at reducing emotional problems combining educational and psychological developments of child at appropriate stage of development. But unfortunately group treatment of these cases have not been very rewarding.

Teaching emotionally disturbed child is a challenge. There are several approaches. The Psycho-educational approach emphasize:

1. Children should develop autonomy and a positive self-image.
2. Each student has unique perception about environment and what is being taught.
3. The inner workings of children minds and the forces of mental and physical development may encourage or deter their education.

The ecological approach considers the environment as problem rather than the child. Problems among children arise because of imbalances in the social systems. Parental conflicts, community disruptions may be reflected in criminal activity. Children behaviours are not disturbed it is more a reflection of a conflict between the individual and ecosystem in which he or she lives. Unless the ecosystem is changed improvement in behaviour will not take place. Of course it requires simultaneous adaptation i.e., the child and environment and not necessarily the child and the school.

The behaviourist accepts that behaviour is learned and it can be treated following learning principles. There is a need for over-all social change in society than mere change in the individual.

The neuropsycho-pharmacological theory assumes use of medications to treat behavioural and emotional problems. But isolated use of medication is not enough. These do not increase student achievement or relationship with peers. Drugs can radically alter behaviour but they do not teach and therefore should be accompanied by interventions.

Role of Special/Resource Teacher

Kauffmann (1985) stressed that "the teahcer must ultimately focus on those factors that can be changed. Teachers should believe that proper classroom environment alone can make a difference in the child's life even if nothing else can be altered and hope that more than classroom can be changed".

The resource/special teacher will need regualr preservice and inservice training to be capable of meeting the needs of the studnets with behavioural and emotional problems. What they should and when?

Behaviour Development Strategies

1. Drain-off of frustration acidity: When frustrations pile up to the point that the student can not continue in a pleasurable activity, sympathetic communication by the teacher may "drain off" a surplus of the hostility-laden emotion.
2. Support for panic, fury, and guilt: When a student is overwhelmed by panic, fury, guilt and other emotions, adults must stay with him or her, provide ego support during the incident, and assist him or her in putting the situation back into perspective.
3. Communication maintenance in moments of relationship decay: When a student is so overwhelmed by frustration that he or she is likely to become uncommnicative and possible enter an autistic state of fantasy, the teacher needs to arouse any and all links possible keep communication flowing.
4. Regulation of behavioural and social trafic: When a student fails to remember the relevant of a social rule or custom, a teacher needs to remind him or her of the basic social conventions, without moralizing.
5. Umpire services: When a student experiences inner conflict over choices or right and wrong or external conflict with peers, a teacher must be

ready to assist decision making or even make decisions that prmote a "hygienic" (emotionally healthy) situation.

Clinical exploitation of life events

1. Reality rub-in: Making the student cognizant of the actual events that occurred.
2. Symptom estrangement: Getting the student to recognize that many of his symptoms are not worth the trouble and need to be let go.
3. Massaging numb value areas: Appealing to potential values (e.g., fairness) held by the student or peer group.
4. New-tool salesmanship: Fostering through words or actions the adoption of a wider range of behavioural reactions to stress than the child currently possesses.
5. Manipulation of the boundaries of the self: Helping the student to feel greater self-worn and broadenig his psychological boundaries to include a sense of affiliation with peer, adults or the setting.

Cognitive Behaviour Strategies

The third approach is cognitive behaviour strategies meant for reducing emotional problems. The teacher models for the student desirable behaviour e.g., I am now going to do math addition aloud and the student models it by self instruction. Impulsivity is reducted by ignoring it and rewarding the alternative reflectively; use clear and definite rules to reduce uncertainity, and setting a time limit for a given behaviour to occur. If such strategies are not useful than self instructional strategies are required to be followed by the child.

The child may be taught how to develop self-instruction to increase attention, reflection, social and academic skills. It enables to self regulation and control. Children can be taught to monitor their own behaviour and performance.

Remediation and tutoring techniques can improve academic achievement. Academic tutoring must aim at (a) support and strengthen academic learned, (b) assist the regular teacher to provide appropriate program for the mainstreamed learner, (c) support the goals of regualr education.

Affective skills can be developed through sociodrama, role playing, play, social learning as a part of normal daily routine. Social learning approach can be followed (Kauffman, 1985) to teach the social and effective skills.

Curriculum for behavioural or emotional problems generally encompass academic skills, community link skills, career/vocational skills, and socially affective skills. The specific topics would include: self control, sex education, drug education, getting along with others. Walker, Mc Connel, Holmes, Todis, Walker and Golden (1983) have developed a curriculum for children's peer and Teacher Skills. Skills treaming the child studying in elementary school has been developed by Mc Ginnis and Goldstein, (1984).

Cognitive Styles Approach

It may be a worthwhile stage to combine the perceptual ability of such children with their learning ability because such children show impulsive behaviour which is not conducive to learning. Attempt to make them more reflective and less hyperactive. Secondly, they should have less anxiety and trauma in dealing with a particular learning situation. It has been suggested that a changed model to be applied for emotionally disturbed to learn and adjust in a better way. By a changed model it is meant a set of logically derived statements of the "if and then" variety which are conditional upon the development stage of the person with whom one is working. Thus, if we know the present stage or conceptual level then we can derive the specific environment most likely to produce progress for the person. The issue is not which environment is best but rather which environment is most likely to produce a desired effect for a specified person or persons that educational environent such highly organised or completely free classrooms are differentially effective with students of varying personality or abilities, is widely recognised. The attempt here is to coordinate and match the environment and person most effectively by use of a theoretical model.

Stage	*Characteristics*	*Optimal environments*
Initial stage	Impulsive, poorly socialised, egocentric and inattentive.	Accepting but firm, clearly consistent with minimum of alternatives.
Moderately disturbed	Complaint, dependent on authority, concerned with rules.	Encouraging independence with normative structure.
Severe stage.	Independent, questioning and self-assertive.	Environment highly autonomous with numerous alternatives and low normatives.

This above model is meant to provide specific environment to deal with specific characteristics of emtionally disturbed child in the normal classroom. Many of the problems of learning of emotional disorders can be reduced by following the procedures outlined here. The frequency, persistence, and intensity of behaviour must be taken into account.

The Role of Regular Class Teacher

The teacher can use classroom management techniques consistently. He should be conversant and trained in behaviour modification techniques.

1. Positively reinforce desired behaviour among ED children. The reward may be tangible, social, immediate or delayed.
2. Do not positively reinforce undesirable behaviour (i.e., giving attention to misbehaviour).

3. Use negative reinforcement only, sparingly to eliminate or extinguish behaviour which is undesirable.
4. Use token reinforcement to decrease disruptive behaviour increase on task and academic behaviour. The student improves.
5. use contingency-contract i.e., agreement in writing that specifies the desired behaviour.
6. Use Premack Principle, i.e., students with ED might get an extra minute to complete the assignments in time. The procedure may be used to increase the strength, frequency and duration of the less prefered responses.
7. Use differential reinforcement to reduce maladaptive behaviour. Rewards desirable and do not reward undesirable behaviours.
8. Ignore disruptive behaviour, it will dissappear.
9. Do not use punishment as it has adverse side effects. This is the bast behaviour modification techniques.
10. Use 'Time out' procedure wherever required to eliminate behaviour while doing so the teacher must ensure that learning environment is rewrding time out refers to contigent removal of the student from a positively reinforcing environment for some predetermined amount of time.
11. Response cost is another token economy. If the response cost is clearly defined and understood the teacher may take back the token for misbehaviour (withdrawal of positive reinforcement) which will decrease disturbing behaviours.

Highlights of the Chapter

Emotionally disturbed children have been viewed differently by teachers, peer groups and parents. The term refers to behaviour disorders that cannot be explained by intellectual, sensory or health factors, but are associated with unsatisfactory interpersonal relationships, inappropriate feelings, depression which is not self-rewarding and is not acceptable to others. These problems range from autisim to psychosis, childhood schizophrenia, psychonurosis and personality disorders. Nearly 1.5 per cent people in the CA 0-21 suffer from ED.

The causes of ED can be traced to Psychoanalytic (anxiety, trauma, distrust, frustration, rejection), environmental (mental illness, maternal malnutrition, anoxia, head injury, separation from parents, parental conflicts, divorce, abuse or neglect), and school related factors (low/high expectations from the student, inconsistent behaviour management, meaningless assignment, reinforcement of inappropriate behaviour).

There are certain behavioural signs (inattentiveness, nervous reactions, failure in school, jealousy and tests to identify ED (teacher rating, peer rating, self-rating, CPI, TAT, CAT, WISC, Bender Gestalt etc.) on the basis of which ED children are categorised as normal, problematic, or referrable.

Emotionally disturbed children have no relationship with their parents and have negative self concepts. They lack feeling of self work, conformity to demands, setting of realistic goals, ability to handle anxiety, are very withdrawn.

Educational provisions consist of using psychological techniques e.g., behaviour modification, modelling, counter conditioning, deconditioning, desensitization, non directive counselling, and emphasizing structuring of classroom atmosphere, use of selected rading materials, group dynamic procedures, directed group activity, supporting self directed activities and recording positive behaviours. Integrated education has been the strategic provision made for these children.

Teaching emotionally disturbed children is a challenge. The special and regular teachers have to be thoroughly acquainted with behaviour development strategies: drain off, support, communication maintenance, clinical exploitation of life events, cognitive behaviour strategies, and use of cognitive style approoaches for effective information processing.

The regular classroom teacher in addition, has to be acquainted with various reinforcement techniques: positive reinforcement, negative reinforcement, differential reinforcement, contingency contract, Premack principle, time out and response cost procedures in handling the ED children.

Review Questions

1. Who is an emotionally disturbed child? What are his characteristics?
2. What are the procedures for identifying an emotionally disturbed child?
3. How would you control emotional disorders among children?
4. What are the different categogires of emotional disturbance?
5. What are the causes of emotional disorders?
6. State the educational programmes and treatment for emotionally disturbed children.
7. Write notes on:
   Psychosis Psycho-neurosis
   Autism
8. How can the emotionally disturbed child be mainstreamed or integrated in the regular school?
9. What are some of the essentials of teaching emotionally disturbed?
10. Discuss the role of the resource teacher in handling the ED children.
11. Discuss the role of the regular teacher in handling the ED children in an integrated setting.

References

Cullinan, D., Epstein, M. and LLyod, J., (1983), *Behavioural disorders of children and adolescents,* Englewood Cliffs, NJ, Prentice Hall.

Feldhussen, J.F. and Treffinger, D.J., (1967), *Teaching Creative Thinking and Problem Solving,* Iowa, Kendeu.

Kanner, L., (1943), *Autistic disturbance of affective contact, Nervous child,* 2, 217-250.

Kauffman, J.M., (1977), *Characteristics of children behaviour disorders,* Columbus, Ohio: Charles Merril.

Kauffman, J.M., (1985), *Characteristics of children's behaviour disorders,* (ed ed.), Englewood Cliffs, NJ: Prentice Hall.

Kauffman, J.M., Cullinan, D. and Epstein, M., (1987), "Characteristics of students placed in special programme for the serious emotionally disturbed", *Behavioural Disorders,* 12, 175-184.

Mattison, R.; Humphrey, F.; Kales, S. and Wallace, D., (1986), "An objective evaluation of special class placement of elementary school boys with behaviour problems", *Journal of Abnormal Child Psychology,* 14, 251-262.

McGinnins, E. and Goldstein, A - (1984) - Skills treaming the elementary school, child. Champaign, Illinoi, Research Press.

Phillips, E.I., (1967), "Problems in educating emotionally disturbed children", in N.G. Harring and R.L. Schienfelbash (eds.), *Methods in special education,* New York: Mc Grand Hill.

Rutter, M., (1978), "Diagnosis and definition", in M. Rutter and E. Schopler (eds.), *Autism: A reappraisal of concepts and treatments,* N.Y.: Plenum Press.

Walker, H. M., McConnel, S.R., Holnes, D., Todis, B., Walker, J., and Golden, N. (1983) The Walker Social Skills curriculum : The ACCEPTS Programme. Texas : Austin.

Chapter 8

Learning Disabled Children

Some children who in most ways seem normal, have difficulty in learning or remembering. They have difficulty in educational performance: copying, writing, listening, understanding, number speech and communication. In the present chapter their problems are discussed with a view to providing an indepth knowledge of:

- the concept of learning disability and its meaning,
- the causes of learning disability,
- the identification procedures,
- the characteristics,
- the general teaching principles,
- the specifics of handwriting, writing spelling, reading, arithmatics, motor ability etc.
- the role of special/resource teacher, and
- the role of a regular classroom teacher.

Who is a Learning Disabled Child?

The enigma of the youngster who has difficulty in learning is not new. But the concept of learning disability has a brief and turbulent history. Some children are quite normal and yet at all times display learning problems. They write 'deb' for 'bed', 'was' for 'saw' and cannot concentrate if there is background noise. The National Advisory Committee on Handicapped Children (USA) defined learning disability as follows (1986):

"LD children exhibit disorder in one or more basic psychological processes involved in understanding and in using spoken or written languages. The disorders are manifested in listening, thinking, talking, reading, writing, spelling, and arithmetic. They include conditions which are referred to as perceptual problems, brain injury, minimal brain dynfunction, dyslexia, developmental aphasia etc. They do not include learning problems which are primarily due to visual, hearing, or motor handicaps, mental retardation, emotional disturbance, or the environmental disadvantage".

Learning disability is an interdisciplinary field and the above definition of learning disabled children was acceptable to professionals.

However, there has been a movement over the last decade to change the definition of learning disability. Another definition was proposed by the National Joint Committee for Learning Disabilities (NJCLD): Hammill, Leigh, Mc Natt, and Larsen, 1981). In 1985, the Federal Inter agency Committee on Learning Disability modified the NJCLD concept and restated the concept as follows:

"Learning disabilities is a generic term that refers to a heterogeneous group of disorders manifested by significant difficulties in the acquisition and use of listening, speaking, reading, writing, reasoning, or mathemetical abilities or of social skills. These disorders are intrinsic to the individual and presumed to be due to central nervous system dysfunction. Even though a learning disability may occur concomittantly with other handicapping conditions or socio-environmental influences and especially with attention deficit disorders, all of which may cause learning problems, a learning disability is not the direct result of those conditions or influences". (Lerner, 1985).

The two definitions are fairly similar. It is safe to assume that a learning disability may or may not be caused by central nervous system dysfunction. The learing disabled have significant problems in learning academic skills that are not due to other handicapping conditions. Many students with LD have a lower than average IQ, many also have high IQ and sometimes reach the gifted range.

Originally children whose achievement was far below the capability were categorised under brain injured children, suffering from neurophrenia, minimal brain dysfunction. It was for the first time that Kirk in 1963 suggested the word "learning disabilities" to describe all the child's behavioural symptoms that arise from dysfunction of the central processing mechanisms. This term described a group of children who had disorders in the development of language, speech, reading and associated communication skills needed for social interaction. Children with sensory and/emotional handicap are exclused from this category.

Prevalence

A more conservative estimate has been made by the National Advisory Committee on Handicapped children. It reports that two to three per cent of the school population are learning disabled. In India one does not have accurate estimates but it may not be far away from the world estimate.

Causes

The causes of learning disability could be organised under organic, environmental and genetic.

Organic

LD arises because of Minimal Brain Dysfunction (MBD). The dysfunction occurs in central nervous system which consists of the brain and the spinal cord.

The malfunctioning is not due to damage, but due to dysfunction which is only minimal. Minimal brain dysfunction arises due to (a) cerebral hemorrhage, cerebral disease because of high fever, head injury, (b) intrauterine environment-premature birth, anoxia, physical trauma, (c) constitutional-genetic-neurochemical dysfunction. It must be noted that all brain dysfunctions are not associated with learning disability and all types of learning disability do not arise due to brain dysfunction.

Hypoglycemia or low blood sugar is a cause of learning problem. Any factor that can cause neurological damage can cause learning problems.

Genetic

Learning problems and hyperactivity run in families. Nearly 20% of hyperactive children had one parent hyperactive. Children with Turner's syndrome have higher incidence of learning disabilities.

Environmental

Maternal factos known to have a negative effect include the use of drugs, the consumption of alcohol and contraction of rubella. Complications during pregnancy such as anoxia (loss of Oxygen), birth injury causing brain damage, and children who received neonatal intensive care subsequently become LD. Learning disability may be caused due to insufficient early experience and stimulation. It is also caused by poor or inadequate instruction.

Identification

Individuals are assessd usually as learning disabled after they start having problems in school. A variety of tests are administered even after certain tell-tale signs. The three indicators of LD have to be identified:

a. Discrepancy between ability and achievement.
b. Low achievement.
c. Scattered assessment profile indicating variable performance in different areas.

There are certain behavioural indices of learning disabilities in children:

- Near average, average or above average in intellectual ability.
- Impulsive behaviour in talk and action.
- Inability to focus on one activity.
- Easily distractible.
- Inability to shift from one activity to another.
- Easy onset of fatigue.
- Wrong or inappropriate perception.
- Reversal in writing and reading and transposition.
- Problems of left and right, up and down orientation.
- Difficulty in understanding and remembering oral message.

- Difficulty in interpretation and remembering visual image.
- Language and organisation difficulties.
- Trial and error approach to work.
- Thinking problem relation to abstract ideas and concept.
- Poor fine motor coordination.
- Clumsiness in thinking.
- Hyperactivity (easily stimulated).
- Hypoactivity (late action with much stimulation).
- Omits, adds, substracts, reverses letters in words.
- Skips line while reading.
- Dos not build letters B-A-T not BAT.
- Unable to follow verbal direction.
- Reverses numbers 6, 9; 36, 63; 14, 41.
- Gets confused with arithmetic signs >, <, –, + ...
- Does not know carry over.
- Get easily disturbed.
- Appears to be moddy.
- Appears to be forgetful.

Early identification of such difficulties are important even from pre-school period so that remedial education can be provided. In fact, the sooner the high risk children are recognised the greater is the chance of prevention failure.

Testing

Assessment of pre-school level children can be made as per DIAL model (Developmental Indicators for the Assessment of Learning). It is meant for 2 1/2 to 5 1/2 year old in the areas of sensory, motor, affective, social, conceptual, language communication in less than 30 minutes. The tests consists of visual and auditory activity, gross motor movements, fine motor movements, finger agility, anxiety, task attention, focus and persistence, social skills, identifying objects, colours, sorting, receiving and expressing language, articulation etc.

Besides the DIAL, there are PPVT, Bohem Test of Basic Concepts, and Early Detection Inventory. The facts remain that children face school failure because their learning difficulties are not detected at preschool age or if at all detected not treated well on time.

At the elementary and secondary level identifications of learning disabilities become relatively easier because availability of instruments, teacher observations and achievement index. Each learning disabled child undergoes neurological examinations, Reading tests, Visual-motor Gestalt tests requiring them to copy various geometric forms, awarness of one's body parts (Draw a Man Test). Gross-motor tests, Fine-motor tests, hyper kinesis, reading problems, otological findings (hearing sounds) and bio-chemical screening. These medical characteristics are necessary to deal with learning disabled children besides intellectual and achievement scores.

This stage of the school evaluation would consist of:

a. Development disabilities.
b. Discrepancy between ability and achievement.
c. Process of child's learning.
d. Analyse why he does not learn by case history, informal test observation standardised test.
e. Psychological test findings.
f. Case history relating to health, development, present activities identifying information, birth history, physical and developmental data, special and emotional factors, educational factors adjustments.
g. Teacher's rating on auditory comprehension, spoken language orientation, behaviour, motor.
h. Spelling errors, informal arithmatic tests, reading tests, graded word recognition test.

The following tests are commonly used in diagnosis of LD.

a. Information reading Inventory—It measures quickly reading skills, reading levels, types of errors, unknown words, related behavioural characteristics.
b. Informal Graded Word—Recognition Test. It measures quickly reading level and errors.
c. Informal Arithmetic Test.
d. Wechsler-Intelligence Scale for Children (Revised).
e. Stanford-Binet Intelligence Scale.
f. Peabody Picture Vocabulary Test.
g. Illinois test of Psychologistic Abilities.
h. Lincoln Oseretsky Motor Development Scale.
i. Vineland Social Maturity Scale.
j. Kauffman Assessment Battery for children.
k. Kauffman Test of Educational Assessment.
l. Wide Range Achievement Test.

The language processing, perceptual processing, and cognitive processing are measured by using Detroit Test of Learning Aptitude.

This test consists of:

Word opposites	—	Vocabulary
Sentence Imitation	—	Repeat sentence
Word sequences	—	STM and attention
Oral Direction	—	Follow complex direction
Story construction	—	Verbal skills
Design Reproduction	—	Drwing geometic figures from memory
Object sequence	—	Primary visual memory
Conceptual matching	—	Relationship between objects
Symbolic relation	—	Problem solving and reasoning

Word Fragment	—	Recognise Parental presented words
Letter sequences	—	Visual memory and attention.

Most definition of LD involve some kind of achievement discripancy model.

Characteristics

There have been many attempts to categories the major characteristics of learning disabled children. One of the earliest attempt was made by Clements (1966) through a Task Force on LD. They observed 10 most general characteristics based on the assumption that L.D. is a neurological impairment:

- Hyperactivity,
- perceptual motor impairments,
- emotional lability,
- general coordination deficits,
- disorders of attention,
- impulsvity,
- disorders in memory and thinking,
- specific learning disability,
- disorders in speech and learning, and
- equivocal neurological signs.

Not all LD children dispaly all these characteristics.

Language

LD children have difficulty both in expressive and receptive language, and relatively more in case of the former. LD children do not have so much of phonological or articulation problems but do show problem in sentence formation i.e., syntax. They do show difficulty in comprehension of meaning and use of pronouns. They have difficulties in understanding and using passive tense, negatives, contractions and past tense, adjectives and adverbs. They fail to maintain conversation and can not argue or ask appropriate questions. So far as written language is concerned they do problems in handwriting, spelling and punctuation. LD children have more of spelling errors than their non-learning disabled peers even when IQ were controlled.

1. They have poor receptive-auditory ability (poor understanding of spoken symbols, requests for repetition, echolaliac confection of directions and commands).
2. They exhibit receptive-visual difficulty (subvocalise reading, read without understanding).
3. They have poor expressive-vocal ability (disorganised thought, inadequate syntax, and dearth of ideas for expression).
4. They manifest expressive-motor difficulties (spelling disorders, drawing disorders, omission and reversal of letters, omission of whole words).

Perceptual and Motor Ability

Lerner (1985) demonstrated that LD children display problems in spatial relations, visual discrimination, figure and ground discrimination, of similarities and differences, auditory sequencing auditory blending and auditory memory. Lerner (1985) further stated that LD children do display haptic and movement as well as have defects in social perception.

They do show problems in gross and fine motor skills (balance, laterality, directionality) and body image and imageness. They can not copy a geometric figure i.e., have visual-motor disintegration.

1. They are unable to identify, discriminate and interpret sensation.
2. They have poor visual decoding (unable to reproduce geometric forms accurately, figure-ground configurations, letter reversals and totations).
3. They have poor auditory decoding (inability to recognise tunes, to differentiate between sounds).
4. They cannot identify familiar objects by touch alone (cutaneous misperceptions).
5. They have poor kinesthetic and vestibular perception (problems in coordination, movement, directionality, space orientation, and balance, difficulties in perception lead to difficulties in concept formation abstraction ability, cognitive ability, and language ability).

Motor Activity — These charactersitics vary according to type of motor activity. These are described below:

Hyperactivity — Constantly engaged in movement, unable to sit still, too much of talking in the class, very much inattentive.

Hypoactivity — (reverse of hyperactivity)—lethargic, quiet, passive.

Incoordination — Physical awkwardness, poor motor integration, poor activities in running, catching, skipping and jumping; walking is rigid and stiff; poor performance in writing, drawing; frequent falls, stubbing, and clumsy behaviour.

Preseveration — Involuntary countinuation of behaviour: this behaviour is witnessed in speaking, writing, drawing, pointing, and oral reading; incorrect spelling, repetition of errors.

Social and Emotional

They are more anxious and withdrawn, have more problems in interacting with teachers and parents, have behaviour problems and are less socially skilled. Many LD students had little insight into nature of their problems and attributed these to luck. They show lower self-concept, more external locus of control, and lower level of aspiration than non LD peers.

- They are quiet and obedient but daydream and cannot read.
- They have frequent temper outburts, sometimes for no apparent reason.
- They are nervous: attention is difficult to hold.

- They jump from one thing to another, and mind everyone's business but their own.
- They talk of self control but cannot work with other children.
- They are emotionally labile and unstable.

Emotional instability arises mainly due to prolonged dependency on the mother and lack of contact with the outside world which generates frustrations.

Attention Disorders

Attention problems go frequently hand in hand with learning disabilities. They have short attention span. Attentional problems are shown to affect student's test taking abilities becuase attend to inappropriate distracters.

1. They cannot sustain attention for the required amount of time.
2. They are unable to attend to the relevant and ignore the irrelevant. They may be attracted to every stimulus that surrounds him.
3. They can be diverted easily from one topic to another.
4. They put excessive attention to unimportant details while disregarding the essentials (attends to the page number than to the printed matter or the picture on the page.)

Memory

Many LD children are passive learners and do not use strategies (rehearsal, mneumonics cues)—(Hallahan et. al. 1985). These children are poor task planners and organisers. They display certain characteristics as regards remembering.

1. Disorder of memory involve difficulty in the assimilation, storage, and retrieval of information, and may be associated with visual auditory, or other learning processes.
2. The LD children have difficulties in reproducing rhythm patterns, sequence of digits, words, or phrases.
3. They have difficulty in revisualising letters, words or forms.
4. Both the short-term and the long-term memory of the LD child are poor.
5. They fail to see the relationship between his present and past experience.

Reading

Nearly 85 to 90 per cent of learning disabled children have reading problems and therefore, have poor academic achievement. These include mispronunciation, skipping, adding or substituting words (Hallahan, Kauffman and LLyod, 1985) as well as problem in memory, reversing letters or words and blending sounds together. They display both oral reading and comprehension problems (Hallahan et. al. 1985).

In case of learning disabled children one finds visual and auditory spellers. The visual spellers write right letters in wrong orders—WTARE-Water. The auditory spellers try to sound outwards: Posishun-Position. There are also omission errors or substitution errors. These defects continue to adolescence and are responsible for learning deficits.

Hyperactivity

Hyperactivity, is used interchangeably with attention deficit disorder (ADD). Hyperactivity is more of a cognitive than a motoric problem. The American Psychiatric Association relabeled this syndrome as attention deficit disorder (ADD). ADD refers to those related behavioural syndromes that are characterized by (1) developmentally inappropirate inattention (failure to complete activities, distractibility, difficulty in concentrating on taks and sticking to play, and the appearance of not listening); (2) impulsivity (difficulty with organizing and with waiting for turns, shifting from activity to activity, acting before thinking, calling out in class, and needing much supervision); (3) and hyperactivity (excessive running, climbing, and moving, awake and asleep, difficulty in staying still and staying seated, fidgeting).

Onset of the disorder must be prior to the age of 7 with a duration of at least 6 months, and without evidence of severe or profound mental retardation, affective disorder, or psychosis. Academic difficulties, conduct problems, low self-esteem, immaturity, poor peer relationships and specific developmental disorders are frequently associated with the ADD syndrome.There may even be another type of attentional deficit characteristic of hyperactive children one involving selective attention. This deficit involves the tendency of a hyperactive child to have the attention captured by the salint aspects of situations to such an extent that the child fails to process more subtle aspects. Further more, hyperactive children may have a greater need for stimulation and may actually be stimulus seeking. Behavioural and cognitive aberrations in these children have their origins in deficits of sustained attention, poor inhibitory control, and faulty modulation of the arousel levels necessary for meetig task demands. This constellation of deficits has been described as an inability to stop, look, listen, and think.

ADD children do not develop intrinsic motivation. ADD youngsters perceive their world less carefully than do their normally developing peers, thereby placing limits on future learning. Available research points to a serious deficit in the higher order mental functioning of hyperactive children.

Prior to the current diagnostic label of attention deficit disorder this syndrome was frequently referred to as minimal brain dysfunction. Recently, it has been called hyperkinetic reaction of childhood. Unfortunately, until recently, our knowledge of hyperactivity was largely based on clinical myth rather than on empirical reality. For example, numerous investigations have pointed out that the majority of children having received such labels do not have demonstrable brain damage and in fact fail to evidence subtle neurological signs. Further, there has been no real validation of a single syndrome that groups neurological academic, and behavioural characteristics or that shares a common etiology, treatment course, or prognosis.

Many treatment approaches have been systematically investigated for use with hyperactive children, but stimulant medication remains the best documented therapy in child psychiatry. Specifying target behaviours for successful drug therapy in these children is critical, and the special education teacher may prove helpful to the practicing physician in documenting behavioural changes in the classroom so as to determine response to pharmacotherapy. Parent ratings of children's behaviour in determining efficiency to stimulant medication may also prove useful.

Educational Provisions

The educational provisions for learning disabled children primarily consist of three types.

1. Day school—where the learning disabled chidlren receive specialised schooling using special teachers essentially on the same curriculum but with greater care and pace. This is a segregated setting.
2. Special class in a Regular School: where LD children are given special isntruction in a self contained classroom by special teacher as well as regular classroom teacher do assist in teaching subject matters. These children receive instruction on academic in these classes but for social activities etc. they are with general students.
3. Since their number is large, and they do not pose organic problems or problems of low IQ, these children are integrated in the regular classroom with resource room facilities (mainstreaming/integration).

General Instructional Techniques

Inspite of differential differential educational provisions there are certain general techniques of instruction. The following instructional techniques have been used and recommended for use with LD chidlren.

1. Use short, brief directions, large print.
2. Use consistent language, colour cues.
3. Write directions or steps on the chalkboard i.e., underline important words etc.
4. Alternate the use of colours for each step in a series on directions.
5. Increase sound level of instruction.
6. Use diagrams or pictorial illustrations.
7. Use an overview of the lesson, ask questions, ask them to read the material, recite and review.

Since LD children lack structure and organisation, they have to be told to, keep daily engaged in the activities; list all future events that need to be scheduled. Provide a hypothetical list to suggest possible events; and plan future events that must be planned, it is time to develop a weekly schedule. Pupils in the upper grades may find useful a schedule that provides for specific subject matter assignments on various types of activities.

Thinking skills can be developed by guiding students collect data by reading, listening, and observing; and discriminate differences on similarities in the data. Teacher questioning can be used to prod the pupil until the ability to make these discriminations improves. Ask the pupil categories and classify the data. Labelling is important during this stage.

Have the pupil recategorise and classify the data in other ways. This continuous reorganisation and restructuring is necessary to integrate new information and new experiences into the pupil's mental structures. Have the pupil make predictions based on the data. Have the pupil generate alternative predictions using the same data. Have the pupil evaluate the alternative predictions by comparing and contrasting possible outcomes and their effects.

Memory ability can be improved by using certain specific techniques, visual and auditory messages can be recalled. Facial expressions indicative of certain materials can be retrieved. Cramming is to be avoided. Certain activities can be practiced to improve auditory, visual memories.

1. Have pupils repeat telephone numbers and street address of emergency service facilities (police, fire, etc.).
2. Have pupils learn songs by listening to the words and tunes.
3. Play games in which the first pupils makes a statement, the next pupil repeats that and adds a statement, the third pupil repeats those statements and adds one, and so on.
4. Have pupils make up rhymes related to subject matter, such as, "In 1492 Columbus sailed the ocean blue".
5. Have pupils repeat oral directions.
6. Have pupils resequence cartoon strips (without words) that have been cut apart. This forces them to observe details in the pictures.
7. Have pupils describe configurations of words that are similar.
8. Have pupils repeat the sequence for a recipe that they have read.
9. Have the pupil practice attending to larger units at one time. For instance, some try to copy one syllable at a time. Encourage the pupil to increase the length of the visual stimulus that she holds in her mind as she write it down.
10. Help the pupil to practice internal auditorisation as an adjunct to visual memory; that is, have the pupil say the letters or words to hersefl while she is translating the written information.
11. Write every other item on the chalkboard with a different colour chalk. This helps the pupil to "find her place".
12. Allow the pupils to copy another pupil's work. Some of these pupils perform better with paper-to-paper copying.

Teachers must be flexible in their approach to teaching reading because of the heterogenous characteristics of learning disabled pupils. A diagnostic prescriptive approach must be used. The reading programme must be matched to pupil's need and abilties. There are several approaches having different degree of relevance.

The Basal reading approach is comprehensive, which uses controlled vocabulary in a sequential manner with adequate reinforcement. Diagnosis is done in course of teaching but it is not so advantegeous for LD children because of its rigidity, individualised nature and lack of provision for removing deficits.

Phonic approach has very limited use especially only for those who had good auditory capacity. Linguistic training also has limited use as it does not aid comprehension.

Language experience approach is most useful as it uses stories personal experiences, child's oral language, incorporates specific skill development, language art skills and makes use of visual motor abilities. Programme instruction is also another viable technique. The other approaches to reading uses multisensory approach and use of pictures. Both the methods have limitations. Because of complexities of both the reading process and learning disabilities, it is difficult to make definitive statements.

Teaching Approaches for the Learning Disabled Children

Teaching Approach	*Advantages*	*Disadvantages*
Asal	1. Comprehensive	1. Limited flexibility in teaching style.
	2. Controlled vocabulary	2. Individualized instruction not encouraged.
	3. Sequential introduction of skills.	3. Lack of depth of material necessary for skill mastery.
	4. Reinforcement of skills.	4. Lack of provision for processing deficits.
	5. Diagnostic and evaluative material usually provided.	5. No choice of analytic or synthetic phonics instruction.
		6. Subject to repetition of the same stories and methods resulting from failure.
Phonics	1. Effective decoding techniques for pupils with good auditory abilities.	1. Not effecive for pupils with auditory deficits.
		2. May be taught in isolation.
		3. Comprehension neglected.
		4. Invariance in English language may cause confusion.

Teaching Approach	*Advantages*	*Disadvantages*
Linguistic	1. Control for irregular spelling in initial stages. 2. Gradual introduction of phonics. 3. Extensive repetition.	1. Little emphasis on comprehension in initial stages. 2. Vocabulary controlled for regular elements and does not utilize spoken language of pupil.
Language Experience	1. Motivates with personal stories. 2. Uses pupil's oral language. 3. Can incorporate specific skill development. 4. Can include language art skills. 5. Good for pupils with good visual-motor abilities.	1. May be limited by pupils' language level. 2. Lacks structured systematic approach to skill development.
Progra-mmed Instruction Materials	1. Small, sequential steps. 2. Immediate feedback. 3. May be boring because of	1. Lacks direct instruction. 2. May be confusing format. consistency.
Multisen-sory	1. Uses more than one sensory input to get message to the brain. 2. Can use an analystic approach or a synthetic approach.	1. Lack of sequential skill development in some programms. 2. Sensory overload experienced by some pupils.
Rebus picture	1. Uses a rebus (picture) instead of a word to simplify initial stages of reading. 2. Well structured materials. 3. Provides for transition to traditional print materials.	1. Format appearing immature for older pupils.

Handwriting

Poor handwriting in the learning disabled has been attributed to numerous causes: Poor fine motor control, poor visual discrimination and memory, spatial difficulties. Manipulative exercises canbe used to strengthen muscles: cutting, modling clay games. Chalkboard practice should precede pencil and paper writing. Proper position for writing habit to develop. Paper should not be placed at a slant for manuscript writing. The writing instrument is held between thumb and middle finger with index finger applying pressure. Graph paper is of valuable help to teach pupils with special difficulties. A creative teacher improves handwriting using certain techniques as detailed below:

In addition,

1. Tape alphabet forms to the floor. Have them reproduce the form with coloured chalk.
2. Have pupils use a stick and their bodies to form the letters.
3. Write each letter in a paper with red marker.
4. Have pupils form letters in wet fingerpaint.
5. Use coloured directional cues such as green arrows and red dots.
6. Teach manuscript letter forms that are oval and slanted slightly. This will encourage left-to-right progression and will facilitate transition to cursive writing.
7. Teach pupils to start all lower-case cursive letters from the line.
8. Help pupils to form an association for a letter they have difficulty in remembering.
9. Have pupils orally describe their movements as the letter is being written. This provides auditory reinforcement.

The various approaches used in teaching by the resource teacher or specialist or classroom teacher have relative advantages and disadvantages.

Spelling

Spelling errors are quite common among learning disabled children. Therefore a systematic work-study technique is used in the following sequence.

"Look at the word—say the word—say the word—look at the word—cover the word—write the word—check your spelling—Repeat". Some of the remedial techniques involve—writing the word on the chalk and then trace it in fingers until it disappears tracing in sand, write the first letter of the word when one listens the word and them pronounce. Ask the children to spell the word properly and clap softly for each vowel sound, if possible by looking at the word.

Arithmetic

Ashlock (1972) made certain specific remedial instruction step for removing arithmetic errors of learning disabled children. Some of the steps are as follows:

Use manipulatives such as bottons and chips to teach number. Use visual material and give reinforcement. Use graph paper for alignment difficulties. Time line, coloured chalks, markings are helpful for attention to cues. A sample problem can be given for each assignment. The size of numbers can vary to indicate more or less. Reduce distractions as far as possible. Reduce number of examples in the assignment and eliminte copying. Use of display charts, abacus, playing cards, calculator, language master are quite useful.

Curricular Concerns

Learning disabled children read in the class as other children. Hence, certain extra care would benefit these pupils. These concerns may relate to four areas; such as:

Auditory Perception

1. Identify classmates from voice when one is blind.
2. Produce a speech sound and ask if they listen.
3. Ask whether pairs of words are same or different.
4. Start naming objects that starts with a particular sound.
5. Practice rhymes.
6. Ask them to repeat oral directions.
7. Tell a sequence of information to improve auditory memory.

Visual Perception

1. Match a geometric design.
2. Ask them to replicate a pattern.
3. Ask them to classify objects.
4. Match, sort and group word cards.
5. Start copying designs from simple to complex.
6. Tell a story with pictures. Then scramble the pictures and ask pupils to tell the story.
7. Recall letters speedily and find a series of letters in words.

Sensory Motor Development

1. Manipulation of object according to directions i.e., in front of, in the middle etc.
2. Use puzzles.
3. Reproduce block designs.
4. Pour water in different containers.
5. Design games.
6. Use tracing, lacing and cutting activities and visual tracking activities.

Social Skills

1. Discuss different emotions through pictures.
2. Explain body language and symbols.
3. Use T.V. for explaining social encounters and social interactions.
4. Identify topics for discussion with peers, neighbours.
5. Remember key points of conversation.
6. Discuss personal experiences that have caused social difficulties.

Mildly and moderately learning disabled pupils can function satisfactorily in the regular classroom with these adjustments. The regular classroom curriculum may require little modification. These are some of the general techniques of remediation but a specific theoretical model should guide the practioner.

The cognitive processing approach provides a way of thinking about how a child learns and offers a framework for teaching. The developmental approach emphasises sequential approach for remediation. Test related approach identifies specific area of deficiency which can be taught.

The specialised techniques approach indicate that the teacher would follow the prescribed order and fashion for a specified period of time. Hierarchy of skills are to be developed in the Skill-Developmental approach using criterion referenced teaching. Published materials can be used for remediation of learning disability.

Behavioural approach refers to behaviour modification approach for manipulations of environmental conditions of learning. Apply reinforcement and change behaviour. Psychotherapeutic approach should build feelings of success and establish a healthy psychodynamic relationship between teacher and student. The major cause of reading failure is dyspedagogia i.e., lack of good teaching. Inadequqacy in the child's teacher and the teaching environment are the answer to remediation.

	Analysis of the Child.	Cognitive Processing Developmental Test related.
Remediation of Learning Problems.	Analysis of Content.	Specialised Techniques Skill Development Materials.
	Analysis of Environment Conditions.	Behavioural Psychotheraputic Pedagogical.

The model of remediation suggested are not mutually exclusive. A teacher can use one or more of the several approaches to deal with the situations. Koppitz (1973) stated:

"... learning disabilities can not be corrected or cured by a specific teaching method or training technique. It is imperative that teachers have a wide range of instructional materials and techniques at their disposal and that they are imaginative and flexible enough to adapt these to specific needs of their pupils."

The Role of Resource/Special Teacher

The LD children as a group are heterogenous. As such they require a variety of techniques approaches as well as materials to satisfy their unique educational needs at different levels of development.

At the preschool level, the environment should be arranged to promote efficiency, accessibility, independence and functionality. Safety is also a factor in the preschool setting. Heavy breakable and dangerous materials should be out of reach of these children. At the elementary level children classrooms should not be noisy, visually distracting and sterile. The special educator and the regular classroom teacher should provide a less distracting environment for students who are overtly distractible and hence learning disabled. Such children can be placed in the centre of the classroom where more often teacher's attention is focused.

Although small group permits individualised instruction yet have demonstrated the efficacy of peer turoring in instruction, seat work and special projects. Care should be taken to select a good regular peer.

Structure in planning the instructional programme is a must for learning disabled children. The curriculum should be organised sequential and routine based so that the LD child can attend to it carefully. For this task analysis procedure is most relevant. This enables the teacher to break the task into components and help the student at each stage.

The teacher should also provide a summary presentation after each sub-plan of teaching so that LD children can learn well in school and this will provide as an advance organiser for learning.

The equipments and materials must be ready to be used in 'dead time' when the LD children has nothing to do. They can not waste their times. There are a number of specific teaching procedures that have been used to remedials academic deficits or failures among LD children. One of the general approach is cognitive behaviour modification. They help children internalise efficient learning strategies by actively involving them in the learning process mostly consisting of self instruction and verbalisation.

LD children lack abilities for metacognition. Hence, teacher can initiate self questioning strategies for students to use while reading: finding main ideas, underline, answering questions, writing down, asking himself the purpose of reading etc. self instructional techniques have been found quite effective for LD children.

Precision teaching is a system of evaluating and improving instruction. It is direct, continuous and precise measure of student progress where the teacher records a wide range of behaviours. They help teachers on track and make accurate isntructional decisions.

As regards teaching contents and materials it should be motivating, non-complex, and appropriate for child's level of functioning, and learning style. Using student's name, talents or interests is one way a teahcer can make assignments more motivating. Illustrations, too much use of colours in the printed page do distract learning disabled children. Educational games capture students' attention and make learning exciting.

Multisensory aproaches have also been applied to teach LD children. Visual, Auditory, Kinaesthetic, and Tactile (VAKT) was developed by Fernald (1943) which is essentially a language experience. He selects a word and goes through feeling seeing, saying and hearing the word. Once the word is mastered the teacher helps them to write a story and then gives him feedback. In this way new words are learned. Children can be taught through association of a how a letter or word looks, sounds and feels. After he learns the works sentence and story writing begin, gradually they begin to read. There are several combinations of multisensory teaching methods.

Direct instruction which includes assessment, instruction and evaluation are used. DISTAR is one of the direct instructional system which teaching sequences are so arranged that errors are minimised, it provides ample practice, and give immediate and positive feedback. Distar includes Mathematics and reading components. DISTAR was used first with disadvantaged children and now with LD. It is a back to basics structured programme. Learning strategies are also used for helping LD children to learn. Computer assisted instruction is also being introduced in the school system for the management of IEP (Lerner, 1985).

Role of a Regular Classroom Teacher

A teacher in a mainstreamed classroom has to make the classroom personalised where individual differences are accepted and valued. Teachers lead students to value and accept personal responsibility for their own learning. They should promote independence, cooperative functioning, and problem solving among all students. Specifically, they—

a. Accept the perception of learner about classroom environment.
b. Provide varieties of options to motivate each child.
c. Encourage independent and small group work.
d. Increase pupil's commitment, control, and responsibility.
e. Informal and formal conferences are held.
f. Ongoing assessment and student evaluation are done to know the each student's progress.

To make these implementable in the regular classroom:

1. A structured programme has to be avoided.
2. Allow distractible student to sit in centre.
3. Use peer teaching and allow the LD child to be tutor.
4. Drive homework on the curriculum taught.
5. Keep close contact with parents.
6. Tailor the programme to student's needs.
7. Make task analysis and lead student step by step for learning.

Learning difficulties are quite pervasive and non-specific, which arise out of several factors and are achievement specific. In regular schools, learning disabled students can be handled well if regular and resource teachers become conscious and sensitive to the problems of these children. The various concerns expressed in the field are mentioned along with tips for relevant remedial measures.

Highlights of the Chapter

Learning disability refers to a group of disorders relating to acquisition and us eof listening, speaking, reading, writing, reasoning, mathematical abilities and social skills. Conservative estimates indicate three per cent of school children to be learning disabled.

Causes of LD include organic (Cerebral hemmorhage, high fever, head injury, premature birth, anoxia, trauma, neurochemical dysfunction, minimal brain dysfunction, hypoglycemia or low blood sugar, hereditary (Turner's Syndrome) and environmental factors (use of drugs, alcohol, Rubella infection, birth injury, poor and inadequate instruction in school).

LD children are identified by their gross discrepancy in ability and achievement, low achievement, scattered assessment profile through tests and observation of behaviours, distractibility, inattentiveness, wrong perception, problem of left and right remembering and organisation difficulties. DIAL is used for early identification of LD in addition to PPVT, BTBC, EDC etc.

Characteristics of LD children include hyperactivity, perceptual motor impairment, emotional lability, impulsivity, disorders in speech and learning, equivocal neurological signs, language difficulties in reception and expression, reading troubles or dyslexia.

Educatinal provisions consist of day school, special class in a regular school, and integrated classroom. In order to teach these children general isntructional techniques (use of shot and brief directions, large print, consistent language, increased sound level of instruction, pictorial presentations), use of memory training strategies, Basal reading, phonic approach, language experience approach, programmed instruction, multi-sensory approaches are used with differential effectiveness. Specific procedures are available for improvement of handwriting, spelling, writing, reading, arithmetic and these are outlined in detail in the text, including curricular concerns (auditory perception, visual perception, sensorimotor development, social skills).

The role of special/resource teachers include awareness and adoption of small group instruction, classroom arrangement, equipments and materials, precision teaching, multisensory teaching, direct instruction and IEP. The regular teacher has to make classrom personalised and accepting, encouraging, motivating, structured tailor made to needs with appropriate task analysis. Both special education and integration are recommended for LD chidlren but the focus is more on the mainstreaming.

Review Questions

1. How would you define learning disability? Describe the salient characteristics.
2. What are the various identification procedures for LD children?
3. State the characteristics of LD children and suggest ways to remedy their defects.
4. What are the causes of learning disability? Can these be prevented?
5. How would you teach learning disabled children? Outline the general teaching principles.
6. What kind of specific techniques can be used to teach LD children most effectively?
7. Discuss the role for the regular teacher in teaching LD children in a mainstreamed class?
8. Discuss the role of the Resource Teacher/Special Teacher in teaching the LD children?
9. What are some of the curricular concerns for teaching LD Children?
10. Do you think LD children can not be maisntreamed and they need special education?
11. Outline the procedure as to how would a teacher teach LD children:
    a. Handwriting
    b. Writing
    c. Spelling
    d. Arithmatic
    e. Reading

References

Ashlock, P., (1972), *Error Patterns in Competition: A Semi-programmed Approach*, Columbus, Ohio: Charles.

Clements, S., (1966), "Minimum brain dysfunction in children" NINDS, No. 3, *Public Health Service Bulletin*, Washington DC, Department of Health, Education and Welfare.

Fernald, G., (1943), *Remedial Techniques in Basic School Subjects*, New York: Mc Grand Hill.

Hallahan, D.; Kauffman, J; and LLyod, J., (1985), *Introduction to Learning Disabilities*, (2nd ed.), Englewood Cluffs NJ: Prentice Hall.

Hamill, D.; Leight, J.; Mc Nutt,; G. and Larsen, S., (1981), "A new definition of learning disabilities", *Learning Disability Quarterly*, 4, 336-342.

Koppitz, E., (1973), "Special class pupils with learning disabilities, Five year follow up study", *Academic Therapy*, 13, 133-140.

Lerner, J., (1985), *Learning Disabilities*, (4th ed.), Boston: Houghton Mifflin.

Mandell, C. and Goldenberg, D., (1975), "For Pre Kindergarten Screening DIAL", *Journal of Learning Disabilities*, 8, 140-147.

National Advisory Committee on Handicapped Children (1968).

Chapter 9

Physically Handicapped: Orthopaedically Handicapped and Health Impairment

There are children who are handicapped physically to the extent they need assistance of others to go to a school. Orthopaedic handicaps need special attention and care. Hence, to give students a clear knowledge about these children an attempt has been made to present physical handicap in two sections:

- Physically/Orthopaedically Handicapped.
- Health Impairments.
  - Under orthopaedic/physical handicaps, the cerebral palsied have been included along with others, their characteristics and causes.
  - Under health impairments, epilepsy, diabetes are included, alongwith characteristics and causes.
  - Special educational provisions and treatment have been presented for the benefit of the students and readers.
  - The emphasis has been on integrated education.

Who is Physically Handicapped and Health Handicapped?

The term physically handicapped has been used in literature in various ways: Physically disabled, crippled, orthopaedically impaired, or otherwise health impaired. Physical handicaps are divided into two types: Orthopaedically handicapped and Health impairments for the purpose of special education (Bigge and Sirvis, 1986). The legal definition of the term orthopaedically handicapped is a severe, orthopaedic impairment that adversely affects a child's educational performance. The term includes impairments caused by a congenital anomaly e.g., club foot, absence of somebody organs, impairments caused by disease, e.g., poliomeyelities, bone tuberculosis, and impairment from other causes e.g., cerebral palsy, amputations, and fractures or burns that cause contractures. A similar difinition has also been adapted by Department of Social Welfare, Government of India.

The legal definition for other health impairments is having an acute condition that is manifested by severe communication and other developmental and educational problems, or having limited strength, vitality or alertness because of acute health problems e.g., heart condition, tuberculosis, rheumatic fever, nephritis, asthma, anemia, hemophillia, epilepsy, lead poisoning, leukomia, or diabetes that adversely affects a child's educational performance.

Certain crippling and chronic health disorders in children are seen as a result of infection after they are born. Some of the common examples are: Poliomyelitis, estomyelitis, tuberculosis, cerebral palsy. Although, the first three do not invariably lead to brain injury, perception, vision and audition deficiencies yet these children demand special educational treatments.

However, there are certain neurological disorders which are not categoriesed as either crippling or a special health problem e.g., aphasia—a language disorder due to brain injury. Hene, from an educational point of view crippling and neurological impairments would include all children with nonsensory physical impairments whether they are accompanied by a neurological damage or not, and whether they resulted in chronic health condition or not.

Basically nonsensory physical impairments may be classified as crippling and chronic health ailments. The cripples have muscular and skeletal deformities which are obvious. They may wear braces, prosthetic devices such as artificial limbs or may be moving with crutches or wheel chairs.

The second category of children are confined to bed for relatively long periods of time and just do nothing. The crippled children are known as orthopaedically handicapped or motor impaired whereas the second category were known as special health problem cases.

A teacher or educator is less interested in the physical aspects of disability but he is more concerned with the manner in which it will affect the child's functioning in learning situation. Hence, this chapter will discuss:

a. Children with muscular or neuromuscular handicaps which significnatly limit their ability to get about, sit in the classroom, manipulate the materials.
b. Children with skeletal deformities which also effect ambulation, posture and use of hand in school work.
c. Children with temporary or chronic lack of strength, vitality or weakness.
d. The categorisation of orthopaedic disability according to extent and severity:

   Mild — < 40%, Moderate — 40% and above
   Severe — 70% and above, Profound — 100%.

Prevalence

It is estimated that physical handicaps occur to the tune of 2%. The most common physical impairments found in school are cerebral palsy, Spina Bifida, and Muscular dystrophy. The National Sample Survey 1991 puts it at 8.939 million in India (orthopaedic) out 16.15 million of the physically handicapped in 80:20 rural-urban, and 60:40 male-female ratio. In 1981 physically disabled were 1.84% and 1.42% for rural and urban respectively. The corresponding figure in 1991 NSSO were 1.99% and 1.58% respectively.

Causes

The causes of physically disabled are many and varied. Brain damage, brain fever, and brain anoxia lead to physical disability. Rh-incompatibility, intoxication, viral infection for the expectant mother also cause physical disability. Similarly, prolonged labour, lead poisoning, accidents may cause damage to the brain leading to neurological disorders. Polio, Burns and injuries are significant causes as per NSSO, 1991 for Indian society.

Identification

Identification checklist for orthopaedically disabled children.

1. Deformity in fingers, legs, hands, spine, neck.
2. Frequent pain in joints.
3. Jerking movement in walking.
4. Amputed limbs.
5. Difficulty in sitting, standing, walking.
6. Poor motor control.
7. Shaky movements.
8. Difficulty in picking holding and putting in some place.

Orthopaedically handicapped students are identified by orthopaedic surgeons regarding degree of disability.

Characteristics

Physically handicapped students generally have average or above average intelligence caused by polio than other crippling conditions. There are evidence of OH being superior when they are currently being served both in regular and special programmes. Dykes (1984-85) suggest 85% of health impaired and 35% of orthopaedically handicapped children are served in special schools or classes. Often their needs vary. The greater needs of the physically handicapped children are in the areas of adaptive equipments. Often they require wheel chairs, crutches, head pointers, arm and leg braces. Technological gap has narrowed down the gap in providing adequate educational instruction to students who can not speak, move or use hands.

Physically handicapped children are passive, less persistent having shorter attention span, engage themselves in less exploration and display less motivation. They are more dependent on adults, and interact less with peers.

Facilitating independence and building selfesteem are the two requirements for the physically handicapped children.

The physically disabled has poor body image, high anxiety, and frustration. They are found to be quiet, conforming, tenderminded and somewhat tense. Social relationships to constitute a problem area for many crippled youngsters. Their capacity for frustration tolerance are lower than normal children.

Some studies are available in India on physically handicapped. Usha Bhatt (1963) studied the physical, psychological, social, educational and vocational aspects of physically handicapped by intending 600 physical handicapped persons in Bombay. 23% of them had left family, 7 per cent had no family. They had less motivation to seek work. 74% were accepted in family, 12% were rejected, 14% were deserted. Friends showed either favourable or indifferent attitude, so did neighbours and caste group. Although in case of the latter two groups approximately 12% and 21% revealed negative attitudes towards the physically disabled. Of those who were placed in some jobs, about 21 per cent of them seemed to be unhappy.

Deb (1967) demonstrated using TAT, poor ego and unconscious guilt feelings and have a strong sense of fear. They are withdrawn and passive and try to compensate their deficiency. They often felt inferior. Mathew opined that the feelings of incapacitation may result in lack of confidence in one's abilities and bring in a host of psychological barriers in personal and social adjustment.

The intelligence of orthopaedically handicapped are similiar to that of normal children. They are less creative than normals. They had better self concept but the sample was very small (n=20), that it is difficult to generalise from a long observation.

In Sehti and Sen's study (1981) they displayed high need resistance scores. They are more interested in the solution of the problem in frustrating situation. One the whole the handicapped children displayed low self appraisal and were self condemning but they had realistic approach to their problems. They are basically intrapunitive, and have poor self-concept.

Inspite of their disabilities, physically diabled children still had some self confidence. The orthopaedically handicapped had better work adjustment. In the educational set up the orthopaedically handicapped need to be given more individual attention in accordance with their improvements. Hence, proper training and evaluation is required.

Difficulties of orthopaedically handicapped arise out of several factors. Essentially children with motor disabilities are not very different from normal boys and girls. Their handicap arise out of three factors:

a. Society's attitude towards them.
b. Child's interpretation of this reaction to his limitation.
c. Discripancy between aspiration and achievement.

Because of neurological impairment and experimental impoverishment they do show perceptual and learning difficulties.

Intelligence for the orthopaedically handicapped children does not basically differ from these of normals except for cerebral palsy. The neuro muscularly impaired children function 10 to 15 points between estimated intelligence. Children with cerebral palsy, muscular dystrophy, and hydrocephalic are in the dull normal classification while other children with the orthopaedic disability were within the normal range.

Because of fear and social insecurity the crippled child apparently retaliates to personal appraisal or criticism with strong projections of blame and hostility opportunities for normal competition are limited and are often rejected by peers. There are 2 sets of reactions (a) immediate withdrawal (b) absorption with self (c) gradual return to reality. Degree of acceptance and adjustment can be provided through satisfying experience and interpersonal relationships. Immaturity and withdrawal are generally felt by children including leadership and self-confidence in school activities.

Educational Provisions

Orthopaedically handicapped children do not need any special situation for schooling. They can be educated well in the regular school alongwith others. The regular classroom teacher can well handle such cases.

Integrated Education

Education of OH children has changed considerably over the past 50 years. The strength for independence and social recognition was difficult. In 1920, vocational rehabilitation were started with physically handicapped children. Public attitudes also began to change.

Programs of children with orthopaedic handicaps have broadened extensively to include the process of rehabilitation. This is studying the total child. Each staff member has to participate and show sensitivity and natural respect.

Special educators need specific preparation for their team work role. The teacher's function include (a) diagnosis of deprived experience and provision of what is essential (b) developmental guidance (c) coordination of habilitation programme, (d) promotion of integrated activities (e) maintenance of reality standards and discipline. Attention should be given both to individual and group in planning differential diagnosis. It means understanding the study of all factors of the child's growth and his development. For example, if a child has IQ 60 and serious emotional problems due to family stress and pressure, it is not a simple case of past polio. In the total programme the vocational rehabilitation counsellor also assumes major responsibility.

In educational planning these children have the same basic requirements as all other children. As a result of their disabilities, they have additional needs. Some of these needs deviate from normal in degree and emphasis, while others require a separate programme.

The questions arise: There are crippled children who are intelligent. There are PH children who have less intelligence, emotional problems, sensory impairments. These two groups certainly require different treatments, based on differential educational disability. Specialised service is required for the severely disabled group while the crippled children with average intelligence can be easily integrated.

In education of these children with motor handicaps premium is placed on intellectual development, academic ability, and facilitating the child's total adjustment to limitations.

1. These children should be taught self-reliance, initiative, and the ability to make choices. They must learn to plan ahead for mobility and assistance. Listening might be a major source of learning.
2. They should be taught how to use the different parts of the body.
3. Teachers ought to see that they develop a workable self-concept. Those children should play, mix with their non-handicapped peers.
4. The school must develop creativity in the children with reference to art, rythm, music, drama, social experience and opportunity for personal development must be encouraged.

It requires orientation of teachers, administration and other school staff to the problems of their children. Education of crippled children should be prepared with a long range objective in mind. Mobility in placement will be an essential plan in the total school programme.

A large number of crippled children can be integrated in regular classroom where convenient hand nails, ramps, wide doors, no door sills and attendance in classroom is facilitated. Regular teacher might require help from a special educator. Special classrooms are located in the ground floor normally for those orthopaedic disabilities where special equipments are provided e.g., standing tables, parallel bars, relaxation chairs.

The following physical facilities may be provided in schools:

1. A short ramp on steps to enable children in wheel chairs or crutches to enter the building.
2. Addition of a handbar by the side of a water tap, in a toilet, or near a section of the blackboard, if the school has this.
3. Removal of desks to make room for the wheel chair to move.
4. Modification of furniture to provide for the comfort of the child with braces.
5. Rubber mats over slippery sections of the floor within the classroom. Problem of children having poor hand coordination can be solved by

taping paper to the desk, devising some means of keeping pencils and crayons from rolling to the floor, providing holders for books.

In other words, with good planning and a little expense many children who would otherwise need special education services can be educated in normal classroom situations. The classroom and equipment provided for these children may consist of—

a. wide door ways,
b. hand rails,
c. nonskid floors,
d. rounded corners,
e. play areas.

The classroom furniture may be modified to—

a. adjusting seats to turn to sides so that the child with braces can sit more easily,
b. providing foot rests,
c. adding hinged extensions to the desks with a cut-out to the child that has poor balance of eliminating the protruding parts over which a child might slip.

In order to make successful integration programme of the physically handicapped children preschool readiness programmes are necessary.

Due to physical disability many preschool children have little opportunity to explore their environment by crawling, playing in grass etc. Many cannot hold the ball, stick. Cerebral palsied can not speak. Hence, right from early childhood growth and development programmes must start. The opportunity for providing first experience should dominate the preschool curriculum. Nursery school experience should be provided to him.

Rich common experiences will motivate speech among children in school. Use of three dimensional objects, raised illustration, familiar objects facilitate communication.

Personal development can be trained i.e., taking out chapals, buttoning jacket, etc. increases the skill development of OH children. Teachers praise and acceptance are significant help for improving personal development.

Gross motor as well as fine muscular coordination programme can be well planned. Play for the child who is crippled can not be overworked e.g., squeezing mud, objects, water running through fingers. Participation in rhythm band are some of the activities for the disabled. Childhood games, action songs and physical skills are important.

Emotional and social developmental activities can be designed in the school. Any are interacting with the child should be responsive, sensitive and understanding of his diability. Teachers should show affection to their children particularly. They should associate own handicapped children with this group. They should describe their own experience.

The intellectual development of these children should be accelerated by using meaningful, purposeful, and interesting materials familiar to the child.

As the child advances to elementary school years, children follow the same curriculum advocated for all children if they are average or above average intelligence. Of course to achieve the same criteria some children need differentiated material and techniques. Skill in utilising his school learnings in his home and community environment is vital for satisfactory personality adjustment. The physically handicapped child gradually realises that he has inability and inadequacy to complete physically with other boys and girls. The teachers have to keep a close watch on visual functioning of their physically handicapped pupils.

Physical limitations, parental aspirations and disappointments, frustrations of the child, and strenuous efforts towards adjustment may result in serious problems of emotional nature. Teachers have to help these children to cope with problems of adjustment.

Emphasis on language arts, language activity mathematics, science, the arts are to be planned to meet the requirements of physically handicapped children.

The teaching methods consists of diagnostic methods as well as prescriptive teaching are used in teaching crippled children. Grouping is not a panacea for all educational problems nor its stability offers security to the teacher. Therefore, there should be flexible grouping.

Cerebral Palsy

Cerebral Palsy is 'brain paralysis'. It is a disability that affects movements and body position. There are a series of neuromuscular disabilities which are characterised by disturbances in voluntary motor action, in the extremities mostly resulting out of brain damage. The sensitivity of the disability depends upon the degree of damage or brain lesion. There are various types of cerebral palsy disorders: spasticity, athetosis, ataxia, rigidity and tremors.

Secondary characteristics appear in these cases because the lesion is rarely localised. Mental retardation, sensory and other defects appear in a considerable number of cases. Approximately half of the cerebral palsy children have IQ below 70, high rigidity and an ataxic. Over half of the spastics and speech defects and nearly 90 per cent of the athetoids and this defect. Almost one third of the total group had seizures and only a lightly smaller per cent had defects of vision. Lack of specific hand dominance contributes to difficulty in learning to read and write.

There are different types of cerebral palsy.

Type	Area of Brain Lesion	Characteristics
1. Spasticity (Muscle stiffness)	Motor cortex and pyramidical tracts.	Stretch reflex, tenseness of muscles, difficult and inaccurate voluntary motion. 70% of cerebral palsied are spastics.
2. Athetosis (Uncontrolled movement).	Basal ganglia and extra pyramidical tracts.	Marked incoordination muscles, constant motion of extremities, speech impaird, poor imbalance.
3. Ataxia (Poor balance)	Subcortical, cerebellum.	Uncoordinated movement impaired balance and sense of orientations in space, movement tremoes, clumsy movements).
4. Rigidity	Diffuse	Widespread continuous muscle tension.
5. Tremor	Basal ganglia	Rhythmic, involuntary, uncontrollable motion, limited to muscle groups.

How to Recognise Cerebral Palsy?

- At birth the baby with cerebral palsy is often limp and floppy and may turn blue.
- Delayed breathing is a common cause of brain damage.
- The child is slow to hold up his head or move around.
- The child may not use hands.
- The child has difficulty in feeding.
- The child is irritable.
- The baby does not respond and is slow in beginning to speak.
- Some children may seem dull and slow moving.
- Fits do occur with some children with Cerebral Palsy.
- The child displays restless behaviour.
- Children have difficulty in controlling this body and have balance problems.

Causes of Cerebral Palsy

There are certain causes which occur before birth and are responsible for cerebral palsy. These are:

- Problems of the mother such as toxemia of pregnancy and diabetes.
- German Measles and shingles (Herpes Zoster) during pregnancy.
- Rh-incompability.

At the time of birth, lack of oxygen creates difficulty for the child to breathe for which he becomes blue and limp.

- Birth injuries resulting from difficult births.
- Misuse of forceps leading to brain injuries.
- Prematurity—babies who are born early and have less than 5 pounds weight.

After Birth—very high fever, acute jaundice, menigitis, encephalitis, head injuries, lack of oxygen, lead poisoning, blood clots in the brain, brain tumors.

The degree of severity depends upon the degree of brain damage.

Characteristics

Cerebral palsy is the result of brain damage. They show emotional disturbances like that of Strauss children. Some of them have impairments perceiving shape, weight and texture. A few others have inability for spatial orientation and judgement. Cerebral palsy chidlren often have difficulty in discriminating figure and background than do normal children. They give more concrete responses than abstract ones.

Nearly 50 per cent of cerebral palsy children have IQ below 70, 23 per cent fall between borderline and 28 per cent fall above average in IQ. Hence, the educational problems become one not only of adapting the programme to the multiple physical and psychological disabilities of the cerebral palsied child and in many cases adjusting to the level of slow learning.

Skeletal impairments in children affect primarily the upper and lower limbs spine and joints. As a result children are unable to walk, sit or stand or use hands. Some children have clubfoot. This is a condition in which one or both feet are downward and inward at the ankle occur most frequently. Congential dislocation of the hips, scoliosis i.e., lateral curvature of the spine appear among some of the children who are crippled or monsensory handicapped. All these conditions are commonly found in school age children particualrly at the elementary grade levels. The incidence of these disorders have decreased because of medical treatment.

There are also a few children in the school who need special care because they exhibit limited strength, vitality and alertness. They delimit the scope of children's functioning in school. Rheumatic fever is a chronic infection of the connective tissues of the body affecting joints, heart and blood vessels. Although rheumatic fever and pulmonary tuberculosis are decreasing, decreasing, diseases like rephritis, infections, hepatitis and infections mononuleosis are creating concern in schools. All these require bed rest and limited activity during which time or programme of instruction in school subjects should be provided.

Educational Provisions

Special Schools

When do we think of placing a child in a special school? When the child has-

1. Special learning difficulties,
2. Needs special kinds of equipment,
3. Needs disproportionately more of teachers time,
4. Needs therapy, and
5. Emotional problems.

The cerebral palsied children cannot ordinarily be placed in a regular class. For mild cases with normal intelligence regular class may serve the purpose but for severe cases special class or special schools are necessary. Cerebral palsied children with mild motor involvement but more severe impairment of intellect, vision, or hearing will be best provided for in classes for the mentally retarded, visually or auditory handicapped. In advanced countries of the world hospitalised instruction or homebound instruction is provided but for a developing country its limitations are obvious.

Children with cerebral palsy may have the learning difficulties of the brain injured child added to the basic problem of muscular coordination and secondary sensory and mental impairment. Curriculum content will depend to a great extent upon what the student is going to be able to do with his education when he completes school or leaves the school.

Education and training of the cerebral palsied children should begin very early, as early as 3 years of age. Early readiness program is designed to (a) stimulate interest and curiosity, provide for meaningful experience, increase language comprehension, develop satisfactory perception and built towards independence. The readiness period may extend over years. Methods of teaching the basic tool subjects may emphasise the meaningful materials and importance of useful reading skills may also be emphasised. Cerebral palsied children with intellectual and perceptual handicaps make acquriing the skills very difficult. For cerebral palsied sometimes silent reading is recommended. The kinaesthetic sense can be utilised in supplementing visual and auditory impressions and children whose motor involvement is not too severe can learn to read words through tracing them. Coloured felt pens are useful for the purpose because the colour gives added clues.

Adequate language and speech development is necessary for the cerebral palsied children. Speech training must be done by a speech therapist but games and exercises which stimulate auditory discrimination can form a part of the daily schedule. A 'conversation board' containing pictures, common objects helps the children learn to read. Non oral students get a deal of satisfaction from learning the 'Morse Code' and they communicate with the teacher by eye blinking or tapping on the desk for dots and dashes.

Handwriting of the cerebral palsy children have improved by giving specific manuscript writing training e.g., activities is space orientation, colouring with lines, tracing and using word boxes with pictures. Teaching materials must be adapted to the needs of invididual students on the basis of their physical problems as well as perceptual and learning difficulties. Pupils in pre-academic classes will learn to match colours and shapes distinguish between sizes and textures and develop the concepts of number through manipulative games and devices which promote eye-hand coordination. Some of the commercial materials available for this purpose are: pegboards, snap blocks, lock boxes, coordination boards, take apart toys, colour cones, junbo beads, puzzles. Materials can be devised to increase motivation and reduce boredom.

The physical aspects of the total educational situation assume major importance for children with cerebral palsy. In fact, physical development should go side by side with academic development and maintenance body posture and mobility, voluntary movement. Physical therapy does contribute to improvement in neuromuscular impairment. The occupational therapists concentrate on the development of the self-help skills of dressing, grooming and abilities necessary for school work. Homebound and hospitalised instructions are costly but are given to cerebral palsy children in case of progressie advanced countries.

These are the physical and educational facilities that are available or can be made available for the education of crippling and special nonsensory health disorders. The important concern should be that he should be accepted, should be helped to be independent and the society must change its outlook in seeing beyond his defect to the person that is there. Theis is a challenge that special educators should take.

For the severely crippled, special units in a wing in the public school building is necessary. The therapists, and the teachers would be placed there for helping the physically disabled children, particularly cerebral palsy. This unit will consist of occupational therapy, speech therapy, physical therapy and other educational services will be located.

The children who need special education because of neuromuscular impairment, skeletal deformities and reduced vitality are provided for in hospital classes, homebound instruction, special schools and special classes. But with some physical facilities and equipment their educational needs may be met adequately in regular classrooms.

These are possible because they do not have impairment in intellectual functioning and can certainly learn through the same procedure as children without disabilities. Unless neurological damage is severe and intense no special method of teaching is necessary.

They require no drastic curriculum revisions. Certain adjustments may be made to increase their vocational and social competency. They may require a little more time to complete the prescribed courses. The goals of education are essentially the same as that for non handicapped conditions.

Integrated Education

Partial integration is possible in special class especially if the unit is desirably located in a public school building.

The child's likelihood of success in regular classroom setting appears efficient when -

a. the child is intellectually, socially and emotionally capable of participation with his peers,
b. the child can participate,
c. the child is not being denied therapy necessary for physical rehabilitation,
d. the curriculum is adapted to most his needs,
e. the physical facilities of the school permit the child to hence access to important educational centres,
f. the teacher is willing to accept the child and prepared to move with one who deviates physically,
g. adequate physical assistance and special supervision is required,
h. periodic evaluation to be included in the child's progress report,
i. the deviant child will not refer the child's progress, and
j. the deviant child will not retard the groups progress.

In 1972, Anderson studied the effectiveness of physically disabled children in the integrated primary school setting. The study showed clear differences in the success of integration whether the child has congenital limb deficiency or additional neurological impairments. The latter showed difficulties in social interaction and learning ability. The study showed physically disabled but intellectually and socially bright do well in an integrated setting. Hence, with structural alternations and right attitudes physically impaired children can be integrated but it is difficult to integrate the neurologically impaired. These findings have been confirmed in the 1970s and 1980s. Hence, the needs of each type of physically impaired children are to be cared for rather than lumping all PH into one group.

What criteria should be used to place physically impaired children in the integrated school? The following criteria seem pertinent:

1. Average or above academic ability
2. Social and emotional ability
3. A desire to be integrated
4. Support of parents
5. Ability to communicate effectively
6. Effective management of contingency.

Hodgson et. al. (1984) schools accepting physically impaired children should ensure (a) preparation of staff (b) preparation of parents of pupils already in school (c) preparation of pupils. The quality of integration should be ensured. Fish (1984) has suggested that other forms of special school organisation should be considered such as providing itinerant specialist help on a short term basis, which will enable a child to cope is a mainstream school.

In fact, most mainstream schools emphasize more of physical access rather curriculum adaptations. At present both are at the cross roads.

These children, either due to gross physical handicap, orthopaedically handicap or neurologically impaired need some adaptive equipments in the classroom. Some of these are:

- Page turner operated with a toggle switch
- Head want to operate a typewriter
- Recorders to replace writing
- Calculator with print out tape
- Eating aids
- Tactile writing paper
- Pencil grips
- Lap trays
- Larger and/or weighted objects for manipulation
- Environmental adjustment in the classroom would include
- Adjustable tables to accommodate a wheel chair
- Wide door ways
- Textured surface to prevent paper or books from slipping
- Storage for crutches.

General Teachig Principles

Teaching children who are crippled calls for same teaching methods but it requires extended sensitivity, creativity and flexibility. The teacher will use his personal knowledge, ability and initiative. A flexible programme is the veichle for translating individual differences of children into a constructive learning situation for all.

The principles of teaching reading to children with crippling conditions are the same as those for teaching all other children. The process is however slow. In addition, unusual physical assistance may be required to be given by the teacher. Adequate perceptual experience of size, colour, texture etc. are to be given. Teaching aids, orthotic and prosthetic aids are to be used. For example, all physical aids, optimum seating and posture, holding a pencil, or a paint brush, turning a page, pushing a bottom or otherwise gaining hand and arm motion will be provided by those best qualified to prescribe. Independent academic readiness materials might include magnetised coloured disks of varying shapes which can be shifted even in gross movement.

Especially for cerebral palsied children oral reading can be difficult even in a group of four or five. A well established pattern of independent silent reading will be an asset to the child who in physically limited. Children working on similar achievement levels can be given common basic reading instruction and reading activities, in which they might read silently for information. All children need not read aloud. Experience charts, labels on objects about the room will help to stimulate interest in reading. Use of scrap books, and charts enable children to build up auditory and visual discrimination prerequisite to reading. Puzzles of various kinds, pasting pictures of several kinds: forms, colour etc. improves reading readiness.

Children with balance problem can use rulers, straightlined markers, cut out to cover a line, coloured pencils improves rapid reading skills. Large charts for children with ataxia and visual problems are useful.

Whether a child is placed in regular classroom or special classroom major problems with cerebral palsied child relate to establishment of communication. Initial efforts to talk would be difficult for the child, teachers, and peers.

A non-oral reading approach is based on providing largely on concrete experience. After reading a sentence, the child will be required to answer the question.

Cursive writings will give most support and resulting satisfaction.

The Regular Teacher

For physical disability the regular teacher need to make instructional adaptations so that the children communicate with teachers well. For Health Impairment he has to know the basic characteristics of disorders, medicine and their effects, precautionary measures, keeping a watch on day to day requirements and develop appropriate expectations so that children do not suffer from identification.

Three factors are responsible for deciding the teaching procedures of physically and/or neurologically impaired children. Task analysis, teaching towards developing independence, and use of computer instruction.

The type of content is dependent upon the degree of physical impairment. Yet certain areas are most essential.

a. Communication skills and language.
b. Activities of daily living, or self care skills (eating, bathing etc.)
c. Community referenced instruction (crossing streets, using money, riding public transportation).
d. Advanced self care skills or home living skills (operating kitchen appliances etc.)
e. Vocational preparation, career awareness, work adjustment skills.
f. Continuity and generalisation.

The Schweitzer Daily living skills programme emphasizes self care and home making skills. The use of equipments has been amply emphasized in the case of neuromuscular and physical handicaps equipments are available and have been designed to assume better positions, ease problems associated with activities of daily living, easing problems associated with locomotion, communication.

Health Problems

Some children have health problems that interfere with their education. Notable among these are rheumatic heart disease, and tuberculosis. There are cases of Kidney ailments and infections such as asthma, eczema, hay fever, chronic health disorders such as: epilepsy, diabetes, migrane headache. But children with chronic illnesses are likely to be enrolled in any classroom.

Diabetes

There are children who suffer from diabetes even from age six onwards. There are some important clues of this metabolic disorder which can be identified by the teacher. In diabetes, the body tissues can neither use nor store sugar, thus the sugar accumultes in the blood. Hence, the child becomes excessively thirsty. He runs to the bathroom more frequently. Energy is decreased as intake of sugar is witheld. He eats much but there is a loss of weight and strength.

For such children, intake of sugar and starch should be limited. At the initial stage this care is sufficient. If not physician prescribes insulin according to the needs of the child, since insulin secreted by the pancrease is not sufficient to utilise the glucose in normal diet. These children should have regularity of diet and meals.

Hence, the child's energy expenditure should be carefully kept in mind by the teacher while planning outside activities. The teacher should teach the child good hygenic care of the lower extremeties, cleanliness, and prompt attention to bruises, erruptions of irritations. Excessive heat should not be applied to the feet. The child should be prevented from scratching the body as this might create injury. The regular classroom teacher may feel alarmed to take so much care and attention but these are essential and the teacher must accordingly plan and draw the program for guiding the diabetic child is his class.

The diabetic personality is described with conflict, hatred of parents yet submission to them, social anxiety, superficial agrrement, fears, difficult sex adjustment, temper tantrums, nightmares. They oscillate between dependency and independence.

Identification of Health Problems

1. Shortness of breath

2. Frequent cough
3. Blue apearance of skin
4. Increased appetite
5. Gets easily tired
6. Restless, inattentive
7. Slow and inactive
8. Irritable
9. Temper tantrums
10. Abnormal thirst, frequent irritation
11. Itching
12. Perspires often
13. Dust allergy
14. Loss of weight.

Epilepsy

What id epilepsy? Epilepsy or seizure is a major chronic health condition which can affect the alertness, vitality and mental health of a child in a manner and to a degree that may severely lessen his ability to function in a regular school situation. This is quite common and is more frequent than cerebral palsy, polio, muscular dystrophy, multiple scelrosis combined.

Epilepsy is the most common neurological disease. In 1870, Jackson defined epilepsy as a group of disorders with paroxysmal and excessive neurocal discharge that cause a sudden discharge in neulogical function. There is a sudden change in intellectual, sensory, motor, autonomic, or emotional activity, limited in length and presumably associated with neuronal over-activity.

One out of 10 or 20 children has atleast 1 fit age 15 but only one out of 50 has chronic fits, a condition known as epilepsy.

Causes

Michael (1994) summarised the causes of epilepsy as follows:

a. Ideopathic-cause not known—30-50%.
b. Genetic—10-20% by inheritance.
c. Metabolic errors—PKU, Maple syrup wine
d. Congenital and peri-natal infections.
e. Encephalitis and menigitis (brain fever) and severe dehydration.
f. Brain tumors—Intra Cranial space occuring lessions.
g. Brain injury before birth at least among 1/3 of epileptics.
h. Cerebral haemorrhage.
i. Drugs and lead poisoning.
j. Cerebral Palsy and epilepsy often occur together.

Brain damage can be prevented during pregnancy. Avoid marriages between close relatives. Anti fits medicines are to be taken for 3 to 4 years to prevent epilepsy occur further.

Types of Fits

Psychomotor

There are several types of epilepsy: psychomotor, petitmal, grandmal. In psychomotor epilepsy the individual is violent, vigorous and is doing some automatic action which appear to others as meaningful but are meaningless. During the seizure the child's behaviour is inconsistent. He makes sucking noises with his mouth, moves his hand aimlessly, strikes a child, tears up paper, move about the room. But the individual does not remember what he has done. Such behaviours include temper tantrums also.

Petitmal

In Petitmal, the child loses consciousness for a few seconds but does not fall. His eyes may roll up or there may be a rhythmic blinking of eyelids. He drops things, appears to be staring straight ahead, or stands still, unaware of what is going on around him. The teacher often thinks that he is not paying attention. He quickly recovers and goes on what he was doing. If he is reading, he will stop for a moment and they go on with the passage. As a rule this does not inconvenience him or to any one to a great extent. But if such seizures occur quite frequently the child is apt to lose the thread of a lesson and be handicapped by gaps in continuity. The teacher should watch for sign that indicate a child is having a seizure and repeat directions. He may have missed or checked to see that he has understood what was going on in the class.

Grandmall

A child who has grandmal seizures has less consciousness and fall rigidly on the floor. This is preceded by a strange sensation kown as aura (warning) and by a shrill cry. His-muscles first tighten, then accompanied by salivation, twitching and tremors may follow. Then comes a deep sleep, come or stuper. The seizure may last for a minute or two and when he recovers he may be dull or disoriented. He may want to sleep for some more time and consequently his school programme may be impaired. In a case such as this, what a teacher can do?

Characteristics

Some children with epilepsy are intelligent. Others are mentally slow. Occassionally fits that are very frequent and severe can injure the brain and cause of increase retardation. Treatment to control fits is important.

Some children may have both minor and big fits or they may have first minor ones and later develop big ones. There is a sign of warning or aura. They may suddenly cry and then are finds suddenly jerks or are thrown immediately. These fits vary in duration.

After the fit is over the child may be very sleepy and confused. He/she may feel body-ache and feel weak.

Special/Regular Teacher's Role

a. Ease the child to the floor.
b. See that he is not apt to injure himself by striking furniture or sharp comers while convulsions.
c. Turning the child's head to one side and carefully placing but never forcing a folded handkerchief or a soft object between back teeth is sometimes advised.
d. Do not use a pencil or other solid object for the teeth an gums may be injured.
e. The teacher should help other children in the classroom to accept this seizure calmly and to understand that there nothing contagious or harmful about in convulsion.

Children with epilepsy do not have necessarily low intelligence due to seizures. They show some signs of maladjustment because social stigma and frustrating environment. Majority of the children with this condition can attend regular school. Normal activity and exercise may actually reduce the frequency of seizures. Incidence is reduced by following ketogenic diet (high fat and carbohydrate) and anticonvulsive therapy.

Treatment

There are no medicines that can cure epilepsy. There are no vaccinations that can prevent epilepsy. However, medicines can prevent occurence of fits if these are taken regularly. Sometimes preventing fits for a long time seems to help stop epilepsy permanently.

Treatment for epilepsy generally consists of four parts (1) identification and eliminating of factors that cause or precipitate attacks (2) sustaining of general mental and physical health and social integration (3) pharmacological therapy that raises the convulsive threshold to prevent attacks (4) surgical therapy for carefully selected patients with seizure of focal origin or for those for whom medication has proven completely ineffective.

The commonly used anticonvulsant medications in pharmacological therapy are Dlantin, Mysoline, Zarontin, Tegretoe, Clonopin, Depakene for different types of seizures. The most significant treatment in epilepsy is the growth of good physical and mental health. A nutritious balanced diet and adequate muscular activity will be paralleled by the relief of emotional stress and the creation of an atmosphere of productive and normalcy.

Educational Provisions: Mainstreaming or Integrated Classroom

The regular classroom will provide most children with chronic medical problems with maximum educational opportunity. These who present physical problems present little limitation of activity and therefore should not be deprived of such opportunity. This of course, requires extra teacher training, planning and ingenuity. Children are very sensitive to their teacher and her attitudes and it should be remembered that teacher's attitude have a contagions effect on the feeling of the total group.

In this environment children will have to face their differences recognize their limits, be assured of their acceptance as they are, and then be given opportunity for participation and enjoyment of class projects. In each they need support and understanding of the teachers.

The human-centred schooling approach should be followed for those children. The child's self concept, his adjustment with others should receive primary focus. The teacher has to participate in overall planning for the pupil.

Special attention has to be paid towards the social and emotional adjustment of the child who because of his disability might feel different, unaccepted, and some what insecure. He may fear the physical and social consequence of such efforts.

The teacher should be aware of their specific health problems, the therapeutic meausres to be taken and the necessary programme alteration. A comprehensive remedial programme is necessary for this group. These factors should be kept in mind while developing programmes for the health impaired.

For helping these children particularly with health impairment standard of achievement expected should be kept at par with the needs of the group and remedical education must compensate the differences of the classroom attainments. Some interesting low level reading books should be on their hand or in library. Teachers can help parents in planning home and community participation for the children.

The 'Buddy' system already referred in case of hearing impaired, visually impaired may also find a place in case of chronic health disorder cases. The Buddy will be responsible to the teacher who will make the necessary adjustments and medical referrals.

No specific prescription can be offered for educating children with chronic illness. Their problems vary according to digonosis, degree of involvement or limitation and supplementary care.

Children do move from one facility to the other. Need for programme continuity, teacher sensitivity, and support as children are transferred can not be over emphasized.

Special Schools and Special Classes

Special schools and special classes for health impaired children are midway between home and hospitalised instruction.

Most special class accommodate physically limited children by offering a comprehensive remedial health programme. Not all children need health programme i.e., health habits, dietary adjustments, rest etc. In a few other cases, special classes prepare them for regular class placement by raising their educational achievement and adjustment. Comparative efforts will be exerted towards developing poise in social relationships by participation in both independent and group activity. Fostering self respect and confidence through achievement in a semisheltered classroom setting will do much towards alleviating fear of inadequqcy in a regular programme.

No child sould be placed in a special school or special class without complete physical evaluation. Normally Health Impaired children are placed in special class according to their types and degree of illness. Teachers should introduce the children to as many aspects of the school programme as possible and encourage them to explore all the ways in which they can prepare for participation with their own class and with other children in school. The school curriculum should also take into consideration the child's need for adjusting to the pace of non-handicapped. Curriculum roads to maturity and self understanding should be explored.

Highlights of the Chapter

Nonsensory physical impairments cover the orthopaedically handicapped health impairments. There are certain neurological disorders which are not categorised as either crippling or special health problems e.g., aphasia, a language disorder due to brain injury. The most common physical handicaps found in school are the cerebral palsied, spina bifida, muscular dystrophy with greater concentration in rural areas and among males.

Brain damage, brain fever, brain anoxia lead to physical disability, in addition to Rh-incompatibility, intoxication, viral infection. Prolonged labour, lead poisoning, accidents cause neurological disorders. Polio, burns and injuries are major causes of physical handicap in India.

Identification checklists of the orthopaedically handicapped are available which includes deformities in movement and motor control. Physically handicapped children are intelligent. "They are passive, less persistent, and display less motivation. Further, they have poor body image, high anxiety, frustration, poor tolerance yet display self confidence.

OH children do not need any special education. They can be educated in the integrated schools easily with adjustments in sitting arrangements and change or modification in physical structure of the class i.e. slipping floor covered with ramps, allowing OH children a seat on the side than in middle of the room etc.

Special schools have been established for cerebral palsied children. These children are detected easily by their conspicuous muscular activities and behaviour. They are irritable, they are limp and floppy. They display problems of balance, control, and movement. Arising out of toxemia, diabates, measles, Rh-incompatibility, anoia, prematurity, these children have less IQ, less ability for spatial orientation, limited strength and vitality and alertness, learning difficulties.

Besides, special schools, hospitalised instruction, homebound instruction, is being provided to CP children in advanced countries. Early readiness programme benefit these children particularly in language, handwriting. For severely crippled special units class in a wing of a school is necessary where speech therapy, occupational therapy, physical therapy and other educational services are available. However, CP child's success in integrated setting is possible when the CP child is otherwise i.e., intellectually and emotionally capable, the curriculum is adapted to his needs, and accessories are provided.

General teaching principles for crippled calls for same teachign methods but with sensitivity, creativity and flexibility. The regular teacher should acquire competence in communication skills and language, activities for daily living, self care skills, community referenced instruction etc.

Children have health problems. Epilepsy is the most common neurological disease arising out of genetic, metabolic, perinatal infections, brain tumors, encephalities and certain unknown causes. They have different amount of IQ ranging from low to average. Fits become major symptom varying in duration. Although the cure lies in medical treatment, use of ketogenic diet, anticonvulsant medications, surgery, the regular classroom teacher can take some cautionry measures when convulsions occur e.g., ease the child to the floor, turning the child's head to one side, carefully placing a handkerchief between teeth etc. These children have social stigma but they can very well study in the regular school. In some special cases, special class/schools work as remedial health programme centre and as a preparation for regular class entry.

Review Questions

1. What is meant by neurological disability? Briefly describe the various types.
2. What is cerebral palsy? What are the characteristics of cerebral palsied children?
3. What is epilepsy? What are its characteristics? How would you treat such children?
4. What are the educational provisions for an epileptic child?
5. What educational procedures can be adopted for the cerebral palsied child?
6. What are the identification signs for physically handicapped children?
7. How do you implement integrated education of the orthopaedically handicapped children?
9. What is the role of regular teacher in an integrated classroom for the physically handicapped?

References

Bhatt, U., (1963), *The Physically Handicapped,* Popular Prakashan, Bombay.

Bigge, J. and Sirvis, B., (1986), "Physical and Health Impairments", In N.G. Haring & L. McCormick (eds.), *Exceptional Children and Youth,* (4th ed., pp. 313-354), Columbus, OH: Merrill.

Deb, M., (1967), *Personality Pattern of the Post Polio Paralytics, A Psychological Therapy,* 6, 100-109.

Dykes, M.K., (1984-1985), "Assessment of students who are physically or health impaire", *Diagnostique,* 10, 128-143.

Fish, J., (1984), "The Future of Special School" in T. Bowers *'Management and the Special School,* Groom Helm.

Hodgson, A.; Ross, A., and Hegarty, S., (1984), *Learning Together,* NFER-Nelson.

Michael, M., (1994), *A Brief Overview on Epilepsy,* Sanklap, 4, (2), 32-33, THPI.

Sethi, M. and Sen, A., (1981), "A comparative study of orthopaedically handicapped children with their normal peers on some psychological variables", Personality study and group behaviour, 1(2), 83-95.

Chapter 10

Speech and Language Handicapped Children

Language is the basis of learning, communication, and thought. Hence, any disorder in Speech and Language becomes a barrier in communication, eventually creating a handicap, reversible of-course through education, training and therapy. The present chapter addresses to issues relating to:

- Meaning of speech and language handicap.
- Identification.
- Causes of language handicap.
- Characteristics.
- Teaching techniques for improving language.
- Mainstreaming and Integration.
- Roles of the regular and resource teacher.
- Educational provisions for the severe cases of language handicap.

Language occupies the central place in the communication system. It is a socially shared code representing concepts through the use of both arbitary symbols (sound, letters, words) and rule governed combination of those symbols (grammar, syntax, semantics). Speech is the verbal presentation of language and writing is the graphic presentation of language. Paralinguistic, nonlinguistic and metalinguistic abilities also play a major role in the process of communication. Paralinguistic refers to segments (sound) of the linguistic code (sentence) to affect or change meaning. It carries the emotion of the speaker in terms of interaction, inflection, emphasis, rate of delivery, pause. Nonlinguistic mechanism relate to body language (gestures, postures, eye contact, facial expression) that carry information. Metalinguistic mechanism include ability to think about content on language.

Speech disorders or impairment include respiration disorders, voice disorders, articulation disorders and stuttering, stammering, cluttering and disordes in paralinguistic mechanism. Speech is a way to express or transmit the meaning of language.

Language disorder is not only characterised by abnormal comprehension and/or production of the symbol and code system (grammatical structure and words) but also by the disorders in the nonlinguistic and metalinguistic mechanism. They may take the form of disorders in reception or comprehension of the speech of others, disorders in gesture, phrasing pattern, personal interaction etc.

Prevalence

Speech and language disorders are the most prevalent type of handicapping conditions encountered by teachers. Nearly four per cent of school children have these problems. The prevalence varies according to type of disorders. The prevalence of voice disorders is often difficult to establish because of voice problems. Wilson (1979) reported that approximately 6% to 9% school aged children have a voice problem of some type. Nearly 3% students in school have articulation problems. Resonatory disorders occur less than 5%. Fluency disorders occur less than 0.8% with greater prevalence in males than females.

Perkins (1977) placed the prevalence of language disorders at 5% of the general population and oral language disorders about 6.5%. The NSSO survey 1991 in India puts it at 1.966 million in CA 5-14 which constitutes 26% of speech and language handicapped.

Causes

Speech disorders are due to combinations of causes rather than due to single cause, such as hereditary predispositions, neurological impairments, physical abnormalities of the speech mechanisms delayed development and cultural or environmental influences. The remaining specific causes are mentioned while describing the characteristics. The important causes include: paralysis, mental illness, illness and general retardation (NSSO, 1991).

Identification

Various techniques are used but one such technique is to know the behavioural clues to detect speech defects.

1. Faulty articulation or pronunciation—substitution (cree for tree) ommission (ate for gate); distortions (ship for sip).
2. Unpleasant voice quality—nasality, (too much sound through nose) hoarseness, harshness (irritation), breathiness (sexy voice).
3. Defective voice—too high or too low; too loud or too soft; monotonous voice.
4. Stuttering, cluttering.
5. Difficulty in understanding meaning of spoken words/sentences.
6. Difficulty in forming oral sentence.

Speech is defective when it deviates so far from the speech of other people that it calls attention to itself, interferes with communication, or causes the possessor to be maladjusted. Language problems should be considered significant if they interfere with communication if they cause the speaker to maladjusted or if they cause problems for the listener "Gearhart and Weigharn (1976, p. 99).

Characteristics of Speech Disorders

Speech disorder occurs when it deviates from the speech of normal people that it—

1. calls attention to itself,
2. interfers with communication,
3. causes the speaker or listener to distressed.

These children due to abnormal respiration have faint voice, sounds are not clear and when talking it appears as if the speech is short, choppy and rhythm is not normal.

Voice becomes harsh, breathy or hoarse. The pitch or loudness is abnormal and not appropriate to age. Either speech is loud or soft.

There are articulation disorders also. These include substitution (red as wed) (s' and 'hissing') (stake as take) distortion, ommissions and additions, (Puhlay for play). Organic articulation disorders have a physical/neurological basis as in cerebral palsy where speech is distorted due to muscle weakness.

Another organic speech order is approxia of speech where sequence of phonemes is not maintained which is related to brain damage. Other articulation disorders include large tongue, cleft of the lip, or palate, malformation of jaw leading to substitution or distortion errors.

Another organic speech order is approxia of speech where sequence of phonemes is not maintained which is related to brain damage. Other articulation disorders include large tongue, cleft of the lip, or palate, malformation of jaw leading to substitution or distortion errors.

Funcational articulation disorders are due to delayed development, incorrect learning, psychological maladaptations, environmental cultural differences. They have also poor auditory discrimination skills.

There are also resonance process disorders or nasality errors. These errors in the tonal quality of speech include hyper nasality of speech, audible nasal emission during speaking and hyponasality of speech. This may be due to upper respiratory infections, and swelling of the tonsils and adenoids. The speech becomes unintelligible, e.g., 'a cold in my nose' shounds like 'a' cold id by dose'.

Prosody process disorders involve improper use of rhythm, timing, information, inflection, stress and phrasing. Two fluency errors are observed: Stuttering refers to abnormal interruption in the forward flow of speech. The second prosody process errors is cluttering that means rapid, indistinct, jerky speech full of hesitations and repetitions with a dominant impression of haste (Bloodstein, 1984). Cluttering appears first in some individuals (Van Riper et. al., 1984).

Causes of Language Disorders

There are several causes of language disorders (Panda, 1993). But considering language impairment from the special educational needs points of view it involves delayed maturation, brain damage, mental retardation, sensory and perceptual impairments or environmental deprivation. Specific language disorders are also mentioned in the section on mental retardation and hearing impairment. Language disabilities are due to minimal brain dysfunction, sensory and perceptual disorders.

Identification

Language assessment can be done by the speech language pathologist on the following areas:

1. Visual Examination of Oral Mechanism

The teacher or speech language therapist can observe the breating and speaking patterns, body muscle tension, movement of the shoulders upward and downward while speaking, head movement downwards to their chest, speech is of short phrases, frequent pauses, slow etc. There are several measures which can be observed.

2. Articulation

Photograph naming, drawing, picture naming activities, noticing beginning and end words, oral reading, conversation are used to observe articulation. Substitution, ommission distortion, addition errors are observed.

The following tests are used to measure:

1. Goldman—Fristoe Test of Articulation.
2. Photo Articulation Test.
3. Templin Darley Test of Articulation.

Similar tests can be developed and/or adopted for use in our society.

3. Voice

Voice, quality, pitch, loudness are observed by the therapist. Optimal and habitual speech range can be assessed. Quality disorders—harshness, hoarseness, weakness etc. are observed due to pathological factors.

1. Phonological Process Analysis.
2. Assessment of Phonological Processes—Revised.

4. Fluency

Speech interruptions, repetitions, pauses, interjections, fear, visible and audible struggle for speech etc. are assessed simultaneously with prosody.

5. Prosody

Prosody stresses on management of stress, pitch and into nation.

6. Language Form and Content

Language form and content are assessed being tests. Which gives us scores on vocabulary morphology, syntax, semantries.

1. Clinical Evaluation of Language Function.
2. Test of Language Competence.
3. Sequential Inventory of Communication Development.
4. PPVT.
5. Test of Auditory Comprehension of Language.
6. Structured Photographic Expressive Language Test II.
7. Developmental Sentence Scoring.

7. *Language components* are also assessed using tests which gives profiles of data. Checklists are also used.

8. *Hearing disorders* are always assessed by speech pathologists where discrimination, perception, processing are assessed.

9. *Residential speech pathologists* also assess social audiological, intelligence, neuromotor functions with proper trainng.

Language Disorders: Characteristics

Language on the other hand comprises of form, content and use. Form includes phonological process, syntactic process and morphological process. Content includes semantics or meaning. Use refers to pragmatic process i.e., use of appropriate language in communication.

Language disorders in preschool and early elementary school aged children are often discussed in terms of pattern of abnormal development of language. Leonard (1986) identified five patterns of developmental language delay in young children. But the two crucial are:

1. Slow language development but will catch up his peers.
2. Very slow language development because of limited intelligence and will not catch up his peers.

Leonard (1986) stressed that mental retardation is a cause of language delay so also autism. Aphasia also results due to brain damage often arising out of serious illness or head injury. Severe hearing impairment causes major obstacle in developing language. Further, language disorder are linked with poor auditory perceptual ability, abnormalities and delays in cognitive development, environmentally, linguistically, and socially deprived language learning environments and nonspecific brain damage (Leonard, 1986) of course with limited supporting evidence.

Language learning disability children show three major symptoms: (1) Language disorder syndrome (2) Articulatory and graphomotor syndrome and (3) Perceptual deficit syndrome. These are seen when the child enters into elementary school and these syndrome constitute nearly 40% to 60% of learning disability.

The other characteristics are related to problems with communicative competence, interpersonal communication, semantics, morphology, syntax, and word finding. The child can not adjust his communication to the needs of listener and environment makes irrelevant statements, superfluous speech. Deficits in semantics include words having multiple meanings, cause-effect relationships, not able to find out appropriate words. There are also multiple communication disorders.

Teaching the Speech and Language Impaired

Techniques frequently utilised in training language behaviours include modelling, imitation, correction of errors, training self-correction, expansions, and extensions. These are used successfully by speech therapist, teachers, and parents in facilitating language development. Modelling and imitation are used in a significant number of language intervention procedures (Leonard, 1986). Prompts are also used in modeling.

Extensions are also used by the teacher. He/she instead of only expanding ommited incorrect features. He elaborates with addition to make the meaning more clear. Another modelling practice is self-correction.

Two approaches have been used to present stimuli and tasks. These are operant behaviour management method and cognitive discovery model. Operant training is structured and use repetitive presentation of a single word, process or concept in an individual training session. The cognitive discovery approach emphasizes creating an opportunity to experience the concept or target word. This is the natural way of learning by the non-language impaired child but language impaired children do not learn by this way to the same degree of efficiency.

The regular teacher serves as a model for appropriate production, a source of feedback, and a facilitator in the transfer generalisation process. He assists the language impaired child from the emotional trauma and ridicule that often accompanies speech and language in the regular classroom. Teachers should see that their (language impaired) self-concepts are not lowered.

Role of Resource Teacher cum Speech Therapist

The Resource Teacher can speech language pathologist would teach proper breathing pattern. The child should be instructed and helped to use short phrase, and correct pause which are beneficial. The use of less number of speaking task would facilitate learning. Girdles, Slings or braces are used to facilitate respiratory ease while speaking.

Speech language pathologist can teach proper voice usage, after identifying student's optimum pitch, and improper phonatory techniques. Use of drawings and diagrams to explain phonatory process are essential. Minimal speaking demands at early stages and use of picture boards, writing, typing, artificial language, artificial speech synthesis, computer, etc. facilitate removal of phonatory disorders in speech.

Speech language pathologist can give appropriate training: such as: Training in auditory discrimination, correct production of target sound, sound imitation, self-correction, allowing successful communication by use of standard teaching materials and techniques such as isolate the sound, repeat the sound, associate the sound, produce the sound by the pupils, practice it and use it in speech.

Nasality errors are the most common type of resonatory disorders. The Resource Teacher and Speech Therapist can tract incorrect articulatory production and teach. Use of motor-kinesthetic cues and amplification than auditory cues, standard teaching materials, and use of nonverbal communication where necessary can also be used.

The most common prosodic process disorder is stuttering for which behaviour therapy, counselling, psychoanalytic therapy, slow speech production training are used. Parental counselling to create and facilitate fluency, and cure stuttering are also simultaneously used. Fluency shaping therapy are also practiced by the child with language deficiency and by initiating utterances with smooth soft vocal production, stuttering is reduced.

The Regular Classroom Teacher

Whatever approach is used, the classrom teacher can use certain tips as follows:

1. Maintain a relaxed rather than authoritarian classroom atmosphere.
2. React objectively and unemotionally to the stuttering.
3. Emphasize a good listening attitude among the class members.
4. Allow the student to complete his or her speech attempts without interruption.
5. Provide opportunities that will serve to build up the stuttering child's self-esteem.
6. Watch for situations in which the stutterer is more likely to be fluent and provide opportunity for those situations.
7. Avoid placing the stutterer in situation requiring rapid oral responses such as oral drills.
8. Avoid allowing the child to build expectancy fears of oral recitations are used. Do not proceed down rows of children or in alphabatical order. Instead, call randomly on children for responses.

9. In calling on students for oral responses, try to select questions for which you are sure the stuttering child has the answer.
10. If the child has just expanced a speech interruption, direct the child's attention to something else other than speech, to reduce development of sound, word or situation linkage to stuttering.

More specifically the regular classroom teacher has to discharge certain responsibilities. He has to—

1. Refer the pupil to speech therapist.
2. Integrate speech and language activities throughout the school day with whatever subject is being taught.
3. Provide a good speech and language model.
4. To improve comrehension use short phrases, sentences and questions when speaking to pupils.
5. Use concrete experiences and role playing the meaning of words, sentences, and stories.
6. Provide visual cues such as pictures.
7. Give enough time to gather their thoughts before they speak out.
8. Give verbal directions, riddles, and display interesting picture and ask them to express or describe.
9. Read stories aloud and ask questions on the story.
10. Repeat words in sentences, use analogies (A dog is to cat as a tree is to ....).
11. Have pupils tell how these are alike or different.
12. In order to improve sentence structure, give them word cards and verb cards to make sentences.
13. Encouraging children to ask questions, role play telephone conversations, use comic strips, picture cards, film strip, puppets, drama to express themselves orally.
14. Have pupils describe their ideal day.

Mainstreaming Language Disabled

Integrated School

The commitment of the whole school staff, parents, and non-teaching assistants, is required if the child is to have the freedom of expression which is so essential for the development of communication skills. It is believed that an integrated setting provides a good language model through able communicating peers. Children whose language is impoverished through lack of stimulation and those who have achieved a certain level of communicative competence and confidence may well benefit from exposure to a language rich environment. Teachers therefore should see that language handicapped children spend a little more time with language competent peers in the mainstream classes. Beveridge and Carti-Ramsden (1987) recommended the use of model called SCORE for language teaching in the mainstream classes. Scores stands for situation, contrasts, order, regulation, and encouragement.

Situation should be natural communicative context of managing the child to make meanings clear by appreciating contrasts. The teacher may use a functional approach or developmental approach or both in an order to help LI children understand language. Language environment be organised which is meant by regularity. There should be adequate liasion, aims, teachers, parents, therapists, pupils. A great deal of fact and sensitivity is required to help LI children learn without embarssment.

Special School

Special school is effective if the teacher and speech therapists are on full-time establishments. Most pupils attending the special schools for language disabled children have achieved excellent results but with poor modelling.

Webster and McConnell (1987) advised teaching language in natural contexts than direct teaching of language. The children are encouraged through shared reading to understand the structure of the text, and then to develop the guesswork strategies using picutre cues and story content to argument any decoding strategies they may have such as initial letter recognition. Later they may be taught that text can be used to analyse, argue, describe, expose, instruct and express. This will help them to learn the text and plan their own communicative exchanges both written and verbal (Beveridge and Carti-Ramsden, 1987).

Speech and language are fundamental processes undergoing all cognitive functioning. In this chapter the discussion has centred around analysing speech defects, deficiency in lingustic structures and various techniques of teaching skills in the mainstreamed classroom. The role of teacher and speech therapist have also been highlighted alongwith provision for special schools.

Highlights of the Chapter

Speech disorders include respiration disorders, voice disorders, articulation disorders, stuttering, stammering, and cluttering. Language disroders are characterised by abnormal comprehension. Nearly four per cent of the school children have these problems. Important causes of speech and language handicap include: paralysis, mental illness, and general retardation.

Speech disorders involves shortcomings such as: faulty pronounciation, unpleasant voice quality, defective voice, difficulty in understanding, difficulty in forming oral sentences, stuttering, stammering. Speech disordered children have abnormal respiration, faint voice, unclear sounds, short speech, harsh voice, substitution errors etc.

Language disorders are due to brain damage, mental retardation, sensory and perceptual impairments, or environmental deprivation. Language assessment can be done by speech and language pathologists using standardised tests for form, content and use.

Characteristics of these children indicate problems in communicative competence, inter-personal communication, semantics, morphology, and syntax.

Teaching language disordered children involves modelling, imitation, correction of errors, training, self-correction, expansions and extensions. These are used by speech therapists, parents and teachers.

These children study in the regular classroom with resource room facilities where the resource teacher and speech therapists teach proper breating patterns, use of short phrases, correct pauses, discrimination training, sound imitation and several speech therapeutic procedures.

The regular classroom teacher maintains a relaxed atmosphere, emphasizes good listening skills, helps build self-esteem, avoids expectancy fears, uses integrated speech and language activities through out the school day, uses visual cues, gives verbal directions, uses concrete experiences, encourages pupils for self expression etc. Besides integrated education, special schools are there for severely handicapped children of this kind where teachers teach speech therapy on whole time basis.

Review Questions

1. What is understood by speech impairment?
2. What is understood by language impairment?
3. How would you identify speech disorders?
4. How would you identify language disorder?
5. Discuss the role of a resource teacher cum speech therapist?
6. Discuss the role of regular classroom teacher of the speech and language disabled?
7. Is special school better for speech and language disabled children?

References

Beveridge, M. and Carti-Ramsden, G., (1987), *Children with Language Diabilities,* Open University Press.

Bloodstein, O., (1984), *Speech Pathology: An Introduction,* Boston: Houghton Mifflin.

Gearhart, B.R. and Weigharn, M.N., (1976), *The Handicapped Child in the Regular Classroom,* St. Louis: Mosby.

Leonard, L., (1986), *Early Language Development and Language Disorders: An Introduction,* Columbus, OH: Charles E. Merrill.

Panda, K.C., (1993), *Elements of Child Development,* Ludhiana: Kalyani Publishers.

Perkins, W., (1977), *Speech Pathology,* St. Louis, C.V. Mosby.

Webster, A. and McConnell, C., (1987), *Children with Speech and Language Disroders,* London, Cassell.

Van Riper, C. and Emerick, L., (1984), *Speech Correction: An Introduction to Speech Pathology and Audiology,* Englewood, NJ: Prentice Hall.

Chapter 11

Slow Learning Children

Slow learning children represent a group who underachieve in the classroom.. While no special educational provisions are required for them, special instructional techniques are a must. The present chapter brings into the knowledge of students:

- the exact meaning of slow learning children,
- causes and their characteristics,
- the identification procedures,
- the teaching principles with regard to curricular and non scholastic activities,
- the responsibilities of the regular classroom teacher, and
- the organisation of the curriculum for these children.

Who is a Slow Learning Child?

Historically, the slow learning child has been described in numerous ways. Ingram (1960) considered them as educable mentally retarded child. Johnson (1963) stated that "slow learners comprise the largest group of mentally retarded persons". Today the term 'slow learner' most accurately describes children and adolescents who learn or underachieve, in one or more academic areas, at a rate that is below average yet not at the level considered comparable to that of an educable mentally retarded student. Intellectually, sow learners, score most often between 75 and 90 IQ—between the borderline and low-average classifications of intelligence (Knoff, 1987).

The term 'slow learner' is frequently used to cover various groups of children otherwise referred to 'dull', 'retarded' or 'educationally subnormal'. In the present circumstances it is used more widely to indicate the fairly large group of children whose learning is slowed down by one or more factors of which limited ability may be one. The common factor with all pupils seen was some measure of educational retardation, the contributing factors being manifold e.g., cultural and poverty, family inadequacies, and parental disharmony. Pupils from such homes as these may well function as 'slow learner' even though their intellectual potential may be considerably higher.

It suggests that retardation of slow learners is something to be remedied, that if given appropriate treatment—usually interpreted as additional lessons in the three R's than their backwardness will be overcome, and they will take their place along the side of the more able. Common experience, however, disprove this. But slow learners with intellectual limitations do need a curriculum and type of extra care in special class although in recent years such a label is not within the domain of special education.

Slow learner is not discussed in the standard special education textbook. In fact, slow learners are not special education students. Slow learners receive additional supportive services, in the regular classroom, curricula and learning. Some slow learners are inappropriately labeled learning disabled to maintain the enrolment of some special education classrooms or because they would otherwise fail in the regular classroom, even though they do not have special education needs.

There is no diagnostic or descriptive profile that characterizes the slow learner. Slow learners are described by their specific academic weakness.

During the last several years there has been increased interest in the education of slow learners, otherwise known as backward pupils in schools. These groups as has been said does not come under special education categorisation, yet because of their incidence in the classroom there is a need for prevention and treatment of backwardness whether they are in ordinary schools or in special education classes. The word "slow learning children" is a broad generic term (Tansley and Guilford, 1971).

Causes

Educationally subnormal children or slow learning children were pupils who by reason of limited ability or other conditions resulting in educational retardation, required some specialised form of education, wholly or partly in substitution for the education normally given in ordinary schools.

These terminologies have less stigmatised effect. They are not based on medical or psychological categorisation but purely on educational needs. The causes of the educational backwardness are: school absence, ill health, unfavourable school and home conditions, and emotional barriers to learning. The cause is not so much of limited ability. Therefore, these chidlren need suitable arrangements in ordinary school. The forms that special educational treatment should take will need to vary according to local circumstances.

Slow learners or backward chidlren may be of three types:

1. Very backward because of retarded mental development accompanied by psycho-social deficiencies. They need special educational treatment outside the ordinary school-special school or special class.
2. Ability is not quite limited but have difficulty in learning than average children—due to school and family or personal factors.

3. They can be dealt with in ordinary schools although they may derive benefits from special classes not limited in intelligence but have problems in reading and writing where as arithmatic and other subjects are high. Their causes may range from specific perceptual difficulties to emotional maladjustments. For them some form of remedial teaching is required.

The slow learning children have IQ as high as 90s but are within 75-90 points. Remedial education benefits these children although in some regular schools there are many slow learning children and hence, a special class for them is sometimes necessary. The children receive education in special class or school but move to a regular school after backwardness is removed.

There has been growing interest in placing slow learning children in regular school. But there is a need to allot enthusiastic and experienced teachers to remedial classes dealing with slow learners. In addition all teachers during training should have some instruction in methods of teaching, the early stages of reading and number and to be made aware of the methods of helping chidlren who cannot keep up with their age group.

A crucial time for getting to groups with backwardness is the last year of the primary school and beginning of junior school (upper primary) CA 7 to 9. Remedial assistance should continue the secondary school. Because the gap between the average pupil and the slow learner widening with age.

Hence, the special class for the slow learning children should have 1:20 TP ratio and a little lower standard curriculum. Usually in our school system they are placed in section C or a special section of the same class.

It is not possible to clearly find out who are backward (CA 5-7) because of limited potentiality for development and those whose emotional disturbance has retarded development. The latter group can not be placed in the classes for ESN or slow learners. Many infant schools arrange for extra attention to be given to these children either by holding reading groups in the head of teacher's room by running a small remedial class. Such arrangements can be most valuable as a first step in the prevention of backwardness. From here one can know who are to be sent to special school for ESN otherwise putting them in ordinary school world lead to a drit, and the foundations given in special school would be lost.

Slow learning or backward children do well in Lower Primary School (7-11 CA) if they follow the infant school approach or if there is a special class. A proper diagnostic procedure is followed by using medical examination, psychological evaluation, educational assessment, social history of family and cultural setting.

Identification

The defects of children who are blind, deaf or physically handicapped are readily apparent to the observers. The handicaps of educationally subnormal or slow learners are not always so obvious. They are less able than most children to meet the normal demands of education and life in modern community or society. Culturally it is relative. In a less advanced society, even they do not draw attention. They manage well.

The period at which their limitations arise are most obvious is that of school years. The normal living demands certain intelligence, capacity for abstract conceptual thinking, intellectual skills, minimum attainment in reading, writing, simple calculation. A proportion of students are so limited in their capacity to learn that they are handicapped to meet the demands of the normal school-learning. Others are learning difficulties and therefore are slow learners. If teaching is not suitably geared to their slow rate of progress and are not modified to use the most effective ways of learning these children fail to achieve success. Hence, there is a need for special educational measure to ensure for these children the maximum progress of which they are capable in the traditional three R's and in practical, social and personal life. These are quite apparent in the context of universal education in the closing edcades of the present century and which started in the closing decades of 19th century. The application of psychology to education and to the study of child development began to have increasing influence. Binet's contribution to mental testing contributed to a large extent to the realisation of differential treatment for children as per their ability and needs. But's forty years of research provided a foundation of knowledge about the extent of backwardness, its causes and the broad lines of treatment for the slow learning children.

Slow learning and/or educationally subnormal children have limited intellectual development. Many of these chidlren grow up in circumstances which limit rather than foster the development of intelligence. Very poor homes rarely provided as good opportunities for the incidental learning as average or good homes do. Skeels and Dye (1939) and Skodak and Skeels (1949) studies showed that removing children from extremely unfavourable environment to one which is very much more favourable would seem to result in quicker mental development during preschool years. Nursery school experiences accelerate mental growth. Unfavourable school and home conditions are responsible for decline of intelligence.

Characteristics

Slow learning children or ESN children showed a characteristic weakness in thinking capacity, finding out relationships, similarity, familiarity, reasoning, observing characteristics of objects, poor development of concept, language and number concepts.

The ESN/Slow learning chidlren also reflect poor verbal ability, the vocabulary is brief, sentences are simple. They have difficulty in abstractions. The abstracting difficulty is also seen in non-verbal tasks such as matching shapes, drawing figures, completing rigs and puzzles, remembering patterns etc.

The children should therefore be taught using thinking and problem solving in practical activities.

One of the most frequent complaints about backward children is the weakness of their memory. Burt (1946) remarked "of all the special mental disabilities that hamper educational progress, the most frequent is a weakness in what may be termed as long distance memory". Dull children need to go over material more times before it is fixed in their minds, and more frequent revision is required to prevent forgetting. There is no doubt that ESN or slow learning children have poorer powers of retention than average children but it would be a mistake to assume that remedy lies in repetition. The quality of imparting initial learning is important.

One cause of poor memory is weakness in attention. These children are restless and distractible. There are evidences of avoidance resulting from previous failure and consequent dislike of a subject. They often glance at words than read them carefully. Attention may be poor because of mismatched or irrelevant materials. The method of presenting learning materials may not facilitate accurate perception of it.

One of the ways in which memory of slow learners can be improved is by ensuring that as many associations are made as possible. These children are weak in this regard. The teacher must therefore pay special attention to getting children to see links which brighter children would probably see for themselves various sensory modalities can be used to present the links and associations. For example the word 'night' can be first sequence of letters n-i-g-h-t. Then visual displaying, speaking, asking him to write down, linking it with light, sight, pight. What is important—presenting the material in a way that facilitates the making of generalisations. Meaningful associations are of great importance. Words can be taught by appropriate actions here, there, down, up, over, under. The slow learner can learn by understanding and then they need more repetition, revision, and practice to retain.

Socio-Emotional

ESN or slow learning children have a feeling of insecurity which arise out of personal inadequacy physical or mental. They are unable to control feelings of aggression or outbursts. The ESN children continuously seek attention and approval of the teacher. They do experience the need for acceptance from the peer groups. The isolated child may withdraw still further. School should provide means for successful achievement which will enhance the sense of selfesteem. These children are more dependent and have limited capacity for taking responsibilities. Opportunities for becoming independence and responsible are to be provided in the school. They are as such not curious. If school can offer security and affection it can go a long way in the education of slow learners.

On the other hand, children whose basic needs have been inadequately satisfied they may be difficult to motivate to learn. They instead are upset by feelings of hostility and jealousy or riddled with anger for their own failures. They use several defenses: immaturity, regression, compensatory activity, withdrawal, fantasy.

These characteristics are not directly related to low intelligence so much as to the educational consequences of low intelligence. Educational and social failures are to be avoided in planning activities in the school.

The teacher in trying to promote social and emotional development must try to recognise the where the child is and start from that point. The child has to learn how to control socially unacceptable expressions of temper, jealousy, egocentricity.

The family is of first importance in creating a sense of security. The child besides other family conditions (disharmony, separation) feels insufficient share of affection or is disappointed then there is an emotional problem. School can provide experience of success but attitude of the family is more important. Parents are not prepared to accept the child's backwardness. Sometimes they are over anxious which contributes the educational backwardness. The emotional growth of every child should be done as carefully and in just as routine a manner as we watch his physical growth.

1. First a congenial teacher-pupil relationship and a relaxed classroom atmosphere which permits a normal, spontaneous expression of the child's personality is necessary.
2. The observer should have intention as well as experience.
3. A systematic observation outline has to be kept in respect of these children.

Physical Characteristics

There are three groups of children who are slow to develop both mentally and physically and there appears to be a slow growth potential resulting in all round immaturity. (1) The ESN/slow learning children are poor in dressing, using drawing and writing materials and tools. They need large practice in climbing, jumping, skipping, dancing, games etc. They also need feelings of success and confidence and improved social development. (2) Many ESN children have better physical development than mental development. (3) Children whose capacity to learn is reduced because of sickness, minor ailments, malnutrition etc. The children can be screened for sensory defects if any which are not easily observed but affect the learning and adjustment of children. Regular physical and motor development activities can be introduced to benefit these slow learners.

Educational Provisions

Teaching Techniques and Principles

1. Individualisation of treatment should be adopted to teach ESN or SL children according to the needs of a particular type of mental ability. This principle calls for skillful teaching which is based on knowledge of children's development and of the ways children learn to give the children suitable learning experiences. It is not individual treatment. It is learning in groups but based on individual needs on the basis of which grouping has been done. This is practicable in an ordinary classroom.
2. Use of appropriate methods of learning. The various aspects of growth physical, emotional, and intellectual should not be considered in isolation but as parts of a dynamic integrated process.
   a. The slow learners are to be motivated. It can be done through a sense of satisfaction through a sense of accomplishment. He can learn if the situation gives him security and confidence. Good techer pupil relationship is vital at all times.
   b. *Learning readiness:* Activities should be planned to provide readiness for learning for preschool stage of all kinds intellectual, emotional, social and physical. The teacher has to recognise whether the child is ready for the next stage by systematic observation of his performances.
   c. *A practical approach* based on meaning and usefulness. The ESN/SL children would be more at home if they can hear, see, and touch and which are within his experience. Teaching which is related to practical human experience is more successful than teaching which involves abstractness, symbols and delayed gratification.
   d. *Concept Formation:* ESN/SL children are capable of making simple generalisations but they must be given ample opportunities to experiment, explore and discuss. The child can be shown or let to discover relationships, similarities, his curiosity is aroused, his interests can be expanded and enriched. In a nurturing classroom he will be willing to experiment and learn by doing. His concepts are to be developed.
   e. *Grading of Work:* In case of ESN/SL children the materials are to be graded to ensure continuous progress and feelings of success. This is real difficulty for the teacher as textbooks are written by others. The teacher can make his own material or analyse the task and make a graded presentation to ensure learning by the slow learning pupil.
   f. *Assessment of Progress:* It is recommended that for the ESN/SL child a cumulative record be kept of his achievements over a period so that individualized treatment is ensured. The child here can compete against himself.

g. *Consolidation:* Frequent repetition, adequate revisions are to be encouraged for better consolidation of the learned material.

h. *Active Methods:* The child must do things with his body, his head and his brain. He must be given freedom to learn and experience. He must experiment and experience.

3. *Cooperation Between Various Professionals*

   In diagnosis, treatment and resarch cooperation between teachers, doctors, psychologists, administrator and social workers is vital. The psychologist can make a contribution by providing a detailed picture of the child's personality, by discovering any anomalies in development, perceptual and conceptual difficulties, intellectual strength and weaknesses emotional abnormalities and by investigating learning difficulties generally, including treatment procedures. The importance of social workers is greatly felt but it has not taken off.

4. *Parent Education and Guidance*

   There are many difficuties that can arise because of wrong attitudes in home. The improvements brought by teachers of ESN or SL children are often nullified by bad home conditions and parental neglect or ignorance. Parents therefore need advice on how to promote development of their handicapped children. The parents therefore are to be guided and in this context a social worker would be of great assistance.

The Organisation of Curriculum

In case, the slow learning children are placed in the special class or special school, the curriculum has to be based on logical, physical and social aspects. The contents however, may vary according to the age and need of the child. The curriculum must be specially designed to assist the total growth as well as to develop basic skills and knowledge. It should not be a mere watering down of the curriculum designed for a normal school. To segregate children and give such a curriculum would be a travesty of special educational treatment. On rare occasions they should be placed in a special class.

However, it must involve (a) central core language and number (b) periphery subjects e.g., environment, creative and aesthetic activities, and practical interests. Both should be related. Time table must keep a balance between core and periphery subjects as well as social and group activities. The organisation should take the following consideration into account.

a. The smaller the school, the more generous should be teacher-pupil ratio. The class size should 20. The school is all age and mixed.

b. The younger the age the smaller should be the class if the teacher is to provide stimulating environment.

c. Some provision should be made for extra remedial work.

More specifically, Tansley and Guilford (1971) suggested that the teacher of slow learners should—

a. Organise the class in small, carefully, selected group.
b. Have wide range of supply of activities e.g. readers, free access to arts and craft materials.
c. Pay particular attention to preparation of materials.
d. Allow brighter children to help duller ones.
e. Encourage children to participate in planning activities.
f. Allow as much as freedom as possible within the well established limits.
g. Avoid rigidity and accept students' suggestion.
h. Be sensitive to children's reactions.
i. Have several periods each week when the class is engagd as a whole on one activity, story, drama, music.
j. Try to obtain parental cooperation.
k. Do not be reluctant to admit failure with an individual child.

Language Teaching

In school verbal instructions and explanations are quite important. Many of the slow learners have retarded speech: articulation, vocabulary, brief sentence, grammatical errors. Emotional reluctance is the chief reason for their backwardness of expression. They need a great deal of speech stimulation through play, and through talking to adults, listening to them. Expression is often lacking in order, sequence and selectivity. Errors in usage are quite frequent i.e., he runned, he catched etc. These children are also poor in remembering messages and listening to instructions, stories and other forms of spoken words. Attention therefore, should be given to listening and reproduction skills.

Poor language may be due to several factors: poor background of speech and language at home, a limited background of experience, emotional and social factors and the limitation of the slow learner's thinking capacity.

These children can develop their language by talking about what they have seen or done, by discussing what they are going to do and how they are going to do it. These are most effective for they evoke stronger feelings of enthusiasm and interest and therefore expression.

The teacher should guide and stimulate the child's thinking about his experiences e.g., what they noticed while conceing to school, climbing tree, making and explaining scrap books, explaining what they learned in television, role playing in a drama in school, listening to stories, puppetry, allowing the puppets to speak to each other, conversation among peer groups. The fact that many children do acquire a better form of speech for use in school does suggest that progress can be made.

Teaching Reading

Reading similarly is not an isolated skill. It is an aspect of the integrated language development programme which includes speaking, writing and spelling. For slow learning or backward children a sound reading programme is necessary. It should consist of:

a. the development of reading readiness.
b. the acquisition of a sight vocabulary of meaningful words.
c. the development of independent reading aided by the use of phonic analysis and other word recognition techniques.
d. the development of speedy, relaxed, silent reading for content and ideas.

a. The Development of Reading Readiness

In the early stages visual method should be used. Teacher should concentrate on the acquisition of slight vocabulary of meaningful words. The classroom should contain plentiful materials to allow activities at different levels of maturity: sand, water, paint, clay, toys, colour, picture books, scrap books, group models. These increase knowledge and interests, vocabulary, powerful expression, improved work habits, social relationships, interest in reading, classification, labeling, visual discrimination by looking at pictures, jigraw puzzles, matching games, drawing and tracing pictures, personal and social development through play.

b. The Acquisition of a Sight Vocabulary of Meaningful Words

The teacher gives written sentences and words and ask the child to draw a picture on the opposite page about what she/he has read. The child was asked to trace over the words and sentence. The teacher makes independent sentence cards and word cards independent of the book. In this way, the child recognises the words. Each child learns comprehension and it becomes an ego involved activity. In this way the slow learning children learned, consolidated their learning, learned vocabulary. The child gradually learns through supplementary materials.

c. The Development of Independent Reading Aided by the use of Phonic Analysis and other Word Recognition Techniques

Backward children are usually deficient in these abilities and require a systematic programme of word recognition exercises of reading progress is to be maintained. It should be a rigid, isolated, elaborate course of phonic drills or word form, and an interesting, integrated controlled attack on the analysis and synthesis of sound units which will lead to continuing improvements in reading for content and ideas.

d. The Development of Speedy, Relaxed, Silent Reading for Content and Ideas

The choice of books is important at this stage to cater for the children's individual interests and reading levels. Backward/SL boys should be little less difficult than their level of understanding SL girls like family situation books, fairy stories and books on animals. With these children particular attention has to be paid for word meaning, comprehension and development of ideas.

Writing plays an important part in reading process and programme. It assists visual discrimination and memory and the relation between visual and auditory patterns.

Some fundamental cognitive incapacity underly reading problems of slow learner. In fact, it requires a significant change in the attitudes. The anxiety which is likely to control the slow learner should be reduced by giving continuous encouragement and initial success. The crux of the matter is motivation. The non-reader is to be persuaded that reading is interesting, it can be useful to him and he can master it.

Remedial teaching must take into account the child's weakness noticed at reading. Silent reading and refresshing are quite significant. Silent reading can be brought by work sheets with instructions. The other method is Kinaesthetic method i.e., tracing and writing words. Systematic work in spelling and a technique of learning would be important in doing so.

Teaching Arithmetic

Arithmatic is a way of thinking about number. Arithmetic teaching therefore is concerned with application of number system to the arrangement, manipulation, and measurement of quanties and the development of the ability to deal with member relationship symbolically and by abstraction in the absence of concrete objects. They should be taught through concrete-pictorial-symbolic modes in addition to general pedagogical concerns being kept in mind. Piagetian approach to teaching number system and arithmatic is quite effective i.e., conservation and formal logical operations.

The Piagetian approach to teaching of concept of number and arithmatic through conservation exercises have been exemplary, e.g., more less, same or less, long and short, heavy and light, fast and slow, middle and end, before and after. The readers are here referred to a book written by the author (Panda, 1993) on this approach. The examples of mass, quantity, number, area, volume, movement are all found in the text.

Teaching Creative Arts

It has been said earlier that most slow learners enter into school with needs of achievement and success to counter act their loss of confidence and sense of inadequacy. Many children are able to achiee success or have it contrived for them in one or other creative activities. On this foundation academic achievement can be based. Apart from this there is a valuable relief and relaxation obtained through touching and handling of materials of moving about and doing. It is as if saying X is frustrated and fatigued in his school work then let him do his painting. There is much to be said in favour of formal work being closely and genuinely linked with creative work. Pent up feelings and hostility or frustration finds a safe outlet in a free drama. The fact that such outlets are achieved in a situation watched and controlled by a tolerant teacher seems to make emotional release all the more effective. Art has therapeutic value.

One of the outstanding characteristics of slow learner is poor concentration. They are often distractible and lacking is persistence. Within limits the ability to concentrate is learnt in the repated experience of absorbing and satisfying activity. Plan and creative work offer conditions for the development of concentration and persistence.

What can the teacher do? The teacher can provide variety of materials and suitable conditions and secondly help and advice regarding their use. The child should be allowed to work more freely and spontaneously.

Knowing Around

Slow learning children can not advance much but their intellectual limitations, often reinforced by social and cultural ones, restrict the range of his experience as well as the depth of his understanding. The child's activities in relation to his environment nourishes his mental growth and language development. Their experience and knowledge can be increased at the initial stage by understanding of the natural environment, why and how things happen exploration, talking and questioning, nature study.

It is said, after Seguin—

1. Teach nothing indoors that can be learned outdoors.
2. Teach nothing with dead things when you can make observations on living things.
3. Nature should be classroom and the school book in case of difficulties.

Of course, the metropolis/urban schools may apply these principles by appropriately having pets and acquarium and by arranging field trips occasionally.

Social Development

This can be looked from two points of view.

a. Personal Qualities.
b. Social Qualities.

The personal qualities of the slow learning children should ensure development of personal hygience, capacity to organise leisure time activities and capable of understanding limitations and of matching the aspirations to the abilities. Social qualities would include getting along with others, listening to and learning from others, as well as avoiding over compensatory behaviour such as showing off, boasting and lying. These can be cultivated during the school years by training mentioned earlier under the social and emotional characteristic heading. Social education must be viewed as an integral part of the whole educational process—in play, in school work, at home. The special/school special class teacher must have some understanding of the child's family and community setting. The regular classroom teacher where the slow learners are found at the early stages of education must be sensitive to these needs and provide directions. The following are some of the cardinal principles.

1. Children can not become socially competent and mentally well if they do not have feelings of success. In school only curricular success is assessed rightly or wrongly.
2. All learning situations and procedures should be so planned as to encourage independent work habits and self direction. Pupils anticiption in learning is a must.
3. Some aspects of social education must be developed step by step procedure, demonstration and daily practice (feeding, dressing, cleanliness).
4. Many children come from home where discipline is inconsistent or non-existent. They have no sense of right or wrong or have poor moral standards. The child therefore has to be taught what is expected of him.
5. The way school and class are run as communities can make a contribution to the development of social responsibility. The discipline system should therefore be consistent and fair and imposition of authority may be kept at a minimum.

Only then development of independence, self reliance and an ability to adapt the changes by the slow learners would be possible. The "regular class teacher" should have all these competencies outlook and experience to handle slow learners in the classroom integrated or otherwise.

Highlights of the Chapter

Slow learning children are not special education students but they represent a group of educationally retarded. The contributing factors are cultural, poverty, family inadequacy, parental disharmony and in a few cases, unfavourable school conditions, school absence. Hence, these children need suitable arrangements in regular schools. Although, some of these children receive education in special school and special class, they finally move to regular school after backwardness is removed.

Identification of slow learning children is not so obvious except for educational backwardness. These children display weakness in thinking, finding out relationships, similarity, familiarity, reasoning, poor development of concept, language, and number concepts, memory. Socio-motional characteristics include feeling of insecurity, withdrawal, immaturity, regression and fantasy.

Educational provisions for these children involve individualisation of treatment, use of motivation and learning readiness techniques, graded materials, concept building tasks, repetition and over learning, parental education and guidance. To enable these children learn better, the teachers have to use small group instruction, readers, language teaching, reading readiness programmes, sight vocabulary of meaningful words, phonic analysis and reading techniques, silent reading for content and ideas, teaching of arithmatics through concrete-pictorial-symbolic modes. Besides these the children are taught to know the things around, creative arts, by exploration, talking, questioning and nature study.

The regular teacher should have all these competencies, outlook and experience to handle slow learners in the classroom.

Review Questions

1. Explain the meaning of the term'slow learning children'. What are its causes?
2. Describe the characteristics of 'slow learner'.
3. How would you identify the slow learner?
4. How would you organise educational programmes for the slow learners?
5. How would you teach the slow learner a given curriculum? Give examples.
6. What would be the roles and responsibilities of the regular classroom teacher in teaching the slow learners?

References

Burt, C., (1946), *The Backward Child*, (2nd ed.), University of London Press.

Ingram, C.P., (1960), *Education of the Slow Learning Child*, (3rd ed.), New York: Ronald Press.

Johnson, G.O., (1963), *Education for Slow Learners*, Englewood Cliffs, NJ: Prentice Hall.

Knoff, H.M., (1987), "Slow Learner", In C.R. Reynolds and L. Mann (eds.), *Encyclopedia of Special Education*, Wiley Interscience Publication, John Wiley and Sons.

Panda, K.C., (1993), *Elements of Child Development*, Kalyani Publishers, Ludhiana.

Skeels, M.M. and Dye, H.H., (1939), "A study of the effects of differential stimulation in mentally retarded children", *Proceedings of the American Association on Mental Deficiency*, 44, No. 1.

Skodak, M. and Skeels, M.M., (1949), "A rinal follow-up study of one hundred adoptec children", *Journal of Genetic Psychologiy*, 75.

Tansely, A.E. and Guilford, R., (1971), *The education of Slow Learning Children*, London: Routledge and Kegan Paul.

Chapter 12

Gifted Children

In the continuum of exceptional children we have so far discussed those who are below normal children, varying in different degrees of handicap or disability. The gifted represent a category which is at the upper extreme in the continuum—representing the superior group. How does a teacher handle such children? The present chapter describes:

- a clear concept of giftedness,
- identification procedures,
- the characteristics,
- the various educational provisions,
- the mainstreaming issues vis a vis the role of a regular class teacher.

After reading the text the students and readers will be able to get a clear knowledge about education of gifted children.

Who is a Gifted Child?

The concept of giftedness varies widely. Concern for the education of gifted children existed even in the ancient Greek and Roman periods. But very little systematic improvement occurred until the latter part of the 19th century. Attention on the understanding and education of gifted children was focussed with the publication of Galton's Hereditary Genius and Lombroso's 'The Man of Genius'. In those days genius and insanity were thought to be closely associated.

After the advent of Binet IQ tests in 1905 and the famous longitudinal study of genius by Terman, emphasis on the gifted became more prominent and especially after 1950 there has been a renewal of interest in the gifted and talented.

The Kothari Commission made a few observations regarding the planning of education of the handicapped as well as about the gifted children. They expressed concern that facilities for the training of the gifted are not available in our country at the moment and should therefore be planned for. This requires an understanding of the gifted and their characteristics, identification procedures.

The number of gifted persons are not very large but the problem is how to define or know who is gifted? Psychologists in the United States began to define giftedness in terms of IQ. A child whose IQ is 137 or above is considered gifted, determined on the basis of a standardised intelligence test. The cut off point beyond which a child will be considered as gifted differed from expert to expert but on the average the child should have IQ at least ot 130 points. This rule of thumb may differ slightly from culture to culture. Somehow or other IQ only did not appeal to the modern researchers as the sole characteristic of the gifted.

One of the most popular definition proposed by US commissioner of education in 1972 reads as follows:

"Gifted and talented children are those identified by professionally qualified persons who by virtue of outstanding abilities are capable of high performance. These are children who require differentiated educational programmes and services beyond those normally provided by regular programme in order to realise their contribution to self and society."

Children capable of high performance include those with demonstrated achievement and/or potential in any of the following areas:

1. General intellectual ability.
2. Specific academic aptitude.
3. Creative and productive thinking.
4. Leadership ability.
5. Visual and performing arts.
6. Psychomotor ability.

The U.S. Federal Registrar in 1975 defined it in a more comprehensive way which included superior intellectual, academic, creative, arts, creativity and cognitive ability. In any case, the term can be explained by considering the characteristics that identified gifted children display.

The definition was slightly modified in 1978, "Gifted and talented children mean and whenever applicable, youth, who are identified at the preschool, elementary or secondary level as possessing demonstrated or potential abilities that gives evidence, high performance capability in areas such as intellectual, creative, specific academic, or leadership ability or in the performing and visual arts, and who by reason thereof require services or activities not ordinarily provided by the school."

This definition has four basic issues:

1. Giftedness is a multi-dimensional concept.
2. It encompasses wide age range.
3. It emphasises potential for superiority.
4. It emphasises the need for special education to fulfil their special needs.

The 1981 concept made it simpler.

"Gifted and talented are those who give evidence of high performance capability, in areas such as intellectual, creative, artistic, leadership capability, or specific academic fields, and who require services or activities not ordinarily provided by the school in order to fully develop such capabilities."

There are several interchangable terms used in the field of gifted. Intellectual giftedness, academic giftedness, creativity talent. Intellectual giftedness can be described as an unusual ability to deal abstract and symbolic learning. They may or may not do well in school. Academic giftedness involves the skills and abilities necessary to perform well in school related tasks. These skills and abilities are memory, logical reasoning and ability to make meaningful associations of facts and ideas. These children have convergent thinking. Creativity refers to an original or unique creation of products or ideas. Talent can be defined as an unusually high aptitude, ability, or level of performance in a particular field i.e., art, music, literature, social etc. There is much of overlapping in these concepts but giftedness or gifted children refer in general to a group of superior mental ability group.

What is then giftedness? Gifted are those children whose cognitive abilities place them in the upper 3 to 5 per cent of the population. The acadeically gifted has an IQ of 130 or above. The gifted children have superior cognitive ability, creativeness in thinking and production and superior talent in special areas. According to Guilford (1950), "the gifted are those students whose potential intellectual powers are at such a high ideational level in both productive and evaluative thinkig that it can be reasonably assumed, they could be the future problem solvers, innovators, and evaluators of the culture if adequate educational experiences are provided".

Prevalence

Approximately 3 to 5 per cent of children population are gifted. Development of this potential is dependent upon the combined efforts of the family, school and community. The incidence of giftedness is equally present in males and females.

Causes

Giftedness is biologically determined (Kitano and Kirby,) 1986, although Gottfried (1984) emphasized a person's SES to be associated with his/her IQ. A midway is Jensen's (1969) threshold hypothesis which suggests that heredity is important in setting the intellectual potential of an individual and the environment determines how much of its realised.

Identification of the Gifted

The identification of the gifted have been done from various angles:

a. Behavioural cues,
b. Teacher rating, and
c. Tests of IQ and Creativity.

a. Behavioural Cues

There 20 cues that indicate giftedness. The teacher plays a vital role in observing these in children.

1. Level of learning of these children is equivalent to that expected of the older students.
2. Reading starts at an earlier age.
3. Awareness of uncommon things.
4. High ability for symbolic thinking.
5. Curiosity behaviour.
6. Large vocabulary for the age level.
7. Mature expressive ability.
8. Ability to apply knowledge in unfamiliar situations.
9. Good problem solving ability.
10. Longer attention span.
11. Dislike for a rigid time schedule.
12. Annoyance with details.
13. Intensive interest in one area.
14. Diverse interests.
15. High energy level.
16. Self-critical and higher aspiration level.
17. Thinking is faster.
18. Poor study habit leading to careless work in certain cases.
19. Requires fewer trials to learn.
20. Extraordinary memory.

No child of course would reveal all these identifiable behaviour but are by and large present in the gifted. Some can be observed more readily and in informal settings.

b. Teachers Rating

Teacher's observation also plays a significant role. To aid the teachers to identify gifted children Renzulli and his associates (1971) suggested a scale which consists of four areas of behaviour.

a. Learning Characteristics:
   - i. advanced vocabulary for age and grade level,
   - ii. independent reading habits, prefers advanced level books,
   - iii. quick mastery and recall of factual information,
   - iv. grasp of underlying principles, ability to make valid generalisations.

b. Motivational Characteristics:
   - i. self starting,
   - ii. persistence in task completion,
   - iii. striving for perfection,
   - iv. bored with routine tasks.

c. Creativity Characteristics:
   i. greater curiosity about many things,
   ii. greater originality in problem solving,
   iii. less concern with conformism.

d. Leadership Characteristics:
   i. self confidence and success with peers,
   ii. ready for shouldering of responsibility,
   iii. easy adaptations to new situation and change in time table.

The teachers can make use of this checklist and arrive at early identification of the gifted. The children's divergent and convergent ability can also be tested using creativity tests. Of course, moderately low relationships exist between creativity and IQ.

IQ Testing

The type of identification procedures recommended by Marland (1972) is given below in order of preference:

1. Individual intelligence test
2. Previously demonstrated accomplishments
3. Teacher observation
4. Group achievement tests
5. Scores on creativity tests
6. Group intelligence tests.

Caution must be exercised if any single index is to be used for identification of the gifted.

Use of individual IQ tests is only a part of the comprehensive assessment programme. It measures cognitive ability. The Stanford Binet and Wechsler scales are used to assess intelligence. To determine intelligence level standardised intelligence tests such as: Stanford-Binet, Wechsler (WAIS, WISC, WPPSI). Progressive matrices, Otis quickscoring test, Cattell's intelligence scale, primary abilities tests are used, depending upon the age level and culture in which the child to be identified is born. Although giftedness can be aroused at any stage of development, yet it is during the school period that has meaning and significance for identification.

To assess special aptitude etc. tests of differential aptitude, Scashore's musical talent test, interest inventories, reading readiness and achievement are usually adminstered individually. Parents reports about the growth and developmental characteristics at different age levels also offer due for such identification. As a matter of fact, teacher's record of pupil behaviour systematically using a checklist of behaviour expected provides comprehensive, objective and overall impression about the children and enable one to draw viable conclusions, regarding presence or absence of gifted characteristics. Recent years also notices use of creativity tests to supplement the identification of the gifted.

Advantage and disadvantages of various identification procedures followed for the gifted children.

Procedures	*Strengths*	*Limitations*
1. Teacher judgement	1. Inexpensive, time efficient, predictive accuracy increased over untrained teachers.	1. Accuracy of judgements questionable: possibility of biased decisions.
2. Informal rating scales /checklists.	2. Quick and easy to administer.	2. Lack of reliability and validity data.
3. Renzulli's rating scale.	3. Well researched; relatively well constructed.	3. No cutoofs given; only one section related to IQ.
4. Individual intelligence and achievement tests.	4. Directly related to identification; scores often used for eligibility.	4. Time consuming.
5. Group intelligence and achievement tests.	5. Time efficient; together predict giftedness fairly well.	5. Good for screening; not for major decision making.
6. Creativity tests.	6. An attempt to measure an important area associted with gifted students.	

Characteristics of the Gifted

The gifted children display certain superior abilities in people from different cultural backgrounds as revealed in general from the studies of Terman.

1. Performance is better in specific problem solving tasks.
2. Greater reasoning ability displayed in problem solving.
3. Action oriented.
4. More productive in individual and small group situation.
5. High aspiration for prestigious occupations.
6. High motivation for physical activities.
7. Learning by visual mode is better than auditory mode.
8. Display goal oriented behaviour.
9. Perseverance is very high.
10. Analytic perceptual ability.

The gifted children have above average physical development. They mature earlier. Baldwin conducted body measurements of 594 children of Terman's gifted group IQ ranging from 130 to 189 (Terman, 1925). These children appeared to be physically superior to the comparison group. Terman (1925) obtained the following physical measure of children.

1. Greater weight at birth.
2. Earlier walking and talking.
3. Earlier pubescence.
4. Precocious detention, early in stage of development.

5. Better than average nutrition.
6. Greater height, weight, strength of grip and shoulder and hip width.
7. Superior motor ability.
8. Less detective hearing and mouth breathing.
9. Less stuttering and nervous symptoms.

Gifted children are academically superior as revealed in learning ability. They usually learn faster, remember it for longer time than the average or normal children. They are highly motivated and have strong drive or initiative in undertaking challenges in intellectual work. Their language and communication ability one high. The mathematical and reasoning abilities are of superior standard besides creative arts and experimenting nature. They often ask curious questions. They have more of persistence and concentration.

The gifted children do show rich language development (Davis and Rimm, 1985); Advanced vocabulary, rapid learning, ability to generalise quickly from principles, tendency to become bored with routine tasks (Kitano and Kirby, 1986); involvement in solitary academic activity and independent ability to learn and experiment, (Bloom, 1982); More task persistence (Bogie and Buckhalt, 1987); Early development of reading, writing, drawing, math (Davis and Rimm, 1985).

The gifted children are well adjusted in home and in school. They are emotionally fairly stable and self-confident. They display a positive self-concept. Their play and leisure time activities are wide and varied. They are quite resourceful. These facts are self-evident from the studies of terman and his associates (Terman and Ogden, 1969).

The gifted children are well accepted in the class. They have a good sociometric index. In special cases, they display special talents in arts, music, painting etc. Giftedness is found without variation in sex.

Ability to express feelings and emotions, enjoyment of, and skills in group activities, problem solving, persistence and self dependence and responsible as well as capable of adapting easily to new situations and direct group activities (Kitano and Kirby, 1986).

The gifted are free from serious maladjustment problems. However, some of the extremely gifted may have adjustment difficulties. They are readily accepted by others in their social behaviours. They are well liked by peers and teachers and they participate in large number of social activities.

They like companions of their own level and who are slightly older than them. They have diversity of interests throughout their lives. They pursue various hobbies and leisure time activities. They are not reclusive, introverted or disinterested in their communities.

Their language development is refined and elaborated. They display independent and original thinking, and high problem-solving ability. They exhibit novelty in expression. These children have the ability to delay gratification. They should therefore be weaned from excessive immediate rewards. They have greater range of interests.

Educational Provisions

Educational provisions consist of early admission of the gifted to provide school experiences as early as possible. Other practices currently used in different schools are described below.

a. Non-graded Classroom

Non-graded classroom is more appropriate for the gifted. The system is like this. The entire course of study in a level of education is divided into a series of units or stages. These are sequentially arranged. Each child in this system is given freedom to complete the requirements of each stage and go on to the next stage at his own pace. This way the duration of the school year can be sufficiently reduced for the gifted in view of the fact he completes the course quite early. This is quite popular in the elementary school years in U.S.A., U.K. and Canada. It appears that this procedures is based on the principle of learning according to ability and its management and monitoring is done through computer and not much of classroom teaching is involved in this system. Tutorial classes are meant to solve some specific learning problems.

b. Special School for the Gifted

Another alternative approach has been to think of providing special treatments to the gifted in the form of opening a special school for the gifted, having a special class in the normal school, for teaching the gifted, partial segregation etc. There are schools earmarked for the gifted in USA but in a country like ours it would be quite difficult for establishing separate schools for the gifted. The constraints may be in less number of gifted children, the linguistic variability, the national ideal for providing education for all. But we have certainly system of identifying good students who may be kept under the gifted category and send them to residential public schools or government schools at State expense.

c. Special Class in a Regular School

There are special classes in the regular schools for the gifted. For the purpose of instruction they sit in a separate room but for social and recreational activities they are kept with remaining students in the school. This permits both academic and social habits to grow. The results of these ability grouping are controversial and unclear. There is a danger of self fulfilling prophecy both academically and psychologically. The teachers of the gifted must be specially trained, specially talented and competent in their fields. Children's intrinsic motivation should be encouraged.

d. Grade Skipping

Grade skipping or double promotion was technique to help the gifted to go to next higher class without proceeding through the normal school requirements on the belief that the gifted child will have no difficulty in delivering the goods in the higher class by skipping the immediately preceding one. This practice was in vogue in public schools and in Government, primary schools but the practice is decreasing in view of the fact that it leaves a gap in knowledge acquisition and allowing the child younger in age to mix up with higher group is not meaningful from social personal adjustment point of view.

e. *Early Admission*

Early admission of gifted children has been in practice in western society to the extent of 6 months to one year on the assumption that the children identified as having higher IQ can keep up with the curriculum demands of the class even though their age is below the requirements of that level. In India such concessions are not yet given. On the contrary, if a bright student does not reach age 14 he is not allowed to sit for school certificate examination even though the child is a position holder in the class.

f. *Advance Placement and Credit System*

Credit system at the secondary and college level takes care of the gifted. Under this system, a degree requires certain hours of course work prior to examination would be necessary for each student. The gifted child can take and often manages more credit in the same time compared to average and slow learning children. As a result he completes a level earlier than other but by satisfying all requirement except for the age required. Graduate and undergraduate schools in Western countries now operate on credit system for all the students.

Arguments are given also against such acceleration procedures on the grounds that mental maturity does not go well with physical, social and emotional maturity. The child may not keep up ahead of in later years when the course demands are high. But if we accept these facts based on insufficient research evidence, we cannot or should not think of education of the gifted.

g. *Mainstreaming or Integrated Education*

These programmes might create a feeling of discrimination among other children but this is what that can be done for the gifted. In fact, there are enricment programmes for the slow learners and disabled. Hence, there should not be any such feeling that the gifted child gets a fell of superiority because of the enrichment programmes are more realistic.

An an educational procedure, providing more meaningful and interesting experiences in the regular classroom seems to be least controversial of the various procedures for educating the gifted. This is also the least costly step and is practised using independent study procedures.

h. Acceleration and Enrichment Programme

Two more popular approaches are acceleration and enrichment Brody and Benbow, (1987). Acceleration strategies enable the gifted to select an educational programme that is challenging and interesting. In this case no special curriculum has to be developed. It does not have any negative effect on social, emotional or academic development.

In enrichment programme students are given additional materials to work within the regular classroom setting. Individual programming and independent studies, using a guest speaker to address the gifted, presenting materials in a challenging and motivating manner, pacing of information, highlighting or telescoping the most important points, avoiding drill exercises are quite effective (Clasen and Hasen, 1987).

Divergent thinking, problem solving and creative thinking can be developed by using Crump, Schlichter and Paek (1988) Talent unlimited model.

Description of the Talent Unlimited Model

Talent Areas	*Definition*
Productive thinking	To generate many varied and unusual ideas or solutions and to add detail to the ideas to improve or make them more interesting.
Decision making	To outline, weigh, make final judgements, and defend a decision on the many alternatives to a problem.
Planning	To design a means for implementing an idea by describing what is to be done, identifying the resources needed, outlining a sequence of steps to take and pinpointing possible problems in the plan.
Forecasting	To make a variety of predictions about the possible causes and/or effects of various phenomena.
Communication	To use and interpret both verbal and non-verbal forms of communication to express ideas, feelings and needs to other.
Academic	To develop a base of knowledge and/or skill about a topic or issue through acquisition of information and concepts.

The authors have suggested some activities but it is felt that teachers can use various activities following the definitions of each talent areas pertaining to level of class and culture.

When acceleration and segregation system do not operate there one is left with the alternative for using enriched materials. Enrichment programmes may consist of:

(a) Provision of instruction in music etc. in leisure time.

(b) Introducing such students to good speakers, new and interesting elective courses.

(c) Encouraging them to undertake activities of their interest, participation in debates, competitions etc.

(d) Making provision for individualised instructions with a view to increase their self expression, skills of enquiry.

Myres (1961) has developed 20 exercises for developing creative abilities of the gifted children. Some of these are (a) combining ideas and elements-try to think of animal that never does ... that might exist in another ... (b) exploring possibilities-write as many as possible for ... (c) what do you suppose would happen, if some one discovered that there is ... write consequences (d) analyses ideas-what would happen if first names are not to be given until one grown up ... (e) seeing relationships-what possible relationships can be there between the following pair of things ... Cocacola-forest fire (f) sensitivity and awareness-sit silently and answer are these things around you which you have never noticed before? Similar exercises can be used by the teachers and parents to accelerate the intellectual development of gifted children.

They should further be made free from peer group pressures while making judgements; and develop independent work skills and habits. Emphasis need also be given for development of critical evaluation and tolerance for different opinions-with a view to examining it more carefully.

There have been a number of approaches to teaching the gifted: (a) Enrichment triad, (b) Structure of intellect model (c) Self directed learning.

TRIAD is more popular approach to teaching the gifted developed by Renzulli (1977). According to this model gifted children are given an educational environment that gives themmore forced on choice for individual instruction.

In enrichment triad (a) the teacher puts the students in contact with areas of study that might be interesting and encourages the student to explore the topic (general exploratory activity) (b) the teacher uses training exercises to develop thinking skills in relation to area of study (Group Training Activity) (c) Individual and small group investigation of real problems. Activities are particularly relevant for the gifted students. This is real experimentation, (Renzulli, 1977). Several skills can be developed among the gifted using computer and research techniques. The gifted students spend nearly half of their time in these activities.

The structure of intellect model has been used to identify the strong and weak intellectual components and develop diagnostic prescriptive programme for remedial purposes for use with the gifted. She focuses on primarily on strong and weak intellectual components, desired from learning abilities test. This should be practised 20 months for 3 times in a week. The self directed learning approach of the gifted is more or less independent study approach using Caroll's model of school learning, IQ, objectives, entering behaviour, instructional process and assessment. The teacher decides at what level the gifted child should start. This is decided on the basis of self-directed having Readiness Scale.

The Role of Regular Teacher in a Mainstreamed Class

Teachers in the integrated classroom should be aware of the gifted child's feeling of isolation—feeling alone in a crowd. There is a need to use flexible grouping to match nearly the different developmental level so that they display similar interests. They sometime face difficulty to accept mistake as others have high expectations. They should be helped to set realistic goals and avoid unnecessary anxiety. They should be made to realise that in classroom convergent thinking is more sought for whereas in specific situations divergent thinking is well appreciated. They should not be unnecessarily concerned with moral and social issues. They should be helped to develop an attitude of acceptance and tolerance of others.

It is desirable to motivate an under achieving gifted for which there is no simple solution. Alternative learning styles, exposure to texts and other materials, avoiding drill and repetitive activities, limiting directions, developing a cooperative attitude are some of the sound practice. Allowing them inquiry skills and organising independent study are some other modalities for motivating the gifted.

Cooperative planning offers an opportunity to the gifted children for developing their potential as against rigid conformity of the typical classroom and its repetitiveness. Gifted children are motivated by alternative choices and they should be involved in planning activities.

Brainstorming is a method of encouraging the development of creative ideas. It requires diversent production. The basic idea is that a problem is raised and then generate as many ideas as possible. Pupils must feel free to express ideas without any fear. The teacher therefore should not criticise ideas, accept all ideas even if these are rural, pupils are encouraged to generate as many ideas as possible.

The problem solving and thinking skills should also be developed with proper guidance. It can be an ongoing activity of the classroom and be integrated to school experience. Activities that require cause-effect relationships, comparison, prediction, analysis, evaluation facilitate thought process. Quantitative subjects such as Science and Mathematics provide excellent opportunities to develop inquiry lessons and research skills. The gifted children may be encouraged to develop independent projects.

The regular curriculum can provide numerous opportunities for creative problem solving, imaginary thoughts can be used to develop potentials of the gifted. Science and Mathematics offer higher levels of cognitive thinking.

One familiar example from the area of Mathematics can be given here.

Level of Thinking	Ability	Example
Knowledge	Ability to identify facts, terminology, generalizations and theories.	Defining addition as more.
Comprehension	Ability to translate, interprete and extrapolate (stating a word problem in conventional form).	Stating a word problem.
Application	Ability to apply mathematical principles to real-world situations.	Determining how much artificial turf is needed to cover a football field.
Analysis	Ability to recognize elements and their organizational relationship.	Figural analogies.
Synthesis	Ability to organise elements into a logical whole.	Designing and constructing a math game.
Evaluation	Ability to make judgements based on evidence.	Debating the values of adding a music teacher to the staff, expanding library holdings, or buying computers for the match department when the school budget limits the choice to one option.

The *regular classroom teacher* should monitor the comments to be sure that praise, smiles, and selection of pupils for desirable tasks are equally distributed among pupils in the class. They should not single out gifted. In such cases they are not accepted by peer group well. No discriminatory practice should be adopted by the teachers.

The regular class teacher must be able to identify the gifted students. They must be familiar with their characteristics. They should use flexible in individualised programme, use various teaching strategies, the respect for student's creativity imagination and personal values. The teacher must be sensitive to needs of the gifted, flexible, enthusiastic and innovative.

The effectiveness of the special educational provisions for improving the achievements of the gifted would depend upon a variety of personnel: the teachers, the parents, the psychologists and community's encouragement and participation in the programme. Current interest in the education in the gifted indicate only a promise for future success but the programme needs constant evaluation and modification.

Highlights of the Chapter

Children possessing IQ of 130 and above are regarded as gifted. The gifted have high general intellectual ability, specific academic aptitude, creative and productive thinking, leadership ability, visual performing arts, psychomotor ability and require specialised educational service not available in ordinary schools. These children are in the upper 3 to 5 per cent of the IQ continuum.

Giftedness is essentially hereditary. They are identified by behavioural cues, teacher rating and test of IQ and creativity. Of course, no child reveals all the characteristics and cues. Teacher ratings are obtained on learning, motivation, creativity and leadership behaviour. As regards testing IQ often individual tests are preferable.

Gifted children are academically superior. They learn faster and remember longer. They have strong drive and initiative with high language and communication skills. With remarkably high curiousity the gifted children school better social and personal adjustment surpass popular expectations.

Educational provisions for them over a period of time consist of nongraded classroom, special school for the gifted, special class in regular school, grade skipping, early admission, advanced placement and credit system, and finally mainstreaming and integrated education with provision of extra care. Acceleration and enrichment programme are must for the gifted to enhance their ability for divergent and creative thinking.

TRIAD is a more popular approach to teaching the gifted where general exploratory activity, group training activity, individual and small group investigation of real problems are experimented upon by the children. The structure of intellect model becomes diagnostic and prescriptive of remedial purposes. The self directed learning approach is an independent study technique for teaching the gifted.

In the mainstreamed class the regular teacher has to follow flexible grouping, alternative learning styles, development of inquiring skills, cooperative planning, brainstorming, problem-solving and thinking skills approaches even though the regular curriculum is being used. However, while dealing with gifted, the regular teacher should not use any discriminatory practice.

Review Questins

1. Who is a gifted child? What are his characteristics?
2. How would you identify gifted children? Describe the procedures.
3. What are the educational provisions for the gifted children?
4. How would you mainstream a gifted child?
5. What are some of the enrichment programmes that you can use for helping gifted?
6. Discuss the role of regular teacher in teaching the gifted in a mainstreamed class.

References

Bloom, B., (1982), "The role of gifts and markers in the development of talent", *Exceptional Children*, 48, 510-522.

Bogie, C. and Buckhalt, J., (1987), "Reaction to success and failure among gifted, average, and EMR students", *Gifted Child Quarterly*, 31, 70-74.

Brody, L. and Benbow, C., (1987), "Accelerative strategies: How effective are they for the gifted>" *Gifted Child Quarterly*, 31, 105-109.

Clasen, D. and Hasen, M., (1987), "Double Mentoring: A process for facilitating mentorships for gifted students", *Roeper Review*, 10, 107-109.

Crump, W., Schlichten, C.L. and Palk, B., (1988), 'Teaching HOTS in the middle and high school: A district level initiative in developing higher order thinking skills", *Roeper Review*, 10, (4).

Davis, D. and Rimm, S., (1985), *Education of the Gifted*, Englewood Cliffs, NJ: Prentice Hall.

Gottfried, A., (1984), *Home Environment and Early Cognitive Environment: Longitudinal Research*, Oralando, FL: Academic Press.

Guilford, J.P., (1950), "Creativity", *American Psychologist*, 5, 444-454.

Jensen, A., (1969), "How much can we boost IQ and scholastic achievement", *Harvard Educational Review*, 39, 1-123.

Kitano, M., and Kirby, D., (1986), *Gifted Education: A Comprehensive View*, Boston: Little Brown.

Marland, S., (1972), *Education of the Gifted and Talented, Report to Congress*, Washington DC, USOE.

Myres, R.E., (1961), *An Experimental Training Programme in Creative Thinking*, Minnessotta: Bureau of Educational Research.

Renzulli, J.S.; Hartman, R.K. and Callahan, C.M., (1971), "Teacher identification of superior students", *Exceptional Children*, 38, 211-14, 243-48.

Renzulli, J., (1977), *The Enrichment Trial Model, A guide for developing defensible programme for the gifted and talented*, Wethesfield: CT: Creative Learning Press.

Terman, L.M., (1925), *Genetic Study of Genius*, Vol. 1, Stanford, Stanford University Press.

Terman, L.M. and Ogden, M., (1969), *Genetic Study of Genius*, Vol. 5, Stanford, California, Stanford University Press.

Chapter 13

Socially Disadvantaged Children

It is true that there are handicapped children of different types depending upon the nature of their handicapping conditions—mental, physical, educational. So also the superior. These children have over the years been subjected to various types of educational programmes and the cry for integration has become the order of today. What about the greater number of children who do not belong to any organic, intellectual handicap category? These are socially disadvantaged groups who had been in the integrated system right from the beginning but were pushed back due to discrimination, neglect, poverty, caste memberships etc. There is a greater need to attend to them. The present chapter deals with delineating.

- Who is a disadvantaged child?
- How would you identify him?
- What are his characteristics?
- How far does malnutrition affect these children?
- What kind of interventions are required?
- What educational strategy are to be followed by a regular teacher?
- How best guidance service in schools help them?

These discussions will definitely equip the students and readers to handle disadvantaged children with greater confidence.

Who is a Socially Disadvantaged Child?

Educators categorize them somewhat arbitrarily into one or more of the following areas of deprivation: economic, racial, geographic, social, cultural, cognitive, and/or emotional. Historically one can identify the roots of this population in terms of their educational needs, but it was not until the mid 1960s that writers such as Riessman and Havighurst had their turns at defining the characteristics that constitute this deprived population. As indicated by Riessman (1962), the terms culturally deprived, educationally deprived, underprivileged, disadvantaged, lower class, and lower socio-economic group, could all be used interchangeably. This is reflected in his classic book, 'The culturally deprived child'. These children have some strength not only defficiencies.

There is a need to develop qualities within this population such as physical orientation, hidden verbal ability, creative potential, group cohesiveness, informality, and sense of humor.

Although Riessman has made great efforts to identify some characteristics that might be construed as potentially positive qualities, he also is cognizant of the negative criteria. The disadvantaged children differ from advantaged class in only six areas: self-concept, motivation, social behaviour, language, intellectual functioning, and physical fitness.

Specific learning characteristics of the deprived or disadvantaged student might include many of the following (1) orientation towards physical and visual rather than to the oral; (2) content-centered rather than introspective; (3) problem-centered rather than abstract centered; (4) inductive rather than deductive; (5) spatial rather than temporal; (6) slow, careful, patient, and persevering rather than quick, clever, facile, and flexible; (7) inclined to communicate through actions rather than words; (8) deficient in auditory attention and interpretation skills; (9) oriented toward concrete application of what is learned; (10) short attention span; (11) characteristic gaps in knowledge and learning; (12) lacking experiences of receiving approval for success in tasks. meeting the needs of the disadvantaged child is relatively new educational approach.

To us the term 'Disadvantaged' means children, who come from socio-economically backward section of the community who can not profit from school because of deprivation of one sort or another, and children who are seen in interiod tribal and rural areas of country where educational facilities have not reacher in the way we find them ina metropolitian area.

In other words, the term disadvantaged would include, children who not only belong to the above criteria but children who are exposed to disadvantaged schools in the rural and slum areas. Hence, both the ecology of the family and the ecology of the institution contribute to educational deficits of the disadvantaged.

Prof. D. Sinha made a strong plea for an ecological model of cultural deprivation (1977). In addition, it is also emphasised that perceived awareness of poverty be it environmental, economic, affective or psychological groups, a number of children in rural and urban slums belong to the category of the underprivileged. One of the prevailing features of modern society in rural areas and slums is poverty of one sort or another, and as such for the education of disadvantaged a new sociological perspective is needed. Our constitutional directives for universalisation of school education will be achieved not only by providing equal opportunity for enrollment, changing the quality of facilities, increasing the teaching personnel and services provided or through shifts in curriculum but significant improvement in the quality of guiding teaching and learning processes. As a matter of fact, when wastage and stagnation would be taken care of, the school attendance approaches 100 per cent of the school age population and the school draws increasingly from the bottom of the pile. The able, the adjusted, the motivated, the upper 30 per cent in ability, have always been in the school and the schools have taught them fairly successfully. Now we have to deal with those who are less equipped intellectually, motivationally, economically to cope with the school culture and expectation and even may seem hostile to what school represents. This segment of the school population is the underprivileged. In fact, if we predict the dropout rates to be reduced in the immediate future, we can in the same tone say that the school population will increase exactly in the same proportion contributing to heterogeneity and children from disadvantaged sections of the community will be more in number.

Causes

Cultural deprivation or disadvantaged arise due to a complex set of conditions which create intellectual deficiency in a child. Some of these conditions are attributed to unstimulating environment, lack of verbal interaction with adults, poor sensory experience, and other deleterious environmental factors generally associated with poverty, low social status, malnutrition, broken homes.

Behavioural Signs for Observation

The term 'disadvantaged' is used to indicate observable behaviour.

a. Progressive decline in intellectual functioning in school.
b. Cummulative academic achievement deficits.
c. Premature school termination and high dropout rate.
d. Reading and learning disabilities.
e. Poor language learning.
f. In adequate social learning and observation in the absence of model.
g. Low attention span and distraction in learning.
h. Lack of proficiency in higher form of cognitive learning and transfer.
i. Lack of abstract and state sequence of events in a learning situation.
j. Inability to classify and form logical concepts, incapacity to verbalise events and solutions.
k. Lack of analytic ability which is esential for learning.
l. They show belief in external factors, i.e.g, luck, chance, late etc. rather than their own self and activity.
m. They cannot delay gratification. Immediate tangible and non-contigent rewards are their need.
n. They have a high sense of avoidance for failure than striving success.
o. They have poor self concept, low achievement aspiration, and low need achievement including lack of desire for self actualisation.

p. Their general behaviour lacks intrinsic motivation. Insecurity and anxiety are very obvious.

Assessment of Social Disadvantage

In order to identify social disadvantage the following scales and tests may be used:

1. Deprivation index—Whiteman and Deutsch (1968). This scale even though developed in USA yet is of relevance after appropriate adaptation.
2. Cultural Deprivation Index—Rath and Samant, (1975).
3. Prolonged Deprivation Scale—Misra and Tripathi (1977). This is most relevant and appropriate but needs shortening in terms of the length of the test. It relates to 15 areas of socio-cultural experiences.

   Housing condition
   Home Environment
   Economic Sufficiency
   Food and Nutrition
   Clothing
   Educational Experiences
   Childhood Experiences
   Rearing Experiences
   Parental Chracteristics
   Interaction with parents
   Motivational Characteristics
   Emotional Experiences
   Travel and Recreation
   Socio-cultural Experiences
   Miscellaneous:

Characteristics of Disadvantaged Children

What are the characteristics of the disadvantaged children? These children show poor academic performance of high drop-out rates, reading and other learning disabilities and have adjustment problems. Socio-economically backward children practically show every such index. They have lower grades, their health is poor, and they have deficiencies in the two most skills reading and language, necessary for success in school. They have minimal training in disciplined group behaviour and educationally they are less ambitious. Children for such environments are apt to have various linguistic disabilities. They also show incapacity in cognitive processes such as: the ability to observe and stating sequences of events, perceiving cause and effect relationships, classifying concrete objects, attributing responsibility to self and in general have poor self-concept. The combination of non-verbal orientation and an absence of conceptualisation very well account for their intellectual deficits and deficit in cognitive skills or in Piagetian terminology, formal logical thinking is absent in all such children or appear very late in the development. The consequences of the cognitive deficiencies are again complicated by their pattern of motivation and attitudes. Psychologists explain that these children have a feeling of alienation induced by family climate and experience combined with a debilitatingly low self concept. They tend to question their own worth, to fear being challenged, and to exhibit a desire to cling to the familiar. They have many feelings of guilt and shame. These children are wary and their trust in adults is limited. They make trigger like responses and are hyperactive.

They are apathetic, unresponsive and lack initiative. It is difficult for them to form meaningful relationships. Although these characteristics are rooted in early childhood family background and social class membership of the family etc. Yet the attitudes of the teacher and the curriculum in the school increase the alientíon of these children. Very often there is a communication gap between the teacher and the students, the objectives of instruction and the actual evaluation of instruction in terms of pupil performance as well as discontinuities in the meanings attached to verbal cues employed in teaching and curriculum materials and the meanings which these children have acquired in their out of school experience. A few teaching-learning problems have also been discussed. Hence, in the educational provisions for the underprivileged, the task of the school should also be redefined not as a cause for contributing to deficits in these children but as an institution in the best position to affect the change. The pre-school programme and compensatory programmes for the education of the underprivileged can work best at the hands of these teachers.

The lower achievement of disadvantaged children could be attributed to atleast five causes: malnutrition, genetic, lack of stimulating early experience, social motivations and cultural values. In addition, the cognitive style or strategy adopted by a group may account for the lower performance of the disadvantaged children. Jensen (1971) has demonstrated that children from low SES use associative learning strategies and evidences are found to suggest that low SES children use sequential processing than simultaneous processing in tasks which demand simultaneous processing.

In India, social and cultural disadvantage is not very clear cut. All low income group children are not necessarily at disadvantage. The high caste is supposed to have a culture superior to that of the low caste Harijan given the same low economic status. The cumulative effect of these widens the gap between Brahmins and Harijans. There are empirical findings which support the cultural effect of a high caste home.

The rich high caste parents showed significantly greater interest in the child's educational progress. They had knowledge of child's educational progress and showed higher aspiration of the children and also made preparations for the child's education. The poor non-orthodox Brahmins were similar to the rich Brahmin which was a bit unexpected. The orthodox high caste and poor low caste had similar but low expectations. May be orthodox parents do not value expectancy so much. No difference in personality was observed.

Panda and Das (1970) examined the rleative effects caste and class factors influencing performance on stroop test and two verbal conditioning tasks. One hundred and sixteen boys aged between 8 to 10 years were used as Ss. They were reading in grades 4 to 6 in the same schools. On the parental income and caste they were divided into Rich (R) and poor (P) Brahmins (H) and Harijans (L). Each of the four groups HR, HP, LR and LP had 29 with comparable mean (from 9 to 9, 6 years) and grade.

Belonging to high caste and to the high economic class seems to be associated with faster reading speed. The superiority of the high caste over the low approaches a statically significant level but it was consistent with an earlier finding and may be traced to the scholastic traditions of in high caste homes. The rich poor difference was not obtained in the earlier study in which the groups were much closer in income. When the contrast in the economic levels is increased, the rich have an advantage over the poor in reading speed.

Sinha (1973) observed that the general performance level of children of schools where children from economically inferior homes went significantly inferior to schools which admitted children from well-to-do and upper middle class families. The test required interpretations of certain perceptual cues. It was also seen that within the same type of school scheduled caste children were inferior to their non-scheduled classmates on tasks requiring simple and complex perceptual skills. Recognition vocabulary, vocabulary of use, length of remark, and complexity of sentence forms in disadvantaged children are all significantly below norms findings which are consistent with Bernstien's differential encoding process. Underprevileged children lack persistence in a school related task and evidence a lower sense of control over the environment than the advantaged children. The achievement discrepancy score is very high in case of the disadvantaged group. Academic achievement is related to a personal style dimension which Kagan has labelled reflectively-impulsivity. The more reflective response tendency is related to higher reading achievement and social class. Intellectual achievement responsible is highly related to academic achievement and children of low SES do not have a sense of personal control.

Many the results supported that with exception to basic intelligence where group difference did not occur between different castes groups, the low caste children did show deficits in personality, information processing modes, and intellectual achievement. And the deficits also indicated progressive or cumulative retardation in most of the measures. Hence, in our cultural background, memberships in low caste and low income family do predispose children to an improverished environment and the consequences of this deprivation are cumulative over time.

Children from low SES and socially disadvantaged homes drop out from schools. Wastage and stagnation is a characteristic of the socially disadvantaged group. Drop out is solely due to cultural disadvantaged characteristics of low caste and rural background. The facts suggest that everything else remaining same the greater drop out rate is influenced by cultural disadvantage or deprivation. There are various causes of drop-outs but membership in low caste/ low income group mostly makes one drop-out-prone in school. Similar trends are seen in all states in India.

Nutritional Deprivation

Poverty may affect intellectual development through physical conditions i.e., malnourishment. Poverty is all pervasie in India and is responsible for social and educational pathology. There is a culture of poverty characterised by the legacy of psychological distortion which manifests itself in profound allenation from larger society and people, feeling in powerlessness and meaningless in struggles. When we live in a society of self advertisement and propagation, these people reamin only conscious of their deprivation. Our attitudes further brutalises the poor and the under privileged. Psychological poverty, intellectual and effective poverty nutritional and biochemical deficiency, institutional poverty: predispose a lower SES child more than any one else for educational under achievement.

Professor Birch and his associates (Birch and Belmont, 1964) have clearly demonstrated that malnurished children were not only of stunted growth and of short height but also were found to be below normal in reading ability and auditory visual integration. Birch suggest that malnutrition might have caused a structural deficit in the central nervous system which affects later intellectual achievement demanding complex integrative mechanism. Poor children are unhappy, have no desire for self-actualisation, they are apathetic distracted and have low n-ach. Because of the ill effects of poverty the poor becomes impoverished in educational achievement.

Nutritional deficiencies constitute most probably the greatest single different to physical health and consequently to mental development and performance in school. Deprived children mostly suffer from malnourishment in one form or another. Current research on the possible connection between malnutrition in early life and mental development was reviewed at a symposium held in Saltjobaden, Sweden in August 1973 by the Swedish Nutrition Foundation in conjunction with World and other bodies. The workshop felt that the complex relationship between nutrition, mental development and the importance of other concomitant or interfering phenomena such as social deprivation and repeated infections and expressed greater need for assessment of the problem and its effects on intellectual performance.

Two studies have been completed by the author and his colleagues on assessing the effect of malnourishment on intellectual performance (Dutta and

Panda, 1977) and on ascertaining the concomitant effects physical anomalies and deficiencies on intellectual performance of low SES children (Spark and Panda, 1971). The former study is based on an Indian sample and the latter on an American sample but both the studies included children from lower SES strata.

In the exploratory study Spark and Panda (1971) the purpose was to investigate the correlates of cognitive performance and achievement in reading, language arithmatic, and intelligence. The study included 538-296 boys and 242 girls, 239 black and 222 white children coming from Powhatan country rural lower SES home and reading in 12 different grades. Measurement was done using WISC and California achievement tests alongwith detailed physical examination by medical staff.

Nearly 2/5th of rural disadvantaged children were under achievers in schools. Boys had more poor attendance in scools than girls. Boys had greater emotional problems, social problems, auditory and orthopaedic problems than girls. Negative relationships obtained between age and each of these measures: intelligence, verbal IQ. Non-verbal IQ and reading comprehension suggested the validity of cumulative deficit notion. IQ scores are lower than the age norm. Arithmatic and reading grades of these children are one to two grades below the grades in which they have enrolled.

Within the class, mean intelligence score and achievement scores measured by California Achievement test were lower in Negro pupils than those in which pupils. Further, the discripancy was in the higher grades. This suggests a similar interpretation of performance different between Brahmin/Harijan studies conducted in India and progressive retardation over age obtained in many studies.

Within the deprived community the girls appeared to be comparatively better than the boys in intellectual performance. There is a curvilinear relationship between sex and arithmatic reasoning and arithmetic fundamentals across grade levels. But in reading comprehension and reading vocabulary than boys across all grade levels children girls did better having physical/orthopaedic problems did not show consistent poor performance in the cognitive tasks. The research findings permit us a general statement i.e., all groups of disadvantaged rural students are characterised by poor cognitive competence, and educational achievement. We essentially came to the same conclusion whether we analysed the results in terms of organismic variables such as: sex, race, grade levels or by dichotomising the Ss on the basis of some behavioural characteristics: social, emotional, physical. Differentation on the basis of physical characteristics offered some meaningful about rural disadvantaged children especially of their educational retardation. Obviously sensory impairments and general malnutritional factors do inhibit school learning.

Dutta and Panda (1977) have observed the consequence of malnutrition on intellectual performance of the low income group children. The study included

360 (180 tall, 180 short) children. The Sweden Conference made it clear that stunting of the child can be considered as an index of malnutrition. All these children came from two caste groups Brahmin (High) and Harijan (Low). The Harijan sample was drawn from both rural and urban schools but the Brahmin sample was only from rural schools. A large number of children were tested with regard to their heights and a distribution of heights was done. Those whose heights fall below Q, were included in the short category and all those whose heights were above Q3 were included in the tall category.

The urban Brahmin sample was not included in this study because of their consistent superior performance in the various studies. Following Birth and Belmont (1964) children who are of short beigh: were considered malnourished and the tall group acted as its control. Each of the children were given a series of cognitive tests including classroom learning tasks, social personal adjustment, self concept, and cognitive style tests. Parents were also interviewed on a parental expectancy questionnaire. The analysis of the data revealed the following results scores on parental expectancy of education of their children, keeping knowledge of chidlren's progress, and making preparation for their educational attainemnt are consistently lower for all the four Harijan groups and short Brahmin children compared to tall Brahmin children. The scores in case of the short Brahmin children is also higher than those of Harijan groups. On parental interest about childdren's academic achievement however, the scores of all groups were fairly close except that of tall Brahmin group.

In school achievement, Brahmin children were better of than Harijan children. Tall Harijan children were superior to short stature Harijan children mostly in rural areas. On test of cross modal coding and short term memory (visual) the effects of malnourishment was clear cut. Short stature children of low/high caste did poor composed to all groups of the respective categories. Brahmin children scored high compared to Harijan children. The colour naming and word reading speed did not reveal significant differences between short and tall groups but superiority of the high caste over the low caste was pronounced. Consistent with previous findings short stature children had lower intelligence as measure by Raven's Coloured Progressive Matrices than the children, and superiority of Brahmin children over Harijans (both urban/rural) got confirmed the data. Malnourished children identified by short stature were inferior in discrimination learning measured by matching of familiar figures and had poor self-concept scores compared to the tall groups. Caste differences were not obvious in these areas, although the Brahmin children had more number of associations to functinal words than that of the Harijan children. These results although preliminary at present to indicate the differential effects of malnourishment on cognitive performance of children and parental expectations. Malnourishment affects adversely the intellectual and affective performance of children. Birth in a high caste compensates to some extent the ill effects of malnourishment.

Discrimination and Achievement

Discrimination, 'social stigma, or institutional racism or casteism account completely for the persistence of poverty of intellect, affective relationship or economic handicaps or in a word deprivation. Experimental validation of the effects of built-in-expectancy on the life of the stigmatised has been shown repeatedly following Rosenthal and Jacobson's (1968) "Pygmalion in the classroom".

Even simulated expectancy regarding membership in a low caste or deprived group has also brought significant changes in teacher behaviour towards the pupils both during teaching (Panda and Guskin, 1976) and evaluation (Panda and Dash, 1980). Discrimination does exist and it does impair intellectual performance of the deprived (Paul Freire, 1972).

The styles of behaviour which are statistically more common among the deprived and which serve to prevent assimilation are escapism alienation, apathy, and timidity, and low learning ability. These are culturally determined characteristics and adaptive responses to a given social situation and not tendencies inherent in the individual. Low SES becomes the explanation for everything and sometimes in a completely circular fashion, for poverty itself.

The question arises should be culturally different or the deprived be brought into an integrated classroom. The U.S. Supereme Courts' famous 1954 opinon was, "Segregation of White and coloured children in public schools has a detrimental effect upon the coloured children. The impact is greater when it has the sanction of law, for the policy of separating the races is usually interpreted as denoting the inferiority of the Negro group. A sense of inferiority affects the motivation of a child to learn. Segregation with the sanction of low therefore, has a tendency to retard the educational and mental development of Negro children and to deprive them of some of the benefits they would receive in a racially integrated school system .... This fact has been amply supported by modern authority.

Many of the deficits observed in the socially disadvantaged are more motivational rather than intellectual and cognitive. The underprivileged children display some significant motivational problems which determine a major aspect of their behaviour patterns.

a. They show belief in external factors i.e., luck, chance, fate etc. rather than their own self and activity. This inability attribute causality to one's own behaviour accounts for poor motivation in any task.
b. They can not delay gratification. Immediate tangible and non-contingent rewards are their need.
c. They have high sense of avoiding failure than striving for success.
d. They have poor self-concept, low achievement aspiration, and need achievement including lack of desire for self actualisation.

e. Their general behaviour lacks intrinsic motivation. Instead it is governed by insecurity and anxiety which are negative motivational factors.

These are explained in terms of learning and motivational deficits, feeling of alienation combined with apathy, unresponsiveness and lack of initiative.

Intervention

Can children come back after a poor start?

Do these studies orient us then to think less hopefully about the fate of the deprived group? An early enrichment programme at the preschool and kindergarten levels may be helpful in arresting or reversing the cumulative deficit. For the Indian disadvantaged tribal children interventions in form of compensatory and high intensity education as remedial measures are also suggested. The writer has also suggested the special requirements of an instructional pattern that will be suitable for the disadvantaged children. The suggestion included modification in teacher training curriculum, changing the life style characteristics of the deprived, use of accelerated learning programmes and changing the motivational and affective climate of the classroom.

Perhaps the answer may be sought in training the deprived children for realistic goal setting, developing self attribution, developing a more analytic way of information processing while in school and giving training for intellectual activities and/or skills where they are deficient. But it is essential that parental education is more crucial in so far as providing an enriched interacting environment in early childhood is concerned.

A brief review of such approach is considered necessary at this point. The Coleman data has proved that integration resulted in improvements in the achievement test scores of black students, i.e., Black students in integrated schools do better than those in Middle class all Black schools. Coleman suggests that the overall gain in verbal ability for Blacks in an integrated school is approximately 1/4 of a SD.

More specifically, the findings obtained in Crain and Wiseman (1972) study were:

- Pupils of integrated schools are more likely to finish elementary and high school and to attend and finish college.
- Students who attend integrated high schools and segregated elementary schools fare as well in terms of finishing high school as those whose schooling was entirely integrated.
- The effects of integration are stronger for both men and women students.
- Students who attend integrate schools scored higher on the verbal achievement test than those who attend segregated schools.
- Occupying a deprived status or a minority status in an integrated.school failed to show social and psychological strain among the pupils.

Optimism concerning the effectiveness of preschool compensatory program such as project Head Start has waived considerably in the last few years. Findings have been consistent that at the end of a year of Head Start type of experience children as superior to children without pre-school experience in both intellectual and socio-emotional functioning. However, the superiority of Head Start children vanishes or is greatly diminished by the end of one year of formal school. In the fact of this evidence some have concluded that compensatory education or Head Start in particular, is a failure. It is unrealistic to expect long term effect of a short term intervention. But it can't be denied that the programs have in fact been successful partially in removing educational disadvantage which economically disadvantaged children might encounter in later life. For this reason the Follow Through Project has been introduced which is 4 year compensatory education programme in U.S.A. school system. Longitudinal data analysis revealed that the followup through programme was not capable of ameliorating all of the negative effects of living in an economically disadvantaged group, however, the programme was highly beneficial to the children who participated in it. The longitudinal and cross-sectional evidence together point to the conclusion that the gains accruing from compensatory education programmes are commensurate with the duration and amount of effort which are expanded on these programmes. Developmental psychologists agree on two basic assumptions; Environmental factors help determine how fast or slowly children develop intellectual ability, and experiences during the first years of life strongly shape children's relative intellectual functioning.

Kagan (1975) from his studies in Guatemala, a non-western culture came to a conclusion— "Children, listless, silent, apathetic infants, passive, quiet, timid three years old but active, gay, intellectually cimpetent 11 years olds". He said that children are more resilent and more malleable, that is more capable of making a comeback after a poor start, than most psychologists have believed.

It seems that the evidences are quite convincing that cultural deprivation and consequent discrimination do create psychological disability which in turn arrests school achievement. It is true that deprived children remain in an impoverished environment which hampers their school achievement. But the school is a part of that environment and school integration is a simple and effective method of cultural enrichment. School integration of course represents a partial solution to the problems of under achievement of deprived.

Every of the assumption and group differences in intellectual activities, affective characteristics, parental expectancies with the terms "Cultural deprivation" or "Cultural differences" is an alibi for educational neglect or environmental insufficiency and in no way a reflection of the natur eof the educational process, which starts quite early in life in family and later on in school. In a country with wide spread poverty, affective impoverishment, ignorance of an effective child-rearing process, it is imperative that the most socially relevant topic for research would be understanding the process through which deprivation or a differences affects adversely the scholastic performance of children belonging to various strata. An outline for a process model approach to research has been suggested by the present author (Panda, 1974). Deprivation is a condition, it mainfests in behavioural characteristics through some processes of interaction. If processes characterising the transmission of deficits could be identified then intervention strategies can be well planned. The present review of the work done mostly in our social context, is quite suggestive in this direction. Remedial effects may be best attained by programme that direct attention to a number specific areas and competencies rather than concentrating effort upon one.

Remedial Measures

Certain remedial measures have been recommended. It is true that deprivation does exist among the socially disadvantaged children due to predominantly.

a. Inadequate early socialisation
b. Mark of opperession
c. Organic deficits
d. Inadequate social environment
e. Culture conflicts and educational deprivation.

In order to reverse the ill effects research studies support certain measures.

a. Early modelling and imitation of desirable behaviour.
b. Language enrichment programme and stimulation at home.
c. Affective attention and acceptance.
d. Providing initial success experience to build better motivation and striving for success.
e. Removal of discrimination attitudes on the part of teachers and other significant members of society.
f. Humanistic approach to teaching the underprivileged in school.
g. Instructional programmes may be geared to their needs and ability level.
h. Giving responsibility, recognition, tangible rewards, positive remarks etc.
i. Exposure to sensitivity training, exposure to literature, discussion and group contacts, role playing, case conferences relating to their problems.
j. Presenting learning materials using images, aids, and providing adequate organisers and drill.

Compensatory education programmes have proved the validity of these recommendations.

Role of Regular Teacher

The following instructional strategies for educating the disadvantaged are suggested considering the objectives of instructions and their entering behaviour to an instructional situation. Basically there is no difference in the way in which the underprevileged children learn. Their learning processes are subject to the same general principles of learning as are the learning processes of the average or normal but with a difference, the rate, the sequence, the type of materials and presentation modes. Hence, the need of a few guidelines is obvious.

a. A continuous appraisal of progress and comprehensive measure of assessment-diagnosis via feedback should become a part of every teaching act and basis of planning the next learning experience.
b. If instruction is to be effective these students are to be simultaneously trained to achieve the three objectives: knowledge, skills and attitudes.
c. Since the students come to the school with cognitive deficit a special hour may be kept aside for remedial teaching language, training in how to increase some of their non-intellective characteristics, i.e., self-concept, level of aspiration, n-ach, sense of responsibility etc.
d. Learning of concepts and ideas may be sequenced before they are presented to the underprivileged group, using more of concrete and life like situations. Training for analytic thinking may also constitute a part of the instructional programme design.
e. The imposition of standardised expectation regarding performance should be replaced by more of individualisation in the rate of learning, exposure to varied materials. Instructions must be given how to pace performance according to their ability. The teacher has to ascertain the pre-requisites before instructing them to move to the next step; and make provisions for acting initial success experiences by the group.
f. For educating the underprivileged giving recognition, responsibokity, tangible rewards, positive affective remarks encouragement have been found to be effective and are to be encouraged in schools. Affective interactions and developments to be supported in a school programme.
g. They also need to be acculturated through sensitivity training, exposure to literature, discussions and group contacts, role playing and case conferences.
h. Self-instructional materials may be used best to their advantage.
i. The curriculum should have direct bearing on their life and work especially for tribal population.

What is needed now is that our schools and educational systems must develop a better understanding of the implications of the social and psychological dynamics of deprivation and translate this understanding into educational programmes, into the training of teachers and administrators and into planning of curriculum and instruction. No single device will suffice to countract or to remedy the complex factors, those are associated with the education of the underprivileged. Administratively the problem can also be taken care of by dealing with acculturation problems and school learning by providing early school experience to these chidlren and following an ungraded sequences or multiple entry system. To unlock the hidden potential among these children, a radical change in curriculum and teaching is required. At least the new curriculum which has been introduced is constructed in such a way that it is related to the psychological realities of the child, is tuned to our social and community life, is geared towards achieving needs and aspirations of our people and the educational climate that is promulgated in the frame-work is more motivating in terms of teaching techniques for which orientation of teachers are conducted in a massive way by NCERT, SCERT and State Department of Education. In a nutshell it is possible to conceive of education as a countervailing force to overcome the deficits accumulated in underprivileged groups or what is currently understood as the broomstick effect. It is true that it is not the educators frunction only to reverse the negative impacts of educational deprivation, social and effective insultation, caste discrimination and economic deprivation. It involves all aspects of the community. The task surely calls for creative innovation all along the line. The crucial pedagogical problem involved is that of understanding the mechanism of learning facility and learning dysfunction and applying this knowledge to optimum development of a heterogeneous population characterised by differential backgrounds, opportunities and patterns of social and intellectual function.

Then what do the psychological studies on deprivation tell us and what course of action is suggestive from these generalisations? Deprivation does exist among a larger section of student community whether we call it as due to inadequacy of early socialisation, organic deficits, mark of oppression, inadequate social reinforcement, culture conflicts and educational deprivation. The various studies that emphasise population characteristics underlining deprivation at the same time agreee on the complex interplay of various intervening processes (Panda, 1974) in causing the performance deficit of the underprivileged children.

A large body of literature deals with trainability of intellectual function and reversibility of early deprivation which was in fact, the concern of Binet and Montessori since a long time. There is little research to support that intellectual functions continues to be malleable into adult periods of life and compensatory programmes are myth. While this may be true largely, it is possible to accelerate the educational achievement of the underprivileged if we attack the issue from a more affective and interpersonal relationship angle. In fact, all learning occur in an emotional climate and this is more so far the deprived or underprevileged. Zigler attempts to account for the changes in the affective state (motivation, task involvements etc.). Affective processes are more manipulable than cognitive processes and as such use of social reinforcement giving attention and approval, building positive expectancies through initial success, elaborate comments and praise, non-verbal attention through a smile, do in fact improve cognitive performance.

An area of research in which data are available is the desegregation of underprivileged children into a separate school system, special school and rural schools. Consistently poor children attending school in poor neighbourhood tend to display poor neighbourhood tend to display poor achievement. Achievement levels raise with desegregation and it also brings about overall icnrease in quality of education throughout the system. Of course in our society segregated classrooms are not available for the disadvantaged but there are schools in rural areas which represents the ecology of a special school, Ashram schools and schools where minority group children are few in a regular school. In such schools, the teachers do hold stigmas and try to have their self-fulfilling prophecies achieved. The belief that "he comes from a SC/ST, or his parents are labourers and that he cannot learn", this attitude of teachers is detrimental to the educational growth of disadvntaged. Hence, each teacher must deal with all students population in equal manner and try to foster their curiosity, creativity and make them all active participators in the teaching-learning process. Teacher's behaviour that is warm, permissive and encouraging can attract underprivileged to the school. The whole educational process has to be humanised and building up of interpersonal relationship can effectively contribute to academic exchange and improvement. Teachers can make a different in the life of the pupils and more so in the life of the underprivileged. We have to engineer what this difference ought to be in our policy, planning and implementation of an educational programme.

For the most part, education of the disadvantaged children can be speeded up by disseminating appropriate method of child rearing systems and values among the parents much before the child comes to school. This will definitely reduce the discontinuities in the norms of children and norms of school. In contrast to the varied, detailed and sometimes adequately designed studies and their reports, it is strange that we psychologists in this country do not take these generalisations to the reach of the common man who contribute to a greate majority of the underprivileged children in school.

An important measure is to make education acceptable to the Scheduled Caste and Scheduled Tribes which constitute a major block of the underprivileged group and make education relevant to them.

Role of Educational Guidance

Education aims at bringing changes which will affect the lives of students is a relevant concern for all educators. In the case of disadvantaged children, the challenge is even greater. The likelihood that these children will overcome the handicaps of poverty in rural and as well as slum areas seems to be related as to how effectively the school personnel assist them. In fact, individuality can be fostered and realised through effective guidance service and the establishent and development of these services can be enhanced by an appreciation of the ecology of the individual and ecology of the school.

The rural disadvantaged children live in an isolated and less densely populated areas. These conditions limit their opportunities for adequate health, social and recreational activities, relevant educational experiences and exposure to vocational life styles which could be a means for changing their future. The characteristics of the rural community further inhibit the learning of new behaviours for coping with urban living. It is the special task of the counsellors and teachers to enable students to discover how they can exercise more control over their life choices. Hence, in each school and for a school complex institution of student personnel services is a must. In small schools, part-time counsellors may be the only source of specialised student personnel services. In general, hopelessness and powerlessness or anomic are so strong among teachers/ counsellors that they should change much more than the students in order to make this possible. One of the most significant contributions that a counsellor can make to any student's identity a introducing a belief in himself as the most significant determinant of his own destiny, which I have referred as intellectual achievement responsibility earlier. In fact, there is much that rural disadvantaged children can learn and do about themselves and their environment, but the counsellor shall work with and through other persons significant, in the lives of these students and help them to develop and realistic self-concept.

Considering from all points of view, guidance activities for the disadvantaged may be organised in small groups of eight to twelve. The information giving, task orientation and counselling type of activities will be more effective in small groups for the disadvantaged because they will not be inhibited before an adult authority as is true of an individual counselling situation. Role playing as a technique is most suitable for guiding the activities of the disadvantaged. Further for helping the rural disadvantaged, guidance service, programme needs be extended through parental counselling, community resources clubs, and referral to a psychologist who should be available at least in each school complex. Guidance must form a part of the entire educational programme which students should perceive as personally relevant for them.

Social disadvantage is a socio-cultural-economic deprivation combined with deficit in cognitive stimulation at home which in then carried away to school. In school, social disadvantage is characterised in terms of achievement deficits, drop out and deficit language and competence. Discrimination and isolation accelerate the deficit process. Remedial educational strategies, guidance, suggested teacher behaviour would eventually contribute to reducing disparities, differences, and deficits whenever they arise.

Highlights of the Chapter

Socially disadvantaged children present a group of children who have special educational needs and are socially and culturally deprived as well as different. These children have cummulative deficits in academic achievement, high drop out rates, and reading and learning disabilities. Ordinarily they were not regarded as handicapped but it is appropriate to put these children under the category of socio-cultural handicapped who have a history of oppression, denial and deprivation of one sort or another. Meeting the needs of disadvantaged children is a new educational approach.

Unstimulating environment, lack of verbal interaction with adults, poor sensory experience, poverty, low SES, malnutrition and broken homes are causes of socio-cultural disadvantage.

Assessment of social disadvantage is done by using (a) deprivation index, (b) cultural deprivation index (c) prolonged deprivation scale besides observable behavioural indices.

Characteristically these children are deficient in all cognitive, affective, and psycho motor abilities compared to the normal child. But their disadvantage is not genetic. In order to achieve education for all, attention to this group of disabled or disadvantaged is a primary step. The National Policy has put strong emphasis on education of disadvantaged groups.

Disadvantaged chidlren are either in the mainstream or at home devoid of care except for certain target groups (SC/ST) where Ashram schools and Kanyashramas are in operation. Educational provisions for these children can be conceived by way of (a) preschool education (b) school readiness programme (c) ICDS, (d) interventions (e) ECCE programmes (f) remedial instruction (g) curricular adaptations (h) motivation.

The regular teachers are to be trained to deal with these children and remove from their minds, the stigma attached to "Disadvantaged". Teaching strategies built on humanistic philosophy, culture specific curriculum, self instructional materials etc. are recommended for use by teachers to mainstream the disadvantaged and thereby provide equal educational opportunity. Educational guidance is a necessary progressive adjunct measure to incentive schemes in operation to deliver the goods but has not yet taken off.

Review Questions

1. Who is a disadvantaged child?
2. State the characteristics of disadvantaged children?
3. What are the educational strategies for helping disadvantaged?
4. What is intervention? What does it tell?
5. Show the relationships between malnutrition and scholastic achievement?
6. Does discrimination affect performance of the disadvantaged children? Explain.
7. How best disadvantaged children can be integrated to the mainstream?
8. How can guidance be used to help the disadvantaged?
9. Discuss the role of a teacher in regular class having disadvantaged children?

References

Birch, H.G. and Belmont, L., (1964), "Auditory and visual integration in normal and retarded readers", *American Journal of Ortho-psychiatry*, 36, 852-861.

Crain, R.L. and Wiseman, C.S., (1972), *Discrimination, Personality and Achievement*, London Seminar Press.

Dutta, T. and Panda, K.C., (1977), *Effect of Malnutrition on Cognitive Competence*, (unpublished research report).

Frerie, P., (1972), *Pedagogy of the Oppressed*, Penguin.

Jensen, A.R., (1971), "Interaction Level I and Level II Abilities with Race and Socio-economic Status", *Journal of Educational Psychology*, 66, 99-111.

Kagan, J., (1975), "Can children come back after a poor start"? *Carneigie Quarterly*, 23, 3, 67.

Mishra, G. and Tripathi, L.B., (1977), "Manual for Prolonged Deprivation and Its Measurement", *Agra Psychological Corporation.*

Panda, K.C. and Das, J.P., (1970), "Acquisition and reversal in four subcultural groups generated by caste and class", *Canadian Journal of Behavioural Sciences*, w, 267-273.

Panda, K.C., (1974), "A process model approach for research into retardates parental family, Theoretical and methodological considerations", *Indian Journal of Mental Retardation*, 71, 14-24.

Panda, K.C., and Dash, P.C., (1980), "Effect of simulated information on assessment of cognitive competence a test of expectancy hypothesis", *Indian Education Review.*

Panda, K.C. and Guskin, S.L., (1976), "Effects of tutors locus of control and expectancy information on tutor behaviour and pupil performance", *Indian Journal of Behaviour*, 1, 36-44.

Panda, K.C. and Lynch, W.W., (1972), "Effect of social reinforcement on the performance of mentally retarded children: A review of research with implications for classroom practice", *American Journal of Education and Training of the Mentally Retarded*, 7, 115-123.

Rath, R. and Samant, C.R., (1975), *Construction of the Scale of Cultural Deprivation and Its Application*, Unpublished Master's Thesis, Utkal University.

Riessman, F., (1962), *The Culturally Deprived Child*, New York: Harper and Row.

Rosenthal, R. and Jacobson, L., (1968a), *Pygmalion: In the Classroom*, Holt, Rinehart and Iwinston.

Sinha, D., (1973), *Age, Schooling and Socio-economic Status in the Development of Perceptual Skills*, (Mineograph).

Sinha, D., (1977), "Some disadvantaged and development of certain perceptual skills", *Indian Journal of Psychology*, 52, 115-132.

Spark, H.L. and Panda, K.C., (1971), "Antecedents of cognitive competence, physical proficiency, and certain achievement retarded measures of a selected group of disadvantaged children in the Powhatan Country School System. A research investigation", Washington DC, Health, Education and Welfare, 1-233.

Whiteman, M. and Deutsch, M., (1968), "Social disadvantage as related to intelligence and language development", In Deutsch, M. et. al. (eds.), *Social Class, Race and Psychological Development*, N.Y.: Holt, pp. 86-114.

Chapter 14

Teacher Education for Teaching Exceptional Children

Development of facilities for education of exceptional children are increasing day by day. Does manpower development, particularly that of teachers and rehabilitation personnel, go hand in hand? Are there such institutions and programmes in our country? This chapter describes the facilities with a historical perspective emphasizing the present state of affairs with respect to:

- Major handicaps: mentally retarded, visually handicapped, hearing handicapped, orthopaedically handicapped etc. in the country.
- Programmes of the National Institutes.
- Programmes of Rehabilitation Council of India.
- Programmes located in selected NGO level.

Special education movement in India is relatively of recent origin. However, the institutions have come up for education, care and rehabilitation during the last two decades in a significant number, if not proportion to the target clientele yet significant enough from near zero base. In the present chapter a review of teacher training programmes institutions in the context of manpower development will be described on the basis of available data, to give an insight into manpower planning and preparation in the field of education, training and rehabilitation.

- The nature and functioning of different national level organisations,
- The courses which are in operation in the field.
- The type of research undertaken.
- An overview of the teacher training programme in described in brief to create awareness among students and readers.

Mentally Retarded

Of all the areas of handicapped, the Mentally Retarded constitutes the largest segment but it is the most neglected field in India. There are a very few institutions of teacher training in India for training teachers of Mentally Retarded: Teacher Training in Special Education, Bombay, B.M. Institute of

Mental Health, Ahmedabad, and All India Institute Speech and Hearing, Kamayani School of the Mentally Retarded, Poone; Bal Bihar Training School, Madras. Alakendu Bodh Niketana, Calcutta; Karnataka Parent Association for MR, Bangalore; Jai Vakeel School for Children in need of Special Care, Bombay; Thakur Hariprasad Institute of Mentally Handicapped, Hyderabad; YMCA, Nizamuddin East, Delhi: Central Institute of Mental Retardation, Trivandrum; North Calcutta Pratibandhu Seva Kendra, Calcutta; National Institute of Mentally Handicapped, Secunderabad and its regional centres. Banaras Hindu University, Jamia Millia Islamia, New Delhi, S.N.D.T. Women's University, Bombay; R.K. Mission Mahavidyalaya, Coimbatore who have undertaken the responsibilities of training teachers for MR in terms of certificate courses; Bachelor in Mental Retardation, Diploma in Special Education; B.Ed. and M.Ed. in Special Education, Post Graduate Diploma i Mental Retardation. The institutes addressed themselves to offer teacher training for the teachers of mentally retarded. These institutes also offer one/two year Diploma in teaching the mentally retarded. Number of students admitted in these institutions are quite limited i.e., about 400 in all in these institutions.

The curriculum includes: Education for handicapped children, psycho-educational assessment; — methods of teaching mentally retarded, behaviour therapy, psychology of the handicapped, medical care of handicapped, occupational therapy, auditory and speech therapy and project work. At present curriculum have been standardised by RCI.

Visually Impaired

Upto 1980, there were four centres for the training of teachers of the blind or visually impaired, one each in Madras, Calcutta, Delhi and Bombay. Each centre is providing specialised training for preparing teachers of blind and expenditure is met by the Central Government on 100 per cent basis. The annual intake of these centres is 50.

The Regional Training Centre for teachers of the blind, Poonamalle, Madras, Training Institutes for teachers of Blind, Bombay; National Institute for Visually Handicapped, Dehradun, Ramakrishna Mission Ashram Blind Boys' Academy, West Bengal; Regional Training Centre of the Blind, New Delhi; Alakenon Bodh Niketan, Calcutta are institutions in India which offer teacher training for the teachers of Blind. These courses vary from 60 days duration (inservice) to one academic year (preservice) and a diploma is given on successful completion of the course. At present there are about 15 such teacher training centres where B.Ed., M.Ed., Diploma and Certificates are given.

Recent centres include NIVH, regional centres and University Departments. Some of these are: Blind Relief Association, New Delhi; Divine Light Trust for the Blindl Bombay: Handicapped Welfare Department, Andhra Pradesh; R.K. Mission Training Centre, 24 Pragana, West Bengal; NAB, Karnataka; Poona

School and Home for the Blind Trust, Pune; R.K. Mission Mahavidyalaya, Coimbatore; Jamia Millia Islamia, New Delhi; Kurukshetra University, Andhra University, Waltier. Mahatma Gandhi Granyo Yog Viswavidyalays, Chitrakoot.

The curriculum that is followed in these institutions include: Educational Psychology, Principles of Education, Education of Blind and Visually Impaired, Methods of Teaching, History of Education and Rehabilitation of the Blind, Anatomy and physiology of the Eye and Eye Diseases, Braille Technique.

These curriculum are almost identifical in all the training institutions and each institution offers practical training and practicals during the course.

Speech and Hearing Impaired

The teacher training curriculum for the teachers of the Deaf currently in vogue at various training institutes: Government Lady Noyce Secondary School, Ferozeshah; School for Deaf and Dumb, New Delhi; Training Institute of Stephen's High School for the Deaf and Aphasics, Bombay; The Centres for the Teachers of the Deaf, Lucknow; Education and Audiology Institute for Teachers of the Deaf, Bombay; V.R. Raja Teachers Institute for the Teacher of Deaf, Pune; provide instructions for a period of one academic year and award a diploma or certificate which enables the graduates to enter into teaching profession. Clarks school for the deaf, Madras; Education Auditory and Research Society, Bombay; Holly Cross College, Tiruchirapally; Institute of Speech and Hearing, Mysore; K.L. Institute of the Deaf, Bhavnagar, Gujarat; Little Flower Convent Higher Secondary School for the Deaf, Madras; V.R. Rina Mook-Badhir Vidyalaya, Pune; Training College for the teachers of Deaf, Calcutta; Sheila Kothavala Institute for the Deaf, Bangalore; Central Institute of Teachers of Deaf, Bombay.

There are also graduate and postgraduate courses in about 15 centres in the country. The instructions include : Audiology and learning aids, Psychology, Principles of education and class management, Anatomy and physiology, History of education of the deaf, sound, curricular studies, Phonetics, Methods of teaching, Arts and Crafts, Problems of the deaf. This course provides practice teaching along with practical and theory classes. On the average 350 teachers are enrolled into the various courses every year.

Orthopaedically Handicapped

The Spastic Society of India, New Delhi; Spastic Society of West Bengal; the National Institute of Orthopaedically Handicapped, Calcutta; Spastic Society, Bombay; offer short term programmes of teacher training varying from 12 seeks to 60 days. Courses include: Medical and therapeutic aspects of the child development, normal psychology and the psychology of handicap, and educational aspects of normal and special children.

These short courses are inservice in nature since no special training for teaching is necessary for teaching the orthopaedically handicapped. These courses are very new and do not have a re-rular intake although each one is equipped with adequate trained personnel. The National Institute of the Regional Centres concentrate on short term teacher training as well as preservice teacher training programmes.

With the assistance of UNICEF since 1979-80 courses were organised for teacher training—one by the spastic society of India and the other by the B.M. Institute for the teachers of Mentally Retarded children. Various courses on Orthotics, Prosthotics, OT, PT, Rehabilitation, Developmental Therapy etc. are conducted by several institutes such as: Christian Medical College, Velore, Seth G.S. Medical College, Bombay; Institute of Social Sciences and Research, Vellore; Patna Medical College, Vikalanga Kendra, Allahabad; School of Prosthetics and Orthotics, Madras; Dept. of Rehabilitation, Safdarjang; All India Institute of Physical Medicine and Rehabilitation, Bombay.

The All India Institute of Speech and Hearing, Mysore

This India Institute established in 1965 in managed by Government of India. It has exceptionally well qualified staff for imparting therapeutic services as well as teacher training the area of Mentally Retarded, Deaf, Orthopaedically handicapped. The graduate degree leading to Bachelor of Science is of 3 Years' duration and the post-graduate degree leading to M.Sc. is of 2 years duration. There is also facilities for advanced research in all these areas of handicap including speech and hearing disorders leading to Ph. D. so far, 246 candidates have obtained the B.Sc. and 158 have obtained M.Sc. degree. The annual intake is 23 and 13 for graduate and post-graduate courses respectively. This institute is an ideal one for undertaking research and innovation in special education in the years to come. The institute brings out the Journal on Speech and Hearing.

National Council of Educational Research and Training (NCERT)

The National Council of Educational Research and Training (NCERT) was established on 1st September, 1961 with its headquarters at New Delhi with a view to improving school education. It is an autonomous organisation registered under the Societies Registration Act, 1860 and functions as the academic adviser to the Ministry of Education and Social Welfare. In formulating and implementing its policies and programmes in the field of school education the Ministry of Education draws upon the expertise of the NCERT.

With reference to special education, NCERT has earlier a department of special education within teacher education and special education cells in all its four Regional Colleges of Education. It is pioneer in running six months key/ Resource Teacher Training at its headquarter and Multicategory Training of Teachers in the four Regional Institutes of Education. Besides, it has assisted in running one week course teachers training of primary teachers, six week's intensive course for selected teachers of PIED. The Regional Institutes of

Education also run B.Ed. and M.Ed. courses with specialisations in one area of special education until recently. These courses are on the process of being phased out. The special education unit is now with the new department on disadvantaged groups.

At the centre, several inservice programmes also being run for Principals of DIET, special education faculy of SCERT/SIE, PIED Block supervisors at various times. The main contribution has been among others implementing of PIED project, development of instructional manuals, promotion of research and documentation, preparation of Handbooks: Hearing impairment, Visual impairment, PIED, etc. It has been also responsible for feeding information to data base for POA 1992 and Policy Guidelines NPE, 1986 and NCTE Committee on Special Education as well as to RCI.

NCERT has introduced MCT programme to prepare manpower for meeting the needs of integrated education in schools. The course is run in its four Regional Institutes of Education and in a few centres e.g., Amarjyoti Trust, New Delhi, and JSS Teacher Training Institute in Bangalore. The course is of one year duration and is not disability specific. About 100 teachers are trained every year. The course structure includes comprehensive coverage for enabling the teachers to develop competency to handle major disabilities.

Emering Objectives of Teacher Training in Special Education

... To develop an awareness that all school teachers whatever the age group of their pupils or level of their work are likely to be concerned with helping some children who have special educational needs.

... To enable teachers to recognise early signs of variable special educational needs.

... To give the knowledge of the part which they can play in the amount of child's educational needs and in the execution of any special measures prescribed.

... To give teachers what special education is like together with the knowledge or range of various form of special educational provision and of specialist advisory services.

... To provide some acquaintance with the school classes and units.

... To give teachers understanding of how to communicate effectively with parent's anxieties and encouraging their continued involvement in their child's progress.

... To give teachers in service training of when and where to refer for special help and knowledge in general terms of teaching to handicapped.

The following skills are to be developed:

... Practical skills in observation of children both individually and in groups to help teachers sharpen their perception of variations in children's learning and behaviour and develop their awareness of variation in children's circumstances (home-school difficulties).

... Appreciation of the educational needs of children with developed difficulties—physical, sensory, emotional behavioural or learning the needs of their parents, and the value of the contribution which parents can make to their children's development.

... Understanding of the practical steps necessary for meeting a child's special needs and an ability to adopt the attitude must suit to dealing with particular difficulties and to appreciate the need for modification of the school or classroom organisation the curriculum or teaching techniques.

... Appreciation of the special services available to children with special needs of their familiar and of the advisory services available to teachers. This might be developed by inviting professionals for the various services to visit the college so that through discussion, the students can learn about the work of teachers in relation to other professionals the contributions which different specialist can make, the services to expect from them, and the kind of question to put to them.

... Awareness of the range of career and professional opportunities in special education and the availability of further qualification in special education and the fact that special education offer the teachers engaged in it an intellectual challenge.

Rehabilitation Council of India, New Delhi

The Rehabilitation Council of India which was originally established in 1986 as a registered society has become a statutory body by promulgation of the Rehablitation Council of India Act, 1992, with effect from July 31, 1993. Its main function is to regulate training, its recognition and derecognition and quality improvement in special education.

Aims and Objectives

The aims and objectives of the Rehabilitation Founcil are as follows:

1. To regulate the training policies and programmes in the field of Rehabilitation of disabled people.
2. To bring about standardization of training courses for professionals dealing with disabled persons.
3. To prescribe minimum standards of education and training for various categories of professionals dealing with disabled persons.
4. To regular these standards in Govervnment Institutions, Central as well as State, uniformally through out the country.
5. To recognise institutions training professionals in the field and recognise the Degree/Diploma/Certificates awarded by these institutions and to withdraw recognition.

6. To recognise foreign Degree/Diploma/Certificates on reciprocal basis and to get Indian Degrees/Diploma/Certificates recognised abroad and to withdraw such recognition.
7. To maintain an Indian Rehabilitation Register.
8. To collect information on a regular basis, on education and training in the field of Rehabilitation of disabled persons from institution in India and Abroad.

The Council has standardised several courses for different categories of manpower requirement in the field of special education.

Training Programmes Standardised by RCE

The Rehabilitation training programme mentioned below are being conducted by various institutes in the country have been standardized and approved by RCI. The Council keeps on updating and adding new training programmes as per requirement of the country.

Speech and Hearing

Name of the Course	*Duration*	*Qualification*
a. M.Sc. Speech & Hearing	2 years	Degree
b. B.Sc. Speech & Hearing	3 years	Degree
c. Diploma Speech & Hearing	1 year	Diploma
d. B.Ed. (HI)	1 year	Degree
e. D. Ed. (HI)	1 year	Diploma
Mental Retardation		
a. Bachelor in Mental Retardation	3 years	Degree
b. Diploma in Mental Retradation	1 year	Diploma
Visually Handicapped		
a. B.Ed. Special Education	1 year	Degree
b. Course for Training Teachers of Visually Handicapped Children at Primary Level.	1 year	Diploma
c. Course for Training Teachers of Visually Handicapped Children at Secondary Level.	1 year	Diploma
d. Orientation and Mobility Training Course	6 months	Certificate

Name of the Course	*Duration*	*Qualification*
Locomotor Handicapped		
a. B.Sc. in Prosthetic & Orthotic	3 1/2 years	Degree
b. Diploma in Prosthetic and Orthotic Engrs.	2 1/2 years	Diploma
c. Multi Rehabilitation Workers	1 1/2 years	Certificate
Multi Handicapped		
a. Post Graduate Course on the Education of Physically and Neurologically Handicapped Children.	1 year	Degree
b. Basic Development Therapy Course for Children with Cerebral Palsy.	1 year	Certificate

National Institute for the Mentally Handicapped, Secunderabad

The National Institute for the Mentally Handicapped was established in the year 1984 as an autonomous body under the Ministry of Welfare, Government of India. The Institute serves as an apex body with specific emphasis on training and research in the field of mental retardation. The NIMH offers specialised services keeping in view the various requirements of the mentally handicapped persons.

The aim and objectives are:

a. To develop appropriate models of care and habilitation for the mentally retarded persons appropriate to Indian conditions.
b. To develop manpower for delivery of services to the mentally handicapped.
c. To identify, conduct and coordinate research in the area of mental retardation.
d. To provide consultancy services to voluntary organisations in the area of mental handicap and to assist them wherever necessary.
e. To serve as a documentation and information centre in the area of mental retardation.
f. To acquire relevant data to assess the megnitude, causes, rural-urban composition, socio-economic factors etc. of mental retardation in the country.
g. To promote and stimulate growth of various kind of quality services for persons with mental retardation throughout the country.

At the Institute's headquarter at Secunderabad, there are six departments namely as medical sciences, psychology, special education, speech pathology and audiology, information and documentation services and vocational training. The

Institute has three regional training centres located at Bombay, Calcutta and New Delhi, while Model School for the Mentally Deficient Children at New Delhi was taken over by the Institute in the year 1986. Some of the Institute's training programmes are also carried by a network of supported and affiliated centres spread across the country.

The National Institute runs the following preservice, inservice, seminar and other training programmes:

a. Three years Bachelor's Degree Course in Mental Retardation (BMR) at Secunderabad.
b. Diploma Course in Mental Retardation.
c. Post Graduate Diploma in Mental Retardation.

The Institute oganises 10 to 12 short term courses every year. The duration of such courses is 3 to 5 days and the courses cover (a) portage programme, (b) vocational training, (c) behaviour modification, (d) appreciation programme for AIR producers, (e) media workshop on disability.

Each year a national level seminar on mental retardation is organised by the Institute which serves as a platform to professionals working in the field of mental retardation to exchange information including parent training programmes.

The Institute provides multi-disciplinary team services for helping the mentally handicapped persons and their parents. Usually all the cases that come to NIMH are assessed by a general service team for psychological, clinical and educational assessments. After identifying the different requirements of the mentally handicapped individuals and their families, intervention programmes are decided which include appropriate referrals, further remediation in special services of the Institute and providing consultancy to organisations such as special schools. The services available include:

— Behaviour modification
— Early intervention for preschool chidlren
— Group activities
— Medical management
— Parent/family guidance and counselling
— Physiotherapy
— Special education intervention
— Vocational Training and guidance
— Psycho social services.

Karavalamban Kendra

This special education centre located at NIMH headquarters at Secunderabad admits about 85 children with mental retardation in the age range of 3 to 16 years. Children are grouped into pre-primary, primary, secondary and pre-vocational levels. Admission is offered for a period of 2 years to children with mental retardation who have been regularly attending the group activity training programme of the Institute. This special education centre also runs group activities for children with mental retardation during the afternoon hours. About 250 children per week benefit from this programme. The children in the morning school programme as well as in the group activity programme are provided systematic training and in addition to participate in extra-curricular activities which include music, dance, drama, sports and other recreational activities. Special programmes such as special olympics are also actively organised. Parents family interaction all programmes is encouraged.

The institute has 12 family cottage which offer stay and training facilities in its campus at Secunderabad. Parents who come from far to places and like to spend time with expert staff at NIMH find the facility of such a service extremely useful.

The Model School which was established in Delhi in the year 1964 by Government of India and later in the year 1986 was transferred to NIMH. About 110 children both boys and girls in the age range from 5 to 18 years are currently on roll. Of them 40 stay in the residential hostel. There are 12 classes at various levels of pre-primary, primary, secondary, pre-vocational and vocational. Apart from regular school programme of training in skills, extra-curricular activities like sports, music, drama and recreational activities are encouraged.

Early intervention services are offered by the NIMH Regional Training Centre (North), Delhi for very young children with delayed development and mental retardation upto 5 years of age. Every month about 40 to 50 children benefit from this programme. The parents are given instructions for home management programme after demonstration of the skill training activities at the centre by the trained staff.

In 1992, the vocational training centre was established which offers services of vocational training to persons with mental retardation above the age of 16 years.

To reach people living in remote areas the Institute periodically conducts rural camps. The activities include (a) screening and case detection, (b) individual assessment and counselling, (c) training of parents, (d) creation of awareness, and (e) reference.

In collaboration with NCERT and Central Institute of Educational Technology, the Institute has produced programmes which are regularly telecast as a part of the school TV programmes on Doordarshan every alternate Saturday. This programme is directed towards parents having children with mental retardation and provides instructions for home management of children. This programme is telecast in different languages.

National Institute for the Visually Handicapped, Dehradun

The National Institute for the Visually Handicapped (NIVH) Dehradun, was established in July, 1979, amalgamatin 9 the National Centre for the Blind. The latter was started in January 1950 with a training centre for the adult Blind, taken over from St. Dunstan's Hostel for the Indian War Blinded. Subsequently, other units such as a women's wing, a workshop for making braille appliances, a sheltered workshop, a central braille press, schools for blind and partially sighted children and a national library for the blind were added.

The basic objectives of the institute are:

- to promote research;
- to undertake the training of personnel; and
- to provide certain national level services.

The National Institute for Visually Handicapped is a registered society under the Ministry of Social and Women's Welfare. Its director is the executive head. The Institute has the following divisions: (i) School Division; (ii) Training Divsion, (iii) Aids and Appliances Division; (iv) Research Division; (v) Book Division and (vi) Industrial Psychology Division.

The activities of the institute include operating schools for the blind, imparting occupational training, running of a sheltered workshop, a braille press, a teacher's training centre, and conducting research on several aspects of blindness.

The institute operates two schools—one each for the blind and for the partially sighted children. These schools prepare the blind children for the secondary examination. It is the task of these two schools to try out new methods of teaching and equipment.

Adult blind persons are imparted occupational training in handicrafts, braille typewriting, braille shorthand, music, book binding, radio engineering etc. by the Training Centre for the Adjult Blind. The institute manages a workshop where blind workers are engaged in caning chairs, manufacturing woollen and cotton textiles, making candles and engineering products. It has four teachers' training centres which offer a one-year diploma course through a common all-India examination. Research on several aspects of blindness is also carried out in the institute. Experiments in occupational and psychological research are conducted for evolving new methods of helping the blind. The Aids and Appliances Divisions is engaged in developing and fabricating aids for the visually handicapped which could be manufactured in the country itself. Factors influencing the work environment of the blind and the visually handicapped are examined by the Industrial Psychology Division.

The Institute has a central braille press which produce braille literature in Hindia and English. The United Nations Children's Fund (UNICEF) entrusted the press with the task of producing braille textbooks upto class VI for free distribution. The library of the institute circulates braille books free of charge to blind readers all over the country. It has now decided to make the material available on tapes to serve other disabled persons not able to read in print.

Model School for the Visually Handicapped

The school provides education to the Blind and partially seeing children upto secondary level. Both types of children are given education through media compatible with the nature of their limitations. Blind children are taught through Braille while partially sighted children make use of magnifying devices to read print. The children are provided free boarding, lodging, clothing, tution and other facilities besides monthly pocket money.

The school is affiliated to the Central Board of Secondary Education for its 9th and 10th classes. The School has opened a pre-school unit.

The Institute has taken up research studies on case study of various disabling conditions and preparations of reports for compelte set of management; effect of exercises in Physiotherapy treatment; innovative method of treatment in management of paraplegia/orthopaedic conditions; consturction of indigenous activities of daily living use of simple mthods in Occupational Therapy; develop simple method of tratment programmes in Occupational Therapy in the Zone of hand funtions; and role of Electromyographic studies round the knee joint in different pathological conditions.

Workshops for Manufacture of Braille Appliances

Various aids and appliances like braille slate, arithmatic slate, plastic stylus, chess board, playing cards, pocket frame, folding stick, braille scale, etc. are produced at low cost in this workshop. The workshop has also produced during the period in collaboration with ALIMCO, Kanpur braille shorthand machines, which were being imported earlier.

The Institute's Braille Press is producing reading materials in braille for the blind on a large scale and braille books are supplied at highly subsidised rates to school children. The press took up printing of textbooks for the states of Bihar, Punjab, Haryana, Uttar Pradesh, Karnataka, Madhya Pradesh and Delhi.

The Library offers free lending services to the visually handicapped readers all over the country. It has 38,453 braille volumes and 4539 printing books. It also has a Talking Book Unit with 105 recorded books. A total of 65 new members were added to the library during the year raising total membership to 1890. The new recorded monthly journal namely 'Chayanika' has been circulated to 160 persons during the period.

Assessment and therapeutic services were also extended to the trainees and students referred for consultation at the Crisis Intervention Clinic of the Institute.

The Institute conducted long term as well as short term training programmes for various personnel engaged in the work for the blind in NIVH and its regional centres.

The Institute has a sheltered workshop and units for rural expansion programmes, management of newly blinded, home management, guidance and counselling, orientation and mobility services.

The courses run by NIVH are: Diploma in Teaching the Blind, Contact cum Correspondence Courses for Inservice Teachers of Blind, diploma Course for Secondary Teachers of V.H., Training Course for Primary School teachers of V.H., Certificate Course Orientation and Mobility Instructors of the V.H. at different times. The other courses are: B.Sc. (Hons) in Physiotherapy, B.S. (hons) in Occupational Therapy, and the 2 years Diploma Course in Orthotics and Prosthetic.

The National Institute for Orthopaedically Handicapped, Calcutta

The Institute has been establsihed in 1979 by the Government of India to:

... Conduct research on early detection, prevention, medical and physical rehabilitation of orthopaedically handicapped children and adults;

... Conduct education and training of orthopaedically handicapped children and adults, training of teachers; and

... Plan economic rehabilitation of orthopaedically handicapped.

The National Institute in collaboration with Spastic Society of West Bengal have conducted a course to train special teachers. The schools that are being started in the National Institute will primarily act as a model in teaching the handicaped as well as training special teachers.

Alimco has located a limb fitting centre in the Institute premises. An orthotic and prosthetic unit is also functioning. The Physic therapy unit is also in operation.

The NIOH has taken up large number of research projects and studies. These include effect of exercises in physiotherapy treatment, occupational tehrapy, and several immature methods of treatment in the management of orthopaedic conditions.

Ali Yavar Jung National Institute for the Hearing Handicapped, Bombay (AYJNIHH)

The National Institute for the hearing handicap has been set up in Bombay. The foundation stone was laid in December 25, 1978. The Institute is functioning since 1981. It has its regional centres in the country.

There is also a training centre for adult deaf which was established in 1962 at Hyderabad which continued to provide occupational training to deaf boys and girls in the area of sheet mental works, fitting, carpentry, electric wiremanship, cutting and tailoring, cutting and tailoring, welding, photography, turning. These students are drawn from all over the country. Recently the institute has made further studies by expanding education and training activities with latest audiological equipments to provide service facilities. Research programmes include early identification of hearing impaired. The courses run by AYJNIHH are: D.Ed. (Deaf), B.Ed. (Deaf), B.Sc. (AST), D.C.D.

National Institute of Rehabilitation Training and Research, Olatur, Cuttack.

National Institute of Rehabilitation Training and Research (NIRTAR) came into existence when National Institute of Prosphetic and Orthotic Training (NIPOT) a unit of Artificial Limbs Manufacturing Corporation of India (ALIMCO) established in 1975, was converted into an autonomious body on 22nd February, 1984 under Ministry of Welfare, Government of India.

Objectives

- — To undertake, sponsor or co-ordinate the training of personnel such as Doctors, Engineers, Prsthetists, Orthotists, Prosthetic and Orthotic technicians, Physio-Therapists, Occupational Therapists, multi purpose rehabilitation therapists and such other personnel deemed necessary for the rehabilitation of the physically handicapped.
- — To conduct, coordinate, sponsor or subsidise research into bio-medical engineering, both fundamental and applied, leading to the effective evaluation of mobility aids for the orthopadically disabled persons or suitable surgical or medical procedures or development of new aids.
- — To develop models of service delivery programmes for rehabilitation of the physically handicapped.
- — To promote or distribute or subsidise the manufacture of prototypes and distribution of any or all aids designed to promote any aspects of the education and rehabilitation therapy of the physically handicapped.
- — To undertake vocational training, placement and social, economic, educational and any form of rehabilitation and any activity to incidental to these.
- — To undertake any other action in the area of rehabilitation of the physically handicapped.

A Regional Rehabilitation Training Centre is also attached to this Institute, besides a leprosy rehabilitation unit.

Rehabilitation camps are organised periodically in Rural and Tribal Areas to make the rehabilitation services available to the physically handicapped almost at their doorsteps.

Medical Services

Patients reporting at NIRTAR are registered at the Out Patient Department and examined by the Duty Medical Officer. They are advised and referred to other Departments as per the individual requirements of treatment and rehabilitation.

A well equipped Operation Theatre is available at NIRTAR for surgery of the Orthopaedically Handicapped people. Tadiological Investigations are done at the X-ray Department. Pathological investigations are carried on in the Clincial Laboratory of the Institute. Physiotherapy Department is well equiped with

Hydrotherapy, Exercise Therapy, Electrotherapy and Heat Therapy. Physiotherapists by using the various physical modalities contribute towards the fullest functional restoration of handicapped. Occupational therapist provides treatment towards functional restoration, giving psychological support, training in use of Aid Appliances and Prevocations Training of the disabled on activities of daily living. Prosthetic and Orthotic appliances are fabricated using standard Alimco components and equipments in the prosthetic and orthotic workshop.

The institute runs several courses:

1. Diploma in Prosthetics/Orthotic Engineering.
2. Degree in Physiotherapy.
3. Degree in Occupational Therapy and

Short term orientation courses are run for:

- Rehabilitation for orthopaedic surgeons and physiotherapy medicine specialists,
- Physio-therapists,
- Occupational therapists,
- Psychologists and Employment Officer,
- Medical social workers/teachers in integrated education vocational counsellors,
- Nurses in rehabilitation,
- Voluntary organisations, and
- Prosthetists and orthotists.

Thakur Hariprasad Institute of Research and Rehabilitation of the Mentally Handicapped, Hyderabad

Thakur Hariprasad Institute of Research and Rehabilitation for the Mentally Handicapped was established in the year 1968. It offers:

1. Special education programmes tailored to meet each student's special needs.
2. Modern Home like residential fortor care mother settings.
3. Health care services.
4. Transitional services from school to work and other programmes.
5. Extensive Vocational and Rehabilitation Programmes.
6. Therapeutic Recreational Activities.
7. Special programmes for children and young with antism and behavioural programmes.

It has made significant contribution in the field of MR in India over the last decade. More specifically, THPI runs the courses such as:

1. Programmes:
    - Diploma in M.R.
    - Diploma in Medical Pedagogy.
    - Diploma in Development Therapy.

- Course for Paediatricians and Clinical Psychologists in Neuro-Kinsiological Diagnosis.
- Diploma in Vojta Therapy.
- Training for para-professinals etc.
- Need Based Training Programmes.
- Certificate course in Vocational Training.

2. Several specialised service wings:
   - Rehabilitation of children under judicial custody.
   - Rural camps.
   - Trainining of school teachers.
   - Consultation services.
   - Resource services.
3. In addition to general services:
   - Behaviour Modification.
   - Speech Therapy.
   - Occupational Therapy.
   - Physiotherapy.
   - Family Therapy.
   - Home Guidance Clinic.
   - Sibling Counselling.
   - Need-Based Interventions.
   - Psycho-linguistic Therapy.
   - Developmental Therapy.
   - Vojta Therapy.
   - Medical Pedagory Therapy.
   - Early Social Integration.
   - Cognitive Therapy.

Highlights of the Chapter

Manpower development is a basic requirement for explanding education of exceptional children. Teacher training facilities in the areas of teaching mentally retarded, visually handicapped, hearing handicapped, stastics, speech and hearing exist in the country and are continued to several voluntary and governmental organisations. Systematic breakthrough have been taken place after the National Institutes and various Regional Centres, university departments in special education have come up.

The All India Institute of Speech and Hearing at Mysore caters to the needs of speech and hearing handicapped by way of teacher training, and research functions. The NCERT has been pioneering and instrumental in bringing education of exceptional children into focus, preparation of modular packages for teachers, IED programme implementation and design and making of short term and one year MCT (Multicategory Training of Teachers) through its various regional institutes of education. Interest seems to be waning over the years.

The responsibility of rehabilitation council is to monitor various manpower development programmes including maintenance of a rehabilitation register. Graduate programmes in speech and hearing, masters level programme in speech and hearing, B.M.R., Diploma in Special Education MR, B.Ed., special education, MRW courses, prosthetics and Orthotic diploma courses, courses on All India basis on Occupational Therapy (BOT) and Physiotherapy (BPT) have been in operation.

The NIMH at Secunderabad basically covers care and habilitation programme in the area of for Mental Retardation running BMR and Diploma in special education (MR) courses, various research, development, extension programmes including running an experimental school in the campus for MR children called "Karavalamban Kendra".

The NIVH at Dehradun, promotes research, teacher training, school education, Braille printing and library and documentation, vocational training in the area of visually handicapped.

The AYJNIHH located at Bombay deals with hearing handicapped, which runs training centres in the areas of deaf, occupational training, and extension programmes.

The NIRTAR and RRTC located at Oltpur, Orissa undertakes programmes of preparation of occupational and physiotherapists, MRWs, CBR programme workers, rehabilitation, and provide services to orthopaedically handicapped and allied health problems. It also runs diploma in orthotics and prosthotic engineering.

The THPI at Hyderabad in a vluntary organisation of repute in the area of rehabilitation, teacher training, extension programmes relating to mentally retarded. Its contribution to bring MR into a policy and national focus have been its major contribution besides services.

Review Questions

1. Briefly state the facilities of Teacher Training in the major areas of disability in India since independence.
2. What are the objectives of Teacher Training in Special Education?
3. State the contributions of the following in respect of Teacher Training in Special Education:
   a. National Council of Educational Research and Training.
   b. The Rehabilitation Council of India.
   c. All India Institute of Speech and Hearing.
   d. National Institute for the Mentally Handicapped.
   e. National Institute for the Visually Handicapped.
   f. Ali Yavar Jung Institute for the Hearing Handicapped.
   g. National Institute of Rehabilitation Training and Research.
   h. Thakur Hariprasad Institute of the Research and Rehabilitation for the Mentally Handicapped.

Chapter 15

Research on Education of Exceptional Children

This text has already presented several crucial issues, problems and discussions on different categories of exceptional children with a view to emphasizing their rights, concepts, measures, causes, characteristics and educational provisions. This chapter will bring into focus certain areas where research in India can be conducted to the vantage of modifying, enriching and applying different educational measures. These are:

- Conceptual Issues in Special Education.
- Service Delivery System and Its Efficacy.
- Curriculum and Instructions.
- Management of Educational Environment.
- Strategy of Research in Special Education.
- Resarch in Piagetian Framework.
- Assessment Research and Identification of Disabled.
- Recent Development of Research Focus in India.

Research and developmental activities in the Education of Exceptional Children have emerged in recent years as areas of concern for educational researchers. Whatever research has been done in different areas of disability is more of an organizational and institutional nature. It is, therefore, a piecemeal academic exercise neither reflecting a view-point based on our socio-cultural ethos nor leading to any viable practical application. Excepting biomedical researchers in mental retardation, researches have predominantly been in the areas of attention, learning and memory, but often dealing with tasks that have less relevance in the classroom setting. A few researches cover the ground in the area of applied behaviour analysis and behaviour modification.

Researches in the area of speech and language disability are rathr more rigorous but are confined to a particular institute and more in the line of therapeutic frame. Research in the true sense has not reached an appreciable degree of acceptance so far as assessment of educability and remediation programmes are concerned in the area of visual, auditory and orthopaedic impairments. The Journal of Mental Retardation, Journal of the Institute of Speech and Hearing, Indian Journal of Disability and Rehabilitation are almost extinct after pious beginning and headway. Disability and Impairments continues with larger input from medical field than from educational sector. The Fourth Survey of Research and the Fifth Survey of Research in Education are eloquent testimony. This then is the picture when we are thinking of research and development in special education in India. There are various constraints responsible for such a backdrop. Lack of trained personnel, lack of institutional support, late recognition of the idea that disabled children within the mild or educable range can be trained, and several other socio-cultural constraints. This situation has slightly changed but is not very conducive to extensive and intensive studies and developemntal activities in the area, primarily because of lack of organised effort by the specialists in the respective areas of disability. There is hardly any interaction and dissemination forum for research. Of course since the 1980's, National Institutes in the major areas of disability (Blind, Deaf, Orthopaedially handicapped, Mentally Retarded) and Institutes for Speech and Hearing, B.M. Institutes of Mental Health, etc. have been focussing attention on research and research based and/or related developmental activities. This is a significant step in this direction. In addition, University Departments of Education at Jamia Millia, Banaras, SNDT, R.K. Mission Institute at Coimbatore and Andhra University, etc. have opened up Special Education Departments. Finally, NCERT, through Regional Colleges of Education and its unit at Headquarters has taken up the challenge of starting systematic research, teacher training and development of instructional material in four major areas of disability. Staff has been trained in and outside the country. It is, therefore against this backdrop we must plan our research which will provide continuity and comprehensive data based understanding of the process in which the disabled child can gainfully be helped to learn within the limits of their educability, feasibility and practical application. Especially, it will also be able to give a picture of education and training of disability in India, based on collaborative national level research wherever the approach is narmotive and at institutional and individual level where the need is specific. Keeping these broad goals and background, a perspective of research has been given with some hints of research areas and topics of interest in general.

Conceptual Issues

Although in the working group report for the education of the disabled, some nine categories of disabilities have been identified for care, training and education in a phased manner according to the magnitude of incidence, yet there is a need for status studies relating to incidence, service institutions, education and training institutions, in terms of physical facilities and resource specialists in each area of disability and their major classification and referral practices in vogue. Such status studies are necessary for programme planning and research undestanding. Experience in observing the identification produces in several institutions reveal that there is no uniformity in assessment and diagnostic procedure. Often it is by intuition, observation of morphology, use of one available test or uses of several tests co-jointly but in redundant combinations. This is not to say that all that is existing is not worthy of doing but there must be a systematic research effort to develop what is called *Learning Potential Assessment Device* which would take into account assessment of cognitive competence and adaptive behaviour appropriate to the age levels based on performance measures and observations of daily living skills. In the socio-cultural context in which disabled children find themselves in India, this is a dire necessity. Any western, or pick and choose method of assessment of disability will be doing more harm than good. The LPAD can be used in all subcultures in our society. The next major thrust in this section should be an understanding of the *Psycho-educational Characteristics of the Disabled* (i.e., the cognitive, affective, socio-emotional, information processing nature, physical and motor activities, perceptual style, etc.) on a normative basis against which deviance can be identified and categoriesed. Such norms are of primary importance for placement of children in a special category and managing special services for them. At present such norms are conspicuously absent in our literature. Another area of concern is the content analysis of school curriculum in each of the major categories of disabled in vogue in our country with a view to developing an uniform curriculum. The existing disparities are so great that no one system will be adequate for all categories of disabled children who are currently receiving education and training in different institutions, voluntary or governmental. Such is the case of teacher training curriculum of the disabled. Only recently the special education unit in the NCERT has taken up the stand and has arrived at a common teacher training curriculum in the areas of visually handicapped, hearing heandicapped, mental retardation, orthopaedically handicapped with a composite course structure. However, the viability of these attempts needs to be examined in relation to objectives of training. The Rehabilitation Council of India has also standardised curricul for as many as 34 courses in the area of disability.

Since language disability has not been spelt out at the moment as a separate area of disability, one cannot deny that language is the medicine for any cognitive, affective or skill learning that takes place. Language deficit is one of the major deficiencies in the disabled. The differential communicative competence and language competence should be studied through development of Language Assessment Kit for the disabled which will eventually help in developing language intervention programmes for different groups of disabled children.

Service Delivery System

It is a fact that deviance is a sociological concept although disability has organic and psycho educational base. More than to disabled children is done by using labels, developing negative expectancy, providing poor observational learning situations to achieve self fulfilling prophency. Some of these are more prominent in a developing society like ours, where pragmatism and progressivism rarely enter into the domain of disability. Rather there is a strong sense of fatalism while thinking of educating the disabled. Against this background certain research problems do emerge. These are: How to parents, community members, teachers, perceive the disabled varying in socio-psychological and physical dimensions? How do other children look at the disabled children in an integrated school setting? How do peers act as models for learning among disabled? Such studies will lead us to examine further by empirical means whether integrated setting in our culture is more helpful to the disabled than the special educational arrangements? What are constraints and resources in making integrated education scheme effective? How can parents and community be changed so that they accept retarded and other disabled children and make referrals for education and provide necessary facilities at home? To what extent resource room planning is effective or a cost ineffective programme? Whether homebound instruction or out of school hours remedial teaching is a good alternative? How far the government and voluntary organisations compare with each other in terms of efficacy in respect to each area of disability? Such opinions if at all they exist are mere speculations. Rsearch fidnings will give direction to developmental planning.

How can peer modelling be more effective by making certain cues salient for the disabled? For all these viewpoints research can only offer meaningful conclusions, conducted on a fairly large scale or using intensie case studied of disabled children and their capabilities as a function of the service delivery system and the parameters of an effective delivery system can till then be differed.

Curriculum and Instruction

Curriculum and instructional procedures can be clubbed as one major area of research concern in the area of disabled. More specifically, first, reading readiness programmes need be develped for each area of disability and level within a given disability area. The existing curriculum for normal children have to be watered down to the level of disabled child and only curriculum research could take such a step with regard to arithmetic, reading, language, social skills, etc. and determine empirically the efficacy of a particular method (s) of teaching these curriculum. Through research we should develop the disability specific instructional technique. Such researches are necessary because the western studies prescribe so many varieties of teaching approach and aids that one really needs to know, which one is more effective than others. Systematic and coordinated research work have been a felt need because ours is not a country of affluence but a growing and developing one. In order to make design of curriculum and methods of instruction effective for the disabled, research in these areas are imperative.

Management of Educational Environment

It has been already stated that disability is often caused by environmental factors and more so precipitated by the environment in which one lives. This brings into focus the place of a disabled child in home, in school, and insociety. The home also has different variations like the delivery systems in school and community. A child who is disabled is perceived and managed in a poor home much more differently than if he is born in a well-to-do home. What is more important in this context therefore is the prevailing attitudes, stereotypes, prejudices and expectancies about the disabled. Before any systematic intervention or educational programme is undertaken, it is necessary to assess the pre-existing status in this regard or else even the best programme is not going to make any difference. Same is true of classroom climate and management of peer attitudes for a better adjustment. Hence, it is necessary to assess attitudes through research, bring changes in attitudes for a better adjustment through intervention, and dissemination of right kind of information about the disabled among the people and parents, develop such material for dissemination. All these aims at providing the disabled the least restrictive environment conducive for their optimal growth and adjustment to living.

The relative merits of isolation and mainstreaming would be another research direction in order to examine the long-term impact that the disabled have upon society and family. What should be the ideal teacher behaviours and parental interaction for these children? What should be the environmental circumstances that should foster development of cognitive-perceptual motor functioning, e.g., tactual, spatial, auditory, mobility, adjustment of the visually impaired, etc. the same logic applies to other areas of disability too. What kind of functional environment will promote learning and adjustment, verbal impact etc.? Parental responsiveness, model behaviours, acceptance of disability as mere difference or not a defect, parental/community participation in care and training many such issues would arise. Research can only show whether they are of trivial, tangential nature or have relevance for developmental programmes of the disabled.

Further, on the predispositional side, biomedical research is imperative to identify and prevent parental influences accounting for incidence of disability and the biochemical screening after birth, dietary habits, etc. that would go a long way in reducing its occurrence in society. Western countries have come up with many answers of which several are universal but others are culture specific, e.g., an expectant mother and women in general in India do not smoke or drink, do not expose herself to too much of radiation but there may be other factors i.e., malnutrition, ignorance about infectious diseases, etc. Hence, investigation would be necessary in this regard to identify culture specific influences which act as predispositions for creating disability slowly but surely.

Strategy of Research

It has been stated in the beginning that disability is a complex phenomenon. It has multi dimensions and multi casuality. Hence, in pursuing any systematic research in this area there is a need of collaborative effort among isntitutions, individuals having expertise in the specific areas of concern, for any fruitful result and development of the disabled. Partnership in research, participation and involvement should be the model as any individualistic orientation is likely to lead toward piecemeal, restricted and trivial and academic resarch. The former method is suggestive enough to accelerate resarch which has been neglected for so long.

Research strategy may take both cross-sectional and longitudinal studies approach. We may rely more on clinical case studies and observation but certainly normative studies are necessary. But no matter what method or strategy we follow our aim should be to understand casual, evaluative, and functional variables in the education and training of the disabled, with focus on studies on post school adjustment in family and society, the ultimate goals of any education and rehabilitation programme. Research in this area would thus provide not only a continuity in thinking, consistency in results but will prepare a sound empirical base in the area of special education which mass media can use of for the benefit of all, and more so for the disabled.

Research in Piagetian Framework

Jean Piaget, Switzerland's noted genetic epistemologist, proposed a developmental and constructive model of human cognition from birth to adolescence based on biological processes. Although his theory has been applied to regular education for several decades, fewer efforts have been made to apply his work to exceptional populations (Wachs and Furth, 1980). One reason for this apparent lack of interest is Piaget's derivation of theoretical principles from observations of essentially normal children, with the consequent assumtion of lack of applicability to handicapped individuals. A second obstacle has been an assumed lack of fit between more holistic instructional goals and strategies compatible with Piagetian theory and the specific step-by-step goals and methods typically prescribed for handicapped learners. Nevertheless, Piaget's cognitive-development theory provides a useful means of understanding and teaching children with special needs.

Attempts have been made in recent years to apply Piagetian research to special education children. Piaget described developmnt of structure in terms of sensori motor, pre-operatinal, concrete and formal operational stages, through interaction with environment.

The sensori motor stages (birth to 2 years) describes the infant and prelinguistic child. The infant manifests cognition through actions on objects, such as giggling the crib to set a mobile in motion. The pre-operational stage (2 to 7 years) is characterized by use of language, symbolic behaviour, and lack of conservational logic. The 2-year old child demonstrates symbolic behaviours by pretending that a broom is a horse and "riding" it. The pre-operational child has not yet acquired the structures necessary for conservation: the ability to recognise that matter is conserved despite superficial chantes in shape or form. For example, when 3 year old is presented two identical balls of clay one of which is subsequently rolled into a cigar shape, the child perceives the remaining ball and cigar as being unequal in size. When asked which is large (or "has more"), the child may attend only to length and select the cigar, or only to width, and choose the ball. The child does not consider the two dimensions simultaneously. Children in the stage of concrete operation (6 to 11 years) have acquired the rules of conservation as well as an understanding of relational concepts. The fourth stage, formal operations (12 and above) describes children who can use abstract rules in problem solving and conceptualize hypothetical terms.

Piaget's theory postulates that although children vary in the age at which they reach a given stage, all follow the same sequence. Piaget's constructionist model has been used to explain social cognition, or children's logical understanding of themselves and other individual in interaction. Children's development of social cognition parallels their intellectual development, progressing through a sequence of stages from egocentric to socio-centric thought. The infant is egocentric, or centered around the self. As children mature and gain experience with the environment, they become decentered. They learn that his self is spearate from the other people, that other people have thoughts and feelings, and that other people's thought and feelings may differ from their own.

Three stages characterize children's development of moral judgement; objectives morality, subjective morality, and interpretation of the act. Children in the stage of objective morality base their judgements of good and bad behaviour on objective criteria such as the amount of damage incurred, for example, when someone breaks a lamp while trying to clean the table. In subjective morality, good or bad intentions become a prime criterion for judging behaviour. At the highest level, children simultaneously consider intent and outcome and develop a sense of moral responsibility for the own actions.

Much of the research on Piagets theory has addressed the invariance of the sequence of stages, the impact of specific training on development, especially on acquisition of conservation; the relationship of social cognition to cognitive development, and the relationship between social cognition and social behaviour.

The instructional principles that follow are directed at the teaching of concepts, generalizations, and thinking procsses rather than at increasing the level of cognitive development.

— Because children's thinking is qualitatively different at the various stages of development, teaching objectives should be matched to children's level of development.
— Learning is the acquisition of higher order structures transformed from and built on previous structures. Thus, learning involves the acquisition of broad general rules or frameworks rather than particular, isolated facts. A such, learning proceeds through understanding rather than through incorporation of rote responses.
— Chidlren are internally motivated by a desire for achieving equilibrium. Thus, learning is facilitated by the presentation of optimally challenging tasks and discrepant events that predispose the child to disequilibrium.
— Children learn best through itneracting with and manipulating environmental stimuli.
— Group interactions may present children with ideas that challenge their own, leading to disequilibrium, reorganisation, and new structrues.

These principles have been translated into more specific guidelines for teaching learning-disabled students. Whether these guidelines are appropriate for other special needs children need to be researched in depth.

Teaching methods consistent with Piagetian principles and guidelines include cooperative learning, hypothesis testing, discovery learning, inquiry and other approaches that encourage inductive thinking. Cooperative learning is an instructional strategy whereby students work together in small groups to complete academic tasks. Potential benefits include gains in a academic achievement, basic skill development, problem solving, and socialization. More research is needed on the efficacy of cooperative learning with exceptional students particularly when learning does not take place in certain groups of disabled children to an optimal or mastery level.

As a group, the educable mentally handicapped children demonstrated greater achieement in language and arithmetic with inductive approaches than matched peers in the control condition. These results suggest that inductive methods may contitute a viable addition to traditional approaches to instruction with mildly handicapped learners. While more researches is needed to validate the efficacy of such approaches for special populations, the approaches have theoretical merit and provide alternatives to traditional deductive methods.

Piaget's theory of cognitive development has had specific application to mild and severe/profound mental retardation, learning disabilities, gifted and other categories (Piaget, 1977).

Although the developmental approach as applied to mental retardation has received serious criticism, research has neither disproved the developmental approach nor proved the deficit position, and probably never will. The application of Piagetian instructional methods with the midly retarded merits serious investigation and offers an exciting alternative to teachers wishing to broaden their instructional repertoire. Most important is application of Piagetian approahces to instruction may provide variety and challenge to the children themselves.

In general, the research suggests that learning disabled (LD) children demonstrate performance inferior to that of non-disabled (NLD) children on tasks designed to measure cognitive development and social cognition. A developmental delay in LD children's attainment of concrete operations compared with non-disabled (NLD) controls over a 3-year period has been obtained.

In conclusion, the available research on cognitive development of exceptional learners suggests, for the most part, that exceptional individuals progress through the same sequence of stages described by Piaget for normal children, although they vary in rate of development and level ultimately attained. Application of Piagetian theory to practice suggest use of strategies that engages children in active problem solving appropriate to their current level of development. Additional research is required to demonstrate the efficacy of Piagetian-derived instructional strategies for handicapped and gifted learners. Such strategies have potential as additions to the instructional repertoire of special education teachers.

Assessment Research

Intelligence as sole criterion of determining school placement, institutional commitment and legal incompetence has been controversial. Primarily this is due to (a) Intelligence is reflected as global intelligence, culture transcedent, and unmodifiable, (b) Instead of socially valued attributes, it is constitutional ability for competent participation in society, (c) Differences in preparative experience for the tests are reflected in the differences in group mean IQ, hence, does not fulfill cultural neutrality requirement. There is a need to measure associative, cognitive perceptual abilities rather than on overall intelligence. In addition to, testing of intelligence and evidence of physical, neurological, or psychological impairments, there are cognitive, perceptual, discriminative, adaptive and emotional functions and client's history are called for inferential generalisations.

The focus of testing behavioural deficits must centre around knowledge of how the child is actually performing within the structure of the community/system. Children are not to be identified as disabled if they are able to function within a sufficient level of social invisibility. They must be able to perform certain tasks. Their activities must be within the "tolerance range" instead of fixed norms, which is a major problem with usual measurement. In other words, assessment must aim at (a) disability, (b) what behaviours are present that interface with individual funtioning within the non-mature range, (c) what behaviours are present that represent the individuals effort to cope with the situation on an "instead" basis. The overall question of an adaptive behaviour approach is far reaching.

Behavioural assessment has been the most rapidly developing areas within the field of applied behaviour analysis, behaviour modification, and behaviour therapy. It is change oriented and has abandoned the standards of age norms for inter individual comparisons. In the total behavioural adjustment of an individual norm oriented assessment is of little value. It is rather necesary to follow the criterion referenced testing and observation index i.e., analysis of behaviour and condition that are relevant for an individual's environment. Three basic parametres are to be considered: onset time, frequency and duration. What is needed, therefore, are inter-observer and intra-observer agreement or "observer drit index".

Assessment in this area should reflect the basic objective i.e., learning deficit both qualitatively and quantitatively. This will enable for potentially beneficial placement of the disabled. Educational assessment should not only assess the child and the behaviour, and environmental contingencies which support the desired behaviour. There is a need for diagnostic psycho-educational report based on testing and observation appropriate for developmental intervention. Informal assessment should include teacher observation, teacher made tests, behaviour rating scales and checklists, precision teaching and formative assessment. Precision teaching not only charts current learning and growth but predicts future learning and growth. Teacher observation and assessment of classroom behaviour can be best accomplished it target behaviours are specific, observable and quantifiable. Child behaviour rating scales can come to help. Educational assessment must aim at educational intervention.

There is a felt need for assessment using both psychometric and behaviour observation-cum case study approach. The tests instead of being developed and/ or adapted at individual level may be undertaken by the respective National Institutes, IASE, CASE, CASP, etc. These tests should be disability or exceptionality specific with diagnostic purpose and be translated into regional and state level languages for ease and efective administration. Checklists of observation schedule and obtaining clinical data should also be developed both for assessing ability and achievement characteristics and levels. Cultural and sub-cultural experience are to find a place in developing tests and schedules with built in flexibility or alternatives to be appropriate enough for sampling behaviour in a pluralistic and multicultural society like ours. Norms are also to be developed for sub-cultural groups. Certification for test users should also be enforced and individual test developer must confirm to these norms or else such tests may be kept away from use with this population for any profitable purpose of identification, placement, and intervention (Panda, 1994).

Recent Developments in Research Focus in India

It is true that recent years have noticed a change from medical diagnosis to multi professional assessment, treatment to education, categorisation to individualised needs programme, Category specific needs (Evans and Verma, 1990; Pandey and Advani, 1995). Yet research in India has not made much headway in the field of special education. Perspectives for education of the disabled has been provided by Narsimhan and Mukerjee (1986), research (Panda, 1974) rehabilitation but most of what is available in psycho educational research on disability are quite limited. A glance at the Indian Journal of Mental REtardation, Disability and Impairment, Journal of the Institute of Speech and Hearing would subtantiate such observations although except for Disability and Impairment, the other two are virtually out of scene.

Quite a few significant studies have appeared under the guidance and involvement of individual researchers than of institutes, big and large. Noted amongst them are the conrtibutions of Prof. A.K. Sen and Prof. (Mrs.) A. Sen at Delhi University with reference to mental retardation and specifically on learning and memory processes (Das, 1968; Goel and Sen, 1985), Psychosocial integration of the handicapped (Sen, A., 1983, 1988) and under the guidance of the present author (Prof. K.C. Panda) on response cost and positive reinforcement (Myreddi, 1995), peer modelling (Narayan, 1992), self injurious behaviour (Peshwaria, 1993), community attitudes (Panda, B., 1992), Integrated education of orthopaedially handicapped (Rath, 1993), Reading comprehension of the deaf (Sahoo, 1995), Personality structure of Blind (Khan, 1990), Isolation effect on learning (Panda, P. 1995), etc. are among the significant ones. NIMH has also researched into skill development in MR. Several research have also appeared o Blind, Blind Relief Association, National Association of the Blind, NIVH and individually (Pannikar, 1978; Panda and Panda, 1995).

The area of disability receiving much attention at the doctoral level research are mental retardation, visual impairment, gifted, hearing handicapped and learning disabled during the last decade but the number of researches are very few and quality wise are only contributory to understanding the disabled.

Researches have concentrated more on learning, memory, attention, personality, community atitudes, efficacy of systems but has hardly are oriented towards interventions but for rew which aimed skill development, development of learning package. National Institutes, NCERT, University Departments have not catered to significant research but contributed more to education and training of personnel for handling the disabled. Efficacy studies, have come up recently (Mani, 1993; Rath, 1993) but researches taken as a whole in the field of special education are in an embroyonic state.

There is no denying the fact that even till now the area of disability has remained as an area of welfare, rehabilitation and care than research, development and education. Both the directions are important and research can well integrate the two to the advantage of the disabled.

Where do we go from here?

This is a question which is difficult to answer but professionals irrespective of speciality in the field of disability must concentrate basically on issues and problems, which are relevant to educational and rehabilitation aspects by and large.

Areas of research would systematically include: assessment test/checklist development in each area of disability; its reginal translation and adaptation; standardisation of functional behaviour checklists even conditions of adaptation from western countries; measurement of change of progress in disabled children as a result of training, ecological intervention, parental involvement, and establishment of cultural norms for clinical as well as research use; prevalence of disability, its incidence in rural-urban set up, incidence rate, socio-demographic antecedents and consequences.

A major focus of our research endeavours must specify comparative studies on diffrent therapeutic interventions and practices, sensory stimulations much early in the process of development and identify efficient procedures for developmental quotient and not merely IQ changes, competence, skills and social personal adjustment would be the primary focus leading to school readiness. Such research areas are painstaking and challenging but worth undertaking.

Special education in our country is an emerging field but there are many sound reseach generalisations elsewhere the field had an earlier origin. It is time for us to think and say on the basis of our own studies whether home based interventions are any way better than the institution based intervention, integrated system vs the special system, efficacy of community based rehabilitation and family studies. Public attitudes, acceptance and awareness are to be assessed and manipulated thhrough various awareness programme since disability seen in home is sustained because of negative attitudes and stigma by the society.

How far rights of disabled are ensured or are they still discriminated against legal background? Diability occupation-fit studies are essential for initiating training using a global socially desirable approach to draw attention or pay a lipservice to the vital areas.

Technology has come in a big way. How can it be used to the advantage of the disabled?—in terms of aids and appliances, classroom learning, teaching, self-learning, mastery learning, evaluation: diagnostic as well as normative, micropocessors and their use in case of teaching the disabled. Many such issues will appear. These are some directions only. While disability specific research is a matter of individual concern these are some of the area that come in any area of disability.

How do we go from here?

The Methodology

Behavioural scientists tend to be obsessed by their methods often at the expense of their results. It is not proper to enter into any philosophical debate on the process nor can any methodological formula for scientific research be formulated. The prinćipal way of attending competence is to do it and develop insight. These methodological issues relate to designs in research, sampling frame and to size, qualitative vs quantitative research techniques. The field of special education is essential fraught with many such issues since researchers in special education have migrated from other disciplines with their well established rigid, hard core or soft-core training and temperament. The field of special education even without sacrificing research ethics, propriety and rigor can still follow a clinical model, a sample size of 1, a single subject research design using withdrawal or multiple base line data; across behaviours, across subjects, across situations, quasi-experimental design can take care of extreme groups in such research, as well as purposive sampling are acceptable practices inspite of procedural lapses and regression, when sample size is not large as it typical in the field of special education. What needed is that researchers in special education should take care of the methodological issues even when they use qualitative research techniques for fact finding, participant observation, interviewing, documentation and review. The fact should remain that it should maintain credibility, transferability, dependability, confirmability, authenticity and fairness.

A Perspective

It is difficult at this stage to speculate and think of research on disability from a futuristic angle yet it is a part of programme building and research planning process. Research in future and particularly in 21st century will be more concerned with avoidance of discriminatory practices and maintenance of human rights so that disabled children have full participation in society. Hence, community research will get our priority besides legislative activism. But this is open direction, what is more crucial for this group is that disability is more often accompanied by mental problems. Hence, research in mental health, psychiatric social work, psychological interventions are and should be points of reference in planning research activities.

In the field of education, the year 2000 will see changes in educational index but what of disabled children? Can improved educational opportunities be extended to this group? Can inclusive education be benefiting the disabled or it is a medium of our self preservation exercise and instinct. If not, research in the next decade should focus on the development of functional skill training, even using computer technology and computer aided instructions:

(a) Allow students to proceed at a more individual pace, thereby reducing stigmas.
(b) Enable developmentally disabled to work at home.
(c) Provide learning aids specifically designed for a group of disability.

In summary, research in the next decade and ahead should focus on:

(a) Identification of available services and resources.
(b) Development of learning potential assessment device test as basis of diagnosis.
(c) Epidemiological investigation of the disabled population.
(d) Research and advocacy of treatment approaches and techniques.
(e) Community integration with a comprehensive care system and a full operational prevention process.
(f) Identification of individually suitable teaching practices, peer tutoring and modelling, education and service delivery system.
(g) Family studies.

These are but a few reflections but there will be many more if really we are committed to the cause of helping disabled children in our society.

Highlights of the Chapter

Research in the field of exceptional children is taking off at a very slow and insignificant level in our country. Virtually it has low priority among professionals. The attempts to implant all Western ideas and principles will not pay divided unless indigenous techniques and procedures are developed through research and development of materials.

Research is in the areas of developing learning potential Assessment Device which is common to all areas of disability. Conceptually, it should focus on psycho-educational characteristics of the handicapped, efficacy of delivery system,s community based programmes, curriculum modifications, developmental research on instructional system, management of educational environment, research in Piagetian Framework with the disabled, assessment techniques based on cultural specifics are in dire need in our country, with cooperative and partnership endeavour since the field of handicap is a complex area and therefore can rarely be handled at an individual level.

Review Questions

1. Highlight the significance of research in special education.
2. What are the critical issues in research in special education?
3. What kind of research can be undertaken in the area of service delivery system?
4. What kind of research can be undertaken in the area of curriculum and instruction?
5. Management of educational environment is a promising field of research in special education—Discuss.
6. What should be the strategy of research in special education?
7. Outline the research perspective in Piagetian framework.
8. State the recent development of research focus in India.
9. What should be the research focus in assessment of exceptional children?
10. What kind of policy research can be undertaken in view of your reading the literature in special education?

References

Das, J.P., (1968), "Mental Retardation in India, A review of care, training, research and rehabilitation programme", In N.R. Ellis (ed.), *International Review of Research in Mental Retardation*, Vol. 3, New York: Academic Press.

Evans, P. and Verma, V., (eds.), (1990), *Special Education Past, Present and Future*, London: The Falmer Press.

Goel, S.K. and Sen, A.K., (1985), *Psychoeducational Research in Mental Retardation*, Agra: National Psychological Corporation.

Khan, A.H., (1990), *Personality Structure of Blind Children and Its Relationship with Their Mental Ability and Educability*, Ph.D. Dissertation, Utakal University.

Mani, M.N.G., (1993), Report of PIED, SRK College of Education, Coimbatore, NCERT.

Myeredi, V., (1995), *Effect of Peer Mediated Reinforcement and Response Cost in the Ehnancement of Learning Among the Mentally Retarded Children*, Ph. D. Dissertation, Utkal University.

Narayan, J., (1992), *Comparision of the Effectiveness of Adult and Peer Model on the Learning and Retention of Performance Skills Among Mentally Retarded Children*, Ph. D. Dissertation, Utkal University.

Narsimhan, M.C. and Mukherjee, A.K., (1986), *Disability: A Continued Challenge*, Wiley Eastern, New Delhi.

Panda, K.C., (1974), "A process model approach for research into the retardates parental family: Theoretical and Methodological Considerations", *Indian Journal of Mental Retardation*, 7, 14-24.

Panda, B., (1992), *Attitude of Parents and Community Members Towards Disabled Children*, Ph. D. Disseration, Utkal University.

Panda, K.C. and Panda, S., (1995), *Development of Education of Blind in India*, (In Press).

Panda, K.C., (1994), "Psychoeducational Assessment in Special Education: Issues and Concerns", *Indian Journal of Psychological Issues*, 2, 1, 1-20.

Pandey, R.S. and Advani, Lal, (1995), *Perspectives in Disability and Rehabilitation*, New Delhi: Vikas.

Pannikar, K.K., (1978), *Vithoba Pannikar Scale of Performance Test for Blind*, NAB, Bombay.

Peshwaria, R., (1993), *Self injurious behaviours in mentally handicapped persons: Motivational analysis and home based behavioural intervention*, Ph.D. Dissertation, Utkal University.

Piaget, J., (1977), *The development of thoughts: Equilibration of cognitive structures*, New York: Viking.

Ralh, K.B., (1993), *Self-concept, achievement orientation anxiety, and adjustment among orthopaedically handicapped and normal children in an integrated educational setting*, Ph. D. Dissertation, Utkal University.

Sahoo, P., (1995), *Development of reading textual material among hearing impaired and normal hearing children*, Ph.D. research work in progress.

Sen, Anima, (1983), *Attention and Distraction*, Delhi: Sterling Publishers.

Sen, A., (1988), *Psychosocial Integration of the Handicapped*, Delhi: Mittal Publications.

Wachs, H., and Furth, H., (1980), "Piaget's theory and special education", In B.K. Keogh (ed.), *Advances in Special Education*, (Vol. 2, pp. 51-78), Greenwich, CT: JAI.

Glossary of Key Terms and Meanings

ABO incompability: If the mother's and foetus blood types (A, B, AB, O) are different then various problems appear. This appears in the second and later pregnancy cases.

Adaptive behaviour: The degree with which an individual meets the standards of personal independence and social responsibility expected for age and cultural group.

Agnosia: Inability to attach meaning to sounds, words, or visual experiences.

Amblyopia: A condition in which the brain will not tolerate double vision and supresses what is being transmitted by the weaker eye.

Amniocentosis: A test that may be done during pregnancy to identify certain genetic disorders in the foetus. It consists of extracting a small amount of amniotic cluid, which surrounds the foetus in the womb, for examination.

Anaphathalmia: In which the eyes do not develop at all.

Anoxia: Lack of oxygen.

Antridia: In which the iris fails to develop and visual acity becomes poor and there is rapid involuntary movement of the eye ball.

Aphasia: Acquired language impairment caused by brain damage.

Articulation disorder: A communication disorder associated with substitutions, omissions, distortions, and/or additions of speech sounds.

Asthma: Chronic condition characterized by wheezing or labored breathing caused by a constriction of the air passages in the bronchial tubes and by an increasing amount of thick secretions in the air tubes of the lungs.

Astigmatism: Blurred vision caused by uneven curvature of the cornea or lens.

Ataxia: A type of cerebral palsy in which lack of muscle coordination results in loss of coordinated movements, especially those relating to alance and position.

Athetosis: A form of cerebral palsy characterized by involuntary, jerky, purposeless, repetitive movements of the extremities, head, and tongue.

Atrophy: The degeneration or death of tissue.

Audiogram: A graphic portrayal of the results of hearing testing.

Audiologist: A specialist in evaluation and remediation of auditory disorders.

Audiology: A science concerned with hearing.

Autism: It is childhood schizophrenia which is characterised by delayed speech, withdrawal tendencies and non-communicative speech.

Behaviour checklists: A list of traits or behaviours that research has shown to be characteristic of a group of children. These checklists are often used to rate children to determine whether they should be referred for special services.

Behavioural contract: An agreement between the client and another person on a goal and a procedure for teaching that goal.

Behaviour disorders: Disorders in which behaviour deviates from a normal range, occurs over an extended period of time, and is extreme in terms of intensity and frequency.

Behaviour modification: Application of principles of operant learning in which the individual's responses are progressively reinforced in the direction of a desired pattern.

Braille: A code developed for blind persons in which a system of raised dots allows the person to read with the fingertips.

Cascade of services: A hierarchy of educational service alternatives for handicapped persons, ranging from the least restrictive regular classroom to the highly restrictive hospital or institutional settings.

Contract: It can occur at any time due to rupture of the lens, even though it is a disease of old age.

Cerebral palsy: An abnormal alternation of human movement or motor functioning arising from a defect, injury, or disease of the tissues of the central nervous system.

Chemotherapy: Administration of drugs to control or aid a problem.

Cluttering: 1. Perceptual disorder reflected in a vebral manifestation of interruption of coding processes. 2. Language disorder characterized by rapid utterance with many elisions, transpositions, and omissions of significant speech sounds and word groups. Speech is generally jerky, explosive and non-melodic, thus obscuring meaning.

Curriculum: A set of learning objectives that are (1), specified as behaviours, (2) written in objective terms that allow observation and measurement, (3) carefully sequenced from the easiest to the most difficult, (4) descriptive of the prerequisites necessary for each objective, and (5) a result of an analysis of each task in the curriculum.

De-Institutionalization: Term used to describe the movement away from placing handicapped people in large residential institutional facilities.

Developmental model: A model of development based on normal developmental milestones.

Disability: A condition due to the reduction of function or absence of a particular body part or organ (e.g., paraplegic, amputce); synonymous with disorder or dysfunction.

Down's Syndrome: Down in 1985 introduced the term to mongoloid form of mental deficiency which is due to an additional chromosome No. 21. known as Trisomy 21.

Dyslexla: 1. Perceptual deficit involving linguistic processing and affecting reading, speech, spelling and other sensorimotor integrative activities necessitating fine coordination. Obsolete: Word blindness. 2. Reading disability, one form of learning disability—Susan Ann Vogel.

Dyspraxia: A sensorimotor disorder affecting the higher levels of neural organization and resulting in deficits in the cortical integration and motor expression of oral language. Imperfect comprehension and memory lapses also may contribute to coding disability. The resulting disruption in programming and sequencing affects all voluntary motor adjustments necessary for speech-respiration, phonation, resonation, and articulation.

Dysphasia: Impairment of an acquired ability to comprehend and express oral language. Aphasia: Total or global impairment.

Echolalia: Repetition of the final segment of a sentence or question, generally practiced by severely retarded children, selectively practiced by young normal children who respond to another's utterance in order to compreh it or to keep up their end of the dialogue.

Ecology: Study of the relation of organisms to their environment. Study and function of nature. The community or individual and the non-living environment function together as an ecological system or eco-system.

Educable mentally handicapped (EMH): Persons of subnormal mentality whose intellectual functioning (existing concurrently with deficit adaptive behaviour) falls two or more standard deviations below the mean on standardized tests. On the Stanford-Binet or Wechsler Intelligence Scale for Children, a score of 65-60 would place a child in the EMH class. The term does not imply feeblemindedness. Synonym: Mental Impairment (MI).

Emotionally Disturbed: Chidlren whose reactions to life situations are unrewarding to himself and unacceptable to his peers and society.

Encephalitis: A condition that causes inflammation of the brain of which may result in brain damage.

Epilepsy: A chronic condition of the central nervous system, charactrised by periodic seizures accompanied by convulsions of the muscles, and, with more severe attacks, loss of consciousness.

Exceptional Children: Those who have physical, mental, behavioural, or sensory characteistics that differ from the majority of children to such an extent that they require special education and related services in order to develop to their maximum capacity.

Fine motor skills: Use of small muscles for reaching, grasping, and manipulation of objects such as puzzles, formboards, cubes, and drawing materials.

Gifted: A term used to refer to children with outstanding ability or potential. The term is usually applied to children who perform in the top three to five per cent on measures of aptitude or achievement in such areas as general intellectual ability, specific academic aptitude, creativity, leadership or artistic ability.

Glaucoma: Severe disorder that occurs when the aqucous fluid does not circulate properly and results in an elevation of pressure in the eye.

Grandmal seizure: A severe type of convulsive disorder involving loss of consciousness and extreme convulsions.

Gross motor skill: Use of large muscles for walking, running and other whole body movements.

Handicap: It refers to problems that impaired or disabled people have as a result of interaction with their environment (e.g. inability of deaf person to hear a telephone or person in wheel-chair to use a revolving door).

Hearing impaired: This is defined in terms of hearing loss: mild 26 to 46 dB, moderate 41-55 dB, severe 56-70 dB, profound 71 to 90 dB, total deafness 91 dB+.

Hemiplegia: Paralysis of the extremities on one side of the body.

Hydrocephalus: A condition of excess cerebrospinal fluid in the brain that results in an enlargement of the head and mental retardation.

Hyperactivity: Excessive physical/muscular activity characterized by excessive restlessness and mobility: sometimes associated with learning disabilities.

Impairment: A condition resulting from diseased of defective tissue (e.g., cerebral palsy, birthmark, nearsightedness).

Individual educational program (IEP): A component of Public Law 94-142 that requires a written plan of instruction for each child receiving special services; the IEP must include a statement of the child's present levels of educational performance, annual goals, short-term objectives, specific services needed by the child, dates when these services will begin and be in effect, and when the child should be reealuated.

Incidence: Refers to the estimates of the numbers of individuals in the population who may exhibit a particular characteristic at sometime during their lifetime.

Integration: Educating all disabled children in regular schools regardless of the degree or severity of their disability conditions.

Labelling: An act of assigning a child or condition to general category or to a particular position in the classification system.

Lead poisoning: Lead is a poison for developing mentál retardation.

Learning disability: 1. "The child exhibits a disorder in one or more of the basic psychological processes involved in understanding or in using language, spoken or written, which may manifest itself in an imperfect ability to listen, think, speak, read, write, spell, or to do mathematical calculations.

Least restrictive environment: LRE refers to the maximum extent appropriate, handicapped children be educated with non-handicapped children.

Mainstreaming: The educational placement of the child in the least restrictive educational setting.

Meningitis: Inflammation of the membranes that surround the brain and spinal cord.

Microphathalmia: In which the eye-ball is abnormally small.

Minimal brain dysfunction: (contoversial definition) Applied to children of average or above average intelligence who have learning disabilities associated with functional problems of the central nervous system.

Mental retardation: Significantly subaverage general intellectual functioning existing concurrently. With deficits in adaptive behaviour and mainfested during the developmental period.

Microcephaly: A cranial disorder characterised by the development of a small head with a sloping forehead; retardation results from lack of space for brain development.

Muscular dystrophy: A hereditary disorder that causes a loss of vitality and progressive deterioration of the body as a result of death of muscule tissue.

Myopia (nearsightedness): Occurs when the eye is too long and the rays of light from distant objects are not focused on retina.

Nasal sound: a sound produced by the blocking of the oral cavity, the opening of the velum and the emission of air via the nasal cavity (m, n, g).

Neurologically impaired: Associated with problems in the functioning of the central nervous system.

Normalization: The concept that all handicapped persons should be provided with the opportunity to live according to the patterns and conditions of everyday life, which are as close as possible to the norms and patterns of the mainstream of the society.

Orthopaedically handicapped: A disabling condition caused by physical impairments especially those related to the bones, joints and muscles.

Oxycephaly: An anomaly of the skull bones resulting in optio atrophy.

Paraplegia: Paralysis of the lower half of the body including both legs.

Partially seeing: Those whose visual acuity is between 20/200 and 20/70 in the better eye with the best possible correction or who in the opinion of an eye specialist need either temporary or permanent special education facilities. Partially seeing people can use ink print in their education.

Poliomyelitis (Polio or infantile paralysis): An acute disease that inflames nerve cells of the spinal cord or brain stem and leaves a residual paralysis or muscular atrophy; is preventable through vaccination.

Portage: It is a need based participatory family training in child care and development carried inside home environment.

Prevalence: The number of individual in the population who currently exhibit a particular characteristic.

Psychomotor seizure: a seizure characterised by many automatic, stereotyped movements.

Quadriplegia: Paralysis involving all four of the body extremities.

Resource Room: A place in regular school where special education students attend for less than 50% of their school day for supportive services.

Resource teacher: A trained teacher to teach the disabled student in the resource room and become a consultant to regular teacher and parents.

Response cost: A procedure in which a response leads to the removal of some portion of accumulated reinforcement.

Rh incompatibility: A condition in which the foetus has Rh positive blood and the mother has.

Rigidity (cerebral palsy): A type of cerebral palsy in which hypertension of the muscles creates stiffness.

Rubella (German measles): A communicable disease transmitted by a virus infection of a woman during early stages of pregnancy produces a high probability of severe handicaps of the offspring.

Severely handicapped individual: One has serious primary disabilities that are cognitive and/or behavioural has the high probability of additional physical and/or sensory handicaps, and requires significantly more resources than are provided for the midly and moderately handicapped in special education programmes.

Slow learner: Children who underachieve in one or more academic area at a rate that is below the average.

Snellen chart: A white background with black letters or symbols of graded size used to test distant field visual acuity.

Spasticity: A type of cerebral palsy characterized by muscular coordination resulting from muscle spasms, opposing contradictions of muscles, and paralytic effects.

Specific learning disability: Disorder in one or more of the basic psychological processes involved in understanding or in using language spoken or written, which may manifest itself in an imperfect ability to lsiten, think, speak, read, write spell, or to do mathematical calculations.

Speech: The physical process involved in producing the sound and sound combinations of a language.

Speech reading: Interpreting the movements of the lips, face, head, and gestures as an aid to communication; also called lip reading or visual hearing.

Time-out: A procedure in which a response removes access to reinforcement for a specified period of time.

Trachoma: Results out of crowding home conditions and as a result of contagious disease of conjunction and cornea.

Trainable Mentally Retarded: Retarded children whose IQ is between 40-60 (earlier 35-55) are ttainable.

Triplegia: Paralysis of three of the body's limbs.

Tuberculosis: An infectious disease characterized by the formation of small modules in the tissue of the lungs.

Turner's Syndrome: A form of mental deficiency which results out of absence of x chromosome in the female (XO).

Underachiever: Any child whose scholastic performance is below that suggested by performance on IQ tests or other indicators of aptitude.

Visual acuity: Sharpness or clearness of vision.

Voice disorder: Occurs when an individual's voice does not present an appropriate and consistent sound as a result of misuse of the voice structures or tissue change in the vocal tract.

Visually impaired: Those whose visual acuity is 20/200 or less in the better eye with the best possible correction or a restriction in the field of vision to an angle subtending an are of 20 degrees or less. The people must use braille and tactile and auditory materials in their education.

List of Acronyms

AAMD	American Association of Mental Deficiency
ADD	Attention Deficit Disorder
ALIMCO	Artificial Limb Manufacturing Corporation of India.
ASL	American Sign Language System
AYJNIHH	Ali Yavar Jung National Institute of Hearing Handicapped
BLAT	Blind Learning Aptitude Test
BMR	Bachelor in Mental Retardation
CBA	Concept Based Assessment
CIET	Central Institute of Educational Technology
CRT	Criterion Referenced Test
CTW	College of Teacher Education
DIAL	Developmental Indicator for the Assessment of Learning, Disabilities
DIET	District Institute of Education and Training
DISTAR	Distinct Instructional System to Arithmatic and Reading
DRC	District Rehabilitation Centre
DRG	Disability Rights Group
ECCE	Early Childhood Care and Education
ED	Emotionally Disturbed
EFA	Education For All
EMR	Educable Mentally Retared
FWCR	Federation of Welfare of Mental Retarded
HL	Hearing Level
HTL	Hearing Threshold Level
IASE	Institute of Advanced Studies in Education
ICDS	Integrated Child Development Scheme
IEDC	Integrated Education for Disabled Children
IEP	Individualised Education Programme
IIA	Initial Teaching Alphabet
ITPA	Illinois Test of Psycholinguistic Abilities
IYDP	International Year of Disabled Persons
LA	Language Age

LD	Learning Disabled
LRE	Least Restricted Environment
NCERT	National Council of Educational Research and Training
NICDR	National Information Centre on Disabled and Rehabilitation
NGO	Non-Government Organisation
NFD	National Federation of Blind
NIHH	National Institute of Hearing Handicapped
NIMH	National Institute of Mentally Handicapped
NIOH	National Institute of Orthopaedically Handicapped
NIPOT	National Institute of Prosthetic and Orthotic Training
NIRTAR	National Institute of Rehabilitation Training and Research
NIVH	National Institute of Visually Handicapped
NJCLD	National Joint Committee on Learing Disabilities
NPE	National Policy on Education
NPERC	National Policy on Education Review Committee
PIED	Project Integrated Education of Disabled
PKU	Phenylkeutoneuria
PLDK	Peabody Language Development Kit
POA	Programme of Action
PPVT	Peabady Picture Vocabulary Test
RPM	Ravens Progressive Matrices
SCERT	State Counci of Educational Research and Training
SEN	Special Education Need
SEP	Special Education Provision
SES	Socio Economic Status
SPL	Sound Pressure Level
SRT	Speech Reception Threshold
TC	Total Communication
THPI	Thakur Hari Prasad Institute
TMR	Trainable Mentally Retarded
TROG	Test for Reception Grammar
UEE	Universalisation of Elementary Education
VSMS	Vineland Social Maturity Scale
VRC	Vocational Rehabilitation Centre
WHO	World Health Organization
WISC	Wecshler Intelligence Scale for Children

Index